The Unsung
Memoirs of socia

The Unsung Sixties:
Memoirs of social innovation

Helene Curtis and Mimi Sanderson

For Pat

Mimi Sand

Whiting & Birch Ltd

MMIV

© Helene Curtis and Mimi Sanderson, 2004
All rights reserved. No part of this publication may be reproduced in
any form without permission. Whiting & Birch Ltd are registered with
the Publishers Licensing Society, London, England and the Copyright
Clearance Centre, Salem Mass. USA.

Published by Whiting & Birch Ltd,
PO Box 872, London SE23 3HL, England.
USA: IPG, 614 N Franklin Street, Chicago, IL 60610.

British Library Cataloguing in Publication Data.
A CIP catalogue record is available from
the British Library

ISBN 1 86177 043 X (hardback)
1 86177 044 8 (paperback)

Printed by Print Solutions

Contents

Preface

THE 1960S IN Britain is regarded as a period of excitement and innovation, a glamorous sequel to the austerities of the post-war period. Carnaby Street and Kings Road caught by the camera of David Bailey, mini-skirts, Twiggy, Mary Quant and the Liverpool sound of the Beatles. While a great deal has been written about the stars of the 1960s less dazzling figures also shook and moved events, set about remedying the ills of the times.

Behind the glamour there was the shock of *Cathy Come Home*, and Rachman's widespread exploitation of tenants. Poverty and debt were on the increase as well as mental illness. And there were cries of isolation from the carers of children and infirm relatives. The 1960s saw an explosion of social innovation. These innovations became, one way or another, part of the social fabric.

This book consists of stories told to us by people who founded or worked in groups or organisations dealing with the underside of the 1960s. It tells how they identified and came to tackle problems not generally recognised at the time. It celebrates their lives, lives not spent in the limelight.

The histories or early annual reports of voluntary organisations give the official story. What we wanted to capture was what it felt like being in at the beginning, what drove a person to start or become involved in setting up an organisation, and who they were. These are subjective stories. If we had interviewed someone else who had been in the same organisation at the beginning, that story would have had a different perspective.

However, common themes do emerge. For example, many organisations got their start by being promoted by socially conscious journalists – a letter to *The Guardian* is often mentioned. The availability of funding from charitable trusts enabled them to develop. A group of people might come together out of self-interest but in the course of time develop a wider network. Even when an organisation gets to the point of employing staff, the employed workers would give extra unpaid service. In the personal lives of these pioneers there are also some common themes such as the impact of World War II and limited education and career choices for women.

We selected, primarily from the archives of the National Council of Voluntary Organisations, thirty-six voluntary organisations started in the 1960s. We did not set out to include every organisation, only enough to span the range of activities. In most cases we contacted the organisation itself for interviewees, with a few we contacted people directly. Almost half a century later, not surprisingly, many of the earliest pioneers have died; some were too incapacitated to be interviewed; and some were untraceable or unwilling to be interviewed.

Inevitably in the course of time these organisations have changed – adapting to meet emerging needs and developing new policies and practices. This can be seen in the Appendix which lists the objects and activities of the organisations as they are today. Some have changed name several times. A few have ceased to operate entirely, in some cases because their work is being carried out by other organisations.

The Unsung Sixties is a collection of stories told in a series of recorded interviews which took place over the period 1997 to 2001. This book does not aim to provide a hypothesis for social change nor does it offer recipes for social change: these are the human stories behind social change.

Helene Curtis and Mimi Sanderson

Introduction

Sheila Rowbotham

THE SIXTIES ARE remembered as a decade of hedonistic individualism in which wild pleasure and wild militancy intertwine. This collection reveals a very different 1960s; a profoundly social decade in which individuals acted with a courageous and idealistic resolve to change how life was lived.

Big changes in British society were at work behind the myriad schemes and projects recorded in *The Unsung Sixties*. The post-war broad acceptance of welfare established a basis from which these innovations could sprout. This foundation was partly material and partly cultural. A key factor was the new common sense which took the expansion of social welfare for granted. It manifested itself not only on the left, but extended through to liberal conservatism.

The educational expansion which was gradually to increase the numbers of working class children and women entering higher education had hardly taken off. Young women in the 1960s were more likely to get to 'teachers' training colleges' than universities. Still something was afoot and the grammar schools and art colleges are mentioned several times.

The sixties saw the beginning too of the expansion in administrative and service jobs which made it possible for the first time for a sizeable minority of young women to support themselves and one baby or even - at a pinch - two. Economics as well as the pill and freer sexual attitudes were behind the new mores of the sixties. There was then a cushion - not a large cushion and not a particularly fat cushion - but something to shield you from going under.

And more than this a mood of hope and irreverence took shape. Though consciousness is notoriously difficult to locate and define, the origins of the shift can be detected partly in the bounce that prosperity and greater security produces and partly in the new social movements of the era. The American Civil Rights movement made news all around the world. Black Americans' demands for political and social rights and their struggles around symbolic spaces, lunch bar counters and transport, were to inspire a generation. In Britain, the Campaign for Nuclear Disarmament took to the streets in a cavalcade of defiance while members of its unruly offspring, Committee of 100, plonked themselves down to be carted off with much publicity by puffing policemen.

The Unsung Sixties documents how, as CND splintered and dissolved as a coherent movement, it sprouted innovative projects and campaigns. One of these is traced in the account by Jim Radford of the Homeless Hostel Campaign which in turn fed into the squatting movement later in the decade. In 1965 the Friends of King Hill rebelled against the policy of putting women and children without men into an ex-Army camp in the woods, leaving the men to sleep in cars outside. This direct action based campaign challenged the survival of the old punitive Poor Law in welfare provision. It was the spark in the tinder box of rebellion against the attitudes of the old establishment. Jim Radford calls it 'do-it-yourself politics'.

Do-it yourself politics were to appear in various kinds of guises; the in-your-face confrontation was just part of a spectrum. Many of the innovations described in this book arose as quiet observations of needs which were being unmet by the welfare state. The range covered is extensive: child poverty, the problems of old people, women living with violent partners, prisoners' wives and those arrested on drug offences, mothers' lack of child care - the list could go on. The innovators were coming at the gaps in welfare provision from many angles, but this collection shows that they shared one characteristic in common – a dogged determination.

Behind the resolve was the tacit assumption that people deserved dignity – a presupposition which would have been impossible without the welfare gains made by an earlier generation. It is there in all the accounts; teddy bears without arms would no longer do for 1960s poor children, nor were people with disabilities any longer to be patronised by the charitable. This change in attitude gave rise to new organisational structures which were not only about getting more but about how human beings were defined in society. The Claimants' Union rebelled against the image of the unemployed as scroungers, the Campaign Against Racial Discrimination connected to the Afro-Caribbean working class' desperation for decent housing and the humiliations of racism, the Campaign for Homosexual Equality initiated a politics of the body. Rights were not abstract or about politics alone, they were active and about sex as well as economics. And this new kind of politics was peopled by the stubborn and the stroppy who refused to recognise officialdom's authority.

The Unsung Sixties is packed full of inveterate individualists of the left and the right; not the 'me first' individualism but the cussed resolution which refuses to look away and will not shut up. Few refer to any party politics; they just were determined to get things done.

Activity, however, fostered ideas and these were partly shaped by oral memory and the accounts provide fascinating glimpses into how alternative visions of community were weaving their way through council estates and concrete jungles. The squatters for instance were sustained by local networks who provided moral and practical support. Moreover a new generation made links with an earlier tradition of working class direct action which had occupied houses when the Blitz left many people homeless. The sixties were to put 'community politics' on to the map, but they did not invent it. *The Unsung Sixties* shows how this too had a history in the Catholic Workers' Movement which stressed that social action meant changing your personal life.

The community arts movement grew out of the art schools which in the 1960s were sites of turmoil and engagement. The purposes of art and the role of the artist were being questioned and Free Form Arts was one of many groups that took these concerns out to inner city slums. Martin Goodrich sums up how they learned to identify issues and needs without imposing solutions. Instead they sought the means of empowering people to devise their own ideas through participating.

This innovative and empowering notion of politics drives the collection, though it is rarely put so explicitly. The projects and struggles chronicled reveal how a precious political space was won during the 1960s. Since then this space has been contested again and again. At times it seemed to vanish entirely, only to open where it was least expected. Tenaciously and against the odds, sustained sometimes only by slender threads, 'do-it-yourself -politics' has survived extreme vicissitudes.

The arena of politics outside government and parties was much later to be theorised as 'civil society'. Its theorists were inclined to present this as a notion which sprang spontaneously out of their own heads. It is often the people who initiated the practical basis for an idea who are frequently wiped out of the narrative of history. While activists and organisers hold no patents on concepts and most would eschew such possessiveness, *The Unsung Sixties* gives credit where credit is overdue. It demonstrates that what was done can provide a stimulating source for thoughts about the scope of politics as well as improving daily life in practical ways.

An ambiguity unfolds itself from all these stories; something which do-it-yourself politics has never resolved. Some of the chapters outline innovation against the state; while others show that people need the state – or to be more accurate they need the resources, skills and protection which are tucked away in bits of the state. Part of the unfinished business of *The Unsung Sixties* is how the sensitivity to need and respect for human dignity that these accounts evince, might become part of a larger democratisation process. A process by which individuals in society would be able to gain a more equitable access to the resources the state controls.

How could the innovators have known that a harsh U-turn was ahead in which society started to head off in the opposite direction and that social inequality and a shrinking public sphere were to constitute the norm for the following generation? They could not see round the corners of time. Yet much of what was done in the sixties did hang on, even if it changed somewhat over the years. Looking back at the unsung sixties thus indicates what might be; this volume is not simply a valuable document of what was done in the past, but a provocation to rethink the present.

Acknowledgements

WE ARE VERY grateful to the Calouste Gulbenkian Foundation and the Nuffield Foundation for the grants given to us to cover transcription and office costs. In particular we appreciate the encouragement that Paul Curnow and Louie Burghes respectively gave us. We also wish to thank the Voluntary Action History Society for administering the grants.

We thank the National Council for Voluntary Organisations for giving us access to their archives, and for permission to quote from their National Voluntary Agencies Directory. We are grateful to the voluntary agencies themselves, whose beginnings are recorded in this book, for their cooperation in helping us to trace individuals involved in the setting up of their organisations.

Our thanks to Susan Hutton for the quality of her transcriptions; and to Caroline Porter and Linda Ryan for making sensible typescripts of our rough drafts.

We appreciate Ruth Valentine's invaluable reading and copy-editing of our manuscript. We also would like to thank Adrianne Blue, Ron Edwards, Helen Hastings, Judy Hildebrand, Ginger Hjelmaa and Joan Minogue for their comments during work in progress.

We thank our families and friends for their interest and support especially Ronald Cohen, Polly Curtis, Sue Henry, Caz Hildebrand and Sophie Humphreys.

We are tremendously grateful to Sheila Rowbotham for writing the Introduction, and bringing to it her knowledge and experience of the 1960s thereby providing a context for the individual stories.

For his enthusiasm as well as for publishing our book we thank David Whiting.

We cannot thank enough all those individuals who helped us at the pilot stage and who do not appear in the text; and all the people in this book who have given so generously of their time both in talking to us and in checking their particular chapters. Sadly we must record the deaths of Dorothy Bennett, David Brandon, Muriel Hackett and Joe Kenyon.

The point of the battle is to win it

Jim Radford
Family Squatting Campaign

> *When the local authority in Redbridge finally realised that smashing out
> the families who were squatting in empty properties with illegal bailiffs
> was just going to get them more and more adverse publicity, and bring
> more and more activists into the area to defend the squatters, they
> started going through the courts. We just waited until Redbridge served
> notice, and then we moved the family out but we swapped them round
> into another squat – the summons was always against a named family
> in a specified house – and the local authority had to start again you see.
> There's all kinds of ways in which the law can be used.*

DURING THE SIXTIES I coined the phrase 'do it yourself politics'
to describe the kind of community action that I was involved in.
The Squatting Campaign that I helped to launch in 1968 was a
classic example of this. It didn't just happen. It was carefully
planned and based on the experience and principles of those who
organised it. Specifically it grew out of the Homeless Hostel
Campaign, and that grew out of the Committee of 100 which was
the direct action wing of the peace movement. Bertrand Russell's
original idea was to fill the jails, and a lot of us went to jail though
we never filled them.

In the Sixties the Committee of 100 had an Industrial Sub-
Committee which I was on, and we realised – well, I realised
certainly – that it wasn't much good appealing to people to adopt
our priorities if we didn't listen and look at their priorities. And so
we began to get involved in other campaigns that didn't seem to
have any direct relationship with nuclear weapons but were
concerns that affected people, and by identifying with industrial
struggles and other struggles people started identifying with us. In
my case it sort of took over. I mean from being a ninety-nine per

1

cent peace activist, most of my activity was going into other areas although I still remained a peace activist. In 1963 the Committee of 100 organised a demonstration at Newington Lodge which was a homeless hostel in Southwark. And that was my first involvement with campaigning with homeless people.

We soon became aware of the nature and scale of homelessness. If a family became homeless and went to their local authority, the local authority had a statutory duty to make provision for them. In the vast majority of cases local authorities were not fulfilling this duty but where they did, they would put families into hostels which were usually squalid and only allowed families to stay for a limited period. In 1965, a year or two after Newington Lodge I became involved in a seminal campaign at King Hill Hostel in Kent. It was an ex-Army camp out in the wilds, big wooden huts, very poor facilities. They put the women in the hostel but the husbands were turned away and told, 'We don't cater for men, we can't have you.' Children over sixteen were also excluded. So the families were dispersed. And then after three months the women and the small children were evicted, which meant in most cases – in Kent for example where we researched it – most of the families broke up and never got back together again. There were even suicides. This had been going on for years and hundreds and hundreds of families had been destroyed. In 1965 there was a spontaneous revolt. One of the husbands moved into the hostel to be with his wife and his children, and refused to leave. The local authority took him to court, and he was sent to jail. So a group of us went down there and got the people in the hostel together. We created an organisation called the Friends of King Hill, which was all the people in the hostel and some outsiders, and we encouraged them and helped them to resist. We contacted all the women's husbands – some were sleeping in cars – and we moved them in *en masse*, barricaded the hostel, and fought a long and bitter campaign for twelve months.

King Hill Hostel served the whole of Kent at that time, including Bromley which was not yet part of Greater London. We were saying, 'Why are you sending people out to this remote place, out in the wilds, a mile walk to the nearest village? Why don't you accommodate them where there's work and where they can be in contact with their families?' They said, 'We haven't got the places.' So we said, 'Yes you have – we've researched it – you've got all these empty houses.'

Publicity was our most potent weapon. If you look at the newspapers of 1965 there weren't many weeks when we weren't on the front page of the nationals. I was the press officer for the King Hill campaign. We had tremendous coverage, the bulk of which was supportive. We made everyone in the country aware of what was going on. We invaded the House of Commons, we camped outside the Minister of Health's house, all kinds of stunts. Every week we were thinking up new things to do. And the result was not only did we get Kent County Council to totally change its policy so as to accept the whole family and to scrap the three months limit, but we compelled the Government through the force of public opinion to issue two circulars directing local authorities throughout the country to do the same. Local authorities were not implementing the fairly vague requirements of the National Assistance Act which required local authorities to provide accommodation for homeless families, and also required them to draw up a plan and submit it to the Government. No one in the Ministry had ever been given the job of chasing up local authorities to submit these plans. We were raising these issues in 1965 even though the National Assistance Act was passed in 1948. Local authorities had cobbled together some scheme of their own but they had never put it on paper and submitted it to the Minister. We changed the system throughout the country because all local authorities from then on were required to accept the whole family and not to arbitrarily evict them.

The King Hill campaign triggered off similar campaigns in other places, so there were hostel campaigns and homeless action groups springing up all over the country. It was during this campaign that our research made us aware that there were a million empty houses in the country. Round about this time Shelter was launched. So it gave Shelter a great impetus, although many people in the charity field were suspicious of us because we believed in direct action: we broke the law, we defied the authorities, we were seen as revolutionary.

During the King Hill Hostel campaign we had thought seriously about squatting the empty houses, but we decided tactically against it because it would be a diversion and our main efforts were on maintaining this fortress at King Hill. But later on, after that campaign succeeded, Ron Bailey and I began to plan the launch of the squatting movement. Ron is a great researcher, he had studied trespass law, he was into legal battles, and he discovered this loophole that no landlord could arbitrarily evict people legally. They did so illegally of course, frequently, but legally they had to take you to court and get an order against a named person. So we planned a campaign very carefully. We started off with token squats, weekend squats. The first one was an old vicarage in east London. The vicar had built himself a new modern house somewhere nearby, and the old vicarage which was a substantial Victorian house had been empty for years and no one knew when it was going to be pulled down. So we just occupied it for a weekend. Just a march, a demonstration that got a lot of publicity. The police were called before we got all the gear into the vicarage. We had people in but without their sleeping bags and provisions. So we were throwing these to the upstairs window because the bottom floor was barricaded. I threw a sleeping bag up, and a rather obnoxious policeman trying to stop me moved in front of me and a trailing piece of string from the sleeping bag brushed his helmet. He promptly arrested me. 'For what?' I said. He said, 'Assaulting a policeman.' This was absolutely ridiculous and outraged the crowd who tried to wrest me free, whereupon several of them got arrested. I didn't resist the policeman; in fact I was appealing through a loudhailer for people to be calm and non-violent. The case was dismissed eventually at Stratford Magistrates Court although one young student got fined.

We got such a good reaction – there were many people who came forward and much good publicity – so we thought, let's get on with it and let's start putting the families in. We held a large meeting in east London and got lots of people there including many who had been involved in the Homeless Hostel Campaign. We also started recruiting people in some of the more squalid local authority hostels – Part 3 Accommodation they called it – and talking to people who were living in absolutely appalling conditions. Some of these places were worse than any slum you could imagine. Eventually we chose Redbridge in east London to squat because they had a major town centre development plan that involved compulsorily purchasing and boarding up more than 1,000 houses in the centre of the town. These were perfectly good houses that had been deliberately emptied pending this development. We had previously made representations to Redbridge, and indeed to other local authorities, pointing out that they'd got all these empty houses – some of which had been empty for seven or eight years – so why didn't they use them temporarily to house homeless people instead of shunting them off somewhere else and splitting up the families. We had got nowhere with these representations, so we announced to the press that we were going to put families in houses but no one knew where we were going.

On February 9th 1969 we led a long procession from Manor Park to Ilford in Redbridge. They were all there, the press and the police. But in the early hours of the morning we'd already taken these houses. A convoy in the night did the work: we fixed them up, we put new locks on the doors and we got the water, gas and electricity put on. We announced to the press, 'These are the houses and they have already been occupied since six o'clock this morning.' That was the start of the squatting campaign in London.

All the squatting that we organised was for families who were really in need, and it was all directed at housing that was mainly owned by local authorities and in some cases the Ministry of Defence. We never knowingly went into any house that was a) owned by individuals, or b) was going to be used. We researched it pretty thoroughly beforehand and we knew exactly who owned the house and what was planned or not planned for it. As the campaign developed we called it the Family Squatting Campaign because we were squatting families, we weren't squatting individuals. We never left a homeless family on their own with bailiffs outside. When we were under siege – in order to protect the family – we would pack the house with whatever supporters we could get together who would stay in the house until it was safe.

The families who came to us for help were desperate enough to do this. The conditions they came from were so bad that this was worthwhile. They appreciated the support we gave them, and entered into the spirit of the campaign and took part. We tried to explain to everyone who became involved that we weren't just do-gooders, we weren't there to do everything for them; if they got involved, we would help them and we would stand by them, and we would get them a place, and provide all the support we could but they had to contribute, they had to become part of the group.

I organised a big public meeting in Lewisham to launch the campaign in southeast London. This brought people together who wanted and needed to squat, and activists who were willing to help. One of the first squats was in a house in Effingham Road, and because I knew that the initial squats would get maximum publicity I found a very good photogenic family with a cast iron case. This was on the front page of all the papers. Next day the local authority housing manager accompanied by the police came round to threaten us. I had all the documentation and I explained to the police what the legal situation was because they didn't know. I said, 'Look, this is the law; if you want to get us out this is what you've got to do, you've got to go to the County Court, and if you do that we'll do this.' So we made it clear that it was going to be a long struggle with continuing publicity. But I also put a detailed proposal to the housing manager and the Leader of the Conservative Council. I said, 'Why don't you leave this family in occupation? If you do, my organisation, the South East London Squatters, will guarantee to you that when you want to pull this house down we will move this family out.' I'd already entered into an arrangement with a housing association that they would help us in this way. The housing manager took this proposal back to the Council and discussed it, and after much deliberation they agreed to it. And that was the first legally agreed squat. Up until that time we'd had campaigns in Redbridge, in Southwark and various other spots, all direct action with bailiffs and battles and sieges going on, but Lewisham was the breakthrough. One of the interesting things about the squatting movement is that the first council to agree to our proposals was the Conservative Council of Lewisham. Of course it was in their interest but they had the sense to see that. We drew up a legal agreement with the Council that they would let us have short-life houses rent free. The people we moved in were not tenants, they were licensees and would pay a weekly fee – they didn't call it rent, it was a license fee – to the South East London Squatters, that's how we financed it. At first all the work was done with volunteers, we would connect up the gas and electricity and make the house habitable, repair any holes in the roof, put windows in and generally fix up but we didn't do any decorating. There are things that people can't do for themselves, things they can. We obviously needed some funds for this work. The licence fee was £2 at first and then it went up to £3 a week. Then, as the groups developed, they employed a handyman who was paid for out of their weekly licence fees. It wasn't always easy. When people came to join the squatters we explained exactly what was involved, and that it was required that they help other people to get houses. These were self-help groups, cooperative groups, everybody had to play a part. There were some people who, once they'd got in a house, wanted to sit back and enjoy it and not fulfil their obligation to the group so there were occasionally problems.

Originally we had called ourselves the East London Squatters because we started in east London. We began with a core group of maybe a dozen activists, of whom Ron Bailey and I were more or less full-time. I chaired that group, Ron did most of the legal research, I did the publicity, someone else organised the transport; Ron and I wrote the leaflets. Different people came at different times but Ron and I were constant. And then whenever we wanted to do anything, we just had to put the word out to different groups and organisations, and announce in the press, and people would turn up, in their hundreds sometimes. I was self-employed at that time, 1968/1969. And it was the reason I didn't make a fortune!

So it grew from there. Having done a deal in Lewisham which gave us a steady supply of short-life houses in that borough, we soon negotiated a similar agreement with Greenwich and crucially with the Greater London Council. The GLC agreement enabled us to use houses in many other boroughs where we immediately set out to create local groups and to manage them. To continue this process of expansion we decided to create a central organisation, The Family Squatting Advisory Service, that would employ workers to set up and support local squatting groups and be answerable to them. That was from December 1970. FSAS was made possible with the help and cooperation of Shelter whose director, Des Wilson, had initially been sceptical about the squatting solution to homelessness. However, following a television debate with me in which he expressed his criticisms with characteristic forcefulness, he had the good grace on reflection to realise that my arguments were sound and to phone me up and say so. I said, 'Right then, let's work together' which we proceeded to do with great effect! As a charity Shelter couldn't get involved in direct action but they could and did provide the money to finance the Family Squatting Advisory Service. This enabled us in the next few years to negotiate legal agreements with twenty London boroughs and to create and develop twenty Family Squatting groups to operate them, thereby bringing thousands of empty houses into use.

In each area we went into and researched we would bring

people together to create a local group. In one or two cases the groups were already there, and they joined us. Chris Holmes, who is now the Director of Shelter, was operating a group in Islington and his group joined us. But most groups were created from scratch. And they all then became part of the Family Squatting Advisory Service, a governing body with a representative from each group. We had a nucleus of four paid staff and many volunteers who set up new groups in different areas and who provided advice, support, leaflets, etcetera. But as each area became established they didn't need the Family Squatting Advisory Service so much. Then in about 1974 it hived off to become the Squatters Advisory Service. We lost or relinquished control.

The Family Squatting Advisory Service dropped the family bit when lots of single homeless squatters got involved. By the mid-Seventies there were different types of squatting. There were still the local family squatting organisations most of which were eventually persuaded – against my advice but by cautious people –to change their name. To become respectable, they dropped the word 'squatting' so they became housing associations in effect. The Lewisham group is still going and is still getting short-life houses from the Council on the same terms but it is now called Lewisham Self-Help Housing Association. We went to their 25th birthday some years ago and they wanted to know who I was. I was their founding father.

Lots of other people followed our example and began to squat including students and single homeless but I was never involved with them. When that first started there were several communal squats in central London – I remember a school in Endell Street WC2 which was full of hippies and youngsters, and got a lot of bad publicity – and that's when people started to be fearful about having their houses invaded. I went along to try and talk to them to see if we could get some kind of cooperation but we couldn't agree. We had expertise and knowledge we could have given them, but in return if we were going to be associated with them we wanted them to have the discipline we had. We didn't want them to destroy the image we had created. By that time we were viewed as responsible people and if we entered into an agreement we kept it. We said, this is how we operate, and we suggest you do something similar because otherwise you're just going to be moved from one squat to another. If you want some kind of stability you've got to enter into a deal. But they didn't want that. Lots of young people were in for the fun, they wanted to take on the world which is fine, but they weren't fighting to win, they just wanted a perpetual battle. I said, no, the point of the battle is to win it, and you've got to know what victory is. No one's going to say, 'All right, you've won, take the house, here's the deeds, and we'll pay you to live there.' I mean, you've got to have some kind of common sense, and the victory you can expect to win is one where everybody benefits, everybody gets something including the owner. However, they didn't agree so we never developed a relationship with them.

I stood down as Chair of the Family Squatting Advisory Service in 1974 because there were too many other things on my plate. I was working at Blackfriars Settlement, and doing the odd campaign as well. All these things that I fitted in, I don't know how I found the time.

From where I stand as a libertarian socialist the squatting movement was totally worthwhile. It upset a lot of bureaucrats and 'we know best' politicians but it benefited thousands of desperate families directly by putting a roof over their heads, and millions more indirectly as authorities throughout the country decided to pre-empt us by making better use of their own short-life houses. Because it was highly visible the campaign changed attitudes and policies at many levels. It inspired a new generation of community activists by showing them that direct action works and that ordinary people can not only buck the system but alter it if they are prepared to organise and to implement their own solutions to the problems that affect them. There were lots of capable people involved and I am proud to have been one of them.

I was named by the insurance man on the day I was born, 1st October 1928. That morning the man from the Pru came round for his penny a week and said, 'Right, so what's all the kerfuffle?' 'Oh we have a new baby.' He said, 'We'd better get him insured then.' In those days you insured in case anyone died, and in those days kids often did. I had a sister who had died earlier that year and that had been a big blow for the family to find money to bury her. So my dad said, 'OK, put him down.' He said, 'What's his name?' So my dad said, 'We haven't decided yet.' 'Well,' the Pru man said, 'I'll put Jim for the time being, that's a good name and if you want to change it later on let me know.' He was probably called Jim. Anyway, he put me down as Jim and that was it.

I was born into a working class family in Hull. My father came from Derbyshire originally. He was one of nine children. His mother had died in 1906, and his father died in about 1914. His family was totally split up by the First World War. He and three of his brothers were in the trenches. Two were prisoners of war, one was gassed, one was killed and one lost a leg. After the war they all moved away. My father had been in the Army throughout the First World War, and then he'd been in the Merchant Navy, that's how he came to Hull, met my mother, and got a job as a dredgerman, dredging the docks in the Humber. All my family went to sea. That's what you did in Hull.

I was the last child. Besides the sister who died aged seven I had two brothers. My mother lost a few babies including twins at birth. I still have one brother; I lost the other during the war. He was a radio operator on a tanker, the SS Cree, torpedoed in 1940.

In Hull we lived in a back street, two up and two down. Outside loo, the coal house, one tap, the garden smaller than this carpet. Very working class, I didn't know the middle class existed till I was in my teens. I knew there were rich people and poor people, and I thought all the rich people were very rich, and all the poor people were like me, like us.

I went to Clifton Street elementary school until the war started so I was almost eleven when I was evacuated. I went sixteen miles out in the country to East Yorkshire, which was a totally new world to me. It was the standard evacuation story, you were sent to school wearing a label and with your belongings in a carrier bag, and your gas mask. No idea where you were going. We were evacuated a couple of days before the war started. We were put on a bus and driven all round the countryside, kids were dropped off at different villages. I think we were given a postcard to fill in so until they got the postcard my parents had no idea where I was. I was a fairly stroppy rough-looking kid, a big hole in my jersey I remember. So I was one of the last to be picked, all the pretty ones got snapped up first. That was lucky for me. The Major lived in the big house and ran the estate for Lord Hotham who owned all that bit of Yorkshire; the Major didn't come down, he sent his old nanny, and she took what was left which was four boys. First thing she did when she took us into the house was to put us all in the bath!

I had never seen a field before. I roamed far and wide, I became very skilled at catching rabbits. I knew where all the orchards were. I was there two years. I loved it. I was well fed and well washed but I had hardly any contact with the family, it was a patronising relationship. We lived in what had been the nursery. The old nanny looked after us. There was a big kitchen, there was a cook, and a parlour-maid and a scullery maid, and a groom, and a gardener. That's how I acquired my veneer of sophistication!

I went to the village school, and then I got a scholarship for Hull College of Arts and Crafts and I went there for two years. Normally you went to elementary school till you were fourteen and then you left, but because I won this scholarship I stayed till fifteen. I liked the College of Arts and Crafts, and I left with a big portfolio of my art. I felt an obligation, having spent an extra year at school, to try and use the skills I'd acquired. Now there were only two places in Hull that I knew about where you could get any work that used artistic skills. One was City Engraving. The other one involved sign-writing, but I didn't want to sign-write although I was always pretty good at it. So I went round to City Engraving with my portfolio under my arm but there weren't any jobs going. I did my duty and went to see if there were any jobs, and then I went straight down to the shipping office because I wanted to go to sea like my two brothers had already done. That's what you aspire to do in Hull, that's how you escape from Hull. Hull was a pretty dreary town, especially during the war.

The Merchant Navy had a pool system during the war so you joined the Pool, and then they allocated you to different ships or shipping companies. But they told me I couldn't join the pool until I was sixteen. So I went round the corner to the offices of the United Towing Company because tugs weren't on the Pool. And they needed a deckhand on a docking tug. So I signed on straight away. After about three or four weeks the chap who had signed me up, came along the jetty and called out my name and said, 'We need a galley boy on the Empire Larch. Do you fancy it?' And I said, 'Yes.' The Empire Larch was a deep sea tug, a Rescue tug, and I wanted to go deep sea, I didn't want to be pottering around the docks. So I signed on that day and joined the ship and we sailed on the 23rd of April 1944.

We left Hull and we went up the east coast to Sunderland right round Scotland and down to Poole, building up a convoy of old block ships, about forty ships. The tugs were there because the old ships kept breaking down and we had to take them in tow. It wasn't until we got to Poole Harbour with this convoy that we realised what the block ships were for. We stopped two days in Poole, and on the 6th of June 1944 – D Day – we sailed for Arromanche in Normandy where we towed the ships into place in the middle of a massive bombardment. While the troops were still fighting to establish the beachhead we scuttled the ships to make a breakwater, and then we built the Mulberry harbour round them. The invasion of Europe depended entirely upon the Mulberry harbour. You can get your assault troops ashore and establish a bridgehead, but the only way that you're going to advance is if you have vast quantities of goods, if you have tanks and guns and supplies and food and petrol, all this stuff has to come ashore, and you can't land that on beaches, you had to have a harbour. We were running back and forth, towing these huge concrete caissons, Phoenixes, and big pontoons that we sank, and big floating jetties. And we built this harbour very rapidly. Ships could come in there and land heavy stuff onto these jetties whatever the weather. For six months the Mulberry harbour was the biggest harbour in the world, in terms of numbers of ships and tons of goods being landed. The vast majority of British and American, Canadian, Polish, all the troops that landed in France went through that Mulberry harbour. We didn't get much recognition but the invasion would not have been possible without this fleet of tugs.

It was a transitional experience for me. We didn't have teenagers in those days; the concept of teenager was unknown to me. From the age of fourteen or when you left school – in my case fifteen – you were either a child or you were a man, and you wanted to be a man. I'd been to sea, I'd been in action, I'd seen death and destruction and survived it and not disgraced myself in any way, so I regarded myself as a man from then on.

When I came back to Hull in 1945 I wanted to go fishing but there was a dispute on at the time so I got a job firing on the railway, shovelling coal on the steam trains that they had then, and when I was eighteen I joined the Royal Navy.

When I joined the Navy you filled in a form which asks your religion. Well, the same way I was born into a Labour family, I was born into a Church of England family, so I just said, C of E although I didn't believe in it, didn't consider it of any importance. Later on when I was out in the Mediterranean, I thought more about it and I consciously decided that I didn't believe in any religion at all; it was all nonsense as far as I was concerned and totally irrational, but because I was down as C of E I still had to take part in church parades. They have a ceremony on RN ships called Sunday divisions when you have to get into your best suit and parade. Divisions finish with prayers. And they say, 'Roman Catholics fall out,' because the Roman Catholics were excused. So they went down the mess to do their washing or whatever while the rest of us had to stand there and sing hymns and shut our eyes and say prayers. I thought, this is ridiculous. I went along to the officer in charge of records and I said, 'I want to change my religion on my card. I want you to cross out C of E and put Agnostic.' So he said, 'Oh, I can't do that. I'll put you down to see the divisional officer.' The divisional officer turned out to be a devout Christian, and he said, 'This is a very serious step you're proposing.' At some point I said to him, 'Excuse me sir, surely I have a right to change my mind about what I believe in.' He said, 'Oh yes, of course you have a right but I don't think you've given this serious thought. I'm going to send you to see the Fleet padre.' The Fleet padre lectured me at length. Listening to this guy who was educated and fluent, I realised he was talking absolute nonsense and although at that time I was reasonably articulate I wasn't well read on the subject. I got hold of Bertrand Russell's essay, *Why I'm not a Christian*, which said exactly what I thought, but he had the words, and I thought, this is me. It was my first discovery that the views I had were totally legitimate and held by people of status and reputation. I got a book on logic and started studying logic, and took to it, loved it. So when I got to see the padre again I was equipped, I knew what questions to ask him, and I knew the terminology. I remember saying things to him like, 'Surely nobody uses the teleological argument any more.' It was quite fun actually, I enjoyed that. The last meeting I had with him, he was obviously very embarrassed because by this time I was able to put points to him that he couldn't answer. So he gave me up as a bad job and they changed my record. And it made me aware that you have to persist, and that authority figures don't always know what they're talking about, and will try and bamboozle you if they can. So I suppose that my politicisation dates from that time.

I also became anti-war when I was in the Navy. I realised that all this energy, all this vast expense on battleships and cruisers, all this money and all this training and skill and effort was for what?

In order to be able to kill somebody at long range! And having seen a bit of war and what it was like, I thought there must be better ways of settling disputes. If the same effort and expense that goes into preparing to kill people were put into avoiding the necessity, it would be bound to succeed. There have been times when obviously it was necessary. I wasn't anti the Second World War – it had to be fought – but if long before that people had put the same effort into peace, maybe it wouldn't have been necessary.

In 1953 I came out of the Navy after seven years having met Jenny by then who was in the Wrens. We were at the same shore base in Wales, a radar training establishment called HMS Harrier. We got married in 1954. We've got two children close together, and then we've got an eight-year gap and then a third one: two boys and a girl. Since I didn't have any skills that were much use on land, I applied to do a Government training course in engineering at Colnbrook which is just outside Slough. I did a six months crash course in engineering, and then I got a job as an engineering fitter, working in various factories in Slough for three or four years.

During that time I became very much involved with the National Secular Society and the Humanist Association, and then I got involved in anti-war activities. I decided to use my developing talent for argumentation and applied for and got a job selling books – an expensive set of educational books for kids – for the Caxton Book Company, door-to-door stuff. I must have been good at it because they made me a supervisor after about two months, gave me a car, and I ended up training other people. I was only good at it so long as I believed in what I was selling, but then I started losing faith in it. So I got jobs selling advertising space, finally going to the *London Weekly Advertiser* as a classified advertisement manager. I was doing quite well there, earning quite a good wage for the time, until they sacked me in 1966 after a short spell in Brixton as a guest of Her Majesty! Although the owner, Mr Britten, a right-wing Tory, thought highly of my abilities he sacked me because I was very active in the peace movement and the Committee of 100, and he obviously didn't like giving me time off to spend in jail!

In 1966 I ran an anti-Vietnam War campaign called the Vietnam Action Group. We did all kinds of stunts, we were out to get publicity. And one of the things we did was the Brighton church demonstration in 1966 when we were arrested for interrupting the Labour Party at prayer. It was all meticulously planned. This was a ticket-only church service, the whole Cabinet, all the Parliamentary Labour Party were there because they start off their conference with a service in the Methodist church. We'd got a friendly MP to give us his ticket, and we'd reproduced it for members of the group. But Terry Chandler, who was the peace movement printer and an anarchist, thought this was such a good idea that he printed a lot more and gave them to all his mates. So a lot of people turned up with similar intent but without the discipline, without the plan. About twelve of us had a plan. We had a statement which I had written, and we knew when we were going to make it. If one person was stopped another person took up exactly where they left off, so the statement got full hearing. We had previously done the same thing in ten West End theatres on the same night during the intervals. The statement made the point that the British Government was colluding in, and supporting, the American war in Vietnam, which was totally unjustified and inhumane. So we got arrested. And because they couldn't get us on conspiracy, they got us under an ancient church law. Under the Ecclesiastical Courts Jurisdiction Act of 1860-something, it is an offence of indecency to interrupt a church service. Nicholas Walter and I were convicted and sentenced to two months in spite of the fact that the head of that church, Donald Soper, was one of our defence witnesses; he said that's absolute nonsense, this is in the best traditions of Methodism for people to speak out against what they see as injustice.

While I'd been in jail I'd been anticipating with my usual forethought that Mr Britten would give me the chop, so I thought what shall I do? And I thought what could I do at home that will earn me a living and leave me free to campaign? I can splice, I'm a very good splicer. So I did some research and invented the double-strength tow-ropes for cars. The link that I invented was a movable cleat. It's non-jamming so it's better than a hook, and I packaged it, and started selling it round garages. I taught my kids, and when they came home from school I'd get them all cutting up rope, taught them how to splice and burn the ends. It earned me a living of sorts. The trouble was, I was so much involved in housing action, squatting and the peace movement that I never had any time. So I earned my living in what other people would regard as spare time. I'd come home in the evening and watch television and splice at the same time. If I'd concentrated full-time on those tow ropes, I'd be a wealthy man by now because they sold well. I also did fluorescent armbands for school kids, and a bit of writing. There was a magazine called *Help* came out about then. It was an attempt to create a glossy, high quality journal for community and social services like a sort of *New Society*. And I wrote a column for them for a year or so for £30 a week.

As the squatting movement developed I made a lot of jobs for other people but I never made a job for myself. I did take ancillary jobs, for instance when I persuaded Paul Curno to provide a base for the South East London Squatters in the Albany, a settlement in Deptford. I then worked for the Albany as a community worker, and ran various tenants' action campaigns, which I would probably have done voluntarily but we managed to get some money for it. And then in 1970 they started these community work courses, so I put my name down, got a grant and went to Goldsmiths' for two years while still centrally involved in the squatting movement.

The rest of my working life was full-time community work, apart from a few years as press officer at Greenwich Council and occasional free lance journalism. I was Director of Blackfriars Settlement for three years, 1972 to 1975. And then I went to Manchester Council for Voluntary Service and ran that for five years. The Community Resource Unit was set up in Manchester with Gulbenkian money and a bit from Rowntrees, and I ran that from 1980 to 1984. The idea of the Community Resource Unit was that someone – me – should go round the country trying to identify and put together issues and people to initiate campaigns that might become models for participatory democracy. There was high unemployment at that time and I became involved with various unemployed groups, and was instrumental in bringing them together to form the National Unemployed Workers Movement. That really took over the CRU because it needed so much time and energy. It was a success in that we had thirty to forty groups throughout England and Scotland who were united, and some of them set up their own projects, but the reason it never took off and never became the threat to the Establishment and the Government which I wanted it to become, was because the Trade Union Congress blocked it. Our argument was, if you're an unemployed bus driver, you've got more in common with an unemployed bricklayer than you have with an employed bus driver; your needs and your interests and your concerns are the same as other unemployed people. We were trying to create power for the unemployed. We had almost three million unemployed and if they got together and used their power they could have made things happen, like pensioners' power. I saw that, and a lot of the unemployed saw that, but the trade unions wouldn't wear it or support a national unemployed union which was a great shame because that could have been a big success story.

After CRU's funding expired we came back to London. I couldn't immediately find an interesting job in community work so I took the job with Greenwich Council. I was their chief press officer for three years from 1985 to 1988. Then a more interesting job came up, a community development job called Unified Community Action in Ealing. The reason I was interested in it was because when I was in Manchester I had thought about and written about this recurring problem in community work: you get local authorities or agencies to employ community workers to help groups in the community, and very often the help they need is to change the policy of the authority that employs the community worker. The issues that bring people together are usually an obvious need like housing, or an injustice. But when community workers are effective the employers tend to say, 'Why are we paying this person to help people to campaign against us? This is embarrassing us.' Whoever had originally conceived the UCA scheme in Ealing had addressed this, and set out that the UCA team would have dual responsibility, i.e. to their employers and to the community they served. I elaborated on this and said, if there are protests – as indeed there were while I was there, and I helped to organise many of them – then I will make it quite clear to the groups I am working with that I would help them to the very best of my ability, but I would also try and help the Council to get itself off the hook by pre-empting it: by telling the authority that if they didn't make changes, this is what's going to happen. But it didn't work very well because the Tory Council that took over in Ealing didn't like any of this especially when I helped tenants to expose gross malpractice in the Housing Department! They couldn't sack me on any reasonable grounds – I would have had every group in the borough up in arms – so they reorganised and made me redundant in 1991.

I did go for other jobs but I was obviously too old at 63. Ageism comes into it. However I continued to provide support and advice to several groups as a volunteer, among them the Community Rights Project. This is an organisation that Ron Bailey originally set up and I chaired for a long time. Under Ron the Community Rights Project steered through eleven pieces of legislation including the Local Government Access to Information Act. We published a lot of useful information: books, pamphlets, leaflets. Ron was more interested in the parliamentary side, and I was more interested in the group development side. CRP was a very useful resource for any organisation or campaigning group that wasn't itself equipped to carry out research.

Currently – in 2001 – I'm involved in the London Alliance, which is the campaign for democracy in London. We supported Ken Livingstone for Mayor. We don't really want a mayor, we want a proper democratic government for London which is now the only capital city in Europe that doesn't have its own elected authority. It's ridiculous. But we've now got this assembly which is a start. Also, because I think there needs to be a Left alternative to the Labour Party I'm involved in the Socialist Alliance here in Lewisham and Greenwich. My eldest son, Steve, is similarly involved in the Hull and East Yorkshire Socialist Alliance.

I'm also very active on the folk singing scene. I have always liked folk music but it's only in recent years that I've been devoting so much time to it, never had the time before. Having been a workaholic for much of my life I'm making better use of my leisure now. It took me seven years to get used to not doing a paid job. I thought, somebody's sure to come and headhunt me. I'll tell you when I gave up looking for a job. There's a little community centre down the road, little tin-pot group, and it's got a residents' association which I'm now a part of. The centre advertised for a community worker – it was a very small job, not much pay – and I thought, well it's on my doorstep, there's nothing they want doing that I can't do and haven't done well. So I applied for that and didn't get it, and I thought, bloody hell if I can't get that job, I can't get anything!

I now describe myself as retired but that doesn't mean that I'm not working. I am press officer for several groups and I think I am still good for a few more campaigns.

£325 to re-house a family

Eileen Ware
Shelter

I would go into a multi-occupied house and there would be a room, if it was 10 foot square you were lucky, and there would be mum, dad, three, four children. You know, the kids sharing bunk-beds, parents in a small bed in the corner, or just lying on the floor. There was one place which Shelter used in an advertisement – it was actually a house I went to – that had, I think it was 21 or 22 people sharing one toilet when it worked. There might be only one sink in the house, perhaps a couple, and very rarely would people have a sink in their own room. They almost always shared what used to be laughingly called a kitchen, but that was often just a cooker on a landing. I am talking about real poverty, and I'm not just talking about one family that I saw like that; I'm talking about family after family after family after family.

SHELTER WAS LAUNCHED December 1st 1966, and I joined in the spring of 1967. At the time there was a very strong housing association movement and a lot of it was church-based, particularly led by Bishop Eamonn Casey who at the time ran the Catholic Housing Aid Society. I think most of the housing associations then had some sort of connection with churches of all denominations, the Catholic Church, the Methodist Church, there was somebody who was a Baptist minister there, there was certainly an Anglican. The housing associations needed to raise money, and I guess they recognised that talking about housing associations is not a sexy way to raise money, not that that expression would have been used then. So they decided that what they needed was some means of being able to raise the money to distribute to housing associations. Shelter was set up as an organisation which would distribute the money. It was quite specifically a fundraising and campaigning organisation, and it would distribute its money to housing associations and to housing aid centres.

Des Wilson was brought in right at the beginning, he had been I think working in advertising at the time, certainly was a journalist, and he devised the launch. One of the things Des Wilson believes very strongly is that if you're going to launch any sort of campaign you have to do a huge amount of homework first, so that when you launch it you know your subject inside out, you know what all the problems might be, and you have built up your support by working very closely beforehand with journalists. I mean I remember Shelter being launched very clearly even though I wasn't yet there and homelessness wasn't something that I had shown any huge amount of interest in before. It was launched with a big bang. But part of the reason for that was because about a week or ten days before, quite unbeknown to anybody at all, *Cathy Come Home* was shown on television, and that was the first bit of really obvious social action broadcasting, and I use that term because it's relevant to what I did later on. There were so many people responding, wanting to help Cathy, that the telephone lines within the BBC just blew, they just couldn't cope with it, they hadn't anticipated it. I think it was the first really big-response programme. And that meant that when Shelter was launched, ten days, whatever it was later, people already were geared up to wanting to do something about helping people who were homeless. And so that was exactly what happened, it was just a huge success right from the very beginning. *Cathy Come Home* was shown again on television I think shortly after the launch. It used to drive me crazy because for the first couple of years at Shelter we were given the rights to show it, so everywhere we went we were showing *Cathy Come Home*, and I just knew the film backwards. I was going to say, it wouldn't have made any difference if there hadn't been *Cathy Come Home*; that's silly, of course it would have made a difference, it would have been harder, but Shelter would still have been a huge success.

It was just right. I mean its success was due to all sorts of things. When Shelter was launched all of the leaflets were printed on brown paper, literally on brown paper, and of course the reaction of everyone to this is, at last an organisation which hasn't spent lots of money on public relations. In fact that wasn't actually true, because brown paper is very expensive to print on. I mean we very quickly reverted to something that made more sense, but it sent out a message. And Shelter's pictures were quite different from the sort of photographs that had been used previously in charity advertising, they were much clearer, they were stark black and white. We did things in terms of attracting attention, but my goodness, everybody would look at those now and just think they were old hat. We had an advertisement, had a picture of a family, and it was an actual quote of something that had been said by the family, who lived in Scotland. The interviewer asked, 'What are you going to do at Christmas?' And the guy just said, 'Christmas, you can stuff it for all we care.' So we used that in an advertisement, which of course meant we got masses of publicity for it, because you didn't say things like this and put it in advertisements.

The voluntary sector didn't think about image then. But Shelter had thought about the whole image. All of the people who worked for it were young, I mean Des never got out of jeans because that was just what he was comfortable in. He is now embarrassed about it and says, 'Why did you let me wear jeans?' But that was actually part of the attraction of Shelter. Everybody who worked for it was young, I was 23, and Des was three or four years older, but nobody was much older than 30. When you went to events and you went into schools, women's organisations or whatever, and when you went on television, people saw a different sort of image of a charity. I organised events at the party conferences at a time when organisations from outside the political movements didn't do that. We would also have fringe meetings at other organisations' big conferences and events. This was something new. I think because we actually saw things differently, because we didn't have baggage with us, we didn't know how to do these things. I'd never done anything like this before. I think because of that we brought a freshness to it, and people were just ready for it, we were lucky. That sort of ethos – of young people doing things – was very strong in America, and I think we helped to strengthen it in England in a very different way. I think Shelter did, yes.

Des Wilson was the first Director. I was one of the first people that he employed once he became Director, and I joined to do media and public relations work. I'm pretty sure there were six or seven of us. The office was somewhere around Tottenham Court Road but we moved fairly quickly to the Strand, into a building that was part of that big Shell building, right next door to the Savoy Hotel. Liz Wills was Groups Director. She had somebody working with her whose job was to go out and set up Shelter groups. The aim of Shelter groups was to raise money like fundraising groups now. The groups were very successful. They were a way of harnessing people's enthusiasm, to get money raised locally. I think to be a big national charity you've got no choice but to do that. It was then the most effective way of raising money. I don't think it works so easily now. Cindy Barlow did administrative work. Pat Speirs, who is now running her own very successful art gallery was the special events organiser, so she would get involved with groups of well-heeled ladies to organise a ball here or a ball there or an art thing somewhere else. I remember there was somebody particularly concerned with raising money amongst private sector corporations. And there were freelancers who helped produce reports and deal with housing issues. It was a very closely knit group.

We were all paid. Well, I couldn't have worked for Shelter if I didn't get paid. I had been working for a local newspaper where I was paid peanuts, but I think I was paid an even smaller number of peanuts when I went to Shelter. Certainly a lot of people were surprised that we were paid, because they just assumed that we came from a group of people who didn't need paying. We had volunteers, yes, and later on volunteers became much more organised. All the people who were out in the field were volunteers and we started to have what we called volunteers' evenings. One evening a week we got together all the volunteers, so it became almost a club and it was a really good social thing for them, but it also meant that we could get huge mailings organised, and a lot of those jobs that are just so time-consuming. We all used to take it in turns to stay late at night and help out, and it was good fun. And students would just ring up and say, 'Look, I've got three months off from university; can I come and help?' We'd have people like that.

Once we got the money in it was distributed. There was a board and the board allocated money to the different housing associations. One of the phrases that we had was £325 to re-house a family. You actually needed £325 to trigger other money, because there were all sorts of grants that were available. The housing associations worked by buying property, converting them into flats, and renting them out at a reasonable rent. So you had this rotation of money really.

The £325 to re-house a family was a very big attraction because £325, even then, was a sum that people could imagine raising. Later, when I became Shelter's Youth Director, we figured out that if twenty-two people did a sponsored walk – I think it was maybe fifteen miles – they could raise £325. Suddenly people began to understand that they could raise that money. A local group, a church, a school, knew that they could actually re-house a family, and it was genuine. Donors didn't adopt a family, they didn't know the family but they did actually re-house a family. That is the sort of thing that triggered enthusiasm to want to do something.

A lot of the things that we did at Shelter were really fun. I mean it was the Sixties so everybody was having fun. It was very much a young person's time, and we were young people, we were being given an opportunity that nobody before then at that age ever got. Of course we didn't realise it at the time. I think when people get that opportunity, you just do trigger off ideas from one another.

What we were doing was actually very simple, there was no intellectual argument about it. I think it was quite a long time before we started to get people in the organisation who started to do that. It was just, here was somebody who was in need because they were homeless; here was an organisation that could actually put them into accommodation that would be much better, but it needed money. So how did we get the money? We would go out and raise it. And I think it was as simple as that. It just wasn't more complicated, we didn't think about anything else. There were people in the organisation who clearly did, I wasn't involved in the financial side of it but I do know that it was extremely carefully controlled, both in terms of spending money, and we spent very little money to raise money, and in terms of how the money was distributed.

If you have local groups of volunteers who get involved in raising money and if the local community has got a housing problem, the local community is going to go to that group because it's promoting the cause of people who are homeless. This was something we had to be quite careful about. I can remember that being an issue that we had to deal with, because the groups weren't housing experts and actually most of us working at the Shelter office weren't housing experts either. We were good at fundraising or public relations or whatever it might have been, but we weren't housing experts. And we had to get people to recognise their limitations. I don't think it was very difficult for head office but it certainly was for some of the groups. Often people could be helped not by re-housing them, but by being given advice so we would encourage Shelter groups to fit in with their local advice network. Increasingly more housing action groups were being set up locally which didn't particularly have anything to do with Shelter, although we sometimes got involved.

We used the term 'homeless' to mean people who were living in conditions that you couldn't by any means of the imagination call home, and who were surviving but they weren't living, they really did not have basic things that made it possible for them to lead anything like a normal family life. We were very clear about our definition of homelessness. There were also obviously people who were homeless and on the streets, actually not as many as there are now, but people who literally had nowhere to go, and there were a lot of other organisations which were working specifically to help those people. But the biggest housing issue that came up was the squatters. I think a lot of newspapers wanted there to be a split, and we worked very hard at making sure that there wasn't. We might sometimes have had views about some of the things that the squatters did, but we were certainly not going to make those public. We worked very closely with people like Ron Bailey and Jim Radford. A lot of people said, 'Oh you've got competition now,' but we weren't prepared to see it as competition. It wasn't competition, because what they were doing was different. It did affect us, because people did get muddled about the two.

Eamonn Casey's Catholic Housing Aid Centre was very obviously a brilliant idea, because so many people had housing problems as opposed to being homeless. I particularly remember an awful lot of people were living in private accommodation. So many people had housing problems, where they needed information, the sort of thing the Citizens Advice Bureaux could provide. But because it was the Catholic Housing Aid Society, although it would help anybody at all, and did, a lot of people wouldn't go to it because they felt that they had to be Catholic to do so. So basically the idea was devised – I think very much by the people involved in the Catholic Housing Aid Society – that they set up a Shelter Housing Aid Centre, SHAC. Initially Eamonn Casey was the person who ran it, until he was made a bishop and went to Ireland. But it wasn't Shelter. It was one of the organisations Shelter gave money to.

I can remember doing one speaking engagement with a group of very well-heeled women, and I recognised that I was talking to a hostile audience, and after I'd finished, one of the women said, 'I don't really see any point in helping these people; if you re-house them they wouldn't know what sort of curtains to put in the window anyway.' Which was the least of their problems. I actually didn't know how to answer it. I mean it was the time when everybody was talking about, re-house them and they put coals in the bath. That attitude was something that went on and on and on. People were just living in totally different worlds, and the conditions that these people were living in were so bad that the coals in the bath and whether they knew what sort of curtains to put up at the window, was almost funny, because, you know, the housing was just too bad to worry about things like that. After a time I didn't even bother to argue with them, they were never going to understand.

I can't remember when Enoch Powell made his 'rivers of blood' speech. But I do remember the day it happened because I was travelling, and I didn't see the publicity, and I went into a school in Birmingham, and I was aware that there was a really strange atmosphere and the teachers were very upset. It was the first time they had ever had any sort of race trouble in the school at all, and they were just separating groups of kids. Around that time Shelter got letters with cheques attached saying, we want this to help a family but we only want it to help white families, and we used to send the cheques back. We just wouldn't use the money. It wasn't a policy decision that was made by any committee; I would have said it was more by instinct than anything else. It was just something that staff wouldn't have been prepared to tolerate.

After a time I became Youth Director so I was working with young people to raise money. The one group that I hated talking to were the students because a lot of them took the attitude that there was no point in helping the homeless, that what you actually needed to do was to let them sink so low that they would be rioting and therefore the Government would be forced to do something. Now that is not an unusual argument, you hear it now, but I just could not deal with it, so I wouldn't get involved.

We had some good fundraising campaigns. One we ran as a competition we called the Young Tycoon, who was the most likely to become a Shelter Tycoon. And I do very clearly remember the kids that won it, they were boys, it was in a boarding school, and one of them had actually persuaded the others to join in with him, so that they set up a cooperative and bought potatoes and some fat, borrowed the school kitchen, and cooked chips to sell to the rest of the kids. I would love to know what happened to him. We did a lot to get people interested in the subject of housing. I eventually set up the Shelter Youth Education Programme, which recognised that young people needed to understand more about housing if they were going to stop themselves from becoming homeless, so it was a preventive programme. It must have been about 1970/1971.

We often used to do things that were aimed at quite young children. There was one fundraising activity which we wouldn't do because I just put my foot down. A lot of schools at that time would have charity drives where they sent the kids home and expected them to bring back sixpence the following day for charity. And it was usually for charity, not for a specific charity. And I flatly refused to have anything to do with that, I just thought it was so wrong. As much as possible we tried to get kids involved. We were very aware that young children wanted to be involved, they wanted to be part of what their big brothers and sisters were already doing, but we also didn't want to exploit them, and there was a sense in which if you got them interested when they were very young they would actually work for you when they were older. We did do things like painting competitions for children. I remember the first painting competition that we had was to draw a picture of what homelessness was like. It was won by an infants' school in Surrey. One particular class sent in so many good entries. I can remember one of the paintings was twenty-two children, three cats and two mice all living in one room, and you could see the people all around the edge of the picture. Another one was signposts, it was a family signpost, and one way it said 'Mum', the other way it said 'Dad', the other way it said 'Children'. And the teacher said the child's parents had split up because they didn't have anywhere to live – in a wealthy town in Surrey. Now that shows how extensive homelessness was. People tend to think of it being in the Gorbals or Notting Hill

I'll tell you another fundraising event which I loved. There was one occasion when Shelter had an awayday to brainstorm and plan the campaign for the next six months. It was held on the day I was going on holiday so I went straight from the awayday out to the airport. The awayday was just after the first man landed on the moon and the second rocket was going to land the second man on the moon, and suddenly the idea hit me. And we had, and this again was aimed at young children particularly, we had a Shelter space race, and we challenged young people to raise money at a penny, an old penny, at a penny a mile, to get to the moon. I can't remember how many miles it is to the moon but we knew we had to see if we could get there before the Americans. So from the second the rocket took off, we had kids collecting pennies and ringing the number through to Shelter Space Stations which were staffed by Shelternauts – our volunteers. And we did beat the Americans.

I think looking back on it, all of the things that I have learnt about campaigning or doing public relations, I learnt from Des. And also from working collectively together as a group. The phrase 'work ethic' makes me cringe, but there was an attitude – I think there was probably an attitude in the Sixties actually – amongst the people there, everybody knew what they were doing and they just got on and did it. I do remember the occasional person who would come along and not do anything, and they didn't last, and I don't mean they didn't last because they were got rid of; they didn't last because if you took that attitude, you couldn't last the course. We really did work incredibly long hours. I mean I can remember a couple of occasions Des telling people they had got to take a week off and go away on holiday, because people were just getting burnt out. And there are some people who say that to an extent we were exploited. I'm never quite sure. I mean I think if anybody exploited people at Shelter it was actually the people who allowed the housing situation to exist, allowed people to live in the sort of conditions that they were living in. That was who we were exploited by; I don't think we were exploited by anybody who ran Shelter, and I don't think that we exploited people either. The job needed doing. And when people nowadays say that they shouldn't be expected to work after five o'clock, if you're half-way through a conversation with somebody who is homeless and it's 5 o'clock, you're not about to say, 'Sorry but I've got to go now'. You just don't do it. It was often questioned whether Shelter was doing work that was correct for a charity or whether it was too political. Des often used to say, well, Shelter's very existence was political, and that's true with certainly most of the charities that I've worked for since; if the situation were different, then the charities wouldn't need to be there, but they do have to be there, so who's exploiting whom?

I don't even want to think about the hours we worked. I mean you were in the office as far as I can remember at nine o'clock. If you're working for that sort of a charity then you've got a job to do during normal hours, but the volunteers are giving their time to Shelter outside their working hours. So it was very rare that I wasn't working in the evenings, because you'd go and talk to this group or that group. Most mornings I would be speaking at a school assembly, and I spoke at hundreds of them. First of all you had to get to your school assembly about nine o'clock. And then talk to about seven classes during the course of any day, and on one occasion I remember I also spoke to a lunchtime group, an after-5 group, and I then spoke in the evening. At the end of it I was hoarse. But everybody was doing it, I wasn't the only one. You had to travel to these places as well. But you didn't think about it, you just did it; it needs doing, and every now and again you got too tired so you stopped.

Des always said he was going to stay for five years, and he did. He would have left in about 1971 so I suppose I left in about 1973. Well, Shelter had a few problems after Des left. And what caused the problem if you ignore all the personalities – and a lot of it was to do with people – was bad judgement and a misunderstanding of the situation. You've got a situation where you have board members who didn't take a particular interest in the organisation but were responsible for it, suddenly realised they had to make a decision about something like who the new director was going to be, so decided that they would go ahead and make that decision. Now, I'm not saying they didn't know about housing because they did know about housing, because they came from the housing association movement, but they didn't understand Shelter at all, and they didn't understand the way it had been run. So when a decision was made about who the new director was going to be, without any consultation with staff, the staff actually said, we don't want to make the decision about this but we want you to talk to us about the sort of person we think should be in that position. It was just this complete lack of recognition of how people who were working in the organisation and really giving their all to it, should be involved in the way that organisation is run. And so the people who had to pick up the pieces after that had a tough grind.

I was born in 1943 in Ballymena. My name, Eileen Ware, is not a married name, I'm not married. I was born in Northern Ireland only because my father happened to be stationed there. He was a conscripted soldier. My parents were both from London. And so we came back to London, when I was a few months old. I've got one brother, three years younger.

I was brought up in Battersea in a council house. When my father came back from the Army, they were re-housed in a prefab till I was about nine or ten, when we moved into a council house.

My mother at that time didn't do anything; my father was in his father's business, a very small business. They reconditioned pianos. He died when I was seventeen.

We were very much a family, I mean we did go out as a family, and my grandparents, all my aunts and uncles lived close by, within walking distance. My mother had two sisters and three brothers, and although my father didn't have any brothers or sisters he had lots of cousins, and we're still in touch. We had a car because my father needed one for his business, so we would go out for the day. We used to go on car rallies, a sort of treasure hunt in cars.

I went to a girls' secondary school in Tooting. That sort of school doesn't exist now. I always describe it as the forerunner of comprehensives because it wasn't secondary modern and it wasn't grammar. It was streamed and the top stream in each year would take the GCE, and I was for some reason in the top stream, and I got five 'O' levels but with difficulty. We also did shorthand and typing. It was a subject you automatically did, whether you liked it or not. It was only a five-year school, there was no sixth form. You might get two or three girls in each year who would go on to do nursing. But basically everybody left at fifteen, an alternative didn't really arise. I left school just before my 16th birthday in 1959.

I don't think that the idea of anybody having a career actually arose. We had even then employment advisers who used to trot into the school, and if you were in the GCE stream, the only thing they could think that you could possibly do was to go into a bank, go into nursing, or – well, I'm not actually sure that there was anything that they saw beyond that. I didn't want to work in a bank. I wanted to be a journalist, so basically they washed their hands of me. Oh they did try to persuade me to be a librarian. I did devour books, that was true, but anybody who knows me falls about laughing at the idea that I should be a librarian because they can't imagine me staying quiet for long enough; I'd be telling people what they should read. My mother, who I would never have described as being a pushy person, on this occasion quite clearly was, because she just got irritated and said, where would you really like to work? All I could think of was the Hulton Press which ran all the big magazines. So she said, 'Well all right, we'll go.' So we walked down Fleet Street and we went into Hulton Press, and she asked to see the personnel person, and when I came out I'd got a job. I was earning £6 a week, and that was a hell of a lot more than anybody else was earning. I think I was lucky. I worked in the office of the editor and the deputy editor, I can't even remember the name of the publication, and they had a secretary who was – I don't mean she was old, because she wasn't – an old-fashioned secretary, Miss Feudiland. It was an incredible name to spell and say, and woe betide you if you didn't get it right the first time you met her. If you started work at 9 o'clock, you were there at 9 o'clock, and I don't mean you took your coat off at 9 o'clock, I mean you were sitting at your desk at 9 o'clock. If you had to go home, your leaving time was 5 o'clock; it was probably half-past 5 actually, if you hadn't finished what you were filing, or the letters, you stayed until you'd finished it. We didn't have electric typewriters so if you made a mistake, woe betide you if there was the tiniest sign that there was a mistake on it. And you always did your filing at the end of the day. It was just automatic. I didn't know any different, that was the way I thought people should behave in offices. So I think it was one of the best things that happened to me, because I actually learnt how to organise.

Then I went to a different job in Lloyd's Shipping Corporation, again for a publication and again I happened to work with somebody who this time was a lot older, but again who was extremely fussy and absolutely meticulous, and again I think it was very lucky. Around the time that my father died, an uncle who was working for Bird's Eye foods got me an interview with the personnel officer there and I went and worked in the public relations department as a dogsbody. The first day I went, the organisation was having a press conference to announce that it was reducing prices, so I just walked straight into a press conference and had to help out at that. So again I was just so lucky, because all of those jobs combined together actually meant that I learnt how to do basic organisation. Plus the fact that I was able to do shorthand

and typing and had reasonable communication skills. I worked at Birds Eye for about eighteen months, but I was still longing to be a journalist.

In the meantime I had become involved in the Young Liberals because was it Cuba or was it Suez? Whatever it was, it was a situation where there was a huge hoo-ha about conscription, and people having to go into the Army. And I got very incensed with something I'd heard on the radio, when somebody had gone on and on about how young people should go into the Army. And then the next question they had was something to do with voting, the voting age. And I got so irritated I wrote saying, if young people are old enough to fight in a war and give their life, they're jolly well old enough to vote. I mean it was just logical as far as I was concerned. I decided that perhaps I ought to know something about politics. I mean this is ironic, because I am now in the Labour Party, but then I didn't want to be in the Labour Party. I didn't know about the Young Conservatives, and I was pretty sure that my parents voted Liberal. I went along to a Young Conservative meeting and it really was all girlfriends, boyfriends, and I wasn't the tiniest bit interested. I went along to a Young Liberal meeting, and they were having a discussion about what resolution they should put to their Young Liberal Conference. And it sort of went round the table, it was just a small group of people, I don't know, a dozen or something like that. Everybody was being asked to talk about something that they thought was important, so I talked about votes at eighteen. So I finished up going to a Young Liberal Conference at the age of eighteen or nineteen and proposing a resolution – the first time I'd ever stood on my feet or spoken –for votes at eighteen which got a huge amount of publicity. As a result of that, I became press officer for the Young Liberal group. And I suddenly got a telephone call from one of the local journalists on the *South Western Star*, it was only a very small paper based in Clapham, who said, 'The editor would like to see you, would you come in and have a chat with him?' For about three weeks in a row press releases I had sent in about the Young Liberals finished up being headlines in the paper. So he said, 'How would you like to come and work for us?' So I said, 'Yes please.' And that was how I became a journalist.

I loved reading, I liked writing. What I never understood until I actually started doing it was that journalism isn't the same as writing. I'm curious, I suppose I am nosy, but I don't think I'm a real gossip. I can always remember one occasion when a child had drowned in a pond and the editor said, 'Go and interview the family,' and I said, 'If you want an interview with the family, you go and interview the family, I'm not going to.' I was just absolutely horrified. I did my three-year indenture. People then were indentured, it's like an apprenticeship. It's a contract, I will work for you for three years, you will train me. But I knew that really journalism was not for me; I liked writing but I didn't like journalism.

And I saw the ad in the paper for Shelter, it was the first job I applied for. I don't think I was even looking for a job, I just saw the ad. I would have said something different at the time, but I think I had realised that if you wanted to do anything about some of the things I was starting to get interested in, then actually you were more likely to do it through a small organisation dedicated to that subject than you were through politics. And I'm not sure whether I still think that, but I certainly did then, and I think a lot of people who were involved in these organisations in the Sixties thought that too.

When I worked for the *South Western Star* which was part of a big group – but I don't think it exists now – the main office was in Hornsey I think. I always remember on one occasion having to take something up to the head office, to the chairman of the company. And we were very badly paid, and we were in a tiny little office that was near as damn it under the railway at Clapham Junction, it was just really awful, with grotty, very old typewriters, and always complaints, not from the editor but from the owners of the newspaper, if you spent the tiniest amount on expenses, and we did only spend the tiniest amount on expenses. I had to deliver this item to the head office, which was miles from Clapham Junction, I mean it took all day, and when I got there I had to wait, and I can remember very clearly, it was in an oak-panelled room. It was still in a pretty grotty area, but it was nonetheless in an oak-panelled room, and I can remember a secretary had brought out a tray that the Chairman had obviously had with a very nice white china teapot, and a nice cup and saucer and some biscuits on a plate, it was just for one – him, not me. I did whatever I had to do, and saw him leave in a chauffeur-driven car. And I've always said, and I still think I believe it, I don't understand why people work for a company like that, to make people like him rich. I don't think I said anything at the time, but you can hear, you can tell how well I remember it, and I don't think I've distorted the memory of it, but it really did get me, and I've worked for charities ever since.

After Shelter I did a couple of short contract pieces of work to do with fundraising, and then went to the Family Planning Association. I was involved in Population Count Down, which I think does still exist actually although the name is slightly different. We were raising money for family planning, and family projects in developing countries. That job lasted for about eighteen months, and then I went to the Volunteer Centre in 1975 to do press and publicity work.

The Volunteer Centre at the time was very small. It was based at the King's Fund and then moved out to Berkhamsted. Ian Bruce had taken over as director and he was expanding it. At the time ITV was trying out a number of programmes for recruiting volunteers and because we were the Volunteer Centre we decided that we ought to take an interest in these programmes. So Diana Leat, the research officer, and I went trotting off to Yorkshire Television, and Cumbria was another one and it became clear that there was a need to get broadcasters and voluntary organisations to work together on the whole idea of volunteer recruitment. I argued that volunteer recruitment was only the tip of the iceberg, because there were other ways in which voluntary organisations and television or radio could get involved in social issues. I had *Cathy Come Home* in mind, because I had that experience behind me. And we persuaded the Home Office, the BBC and the then Independent Broadcasting Authority, all to put money into a pot. So I spent the next ten years getting the voluntary organisations and broadcasters to work together. Eventually I left and spent a year, well less than a year, working with somebody else who was thinking of setting up a public relations business. It just didn't work out, we had different characters.

I saw the job at FullEmploy advertised, applied for it and got it. And again, I finished up changing the job once I got into it. It was about black economic development, and it was partly a training organisation that did a lot of work in trying to get companies or employers to recognise their responsibilities in terms of black people generally. I started off doing press and public relations work for them, but in the end finished up working in the chief executive's office with the job of getting the issue of black economic development raised without necessarily talking about FullEmploy. So I was working with politicians, I was lobbying, I was working with companies, I was dealing with the media. The organisation got into financial trouble, partly but not exclusively, as a result of Government changing its funding for training agencies, when a lot of organisations bit the dust. I then started freelance work.

Most of my personal life has tended to be work really. Because most of the things I've done have been fun. I started to live with the person I'm living with now about five years ago, but for donkey's years I lived by myself quite happily.

In my spare time I read, cook. I mean the same as it's always been, the same as when I grew up, spending time with friends, and eating, and, partly because my partner who works for a trade union is so busy we don't get a chance to go out as much as I would like, to things like cinema and theatre. Oh, we do often go to listen to music, jazz. But most of it is good friends.

Anybody that I know who works for anything connected with the voluntary sector or for a non-profit organisation, does not do it as a way of making money and it's certainly not as a way of getting much spare time. It's very very easy to get caught up in doing an awful lot of work that you don't get paid for, and I can't afford to. I mean I have got to earn money but I'm not interested in earning masses of money. Three times I've actually dropped money to do a particular job that I wanted to do. I would always have rather spent my time doing something I was interested in and wanted to do, than earning the money. If you actually had money, if you had real money to lose, you would think twice about that. But you take chances, and you're prepared to take chances, because on balance you're still going to gain more. I really am not a gambler. I buy my one Lottery ticket, twice a week. But no, most of the time I don't even check it, I've no anticipation that I might win at all.

A kind of sixties passion

David Brandon
Centrepoint

I think one of the interesting things about going back after 40 years, I've been 45 years in homelessness altogether, is that very little has changed. I went to visit a place I hadn't been to for 30 years, I could have picked up my soup ladle and carried on. It's absolutely incredible how resistant to innovation and change homelessness is, it's quite astonishing, yes. Each generation has to rediscover it afresh, you know, and that's incredibly annoying because it means that we don't learn from previous generations, in fact we make exactly the same mistakes. Now I find that heartbreaking that we do that. I can hardly bear it.

IN 1965 PROBABLY the most famous TV programme ever was produced, *Cathy Come Home*. I helped and also appeared in it. I don't think you can really imagine the impact of this programme. It had an astonishing impact. So from that came a lot of the work in the homelessness field like the development of Shelter and the Cyrenians and St Mungo's. There was an enormous energy around homelessness.

By the end of the Sixties I had just qualified as a psychiatric social worker and was working for Christian Action in a shelter in Lambeth, South London. And I and several others got involved with Father Ken Leech of St. Anne's Church, Soho, and he began to talk in the summer of 1969 about a homeless project, which wasn't called Centrepoint then at all. This project was to be in the basement of St. Anne's Church. The entrance was in Shaftesbury Avenue, although the church entrance was in Dean Street. Ken was a guy I had known for five or six years or so, and he was mostly interested in drugs whereas my interest was mainly in homelessness but obviously there's an overlap, particularly at that time. And we discussed the setting up of the homeless project, and the people that might be involved in it. Ken was not involved in Christian Action but because we were both socialists and Christian Action was a left-wing Christian organisation, there was a kind of fellow feeling, not just personally but also organisationally. We came from the same kind of background. I wasn't a Christian in those days, but I had been one. So there was a lot of discussion, and in about that same year, 1969, I came to do a seminar, one of a series of seminars on homelessness in St. Anne's Church. Part of the process of setting up a new organisation was to get people's consciousness raised and be concerned about what was happening immediately around them in Soho. This was an astonishing experience because this seminar, which started at 8 o'clock, finished twelve hours later. I never was in a situation like it, I mean it was absolutely extraordinary the enthusiasm, the passion. I don't think you get that now, it was a kind of Sixties passion. Things are very different now, you know, much less energy, much less passion. I think it is very very difficult to innovate now. I think that will change in the next few years a lot, but the mood of things now is really hard.

A few years after our discussions and seminars, so it would be 1974, comes the occupation of Centrepoint, the tower block of offices and the protest was a real seminal protest. I was not inside but I was outside when it was actually being occupied and the police were around. It was one of those defining moments, wasn't it? Centrepoint, the big block of offices on Tottenham Court Road built in I guess something like 1966 or so, was the unacceptable face of capitalism. That's a quote from the Seventies but we'll use it retrospectively. A group of people I knew including Ron Bailey who was the squatting guy moved in there. It was a protest against this ugly side of the Sixties, and capitalism. It was also in a way quite romantic I suppose, and we were quite romantic in some ways not about homelessness but about poverty, no, not about poverty, about what was possible. I think that we were wrong in a sense. We didn't understand about the backlash, the way in which this society can protect itself very effectively, we really didn't understand about that.

Centrepoint – although not yet called that – started with seven Volunteers. Each night there was a Volunteer with a capital V in charge who had a group of volunteers with a little v as helpers around him, or her. I was the Volunteer responsible for Tuesday night. What that actually meant was that I worked incredibly hard. I mean I'm a fairly industrious person and I work very hard now, but in that year, or those two years, I actually slept hardly at all. It was astonishing what I did in terms of output. I wrote a whole range of stuff on homelessness which was published and I ran a fifty-bed women's hostel which I started for Christian Action at 59 Greek Street. Christian Action squatted there, we moved in without permission in fact, which annoyed the Anglican Church very considerably, but they weren't about to evict fifty homeless women onto the street. Ironically, that building at 59 Greek Street has just been taken over by Centrepoint.

But back to the beginning: there were seven Volunteers; Ken was one and myself and five others. We rarely met as a group because we were very busy and we were absolutely shagged out by the time we lost a night. At the same time I was running the fifty-bed hostel for women, training as a psychotherapist, travelling the country promoting groups and doing research. During that time my marriage nearly broke up because I was never at home. I lived fifty miles away in Shoreham-by-Sea near Brighton and it wasn't on my route.

Centrepoint started in the basement of St. Anne's, Soho, very rudimentary, camp-beds and things like that. We took in twenty people a night. We didn't have much idea of what we were doing. We didn't know the kind of pressures there might be. And so the rule quickly became that people could only stay three nights there. Now the difficulty was that there wasn't much of a network, you couldn't very easily find out where there were vacant beds. We were inundated and having to turn away people at the gate, a rather harsh gate.

We would come on duty through the main entrance, the Dean Street entrance, and discuss with Ken, who was the unpaid director of the project, about what had happened and what was going on. None of us were paid. I was paid for my work with Christian Action of course, so I didn't need to be paid, the question of payment never, never came up. I mean we were just friends of Ken and friends of each other and we trusted each other. So we would come on duty about half-past six I suppose. And there might be other volunteers around, it was an informal, rather anarchic system. We would have a chat and tea, and then at about quarter to seven, seven o'clock we'd go down to the crypt.

You couldn't get from the church building into the crypt, you had to unlock the gates from the Shaftesbury Avenue side and then go in. The gates were always locked. Then we started getting things ready and did the cleaning, although cleaning would usually have been done at the end of the shift in the morning. There were usually about five or six of us on duty so that making the soup and laying out the food would be delegated to some of the volunteers. There's a long tradition of vegetable soup in homelessness. In those days we had bacon bones as the stock but we wouldn't do that now with vegetarians, most of us are vegetarians. The task of the capital 'V' Volunteer was to handle the phone and referrals and police enquiries and things like that. The police took an enormous interest in new projects for the homeless because they were looking for runaway youngsters. And quite a number of the people there were runaway youngsters. So we had a difficult issue to balance. We would ordinarily accept the age that people gave even though it wasn't true, you could see that somebody wasn't eighteen. Everybody was suddenly eighteen. But we in a way didn't want to know, not because we wanted to save ourselves a problem and trouble but we didn't want the police to come in heavy-handed.

There were a lot of problems so one of the jobs that a person with a capital V had was handling the gate. We would switch the bell off until eight o'clock. And at eight o'clock we would come to the gate, which was immediately on Shaftesbury Avenue, and there would be a group of nine or ten people out there already, queuing up, all claiming to be first. We would actually talk to the more vulnerable, the younger ones. The other thing too is that we would want to make sure that people who had actually spent three nights there were not being admitted. That was pretty difficult, in the early days virtually impossible. And people used to exploit that quite a lot. We weren't draconian on that, I mean some people just needed the help. So we were making decisions about young vulnerable people, they were our priorities and we would talk to them first, we wanted them off the street for the night, and with the others we'd make referrals to somewhere else. You didn't want people who were very very drunk and people who had a history of violent behaviour. So we would have a kind of haggle at the gate, the other side of the gate. The gate was locked during this haggling. And that was the responsibility of the senior Volunteer to do that because that was crucial. You've got to remember of course that I knew pretty well all the old-timers in that area, most of us did, we knew people by sight, we knew who they were, living around

Trafalgar Square and Piccadilly Circus. So there was a lot of hassle and effing and blinding. And then we'd let people in and we'd lock the gate.

In the beginning we took in around twenty and it went up to twenty-five. There were fire and hygiene regulations, but we wouldn't take too much notice of that. We were learning on the job, you know. There wasn't a night shelter within a considerable distance that we didn't know, because really 59 Greek Street where I worked, and the hostel of St. Barnabas, which was just over the road, were increasingly not direct access. They were what's called secondary services. The percentage of direct access during any particular week, was minimal. So here was Centrepoint, a centre which was tremendously direct access, you can't get any more direct access than a night shelter. The direct access centres are very difficult to run, much more difficult than other kinds of homelessness projects I think. So that gate and lock were very important, you know, it was the valve into the centre. And then we'd take them down the steps, into the crypt. Now when we got to an agreed number, we would say no. And we would go to the gate sporadically and explain to people that we were full. And we might take one or two more people if there was somebody who was very young, if there was an obvious thirteen- or fourteen-year old, we would take that person, and make enquiries when we were worried about somebody. But basically we would say no, and get effed and blinded which is what the business is about, that's what happens.

Increasingly we would go for the young ones until as time went on we insisted that people were twenty-five and under. Because we were making it up as we went along, we were deciding in those first few weeks, months, what was working, what wasn't working. We decided at the outset that Centrepoint had to be a dry shelter, that you couldn't come in with alcohol. Some shelters allow alcohol, and there are really difficult arguments about what you do. It's not so bad in London but in small towns, if you have a dry shelter you tend to get alcoholism outside the shelter. Like we do on the steps of the university here in Cambridge. So six of one and half a dozen of the other, it's very difficult to work out what's the best strategy on that.

The crypt was a large room. There was a Formica bar and stools, a bit like a café, where people had chunks of bread, not sliced bread, and salt and pepper, and these bowls of soup which were pretty nourishing, and cups of tea. We didn't have coffee in those days, these are the Sixties, this was tea, mugs of tea. And that was really about our only financial outlay, I think, because the beds and the stools – everything was got from various churches. The actual amount of money sustaining Centrepoint, doing that night shelter, that single night shelter, was certainly under £500 a year.

And then we'd settle people down. They'd been out on the street so they wanted something to eat first, and then they settled down with their tea, and volunteers would talk with them. I think the interesting thing about that perception of talking was that the volunteers called it counselling. They wanted to be counsellors. I suppose as somebody who is a psychotherapist by one of his trades, I ought not to be saying this, but I will anyway. I think the counselling was much more to do with the volunteers' wishes. When you actually research the homeless users' perception of what was happening in those conversations, they described it as chats but the volunteers always described it as counselling. I think those two words are significantly different. The word 'chat' denotes something which is not terribly important, and the word 'counselling' denotes something that in the view of the person is very important. Now to whom is another question. So we settled people down round about half past ten, eleven o'clock. There was no television there, I think there was a radio going. There was only the one big room, you can imagine what that was like, it was pretty bleak, with beds which looked like ex-army beds which I presume is what they were. And then at the back were toilets and a wash basin, we didn't have showers at that point.

Some of us would go off about midnight, one o'clock in the morning, when things had calmed down a bit, and a couple of volunteers would stay on. And in the morning they got up and there was breakfast, there was tea and there was toast, and there was a bit of cheese. I don't think it was very much. And they were expected to be out by something like eight o'clock, initially, and then it got extended to nine o'clock. Now, you've got to remember that when they left there was a whole variety of information services and day centres like New Horizon which were just opening up so we weren't putting them out on to the street to nothing. So in the morning those two volunteers who were on would try and make phone calls to agencies, to make referrals for more permanent accommodation. What I'm interested in is how the day has shifted. I find now that it's no good ringing people before half-past nine in the morning because they're not there. I remember that people were in their day centres from half-past eight in the morning onwards, and so there wasn't much of a big break, you could send people round for help with accommodation, help with most problems. So in the morning there might be two or three people who were regarded as vulnerable by the volunteers and picked up by the Volunteer in charge, and held onto until phone calls were made. That might involve somebody who wanted to go home after just a couple of nights in London and who had decided that running away from home was not what he wanted.

I don't think we took in any women. We didn't have to because I ran a women's hostel so we could have them round the corner. The proportion of homeless women has rapidly expanded but in the beginning the users of Centrepoint were males and mostly young males.

People who stayed couldn't book for the next night, they had to get in the queue again. If we considered them to be terribly vulnerable there might be a note to re-admit them in the log book which also listed all the telephone calls we'd received.

At Centrepoint we kept records of everyone who came in. We only had a card, just a single white card like a postcard, which went into a box. And we also had a cork board with photographs sometimes of missing people whose relatives were looking for them. And also we kept a book, a ring binder with information about local police stations, hospitals, accident and emergency. I mean it was pretty primitive, you know, in the beginning.

The volunteers were good people. They were church people, not necessarily from St. Anne's, from Soho churches of different denominations, but mainly Anglican. They were social workers who were fed up with working for Westminster Council and the London County Council, well the LCC went in 1965, but they were from that kind of background. There was an accountant and an estate agent. A lot of them were people who would have become social workers but there wasn't any money in it, and so it was about expiation to some extent. I'm not knocking that. They were good people. I say that with a sardonic edge to it. I mean, there wasn't any way in which they were really going to understand what was happening to these youngsters, to these people, the kind of world that they actually lived in, and the poverty and the chaos of it. Amazingly enough they lived considerable distances away. I knew a couple who used to come from Guildford for example, which was quite a way into London. Centrepoint was famous, Ken and myself and others were on TV, radio, right from the start.

There was overlap of people working at Centrepoint and in the squatters organisations and other organisations dealing with the homeless. These were the same people. I mean, it wasn't like it is today, it wasn't fragmented. You could have assassinated fifty people, and that would have been it. You just had to put fifty people up against the wall and shoot them. You can't imagine how few people there were. In terms of innovation it's hard to underestimate how few people are involved in radical change. One of the things I've learnt over the years, certainly from Centrepoint days, is that conservatism in the form of Thatcherism or its new version, New Labour, is actually about relying on the fact that 90 per cent of the people will do nothing, and if you can't rely on that, then you're in real trouble. I mean I'm absolutely convinced, at the university where I work and elsewhere that most people will do nothing under any circumstances, and that that's how things stay the way they are. There are lots of reasons why people are not doing anything but for many it's their preferred strategy given any circumstances. So we were in a world where we thought everything was going to change, and we were wrong, frankly, we couldn't have been more wrong. But I don't have regrets about that. I think that we had a kind of hope, the revolutionaries that came out of Centrepoint, the tower block, at the end of the occupation on a Sunday in January 1974 to huge crowds and police all around.

Centrepoint was first-level housing for young people so there wasn't a lot of competition. It was in an enormously good position, it was going to grow and expand and develop and become a housing association-type body. The relationship between Centrepoint and Crisis at the beginning was really difficult; my perception was that Crisis was an organisation that took its numbers out of the telephone directory, and I said that a number of times on TV. I mean as somebody who knew about the figures and the statistics for homelessness, their figures were just unbelievable. I think at one point they produced figures which were actually greater than the number of teenagers living in inner London at the time. And they got to the situation where nobody believed a fucking word of what they actually said. So there was a tension there between Crisis and Centrepoint. There wasn't a tension between Centrepoint and a whole range of day centres, mostly church facilities, because we needed each other. People needed Centrepoint to provide the basic three nights to give them time to work something out.

Some individual police officers definitely hated us but not the transport police. We've still got that problem, but only with individual police officers. Today the Metropolitan Police recognises the problems of homelessness, then they didn't. I think the big enemies, the people that we had a real problem with, were the social workers and the staff in the big hospitals that ringed London, who were sending in really disturbed young people, discharging them on what was called single ticket aftercare. They were given a ticket at the gates of the hospitals to go on a bus to Trafalgar Square, and they were in a hell of a state. Somebody who was completely psychotic, you know, twenty-two years of age, and who had been discharged from one of the Epsom hospitals, Guildford or Godalming or wherever, and sent into central London. We'd be talking with a social worker over the phone and saying, 'Why are you doing this?' 'Well we don't have the beds.' 'But you can see the state that this guy is in, we ain't got no facilities here. Soup and comfort is what he's going to get, I mean this guy's in a hell of a state; you know what the situation of the inner London psychiatric services is like.' And the social worker would say, 'It's hospital policy, single ticket.' That was quite common. And then there was the whole thing about children, it was very difficult, we had kids as young as thirteen. Very difficult ethical dilemmas for us, because we knew that it was probable that terrible things were happening at home. What did we do? We could be in trouble ourselves with the children's legislation for not declaring them. So it was very very very problematic.

I suppose that I'm an agnostic, I really don't know whether our 'help' is effective. I'm surrounded I guess and always have been by people who are kind of Jehovah's Witnesses in help and I never was able to believe it, you see, and I'm always, both for myself and for other people, constantly wondering about whether I do any good or not. What Centrepoint was trying to do, what Ken was trying to do was to move from a kind of sentimental muck – these poor bewildered soul-sick people, et cetera, the whole rescue thing – towards a more structured understanding that people were becoming homeless because dishwashing machines were replacing kitchen porters in big hotels, the markets like Covent Garden were being redeveloped so the tourist could have a place to go, and lodging houses of 700 or 800 beds were being demolished or refurbished as hotels. So we wanted to look at what was happening in the social and economic structure that spewed people out. At Centrepoint what you had was the meeting of what Karl Marx called the *Lumpenproletariat*, with the middle-class volunteers who lived in the constipated stockbroker belt. So it was in a way black comedy. And being someone who came from the kind of hellhole category, who was born in poverty and in violence and with homelessness, but had also trained as a professional, I was actually one of the few people who knew what it was like to be on both sides of that. But also Centrepoint was born out of an extraordinary kind of hope, there was a buoyancy and a hope which doesn't exist now. I mean, everything was up for grabs. I had the sense in 1969, 1970, of London being the centre of the world in terms of ideas. I mean we were just zonked with the ideas. Almost every week there would be something else. It was like being in a chocolate shop, being told that you didn't have to pay for the chocolates. Centrepoint was for me part of that.

Leaving Centrepoint happened pretty naturally really. I got more and more busy with other things, and Centrepoint got more and more popular and more and more volunteers, so it wasn't necessary that I volunteer after a bit of time. I maintained contact. I'm still very friendly with Ken Leech. But I suppose in some ways I'm seen as a fairly spiky individual, a hedgehog in a nest of moles. And I'm always reflecting, whether I work inside an organisation or outside, about what we can do to do it better. I think that's quite disturbing for people to have around. I was quite tired as well, you know.

My full name is Allen David Brandon. My mother's name was Ellen, so she altered it by one letter. I was born in January 1941 in Haverhill in Suffolk, where my father was in the Royal Air Force.

My mother's home where we were brought up was Sunderland on Wearside, so that's what I look at as really my home. My father was in the RAF from 1936 to 1945/6. His mother was a minor actress who probably had an affair with Charlie Chaplin. So he was kind of fallen middle class. He had done very badly at school and he didn't have any exams. Then he married my mother. And whoever is up there organising all the marriages has a very bizarre sense of humour, because those two should never even have been in the same town together, never mind marrying. My father was extremely violent. He didn't drink but he was like a very large five-year-old. He hit, well more than hit, we're talking about the use of chairs and implements, and smashing things. So we were brought up in some poverty because my father could never hold down a job for very long, and when he did hold down a job, which he did as an insurance agent, he lost money. He was incompetent really but he was also a very charming guy.

I have a younger brother, Eric, who still lives in Sunderland, was in the Fire Service, and retired a couple of years back, has done well for himself. Both of us are like my mother, terribly industrious, very hard-working.

We lived in a prefab in the Grindon area of Sunderland for ten years. I always thought Charlie Chaplin's *Easy Street* film was a documentary because I lived in that street. Then we were resettled about two miles away to one of these soulless council housing estates about four miles outside the town. Not a good place to live, just no character to it whatsoever.

My mother made dresses and then specialised in loose covers. She made a good business out of it. But my father was impecunious; I always think of Mr Micawber when I think of him. I mean whatever money there was, he could spend it. And he was a very destructive person. I think people make a distinction between physical and intellectual violence. My father was both. He could talk for five minutes on any subject that you cared to name, but not more than ten minutes. So he gave the impression of erudition and actually it wasn't. He had correspondence with George Bernard Shaw and people like that. I met Aneurin Bevan twice and yet we didn't have enough to eat.

Both Eric and I went to poverty-stricken schools where virtually nobody passed the 11-plus. Well, I managed to pass it and Eric did not. And I went to a middle-class world which was completely bizarre. I really didn't understand it then. We didn't have any money so my mother had to make me a uniform, the whole thing. And I was the only person on this large housing estate who went to that school, so I was a figure of fun, and there was a lot of mockery. If you are a working-class, lower-working-class kid with no money, then the only route out is to become an examination-passing machine in this country, which is what I effectively did. But my brother went into the Royal Navy which is another route in Sunderland to get the hell out of it. My schooling was very narrow, very disciplined. There were a lot of good things to it, but it was a struggle. I mean I was virtually financially self-sufficient by the age of twelve or thirteen. And those are long hours, you're talking maybe ten, fifteen hours a week of work, and on top of that you had to do schoolwork and A level work.

I was very unhappy, and I was getting kicked around a lot, and I was very angry about it so I was in trouble with the police. Not formally. My brother was in trouble with the police formally but I wasn't. I was extremely lonely and isolated there, I didn't know anybody you see, nobody from the school lived in my part of town. I was a strange, rather isolated, aggressive gangly kind of soul, who was an extremely good chess player, and was a killer on the school rugby union team, but outside those two things I didn't know anybody. I couldn't go on school trips, I didn't have the money. I was actually in the top stream in the school, which meant even more that there weren't people like me, and the kids were reasonably well off, you know, and you couldn't compete with that. I had a long stretch of illness, I was in hospital for quite a long period of time when I was about twelve. I'm not sure what that was about really, but I finished school. I used to get beaten a lot at school, so I was going from one beating to another. I used to get beaten, you know, caned, so my life was about getting beaten up.

I was in grammar school for seven years, and I don't recall going into anyone's house. Well I couldn't bring anyone home. We didn't have anywhere for them to go. And anyway I lived in a different direction from everyone else. I lived inland, everyone else was living towards the sea. I remember going out with a girl when I was about sixteen. We had gone out to the pictures, and it hadn't gone too badly, and she said, would I come to a gymkhana in East Boldon. Well, East Boldon was like Knightsbridge. I knew where it was but I wasn't quite sure how to get there. And I had no idea what a gymkhana was, I thought it was maybe something to do with climbing ropes. So I agreed, and I went Saturday morning to meet her there. It was a completely humiliating experience. I mean talk about Thelwell ponies! For me middle-class people, they were much better than we were, you know, the message was, they were much, much better people. Firstly there was the piano. I saw where people lived from the outside, especially when their curtains weren't closed. I'd never been inside any of these houses, but they were completely different from public housing, and there seemed to be a piano, and so one of the marks was that these people actually had a piano. And the second was that they had ponies; of course they didn't, but they seemed to. At this gymkhana, well there weren't any pianos but I absolutely knew that these people had pianos in their houses. And they talked a strange language, a very strange language, and made references to things I had no idea what they meant, including the word gymkhana, which I'd never heard before. So we never went out again, that was it.

Sometimes I would run away in school time but it would mainly happen weekends when my father was around. Friday evening was a particular crisis time which it is in a lot of families. And my father was completely unpredictable, you didn't know what actually it was about sometimes. You were sitting there, things were getting smashed up, and I couldn't figure out what had actually happened to be the trigger. We would be sitting there at five or six o'clock in dread, expecting this hurricane to arrive from work. I never really understood what he was about. He went in and out of mental hospitals as well. But then they got divorced, they separated when I was about seventeen. My father had cleared off with another woman from about fifteen miles away, and he lived over there in a caravan. We didn't understand what was actually happening. Then he would come back, get angry, and then go away and come back, go away, come back. When I was fifteen, on a Saturday morning he came back and he attacked my mother. I came in the back door and he had hurt my mother and tore a lot of her hair out, and there was blood all over the place. You get to be an expert about injuries. If you don't get a lot of blood, then you worry. I said something like, 'Don't do it Dad,' and he turned his attention on me. He had smashed up the kitchen, he used to throw everything against the wall, just senseless. The kitchen would be ankle-deep in eggs and cans and it would take ages to put right. So he turned to me and that was the first time he lost and he broke both his wrists. He got a friend to write to the headmaster to say I was a violent and uncontrollable kid. The kettle calling the pot black. So I got a reputation at school as being a complete psychopath. But when I was around, that was the end of the violence at home. That was the big turning point. I suppose as life's gone by I've become more angry about my mother because I think there were a lot of things that she could have done and didn't do. Life is more complicated. They were two extremely strange people. And I think with another woman my father would have been very different. But my mother was from incredible poverty, we don't have poverty like she was brought up in. Her parents beat her up on the day that she got married because they knew that they were losing her bread money. She didn't do anything to protect us from him. And she was a hard woman, she was a specialist with our kids, her grandchildren, of the cuddle-with-no-arms. It was extraordinary. She could not touch, she was not capable of it.

When I was about twelve or thirteen I started running away from home. I ran away from home quite a few times, initially to quite close places like Durham City and Houghton. I would get picked up in the middle of the night by the police and brought back. As soon as the police left my father gave me a leathering for causing Mother and him inconvenience. Then I started going longer distances, getting to the Cock of the North which was a famous pub on the A1 in those days, and getting lifts down to London, mainly to London, because that's the place I knew of. I was sleeping rough in the City of London, and also along the Embankment.

My experience of other homeless people was pretty good, it was quite positive. I found that mostly young people gave me support, for example in a lodging house it's learning to sleep with your shoes underneath your pillow, which is standard practice, otherwise you get them nicked. And if you lose your shoes you're in real shit. It's just simple things like that that people help you to learn.

And I would be there quite a bit of time, and then be picked up by the police and sent back by coach. It was quite a long journey, you know, the country was bigger in those days, it would take twelve hours, maybe ten hours through the old Great North Road to the north and Sunderland. So, that was quite exciting and it was frightening. There are some advantages to my upbringing in the sense that I am completely unafraid of physical violence to a frightening degree. I would take on situations, and I'd be completely unafraid. I think I have an understanding of it that very few people have. I'm interested in the difficulties that professionals have in understanding violence and what it's actually about, and the chaotic aspect of it. I really believe that there are a lot more dangerous things in the world than violence. I mean I think that the worst thing my father did to me was not violence, it was the constant river of sarcasm.

The big advantage that I had was that I didn't know the script. It's a bit like being a foreigner in a different country. I was never around people for the first nineteen years of my life. Most of my time was spent trying to stay alive so I was on my own a lot. The big advantage I have now is that I don't know what the agreed answers are supposed to be, which makes enormously good food for innovation.

I've been in seven different professions. I was in nursing, that was my first. I was a journalist, I worked on *The Sunderland Echo*, so that's two. I was an administrator with the London County Council. I'm a social worker, an academic, a Zen Buddhist monk, a writer, and I've been a broadcaster, and worked at Channel Four. I've probably missed out some. Yes, therapist is one I missed out. I actually know deep down they're really a load of rubbish. I agree with Bernard Shaw who wrote that every profession is a conspiracy against the general public, and the knowledge base of most of these professions is so limited that most of their skills can be learnt in a concentrated weekend. Not brain surgery though. That takes a week.

I got my A levels. I decided to take a year off, which is when I did nursing. I wanted to earn some money and I also wanted to work abroad. I came back and went to the University of Hull to do a degree in social studies. I met my wife there and she was my main subject, which was good. We got married when we left university.

My initial job in the London County Council in 1963 to 1965 was working with old people, running old people's homes. But my main job was to close the big institutions, the workhouses, and develop a network, get more old people's homes. It was an enormous challenge, and I enjoyed it a lot. Then I got the offer of a job over the other side of the river. For eighteen months or so I worked in the Welfare Office for the Homeless underneath the Charing Cross Bridge beside where the Embankment tube station is. My office looked into the green taxi cabs café. It was an advice service and later it was taken over by Turning Point for drug issues.

The responsibility for the Welfare Office for the Homeless had been transferred from the London County Council to Westminster Council. The London Government Act which came in on the 1st of April 1965 made a mess of homelessness, it really did, because the twelve inner London boroughs couldn't get their act together. It was extraordinary for several months, extraordinary. *Cathy Come Home* is about a particular period in time, it was typical of homelessness in London, which was a complete mess. And I was very very angry because Westminster had its agenda, and wanted to disperse homelessness in various ways. And then Jeremy Sandford came into my life on a Vespa scooter, and talked, and made tape recordings of me talking about homelessness, and got figures and other information. I helped him, along with others. I actually suffered a lot from that, eventually got the sack as a consequence. So I had to move to West Sussex, I went down to Shoreham and I worked there from 1965 to 1970. But also in 1968 and 1969 I was at the LSE training as a psychiatric social worker which is why I was in London, and seeing Ken Leech. At the end of the course I felt that none of the stuff that I had been taught worked, which is why I trained in psychotherapy. And then much later, I realised that what we were actually doing was manufacturing a psychotherapy business which was going to be a huge business. So I packed that in some years back, I just packed it in, and did different things.

My wife wasn't working at that time. She did later, she had been a part-time teacher. The kids were very young and things were difficult. And also I wasn't at home much. It was quite a short period in our long relationship, but it was the most difficult. And I had a breakdown because I kept on going, so I was in a hell of a state myself. After I finished with Centrepoint I was doing more with Christian Action. And then a number of things happened. Firstly, I moved to become an academic at Hatfield. I needed to get out of homelessness. It was too exhausting, I was in a shocking state, and I needed to start taking up the strings of the family again and being a husband. I had finished the training I wanted to do at the time. So we all moved to Hatfield from Shoreham, and I became an academic, and more or less at that same time I got research money. We stayed in Hatfield for three years.

When we left Hatfield, we went to Preston, we lived in Preston for seventeen years from 1975 till 1992. We did three things. I was an academic most of the time in charge of the social work courses at Preston Poly, which is now the University of Central Lancashire. I was Director of Mind in the northwest for eight years. My wife and I ran our own training consultancy business. And then I came back into academic life. I was at Salford for a year, and then I came to Anglia Polytechnic University here in Cambridge seven years ago. I'm Professor in Community Care. What happened was that the Social Services Department here decided to make my life very very difficult, and every time they threatened me, the university promoted me. I've never understood why they did that but I never complained.

I'm leaving the university. I've got six years to retirement at 65. I've no idea what we're going to do. No idea. I think that there are horrendous problems, and they can't be tackled inside an academic setting. One of the problems with the English is this enormous division between theory and practice which, unless we heal that, we're not going to do well in the long run. I would like to do some innovation, I would like to think up some new ways, new systems.

I have two children. Stuart is a writer, did a book about special needs a couple of years back, which included a libellous description of his father. Toby has just got his doctorate at the LSE, and is an academic working in Durham University, in exactly the same area as his father and mother. I managed to get them all eventually. Played a waiting game.

A problem that shouldn't be

Bill Shearman
Crisis

In the mid 1960s the East End of London was very much a one-party State. Occasionally the East End would get a Conservative councillor in one of the boroughs. I believed the Conservative Party – the Tory Party as I prefer to call it because I am philosophically a Tory which is quite a bit different actually to a Conservative – had to become socially relevant to the area as this was a way of gaining credibility with the people. The way of showing this was to be concerned with the areas of social need, social concern. What I did is I founded an organisation called the ELCA, East London Conservative Association, and I was fortunate enough to get Iain Macleod involved, and he became the backer of ELCA.

I HAD A young friend in the Young Conservatives who was only about fifteen at the time. His sister was involved in a Catholic social organisation which was based in Cable Street looking after people in skid row, alcoholics, meths drinkers, and she took him along. He was absolutely appalled. Then he took me along. Cable Street was derelict land. He took me to a shack, and in the shack there was a bed with this fellow lying there and a girl looking after him. Of course all around that area people were sleeping rough and swigging alcohol. The smell was unbelievable. You're talking about in the Sixties – a rich Western country – and it seemed to me this was a problem that shouldn't be, I used to call it an obscenity.

This was something to get involved in so I spoke to Iain Macleod. He said this is a marvellous idea, we should all have a meeting about it which we did. We were all Tories at the time, left-wing or one-nation Tories. We had a meeting down at Iain Macleod's house, and during the course of this particular meeting we decided that homelessness was a major initiative we could take action on but it should not be a Tory organisation. The idea was to solve a problem and at that time it looked as though it was a

52

problem we could solve. I mean if anyone had told me that thirty-odd years later I'd be speaking to you about Crisis – a massive organisation with computers, budgets, Christ knows what else – I wouldn't have believed it, I would have thought the problem would be solved by now. There were already agencies operating in that area of concern: the Salvation Army, a Methodist mission in East London, and the Simon Community who were doing some sort of utopian refuge schemes, and I don't mean that in any critical way. We decided in fact that we should bring this issue to the forefront of society's consciousness.

This is very very important: Crisis at Christmas as we were called then was not just a question of raising awareness about homelessness and of raising a large sum of money which would go to the agencies working in that field, but what it would also do in fact was unite society. The idea was to underline the humanity which crossed all political boundaries. The idea was that it should unite everyone to focus for one day of the year on homelessness, to our mind the worst problem of all. The idea was to make it multi-political, not non-political, so that all the political parties and all the social agencies, all the churches should send representatives onto the committee and be involved in making one huge event on the Sunday before Christmas. During this discussion Iain Macleod and a man called Michael Spicer, who's since been a Minister and now is Chairman of the Parliamentary Party, as well as lots and lots of people, all said, 'You must do it.' Iain Macleod said, 'I'll give you £100 to do it, but the first thing you should do is find someone else to join with you so it won't be seen as Tory.' The local Labour MP, Reg Prentice, also gave me £100. Fortunately at that time a friend of my wife's was going out with a young curate, Nick Beacock, at St. Barnabas Church so I asked him to be the chairman because I knew he was a member of the Labour Party. Nick also got the vicarage for us, so Crisis at Christmas started at St Barnabas Church. This would be 1967. I don't know how we did it because Crisis at present, to be honest with you, doesn't seem to be able to do what we did virtually on a voluntary basis. I worked on it I think two months, maybe ten weeks. Our idea was to have four sponsored walks into Hyde Park: one from Upminster, one from Redhill, one from north of the country, I can't remember where, and one from Windsor. At the same time to get publicity there was to be a symbolic walk with all the politicians, from Cable Street into Hyde Park. So I organised all this.

Nick Beacock was the Chairman and I was the organiser. We had a big room in the vicarage in Browning Road in East Ham. There was a desk in the middle of the room and I had one phone one side, he had a phone the other side. There were plenty of settees and couches and tables so you could get a lot of people in. Masses and masses of people came in: Young Conservatives, Young Liberals – there weren't any young Labour or young Socialists – people from the agencies, they all helped. Simon Community sent people along to help, the Methodist Church came along to help. And every evening people used to come from work to help distribute God knows how many sponsorship forms for the walks. We sent out sponsorship forms to everyone under the sun: members of the Catholic Church, the Methodist Church, the Church of England, all political parties, even members of the Socialist Party of Great Britain – one member, Brian Tully, even sat on our committee. We sent out press releases, and we had a press conference which practically no one turned up for!

The whole thing was *ad hoc*. There was a constitution but you were on the committee if you came along to the meeting which is the right way to start and build up an organisation. You didn't have to go through secondings and proposals. There was no bureaucracy. That all came later. We got Lord Soper to come in as honorary treasurer. He stayed with Crisis until he died, and so did Iain Macleod. But Iain Macleod was the most important person, he used to attend our committee meetings, God knows where he found the time, I mean he was a front-bench spokesman at the time, he used to come down during the day to see us, he was marvellous.

The target was to make this particular Sunday before Christmas a huge successful event, and to involve as many people as possible. And the ideal was that people can put away their differences for at least one day of the year. If they want to argue and kill each other for the rest of the year OK, but one day a year you can do it. And those religions who gain their inspiration from Christmas or us secular people who enjoy Christmas as a spirit of goodwill, this was a way if you like of underlining and amplifying that particular view. That was basically the idealism behind it. And what should come after that is some sort of transformation where people would end up being more tolerant of each other, and understand other people's positions better. I think that happened in a small way. People didn't say, you're a member of the Conservative Party, you're the enemy. If you can't do away with all your prejudices at Christmas, if you cannot suspend all your disbelief, and you can't work together for something like homelessness, then there's not much chance for society. And anyway, what one always thought was that it's humanity that binds us all together as human beings on this planet, it's far greater than any differences we may have like whether we should nationalise private firms or what have you.

I did it because it stretched me. In those days I was quite a forceful personality, I could speak pretty well – this sounds very immodest – and I was phoning up every damned contact I knew: all the people in the Bow Group, Lord Soper, nuns and speaking to universities and at Tory conferences. I was trying to get all these people to work together, being skilful enough politically to stop them arguing about politics and getting upset. Looking back, I don't know how the hell I did it. I suppose I used to start in the morning at about half-past eight and I used to get home about eleven o'clock at night. And it was exhilarating.

The aim in 1967 was to raise £50,000 at Christmas. I don't think I've ever worked so hard in my life, and I enjoyed it with people coming in and helping. When the walks actually happened, we got very little publicity except for one back-page in the *Mirror* about the candlelight rally in Hyde Park where Iain spoke, I spoke, the Young Liberal leader Eric Lubbock spoke, Reg Prentice spoke, a lot of people spoke. And after the event we had a drink with Iain Macleod in his flat in London. The money wasn't anything like I imagined it would be, and neither was the publicity. Iain, who had far more wisdom, thought it was a huge success, but I didn't. I was very depressed because we didn't make £50,000, we only made £7,000. But £7,000 in those days was worth about £40,000 now. All the money was distributed: the Methodists had £2,000, the Simon Community had some, I can't remember which other agencies had it. And they were obviously pleased.

In 1968, the second year, we didn't do the walks we did something called square-bashing, an army term meaning drill. The idea was that you got sponsored for going to as many squares in London as possible in a day. We raised about a thousand pounds but I didn't put in the same effort as I had for the first event. Iain Macleod then said to me, 'Bill, you have a lot of imagination, really give it a go.' Which I did, because I came up with the idea of a reverse pilgrimage from Canterbury to London, and that was newsworthy. We did the square-bashing as well and we did carol singing. I don't know how I organised it because by this time I also had a job and I was doing all the work for Crisis in the evening. Anyway 1969 was a huge success. It got massive publicity.

Crisis didn't hold its own 'Open Christmas' providing food and shelter for the homeless until the 1970s. But there were certain things we did do even in the first Crisis at Christmas. For example Tim Sainsbury was a member of the Bow Group and so was I, so I phoned him up and asked Sainsbury's to help. And Sainsbury's supplied a hell of a lot of food to the people who were using the agencies – like the Simon Community and the Salvation Army and the Methodist Mission in the East End – as well as snacks for the workers as part of Crisis at Christmas.

Obviously there's a lot of awareness now about homelessness which there wasn't when Crisis started. Crisis now is involved in practical steps, a lot of which are within the spirit and philosophy of the original concept. For example Crisis is developing projects like Stepping Stones which provides sheltered accommodation to help people to reintegrate into society, sort of a ladder back into where we all are. However 1969 was the breakthrough, and it never looked back really, it's been going 30-odd years. But I am very suspicious of institutions even if that institution is doing lots of marvellous things. My big criticism is that when something is founded out of a concern for humanity and the aim basically is to go out of business, why is it still there? Crisis will tell you that its aim is for Crisis not to exist but you get the suspicion that the problem of homelessness is supplying lots of careers for lots of people. I'm not saying it's wrong to have a career in an area of social concern but institutions tend to have – without the people involved even knowing it – a prime purpose, and that is the survival of the institution. So if they run out of problems, they look for another problem to address. This is the danger of institutions, and this is the reason why I walked away. Also I had had enough, and I wanted in fact to make money. I wasn't a wealthy man, I had to make my way in the world, and I wanted to do other things. I'd done my bit, I was pleased with what I did because I knew that it would continue. After that I never had anything to do with Crisis until they involved me again for their 30th anniversary. I was the founder who they had heard mythical stories about, but who no one had ever seen. So that's basically the story really.

When I go to Crisis now, and I see the computers and the massive organisation, the budget … I mean we did all of this on a shoestring from an office in the vicarage. I was only paid for the first period, 1967, and that was only about £10 a week for eight weeks. Obviously if you want to supply professional services you have to have structure. But I've always been suspicious of structures, and suspicious if you like of the State.

I was born at 885 Romford Road, East Ham in East London in November 1937. My father's name was Victor Arthur Shearman, my mother's single name was Eliza Blaney. But she was always called Joyce because my father said she gave him so much joy.

My grandparents on my father's side had fourteen children and my father was the youngest of seven sons. People think that Shearman is a Jewish name but it's not actually, it means shearing sheep. My mother's family are of Irish extraction. I don't know how they arrived here. The only thing I know about my maternal grandfather, who I never met, was that he was a bookmaker and he ended up being hit on the head and he died in an institution. My mother had a sister and two brothers, not the huge family that my father had.

My mother before she married was a forelady in the print trade at Waterlow's where she stayed until I was born. My father, who left school I suppose at fourteen, started a business as a builder and decorator and he built up the business quite well. Then he went into the Navy and served in a Corvette as an engineer, he was a petty officer. He did the Atlantic convoy, the Russian convoy, and I can remember those times quite well really. He had a brother-in-law who looked after the business so during the course of the war, because of war damage, he ended up making quite a bit of money which he subsequently lost, but that's another story. Well he didn't lose it all. After the war he ended up building flats in East Ham. The biggest memory of the war years was being taken out of bed when bombs fell. My mother would pick me up, take me out into the hall, sometimes into the shelter. We had an Anderson shelter but strangely enough we very rarely went in the shelter. People used to prefer to stay in the hall for some odd reason, strange really.

I was the eldest. My brother came along in 1944, he was a wartime baby, Victor Arthur, named after my father. And I've got a sister – she came along in 1947 when my mother was forty-two incidentally – and her name is Joyce Lena.

My father bought our house which was on the Romford Road, a main road, in I think about 1935 for £300. He used to have a tenant in the upstairs flat. Downstairs we had a bedroom, a sitting-room and then a big kitchen, hardly a garden although Mother used to keep chickens. Lots of people used to keep chickens in those days. Eventually my parents moved to 806 Romford Road to a house across the road, and I stayed there until I married. During the war my parents had a bit of money, so they paid for me to go to a local Catholic school in Forest Gate. And to cut a long story short, I got expelled from that school. I was told it was because of my swearing. One of my grandfather's sisters had married into a wealthy family on the Isle of Wight and they owned the Crab Hotel in Shanklin so I was sent down there and I ended up going to a local school where I wasn't very happy. My aunt said to my father, 'Why don't you send him to boarding school' which turned out to be the Ryde School, Isle of Wight, quite famous actually. This was 1944 so I was about seven. I remember being dropped off, and the teacher trying to be kind, a nice woman called Miss Turner, and she said to everyone, 'You've got to be kind to this small boy because he's come from war-torn London, bombs falling all over the place.' So obviously what the kids did was the opposite. Anyway, I ended up losing my temper and having a fight, and I happened to be fighting a boy who was in the junior school, and I was a prep boy, and to fight someone in the junior school as a prep boy you were considered the hero. And that was the end of the problems I had at boarding school to be honest with you. Although my popularity in boarding school was based on having the record number of canings and always getting into trouble, I didn't get chucked out of that school. When I arrived I had had a disrupted education because of the war so I was behind a lot. And I was behind not just in academic work but my writing was very bad and I was behind in the way I spoke; for example I used to say, 'I are' instead of 'I am'. And because I came from the East End, I was sometimes called an East End guttersnipe. I wasn't given any credit for being academically any good for a start. If you ain't going to be the school swot, OK, at least you can be the big hero of the school by being the naughtiest boy, and then you can make people say, 'Oh my God! did you hear what he's done? He's walked out of the window, he's walked along the ledge.' It's a way of gaining acceptance, leadership. I was there until King George VI died in 1952, fourteen or fifteen. Then my father sent me to a local school in Ilford which was called Clark's College and I enjoyed that very much. I did OK academically, nothing to write home about. But I got turned on to knowledge.

I've always been an individualist, I think it's in the genes. My father was the same. My father was built totally different to me; he was shorter than me, he was built like a tank, and he was a champion boxer and a champion swimmer. It was absolutely marvellous as a kid when people would come up and say, 'Your father was in the Three Rabbits Pub and he laid two people out.' I'm not saying this is a good thing for him to do but he was an absolutely marvellous man, he was the kindest man in the world. In the East End in those days if you were building up a business and employing men, and if you didn't have that sort of toughness, I don't think you could possibly have a business. He wasn't like that to us or to Mum. I was very very lucky with my parents because I knew I was loved.

My father was a member of the Liberal Club in East Ham. He didn't join because he was a Liberal, he joined it because all the local authority officers, sanitary inspectors, building officers, they all used to go there, and all the local businessmen used to go there. And he became a Mason as well which I never did. My brother became a Mason but it's not for me. My father used to go out practically every night and my mother never seemed to worry. But he wasn't perfect, he drank a lot and he gambled a lot. My father was also very interested in politics and history, and he used to have a weekly publication on ancient history, and he also had the books on the Bolshevik Revolution. He was influenced by his tenant, Mickey King, who was a Scottish Marxist but he never went that far. When my father came out of the Forces at the end of the war – like I suppose nearly every ex-serviceman – he voted for the 1945 Labour Government. So I wouldn't have joined the Tory Party then.

I left school at seventeen and I had no real idea what I wanted to do to be honest with you. My father wanted me to be a quantity surveyor so he got me a job with some quantity surveyors over in

Kensington. There were two partners, a fellow called Walker and a fellow called Ward. They were in a long building and they had their offices at either end. Anyway, there was a girl working there who must have been in her twenties I suppose, and she was the daughter of Walker and she was married. To cut a long story short she liked me for some unknown reason. Anyway I was putting my arms round her and doing things that I shouldn't do when I looked up and it was her bloody father watching me. So I had to leave that job. I was terrified that my dad would find out. But there was no need to worry because all they did is give me three months' money, and apologise to my father that they were so busy they didn't have the time to train me.

After Walker and Ward I got a job in the docks with a meat company while I was waiting for my National Service to come up. I got called up in 1956 when I was eighteen. That was the beginning of getting together my philosophy really, that period of National Service. When I was doing my National Service I came across the sort of thing which upset me in a human way. It's difficult to explain. National Service is very brutal, and if you're in the Army they claim it's done for a purpose, they have to condition you to be a soldier by screaming and shouting at you, terrorising you in a sense. Lots of people got recruited who, even though they were assessed, should never have been called up not because of any physical reason but for mental conditions. When I did my National Service there were two boys who should never have been called up. It was the old thing I had right from boarding school, anti-bullying. I would look after any person who was a bit strange and I would learn from them, because they would give me an insight into things that they liked. I mean one fellow in the Army taught me about art, made me appreciate modern art. So when I saw this bullying in training it moved me, it moved me along, made me question how society is.

I was with the Army in Singapore and Malaya from 1956 to 1958. I also did some social work with the Baptist Church looking after children in villages or kampongs as they're called in Malay. Everyone else thought I was mad. There was only one other friend of mine who joined me. But I didn't mind people thinking I was mad, in fact I quite liked it. I had a wonderful time there, and I had the opportunity to read a hell of a lot.

First of all I was influenced by secular humanism which had its trinity of organisation, technology, education. And what people like HG Wells and Thomas Huxley advocated was basically state control to build the utopia, make things better. But I had a great distrust of authority. Even more so in the Army then because I suddenly realised – and not just me but most of us national servicemen – that the officers in those days were either crazy or incompetent. I didn't like the left-wing premise which vested authority in institutions. Then I read *The Open Society and its Enemies* by Karl Popper, and that was the biggest demolition of Marxism that anyone has ever written. And then I read a book by Koestler about individualism, made a great impression on me. He said, if you get one madman in society running around with a gun, how many people is he going to kill? Ten, twenty, fifty, sixty, a hundred? You get a nation going mad, you'll get six million. So he believed that it wasn't some man's individualism which was going to destroy mankind, it was when people become subservient to a set of ideologies, and in the name of that ideology normal rational people will commit barbaric acts because they absolve themselves. The fact is, we've got to realise that any view we have, be it in science, be it in philosophy, be it in any area of activity, it is tentative, it's not absolute. It's only good until the view is proved to be wrong.

When I came back I decided to join the Tory Party because I had learnt about the idea of pragmatism, the idea that if it ain't broke don't fix it. But the great thing really was that the Tory party offered you the greatest individual freedom. It's what Bolingbroke said, the difference between licence and freedom, you know, there's got to be a point. But basically I think I believe in freedom, and what the State should do and what the law should do is obviously try and bring about equality of opportunity as much as possible. In other words give everyone the same stepladder, give everyone the greatest freedom of opportunity, have a society which is broad enough to judge people on wider criteria. In other words not just saying, 'Oh this man deserves respect,' only because he's made a million pounds, or conversely a scrap dealer who has made a million pounds saying he knows best.

When I came back I lived with my parents and I went back to the docks, and then I chucked that in. What I really wanted to do was to start my own business which I did, selling mail order clothes, and at the same time I did some work for a catering company at the racecourses. I didn't do any of the cooking, I was just the management and did the accounts and the figures and what have you. That was going well and my business was going well. I had joined the Young Conservatives in 1958 when I was 21 and I had just been elected Chairman of the local Young Conservatives. Then in fact something happened to me which again changed my life. I crossed the road and a car hit me – I don't remember it – and threw me right up in the air. I got rushed off to hospital and I suppose I was on the danger list for about twelve hours or so. Anyway, I was in hospital for nearly a year, and I think being in hospital made me a better person because I decided that if I was going to achieve anything in this world I would try and do it without being a total shit. I was going to behave in a way I thought appropriate, and there were and are certain things I just can't do. I haven't always kept that but I tried.

I met my wife while I was in hospital and we got married in 1962. After I got married I formed the East London Conservative Association, and I fought the 1966 General Election as parliamentary candidate for West Ham. I fought again in 1970. In 1974 I became the founder Chairman of the Tory Reform Group for one year and then I left the Tory Party when Margaret Thatcher became the leader.

In 1968 – the year before I left Crisis – I worked for Powell Duffryn, a big group of companies, and after four years I joined up with an ex-banker, a personal friend, and we built up a series of companies, one covering banking, one taking stakes in companies, being company doctors, and one marketing. When we split the partnership I ended up with the engineering company. I got a reputation as being marvellous at business and then I became a victim of my vanity. People kept asking me to help them, and my vanity got the better of my expertise, and I was asked to go into a big building company. To cut a long story short I thought I had saved it, but I hadn't; the banks asked me to guarantee it, and then they put a receiver in. So all my business empire fell down flat. I nearly became bankrupt, I lost everything. And since then I've got 101 different things on. I haven't made my fortune but I've survived by doing consultancy work and various deals. I suppose my final ambition actually is to write a book. I want to write a philosophy book, not political philosophy, not ethical philosophy, but philosophy about the nature of reality.

I've got three children. My wife is a better manager and a better business person than I'll ever be actually. She was an absolutely wonderful, absolutely marvellous mother, because she didn't work until my youngest son, born in 1965, was five, and then she worked from ten o'clock to three o'clock. So as far as the children were concerned, she wasn't at work. She worked for the local authority, now she works full-time as the members' secretary for the Newham local authority, which is quite ironical because it's a Labour authority now. Fortunately all three children live locally so we see or have the grandchildren to stay most weekends. I've taken all my grandchildren away individually, they've all gone with me to the Isle of Wight for four days, just one-to-one. Children teach you so much, and one-to-one is absolutely marvellous for a kid whoever it is they're with, whether they are with their parents or their grandparents. So you build up a bond with them. They tell you things they won't do in front of their brother or sister. And they think for that period of time they are special.

We never knew what problem was going to come in

Rosamunde Blackler
GALS (Girls Alone in London Service)

*I don't give much thought to the old work because it's such a long time
ago. When I retired to Malvern twenty years or more ago, it didn't take
me long to discover that nobody, certainly not the people I came across,
was in the slightest bit interested in what you might call difficult youth.
I remember a very charming man who lived next door to me said, 'Lock
the whole bang lot up, that's what I say.' And that was the attitude here
so I soon learned to shut up. I did manage to get an article into the local
paper – this is going back maybe more than twenty years – and my aim
then was to form in Malvern a group of the Friends of ALS (Alone in
London Service) as it is now called, and have a few coffee mornings or
what have you, and send some money. Not a single sign of interest. I
didn't know many people then but anybody I ran into said, 'Oh poor you,
what a way to work.' It was incredible.*

*I used to feel, there but for the grace of God go I. That was always my
motivation. Because I really was a very naughty girl myself. I think
that's where the sympathy came in, because I could see myself, if I hadn't
been so fortunate in having a good well-off home behind me, I would
have been one of these little things who had run away from home and
gone to live in a squat and maybe fallen for a baby. I knew that.*

GALS STARTED BECAUSE I was working for the YWCA and had set
up their Accommodation Advisory Service and knew I had to get
out. I came to blows with the very powerful YWCA London Area
Committee. I have to admit that I was an absolute pain in the neck.
I remember standing up at a huge national conference and saying
something like, 'You can't have a whole lot of frumpy holier-than-
thou people telling these with-it young people what to do, they
won't take the blindest bit of notice of any of you, no wonder the
numbers are falling off all over the country.' I was ostracised by

many after that. So all the time I knew I had to get out, because it went against the grain with me to be associated with the YWCA. I wanted to have my own show. That's what it was. Where I could help the sorts of people I wanted to help.

I had met through my work at the YWCA a number of important and good people, and I knew that they knew I was a good worker, if I may be so bold as to say so. People like Pat Brown, an Islington Labour councillor; Mary Hamilton, the Chief Probation Officer at Bow Street Court; Mary Peyton, later Lady Peyton, the wife of the former Minister of Transport. I met Mary when we were both members of the Women's Group on Public Welfare, one of the most high-powered committees on which I ever served. She was marvellously helpful and supportive throughout the time I worked with GALS. Then there was Dr James Hemming, the educational psychologist; and Dr Oscar Hill, consultant psychiatrist at the Middlesex Hospital; and Cy Grant, the Puerto Rican guitarist and folk singer; and Greta Bennett of the London Union of Youth Clubs. So I asked all these people individually, went and called on them and said, 'Look I want to get away from the Y, I want to help kids in trouble, homeless young people, but not the sorts of girls who go to the YWCA whose parents can pay for hostels; the ones who arrive with nowhere to go and no money and maybe pregnant or running away from ghastly homes and so on. Would you be prepared to come on to a committee to support me?' And so, by just a wonderful piece of luck, all these people agreed that they would form themselves into a committee, that the organisation would be called GALS, Girls Alone in London Service, with Lady Peyton as President and I would be appointed its one and only member of staff as director with a free hand. That's how it happened. Later, Colonel Peter Goddard MBE, a retired army officer whom I met through the Institute of Chartered Accountants, agreed to be our honorary treasurer; and Patrick Bromley, an enterprising young Islington businessman known to Pat Brown, offered to take on the Chair.

I mean it was wonderful. It was just fantastic.

But at our first AGM I got ticked off by Cy Grant in front of the committee because of my first report which I had written entirely on my own. He stood up and said, 'Look here Rosamunde, you'll have to do better than this. I very much object to this word 'coloured' being used to describe some of the black clients that you have had.' He said, 'Do you not realise that to use the term 'coloured' about a black West Indian girl is an insult?' And I said, 'No, I'm terribly sorry, I didn't realise.' But he taught me a lesson that I've never forgotten.

But to get back to the beginning. I suppose you can say it was fate really, these things obviously are meant to be, and they get you on your way. A man, a very nice old boy, asked to see me and he said, 'I've read about the work and I know there are lots of young girls in trouble. My wife is dead and I would like to do something before I die that I think would please her.' So he said, 'I like the sound of the kind of work you do, helping girls get off the streets and so on, and I'll give you £1,000.' And that was our first bit of money.

I'd never had any money, people always think I've had plenty. Never have. And I'm better off now than I've ever been really in my life, because I have my husband's pension, but that's beside the point.

I was looking for premises in the King's Cross area, because even in those days it was known for prostitution and girls arriving penniless and homeless at the station, and people on the lookout for them. Wandering around Exmouth Market I suddenly came across an old printing works and attached to it a little three-storey unoccupied house, number 69 Rosoman Street. So I went to see the owners, and I signed the lease in my own name. The rent, I mean these days it would be laughable of course but if you had no money it was still money. I gave up my YWCA flat and moved into that ruin of a little house. There was no money to pay me a salary or anything so the committee said, 'You live there rent-free until we can pay you some money.'

And that's really how GALS started, Rosoman Street. The ground floor had been a little old-fashioned tobacconist shop, I think belonging to Finlays, one of those chains that used to be all over London, and I looked around and thought, the whole lot's got to come out. The basement was just piled to the ceiling with rubble and rubbish, hadn't been used for years. There was a reasonably respectable two more floors above that, including the attic. So I moved into the floors up above, and I lived there – GALS hadn't opened or anything – whilst all the renovations were going on.

And I look back now and it's crazy, but it was really a wonderful adventure.

I really had a free hand. I found local builders and people who would cart the rubbish away so eventually we had the old tobacconist shop cleared out. I was a fool because it had what apparently was quite valuable, very old, very dark wooden panelling, frightfully old-fashioned with all its drawers and things for tobaccos. Somebody over the road was smarter than I was. He came over and said, 'You wouldn't let me have that wood that's being stripped out, would you?' I didn't think anything of it at the time, I was jolly glad to get rid of it because I wanted something modern and clean looking. We knocked through the two little front rooms for a walk-in advice and counselling room, with a tiny private office behind where I used to sit. The basement we eventually cleared, and made into a modern kitchen, and the coal cellar we made into a bathroom for the girls. There was another bathroom upstairs which of course I had when I was living there.

In the meantime the treasurer, Colonel Goddard, and I worked frightfully hard. I'm no typist but I had my own typewriter and I knew how a letter should be presented. I used to spend hours and hours because I wouldn't send letters out unless they were perfect. That won't do, I'll have to do it again. And I used to sit there alone, completely alone sometimes falling asleep. We approached all the livery companies and one of them gave us a couple of hundred pounds. And we approached the London Boroughs Association.

Islington Social Services sent the first clients in about a year's time when we actually opened the doors. Now that was a triumph, because Social Services were a law unto themselves in those days, and very much looked down on anything sort of amateurish. So my first client was sent by Islington Social Services because she was just sixteen and they weren't going to bother with her, you see. And that's why a lot of the girls came to us from Social Services. And Centrepoint sent masses of people to us because Centrepoint only put people up for three nights. Another source of supply was the Birkenhead Street Hostel for Destitute Women just opposite King's Cross. It was a DSS hostel and if they were too young for the women's destitute hostel, they were sent to GALS.

We never knew what problem was going to come in. Some were dreadful. And many girls had run away from the North, that seemed to be a thing to do, it always has been hasn't it, to get to the bright lights of London. We obviously had to find out if they were under-age because we weren't supposed to deal with them if they were. We used to do our darndest with under-age girls, to get them back home before we called in anybody. We were very reluctant, very reluctant indeed, to hand them over. Not always. There were some who were nasty little pieces of work – that's a horrid thing to say – but there were some you thought were as hard as nails so you didn't feel quite so sympathetic. I know one shouldn't, I learnt that years ago, not to become emotionally involved, but every now and then you would think, oh my God! But, no, we did try terribly hard, but there were occasions when we would say, 'Look, if you won't tell us your age or where you've come from, you are going to have to go to the Social Services. But if you tell us where you've come from, perhaps we could give you your train fare and we can get you back home, or telephone your mum.'

You have got to remember that even in the Sixties and Seventies it was still a disgrace to have an unwanted pregnancy, to be having a baby, and girls were still being made to marry the father. But abortion was beginning to be better known about, and so there were girls who came in the hope of finding some place where they could get one. I mean it wasn't easy as it has become since of course. There were still things that people were ashamed of, and girls fell out so easily with their mothers who were probably much more old-fashioned in many ways than they are now. And then there were the drunken fathers and the abusing fathers. I have to tell you here quite frankly that I personally am in favour of abortion. I think that rather than bring an unwanted child into the world with possibly no money, no love, and to have a hell of a life, it's surely better really to abort it. But I have always felt that way. We sent them to places like Brook Advisory Service.

Our main purpose was, well, to come to the rescue really. Young girls can be so stupid can't they, do such silly things like falling for all sorts of promises. And it's so much worse in a way for girls because of this awful pregnancy trap. And of course they had no idea at all in those days, they had no idea about how to obtain birth control.

Then my old pal, Eileen Eisenklam, who had worked with me in North Kensington and at the YWCA got in touch with me and said, 'If you're going to have any jobs, can I come and work with you?' She was a qualified nurse and had just taken her social work qualifications at LSE, and was really far better qualified than I ever was. Incidentally, I had by now attended a course at Morley College and had acquired the qualification for youth and community work which had been newly authorised by the Department of Education and Science. This meant there was now a recognised salary scale for qualified youth workers. Anyway, Eileen came after GALS had been running for nearly a year and we were beginning to get known. I knew the local trades people, and Father Laister at the Roman Catholic church used to come and say, 'Are you sure you know what you're doing? These people are tough out here you know.' And I had a lot of that. And I said, 'Look I've already spent nearly twenty years in the back streets of North Kensington, I know what I'm letting myself in for,' which I did. And that was the challenge really. So then when Eileen came I really did become, you might say, the director, and she was the counsellor. She was a wonderfully efficient person and a very good counsellor.

We thought, right, now what we really need to do is find more central premises near the station, maybe Euston or King's Cross, and move. I'll move out, if I ever find anywhere to go, and make 69 Rosoman Street into a hostel and then we will appoint a warden. And if we can find a walk-in advisory centre near one of the stations, any homeless girls we can't place elsewhere – remember we both of us knew the hostel situation in London like the back of our hands – we'll put up in our own hostel.

I got in touch with somebody or other at British Rail, and told them what I wanted. And I had a phone call saying, 'Sadly we still have no premises. However, we have one suggestion to make to you. Would you care to meet one or two of my colleagues for tea at the Great Northern Hotel behind King's Cross Station?' So, I went. I remember sitting there and one of them said, 'Would you like to be mother?' They said, 'We're terribly sorry, we think you're doing a great job of work, but we've got absolutely nothing near King's Cross. However, we have got something we would like to show you, although we don't think it would be suitable, just outside Euston.' They said, 'When we've had our tea, if you wouldn't mind walking down the Euston Road, we'll go and have a look.' So the four of us, there were three men and myself, walked down the Euston Road and we stopped outside West Lodge, part of the famous old gateway. One man got out a huge key, and he said, 'Now this place has been used as a storage dump – brace yourself before we go in – but it would be available to you for a peppercorn rent.' We could hardly get in, it was filled with rubble, rubbish, but there was this wonderful wrought iron staircase going up to a floor above, where there were floorboards missing, and lots of pigeons. I mean shades of Rosoman Street, it was just the same really. But I knew I would have it as soon as I saw it. And he said, 'We'll help you get the rubbish out, make it reasonably presentable, and then you can have it for,' whatever it was, £150 a year, some peppercorn rent. And so I said, 'I'll take it, yes.' And you see here again, this is where I was so lucky, I didn't have to go back to the committee for their OK. All I had to do was say, 'OK,' and then when I next saw the committee, 'I've found a wonderful place outside Euston.' Do you see? I mean it was quite incredible really when I look back, when I think of all the red tape that can exist in some of these things. And so, that's how we got West Lodge.

Once we opened West Lodge, we had four or five beds ready at the house in Rosoman Street. I had moved out by now and found myself a flat out near Croydon. And we got a warden through a hostel for destitute women in Soho Square. There was a wonderful woman running that hostel, and she said that sometimes she had women there who were only destitute because they were down on their luck, and really could be very good workers. And she knew of one who she thought would be good as the warden at Rosoman Street. The attics up at the top had three beds and there were three, I think, or even four in the big room below, and then the warden had the flat below that, and then the counselling offices, and then right downstairs in the basement there was a kitchen with a huge table, and a bathroom in the old coal cellar. I remember buying the furniture at some place like MFI just beyond Crouch End, buying a whole load of cheap little wardrobes, little dressing-tables, and beds, and having it all delivered.

I was with GALS for seven years and it was well established at Euston as a registered charity and the hostel was going fine. We now had a splendid secretary and two new counsellors. And then I had to leave. I was sixty-five you know by then. I started much too late, but then I was of the generation which had to start late because there was nothing doing much when I was a girl.

I did go to one more meeting of GALS, must be about six years ago, I went to stay with Eileen Eisenklam in London. I thought, well I'll go to a meeting, after all I'm supposed to be vice-president – I was elected vice-president for life at my last committee meeting – maybe I can pop into any of these meetings, even as a sponsor I can go. So I went, and the chairman said, 'I don't think I know you.' I had sat myself down at this small table, it was a staff meeting. And, I said, 'The name's Rosamunde Blackler.' 'Oh, have you any connection with us?' And so, I said, 'Well yes, I did have in the early days,' I was very subdued. And there was somebody there who said, 'Oh yes, Mrs Blackler did a tremendous amount of work, got this place going.' And the chairman said, 'Oh really?' And went on with the meeting. And made no further attempt to come and talk to me. And so at the end of the meeting, I had a cup of tea with one of the youth leaders, and left.

———————

I was born on 13th April 1913 in Bromsgrove in Worcestershire so I'm an Aries. Astrology is one of my hobbies. A sister and brother came after me, I was the eldest. My mother was very musical so I was christened Rosamunde after Schubert's *Rosamunde*, Rosamunde Rushworth-Lund. My father was the curate to Bromsgrove parish and he was also a medical student because he wanted to be a medical missionary in the Far East.

My father was a shy young curate when my mother met him. I think they met in Lucerne, where she was on holiday with her parents. He was obviously clever, he had already got a Cambridge MA and was just entering the Church. Later he went back to Cambridge and then to St. Thomas' and qualified as a doctor. An idealist, an absolute idealist, a great classical scholar. We were always being told about word derivations, not that he played a great part in our childhood, no. I think he was probably rather a reclusive man. I believe my parents were rather poor, really struggling when he was a medical student and a curate at the same time. But from about 1918 on we always lived in the most beautiful houses, country doctors' houses all over the place. My father was a restless man, I don't know why, and he never settled for longer than five or six years.

My father never became a missionary. He gave up the Church, and for practically the whole of our growing up time we simply thought of him as a GP, a country doctor. I think he was probably a popular man with his patients, but he and my mother were not terribly happy. My mother played the piano beautifully, so we were brought up in a musical atmosphere. My mother was never very strong, a very delicate woman, although she pottered a bit in the garden. I think she was very very highly strung. She had awful circulation trouble, and I imagine a bit of heart trouble with it, and died in her fifties.

My father came from the north, from Yorkshire, and we never knew those grandparents. His mother had died when he was a child and he didn't get on with his father's second wife. I would say that he probably wasn't a really happy man. When mother died Pop was then practising down somewhere near Southampton. We didn't see a great deal of him, my sister or brother or I, and when he died, we all went together down to the funeral – we were in for a dreadful shock, the three of us. The solicitor said, 'First of all your father married again last year, and secondly he has left everything to his widow.' But, I must be fair, this woman was very nice, I think that she had made him happy in the last years of his life, and she said, 'Look, I know it must be awful for you, but would you all like to come and choose a couple of items of furniture from your father's house that you really think should be yours?' And so we did.

My maternal grandfather, James Woodyatt, was a terribly successful Worcestershire farmer who became vice-president of the National Farmers Union, and he had a number of farms on the edge of Malvern and he owned a lot of property in Malvern. I was the eldest grandchild and he spoilt me from the day I was born. And everything really material that I had, I had from him. He taught me to drive when I was only sixteen, and that was pretty progressive, and he gave me a car when I was twenty-one. He was wonderful. I adored him.

My sister and I were sent away to Cheltenham when she was seven and I was nine. In those days we lived in a beautiful house, right on the cliffs at Cape Cornwall near Land's End. We had been allowed to run wild as children, we were absolute tomboys, which was rather incredible in those days I think. When we went to Cheltenham a practice was bought for my father by my maternal grandfather, in Tetbury in Gloucestershire, to be near Cheltenham. We had a lovely house in Tetbury.

We were only at Cheltenham for five years, and then my father moved to Southwold in Suffolk, where again we had a rather lovely house on the village green. We were whisked away from Cheltenham and sent to St. Felix, my sister and I, where my father was the school doctor. My brother was sent to Harrow so we really had a pretty affluent upbringing. Although I don't think my parents ever really had very much money, I think my mother's father was always there to help out, and probably paid for some of the schooling.

I was very athletic when I was a girl, and it was much more

important to me to get into school teams than to do well. I was quite good really at cricket and I was in Cheltenham College Junior before we left there. I think I was quite bright but I never worked terribly hard. So I got all the exams results and everything that I should quite easily, but sport, at both schools, was more important to me than work.

I was reasonably happy at school. I wasn't a blue-stocking by any manner of means, and I think I probably was a bit of a show-off, a silly sort of cheeky kind of girl who probably was rather annoying to some teachers, trying to be funny in front of the class. I did have some very good friends at both schools, but it's so long ago, practically all of them have died you see, and one loses touch as you know. On the last day at St. Felix, the headmistress made a point of seeing each leaver separately. We all used to dread it because it was said that she kissed you, and everybody went, urghhh! And so, she did of course, even though she had never had anything to do with any of us before. I remember her saying to me, 'Now Rosamunde, you are very good at games dear. I wonder if it has occurred to you that you might possibly like to become a games mistress.' I mean this was the last day at school. That was the only thing that was ever said to me about a career, university, anything. There were two or three swots as we called them who were going to Cambridge, or going to university, who had done frightfully well and got Higher Certificate and so on. I wish, looking back, that I had done that, but I didn't. The thing to do was to go to France or Switzerland when you left school, and that is what I did. It was only afterwards one thought, why didn't anybody ever say, look, you are quite bright, being a games mistress isn't going to get you very far unless you're going to aim at being a great sports instructress. Nobody ever said a word. Not a word.

I went to the University of Lausanne but again I didn't work. I did learn very good French. And when I was out there, my mother, who wasn't at all well, was sent out to live in the mountains for a while, and this just fitted in very nicely with me being in Lausanne and my sister just about to leave school, so we had a couple of years up in the mountains skiing, living with our mother. And that's when we were eighteen, nineteen. Nothing like skiing, I think it's absolutely marvellous. I haven't done any since. My husband and I, we never could afford to go with our children.

When I came back, I didn't know what I was going to do. I taught French in a private prep school in Kidderminster and I was supposed to be helping the children with their games. When I look back, when I think, the amateurishness of it all then, some of these fee-paying places. Anyway my grandfather then paid for me to go to a very expensive domestic science place attached to a fashionable girls' school in West Malvern. It was frightfully snobby. You could go for a year and learn everything about running a home. And I went to that. And mind you, it has stood me in good stead, because I learnt all the basics, of how to make pastry, bread, the lot. But it must have been the end of an era because it was assumed we were all going to have servants and staff in our homes, and so you had one month of being kitchen maid, one month of being a parlour maid, one month of being a cook, and when you were doing that you wore the appropriate uniform and you did everything that a maid would be expected to do in your own home. So if you were a kitchen maid you got up at six in the morning and swept out the fireplaces, and if you were a parlour maid you waited at table and learnt everything about how a table should be laid and which side you placed the cutlery. I did it for my grandfather, and I was very pleased because I did well and he was so proud that nobody had ever had such high marks before. I really worked for him, and it's the first time I had ever worked in my life, really worked.

I think it was 1935 or 1936 I was married from my parents' home in Desford, Leicestershire and I was married by my godmother's husband who was a Canon of Worcester Cathedral and who had christened me as a baby.

Stuart Blackler. He became the rock in my life, because I was a bit of a madcap. Remember I had a car, and a certain amount of money and I chased around. I could have got into all sorts of trouble, there was no getting away from it, really, when I look back. Anyway I met him, and he was a good ten years or so older than me. I think it was a case of more or less love at first sight, because he was working in London then and he drove down to see me the next weekend, and we got engaged pretty quickly after that. He was a banker, and he came from a very very good family, then living in south Wales. Everybody liked Stuart. You could see he was a man of integrity. And of course later, as years went by, I rebelled against the dullness of it really, I have to admit now. But I've had to eat all my words in later years.

We lived in Stanmore, and I had my first baby about a year later, and of course it was war then. And the other two were war babies born in 1943, 1944. Stuart, being in a bank was in a protected reserve occupation, and he tried desperately hard to get away and enlist, but they didn't allow qualified accountants to go. He worked for the NatWest and he ended up in Berkeley Square. But before that we moved down to Surrey, and I was fortunate in getting my two little ones into a nursery school in Godalming as soon as we arrived. We were only there for five or six years and had the nicest place, and all the children say it was the happiest time in their lives, and also it was the happiest time in our marriage. And I then started doing voluntary political work for the Conservative Party.

I hadn't a clue about anything, but they sent me and I didn't know it, to the working class area of Godalming, which was a small town called Farncombe, where there was no branch or anything, and I soon discovered that nobody ever went near them because they were working class. And that was the beginning of my anti-snobbery attitude. I worked awfully hard there. It was Farnham constituency with twenty-three branches, safe Tory seat, a huge majority. I became constituency chairman later, which was pretty good going. But I had an altercation. You see something happens to me at committee meetings, and I spoke out. I said, 'How is it there isn't a single working-class person on this committee?' Something like that. And there was a ghastly hush. I know it ended up with the chairman of the Goldalming branch saying, 'Well if Rosamunde Blackler thinks she's so marvellous at all this kind of thing, I suggest we vote her into the position of secretary; we're just going to have a general election and I am sure she will show us all how to do the work.' So I said, 'Yes, OK, I'll do it.' So I was landed, not knowing a thing about it, with a committee room for Godalming for the general election in 1951 I think it was. I worked like a slave of course day and night, day and night, for weeks, with all the electioneering and envelope addressing, and hundreds of volunteers, and God knows what to be done, cars to arrange, and everything. And I mean it served me right. But, after that I founded a twenty-fourth branch in the constituency, entirely working class, in Farncombe, and it exists to this day, and with a working-class chairman, and I thought that was worth doing really.

Well then, my husband was appointed manager to the Ebury Street branch of the National Westminster bank in London. And over the Ebury Street branch there was the most beautiful flat, huge flat. So we moved up there.

My MP in Surrey was Sir Godfrey Nicholson of Nicholson's Gin, a wealthy man. He was nice, I liked him. Anyway, he liked me, and he should do too because I did a hell of a lot of work for him. His Nicholson's ginnery, distillery, is in Shoreditch, and he knew I was rather anxious to go into politics, so when we got to London he said, 'Look here my girl, I am Chairman of the Shoreditch and Finsbury Conservative Association, such as it is.' It was an absolute dead loss of course for Conservatives as it was one of the strongest Labour seats in the whole of the country, and certainly in London. He then introduced me to the Shoreditch and Finsbury Conservative Association and said, 'This young woman has done some very valuable work for me in Surrey and has been speaking at meetings and I strongly recommend her to you as one of your London County Council candidates for the 1955 election.' I was adopted, you know, three people stood in those days, I don't know if they do now, for the Greater London Council, then the London County Council. I then started doing a lot of home visiting, Care Committee home visiting, and that got me into some of those ghastly tenements because I mean, in those days it was pretty awful round Hackney and Shoreditch. A great friend of mine and her husband drove me in a car with a loudspeaker and I went round a lot of the blocks of flats and yelled and shouted and a few children would come around and one or two men heckling. And I also stood up on fruit barrows in one or two of the markets and yelled. Well, my two fellow Tory candidates didn't like this at all, because they said, 'We haven't a hope of getting in, why go around making a fool of yourself?' So I suppose I fell out with them really, because I said, 'I'm sorry, but I come from a terribly efficiently run constituency where people work to get in.' The editor of the *Hackney Gazette* wrote in the paper, 'At last a Tory live wire in Hackney.' When the election came I got a thousand more votes than the other two. And I knew this was due to hard work. But then, Stuart, my husband, stepped in and said, 'Look, we're not rolling in money, we never will be, and I am not prepared to subsidise the Conservative Party to the tune of the use of my car and about £2.50 a week on your expenses. Sorry, no more of it.' So I said, 'Right, well, I've found out through working in the slums with the Care Committee work that I get on terribly well with working-class teenagers and some of them have such a hell of a life. I'm going to work with rough youth. I'll make a career there, and get a salary.' So, I gave up the politics.

So this is how my career started, all the rest had been voluntary until then. How on earth do I get youth work? I hadn't a clue. I looked in *The Times*, and I saw an advertisement, 'Youth worker wanted for North Kensington Youth Club.' And I applied. It was £500 a year, and I got the job for the obvious reason that nobody in their right mind would ever apply to run a youth club in North Kensington, as it was in 1955. And I thought it was terribly clever, I'd got this job as a youth worker. And, my goodness me, it was a youth club, 500-strong, it was at the North Kensington Community Centre which was then the largest community centre in London. I've always got on well with the kids you see, I'll shout at them and swear at them, but I can control them really. But it worked, I was lucky enough to get away with it. I caused a riot there one night, again through my ignorance, and through this rough approach of mine. Some big boys kicked over some stuff in the canteen, and I said, 'Pick that up'. 'Pick what up? Can't see nothin.' So in the end, when everybody was beginning to turn over tables and things, I stood on a billiard table and yelled, and unfortunately I used a word with a double meaning. I said, 'Can't do that,' and they thought I'd said cunt. And they went mad, the whole place was wrecked, wrecked. Had to have the police of course, the police, dogs, everything. And not a girl or a boy to be seen when the police arrived. All I could do was think, where's my car, get me home, get me back to Ebury Street. Never ever again, thank you. I really felt finished. But the next morning I thought, I'm finished if I don't go back. So I went back. And, it was the making of me. In some strange way it worked to my advantage, because I was able to say things like, 'Oh shut up there, you know what happens if I start shouting at you. We don't want the place upset again.' Somehow I got away with it, and it worked. And I never had any more trouble after that. But it was terrifying, absolutely terrifying.

I became the warden myself the following year, but I wasn't there for very long before I was approached by Miss Mollie Mann, a wonderful woman, District Care Organiser for Notting Hill Gate area. And she knew I had done Care Committee work in Shoreditch, Hackney. She came to see me and said, 'Look, you wouldn't like to try an experiment would you, working with some of these kids, some of these fourteen-year-old girls?' And that's how the Avondale Project started. It started in Avondale Park School in North Kensington in 1957 which was very much what one used to call a slum school, twilight area school. The idea was to work with all the school leavers in their last term, and I had a free hand – it had never been done before. I went into the schools, only one to begin with, once a week during their last term of school and held discussion groups with all the fourteen-year-olds who were just about to leave when they reached fifteen, on anything they wanted to talk about. And Miss Lidgey, the headmistress, looked a right old dragon of the old school, hair screwed right back, a ramrod of a back, and very strict, but she was wonderfully understanding. She didn't interfere at all, she said, 'Go ahead dear, do what you like with them.'

It was seven years' work you see. To begin with I think I only got a little money for the petrol. It was voluntary in a way but it led to being paid a bit by the Gulbenkian people who agreed to grant aid us.

In every single group that I ever had, during the first lesson, there's been the wag of the class who stood up and imitated my voice. I waited for it, I mean it was quite funny really. At first it upset me a bit, but I soon learnt how to deal with it. I said, 'Oh that's good, now let's see if I can do your voice.' What they wanted to talk about was always the same over the years: personal relationships. I used to say, 'Think about what you would like to talk about, and maybe I know a bit about it, or maybe I don't, or maybe you can tell me.' And always it would be 'Boys please Miss.' And so I said, 'What about boys?' And there would be silly giggles. I hope it was helpful because there were lots who stayed behind to have a little private chat afterwards and said, 'I'm not pregnant am I? I let my boyfriend...' do this that and the other. You can see the rudiments of how GALS came about can't you? I visited every single home, and I found out quite a lot of things that the school didn't know. The school always knew of certain bad families with drunken fathers or no father at all and so on. But there were certain things that they didn't know and you noticed straight away in these horrible little flats I went into all round Ladbroke Grove, North Ken, White City Estate, dreadful some of them were. There was nearly always a man either reading behind a paper or looking at the telly, which was then coming into every home, who never switched the telly off and never put the paper down. They couldn't care less about their daughters. And here one was trying to help a girl who was just about to leave school and talk about what she might do or might not do. And you did find out. Perhaps you would say, 'Where's your dad?' 'Oh, I ain't got one.' 'And where's your mum?' 'Oh, she'll be out at the pub, she never comes in till twelve.' Little things that were of great interest to the school. And then other things. 'Where do you sleep?' 'Oh I get in with me mum and dad if they'll have me, otherwise I have to sleep on the floor.' And that made the headmistress realise why a certain child was always so tired at school, black-eyed at school. So we did unearth certain things that weren't already known, simply because we went to every family. Some were very nice, very respectable, very pleasant husband and wife, you know, nice tidy home, and meal ready when the children got home, and others, oh, absolute dens of iniquity, you know. And so I went into masses and masses of homes like that.

In 1964 my husband, who was ten years or so older than me, retired, and there was no question at all, the moment he retired we were to live in Spain. I was the little woman. But the point is, I wasn't a little woman. I had then had a book published about the Avondale Project called *Fifteen Plus*, which was amazingly successful, and that enabled me to meet all sorts of interesting people. Well, then along comes my husband's retirement and before I know where I am the furniture is in store and we're off to Spain. I thought, well I am the man's wife. Anyway, I gave everything up, I thought, right, the Inner London Education Authority has taken over the Avondale Project; I go like a dutiful wife out to Spain. And I came back nearly a year later. I knew I was going to come back. I didn't know how I was going to get back or what I was going to do, but I knew it. One day I just got on a plane and flew back. I went to stay with some friends. I had no money, when I say no money, I had probably got £100 in the bank and that was all, no job, nowhere to live. But I had two great friends, one put me up in Stanmore, and the other one put me up in her very nice little house in George Street off Baker Street. I looked around and found myself a bed-sitter and straight away got the job at the YWCA.

Miss Bailey, who was a wonderfully strong woman and the London area YWCA secretary, said 'Look Rosamunde, we're going to try an experiment here with having a counsellor adviser to go round to all our Y hostels for girls in the London area to get to know the girls, see what their problems are. Would that interest you?' She said, 'It will be a different type of girl obviously to the ones you've worked with, but you get on well with the young and maybe they will trust you and maybe you can help them a bit with their problems.' So I thought, well, thank goodness somebody has offered me a job. So I said OK, yes. But I was always anti religious establishments. I was terribly critical of organisations, like the YWCA, any church youth clubs. I used to say, 'No wonder they don't come here with all these goody-goodies around.' Anyway, there I am at the Y, getting on pretty well but, all the time I was thinking, this isn't good enough, you know, I can do better than this. And then, they said to me, 'Look, we've taken over the trusteeship of the old London Council for Welfare of Women and Girls in Baker Street. If we make you director and give you a free hand, do you think you can build it up for us as a new YWCA project?' And so, that's how the YWCA Accommodation and Advisory Service came into being. I did do a very good job there I know but I still wasn't happy. So I began to talk to the people who became the committee for GALS. I've told you that story.

Stuart and I had become legally separated. The children had grown up and gone, and I lived completely on my own in London when I was doing most of this work we've been talking about, and coped entirely on my own from 1964 onwards until I retired. Yet, when Stuart came back from Spain about eight or nine years ago now, we had a reconciliation. He rang from Spain and said, 'Do you think we could get back together? I know I'm getting an old man now, but, maybe you could do with some companionship too.' Something like that. And I met him, he flew to Birmingham and I met him there. He sold up, came over here and we were together about three years when he died in 1993. I reckon he had had a good time out there, and I reckon he was getting an old man and maybe a lonely old man. I think he probably wanted to think that everything had been put right. Well I was still his wife, we were only legally separated, we weren't divorced. And so thank God for that, and also because I am entitled to the bank pension, and without that I would have been really, well having to ask for Income Support. Because half the jobs I did over the years I've had only pittances, little bits of expenses, you know, and 'Sorry, we can't afford to pay you anything yet, but we'll give you your bus fares.'

I must admit it's only in the last perhaps two years that I've begun to be much more aware of my age. Until then I've always been very active, walking on the hills and gardening, driving the car without turning a hair, seeing my three grandsons and my daughter and my son whenever possible and flying out to Australia to visit my other daughter. Retirement was great fun in the early days but not any more, no, not any more. And so talking about GALS is very stimulating you see.

Voluntary poverty

MT Gibson Watt
The Simon Community

Usually sitting in a corner of the front room commenting on everything that went on would be Fred who had had the first prefrontal lobotomy in this country. He is a chronic mumbler and has a very wicked sense of humour. Sitting next to him might be a guy who has come in off the streets and who is catatonic schizophrenic and who is sitting there in his own shit. Every so often the workers or maybe the residents might come and just very quietly put a roll-up into the hands of the catatonic schizophrenic or give him a cup of tea and help him to drink, and just talk quietly to him for a few minutes, and then go off.

St Joseph's was originally a four-bedroomed family house in Malden Road, Camden Town, London. You go up a few steps to the front door, and downstairs there's an outside area which is often really smelly because there'll be rotting sacks of veg down there – too bad for anybody to eat – or maybe somebody has really messed up on a mattress and it's there until it gets taken away. But the basement was nearly always smelly from poor drains, certainly before the house was renovated in the late Seventies, early Eighties. I'm talking now about what the Community was like in the 1960s.

In the narrow passageway there is likely to be anything up to six or eight people who are all street drinkers, munching big fat jam sandwiches and drinking mugs of tea, and standing or falling about, and generally trying to tap you for ciggies. In the kitchen there usually is somebody who is sober, cooking. His assistants may or may not have come in off the street, or may or may not be kids straight out of school learning to work in the Community. They help the cook for the day, keeping big urns of tea brewing, making sandwiches for the tea run and the soup run, and trying to keep the place clean. One of the problems in the Community has always been that nobody can tell who are the workers and who are the residents.

And then still on the ground floor there is a tiny little backroom and that is the office, and that's where Anton and I sleep on a single bed. The office is open to all during the day and that's where the drugs are kept, all the files, the desk. And when Luke was small he lived in a cardboard box on the top of the filing cabinet.

You go upstairs to the main room and there might be ten people in this room which is, I don't know, 15 feet by 12 feet. There are desks and telephones and charts and pictures and promotional material and books all over the place, everyone busy dealing with the admin of the Community in a wider sense, not just the house admin. And dealing with the media. Anton is very media-friendly, and journalists love him because he is good TV, he knows what makes a good story.

In the bedrooms above there are any combination of people. A young woman with obsessive compulsive disorder who cleans her face with sandpaper about 500 times a day so her skin is just raw and peeling. We had one woman who was in and out of the Community for years, who ate cutlery and every so often it would all get too much and she would have to go into hospital and have it removed. And people coming off drink, people who have brain damage, people who are just very lost and frightened and lonely and isolated. Some of them very lively and noisy, some of them very timid. And cars and vans drawing up and bringing in stuff picked up at the markets, or clothing and furniture, and ferrying people across London to different houses and to our farm in Kent.

Anton needs only three hours sleep a night so he is usually up about 6.00, and he usually goes to Mass. I am probably struggling to get up after 7.00. Everyone has breakfast at about 8.30. Breakfast is tea, porridge a lot of the time, toast, cereal. Occasionally Sundays might be a cooked breakfast, or if there had just been a Harvest Festival and there were lots of nice things, there might be something different. At the same time there is the breakfast meeting where you discuss what people had done, what they are going to do, and where they will be working. And then soup for lunch, and then an evening meal about 6.00. Anton is famous for his midnight soups, because he won't go to bed till 2.00 or 3.00 in the morning, and so at about 11.00 he comes back in from a soup run and then makes a soup stiff with pepper or curry, and people pile in and there is a big cook-up in the kitchen, and anybody who is around gets caught up in that.

THERE HAD ALWAYS been homeless people, and a long tradition of lodging houses and projects for the homeless run by quasi-religious groups like the Salvation Army. But the model for the buildings as well as the experience of being in them was really

Victorian. After the war people thought that homelessness would be abolished with the advent of the Welfare State. What became apparent to Anton and others was that there existed a group of people who had other reasons for being homeless than just lack of accommodation. They were the people who he called the 'socially isolated,' people who found it difficult to fit within the mores of whatever society existed, who today might be described as socially dysfunctional.

In the late 1950s/early 1960s Anton Wallich-Clifford was a probation officer in Bow Street Magistrates Court, and he was beginning to realise that the homelessness of the socially isolated was a problem which had not really been foreseen. Anton had strong religious faith and he was very tied up in the whole concept of the suffering Christ. He believed that one should see Christ in everyone, and that led him naturally enough to want to spend time with people who were homeless and see what they did and how they managed on their own. So while he was a probation officer he went out at night and spent time with some of the groups of meths drinkers in the East End and other homeless people. He was just this vague figure on the outskirts who occasionally lumbered along and sat, and the bottle was passed round, and whether he drank or not nobody really noticed. The meths drinkers in those days were largely ex-Services, and had been in the war and had names which reflected the exploits – Tobruk and Benghazi for example – that they had been involved in. Anton felt that if people were that damaged you could not expect them to go through the standard process of rehabilitation. He got the opportunity to work in a half-way house in Southampton so he left the Probation Service and moved in and ran this half-way house for a year. I think that really clarified his ideas about the vital necessity for long-term unconditional support for those people who could not cope with a rapid process of rehabilitation, or who could only exist.

Anton felt that people had to live in a community. His first idea was that he would create a village setting where a lot of other like-minded people would come and rent or buy and live in perhaps a manor house and a variety of cottages. There would be mixtures of people who would share their lives on a long-term basis with people who had been homeless. In the main cities there would be projects which would take homeless people through into the central long-term community where they would be given the length of time necessary to re-learn or learn social skills that they never had. But it was very difficult to get planning permission. He had found a manor house in Kent and had hoped that they were going to be able to take that over, but there was such a public outcry that it fell apart. By this time, 1962 or 1963, he had moved into his mother's flat down in St Leonards on the south coast with an ex-prisoner and an ex-mental hospital patient and formed a sort of mini community.

Anton's mother was an extremely religious and pious woman. His father had died when he was two and his mother had always hoped that Anton would become a Catholic priest. In fact he had been in a seminary up to the outbreak of the war. After he came back from the war where he'd been in the RAF, she hoped he would go back into the seminary but he never did, and he lived with her for virtually all of her life. She had a great heart and great empathy, and believed that everyone should be welcome. Anton got that from her. She was perfectly happy for him to fill the place with any sort of people under any sort of circumstances.

Having failed to get the manor house in Kent Anton decided to trundle around the country talking about what he wanted to do. And by Palm Sunday 1964 he decided to have a rally in Trafalgar Square to talk about homelessness. There was beginning to be a lot of rumbling about the problems of homeless families, and the obscene and Victorian ways in which they were dealt with. Husbands and wives were separated and only allowed to meet once a week socially, and the women and children were put into old army camps with just blanket walls between them and the next family. *Cathy Come Home* was made in the later Sixties on the basis of that. So there was a big rally in Trafalgar Square, and as a consequence an elderly woman offered Anton St. Joseph's House in Camden Town which had been a Catholic Worker house in the Thirties. Since then it had been kept continuously by people who were Catholics and who were concerned about poverty and homelessness. Anton felt this was a very good omen and took over the house in September 1963. But it meant that the work got turned around. Instead of what he had seen as an experiment of interested, like-minded people who would come together through their common beliefs, he found himself taking over a house which already had a resident in it, Miss Nicholson. She was very elderly, confused and deaf, and she lived in the basement of the house where she had lived for about twenty years. She wouldn't come out except at night, and she always wore a coat and a woolly hat and she looked like a gnome. She would clank along the corridor with her slop pail, shuffle shuffle, clank clank, and she would wail in the middle of the night 'Wooooooah!'

After the first house Anton quickly acquired a hotchpotch of places. There was a Catholic priest who had a house in Rochester for single-parent mothers, and there were various other projects. Anton also acquired a place in Slater Street in the East End for the meths drinkers. It became apparent that this diversification wasn't going to work, they were too stretched. Because Anton had never intended the Community to start in that way, he hadn't really thought through how his beliefs and ideas would need to be applied in practice, that just putting a whole group of people together and expecting for it to work was no good; you had to have some coherent ideas before you did that. And so in 1965 they retrenched and actually hived off these other projects. The Community ended up with just St. Joseph's in Malden Road where there were thirteen of them for about a year.

Anton and the other core members beat out the principles of community living based around Anton's ideas and beliefs. They needed to work out how you go about creating an environment which allows you to share completely but still recognises the difference between those people who are coming in as volunteers – in Anton's terms the socially adequate – and how they work with people who are socially inadequate. The theories were fairly straightforward but Anton evolved quite a complex methodology in order to recreate some of the processes that people would have gone through had they been well parented, although there was no pretence that this was a family. One of the things that he believed very much was that all these processes had to be explicit. It was not, we are doing this to you; it was, we can do this, and this is how it's done.

The breakfast meetings are an example of the methodology in practice. Most people learn to communicate through interaction with the family through questions like 'Oh what happened to you yesterday?' and 'Where are you going today?' 'Oh I'm going there, shall I give you a lift?' You have this sort of management of your life that goes on through informal discussion, often at breakfast or at the evening meal because traditionally that would be the place where, in a healthy family, these sorts of things would happen. Everyone was asked what they had done the day before and the workers' job as the influence leaders was to try and make it work as naturally as possible within the confines of a structured setting. If somebody couldn't say, or if somebody was too shy, the workers and after a short time the residents would pick up the skill to say, 'Didn't you go to so-and-so yesterday?' If someone can't respond they can nod or they can flick their head. And then you go around and do the same thing with what's happening that day. And so the workers or, within a short space of time, the residents who get it become involved in making the links on a day-to-day basis. They make sure, for instance, that if someone has never been to the DHSS somebody goes with them who has been before and who knows what to do. You also would deal out the chores so people have to chip in. It's a very simple structure but it's a very powerful one. It's such a simple way of enabling people to talk about themselves, to talk about their needs and their desires and their hopes, and to interact with other people in the process of doing that.

After working out all of these principles the Community started to expand very rapidly. Anton and some of the others started travelling round the country. Some of those initial contacts were through the Catholic network such as the Dominicans and the Franciscans and Catholic student unions. Anton would get them involved in helping to set up meetings. Communities were set up in Edinburgh and Glasgow, Oxford and Cambridge, Exeter, Liverpool. The Community also acquired a farmhouse outside Canterbury. There were various houses that the Community had access to in London because local authorities had started to allow charities to have lots of their properties on short-term tenancies while they were waiting for them to be bulldozed. And so for about twenty years there was an almost endless supply of properties that you could shuffle around in.

I joined the Community full-time at the end of 1967. I had got involved through their Edinburgh project. I was raised in a Scottish mediaeval Catholicism, which I'd disliked very much but I was idealistically committed to the ideas of the Gospel and the Sermon on the Mount. And the Community was a great revelation to me; it fitted exactly with what I felt, the way I felt that I should live my life at the time. And so I joined and went down to the training course that the Community was running, and even though Anton was twenty-five years older he and I clicked. I don't believe in any supernatural stuff but we could seamlessly follow each other's thought patterns without even being aware of it. I didn't realise that was happening to begin with but Anton picked up on it. And so we had a whirlwind romance and it wasn't just a romance with Anton, it was a romance with the Community and the whole idea of the Community. We married very quickly and spent our honeymoon staying for three nights with a worker priest in Paris, visiting the Emmaus communities. When we came back to London we started a new Simon Community project working with drug addicts.

People who worked with alcoholics or drug addicts would often say, 'We'll work with you from the point that you come off.' That's not so common now, but in those days that certainly was the situation. And Anton believed that you couldn't do that. He believed that if people were in need and in pain you had to work with them as they were and hope that the work you did with them would enable them to get control of whatever was going on.

Our drug project was in a house just opposite St. Joseph's in Malden Road, it was one of those short-term properties. ED Berman was next door setting up Inter-Action. It was always fun when you took over a new house because you had no idea what was in it, if there were going to be electrics, if there was going to be water, if all the toilet fittings had been smashed. You went in and did a very quick rehab, lifted up the floorboards to see if you could find the stop-taps and checked that there were no rotten floorboards people could go through. People would slap paint on because the rooms were usually fairly grimy.

One of the things Anton evolved was the tier structure: first tier would be the reception house where people would come in straight from the street. If you were at first-tier level, doing nothing at all would be acceptable. But by the time people got to the second tier they would be expected to be integrated into something even if it was just going out with the guy who drove the van and keeping him supplied with ciggies. Anton was brilliant, he was always inventing new titles, and everybody had some function even if it was very limited. Most agencies had criteria for the sort of people they wanted because they wanted to succeed in rehabilitating people, and so we ended up with people who had been in every agency and nobody wanted them because they were not amenable to the rehabilitative regime. But the Community still had to make assessments of people, and we would always move those people who we felt were capable of being rehabilitated on to the relevant agency. So we tended to end up with people whose difficulties were so great that they would be with us on quite a long-term basis.

With drug addicts you had to shift your schedule because they were never functional at breakfast. So you would have a lunch meeting or you would do the breakfast meeting at dinner time. We got through vast quantities of custard because many of them didn't have much of an appetite but they could eat custard with sugar. There were about sixteen people living there, all bundling in together and cooking and cleaning. In some ways it was a bit harder, some of the people we had were very ill and they weren't able to do so much for themselves. There was one elderly woman who had been an addict since her twenties, and she was on horrendously high amounts of heroin and really quite frail. But still, the processes that went on were the same as in the rest of the Community. And some people did eventually come off but that was not the primary purpose. If people responded in any of the projects, if they came off, if they managed to climb their way back into society in some sort of stable state that was a great bonus. However Anton always believed that one should guard against the pressure for some sort of success.

In the early days when I joined the Community, the idea of the group therapeutic process was paramount. Everything would stop for talk, and you might go on for twenty-four hours. Say somebody was caught stealing again. 'That's it, he's got to go,' and we would go through the process of discussing and working through it until there was a resolution which everybody could live with. Eventually non-stop group therapy became less of a feature of the Community's work. I think that living a life in that way requires so much of you that in the end you burn out.

I suppose one of the most common reasons for being thrown out was being a persistent thief within the Community. Another common reason was drunkenness. Unless it was a wet shelter, most of the houses have a no drinking on the premises rule. You could come into the house drunk but you had to go to bed and you had to be fairly quiet, and if you were very obnoxious you'd get chucked out for the night, and you came back for breakfast. But if people were into a big drinking binge they might get bounced out on the basis that the quicker they got to the bottom, the quicker they would get picked up again. There was not much violence. I can only remember one or two people in all the time who were permanently banned for violent behaviour. But all other behaviour was tolerated like bedwetting which is a very common way to get chucked out of hostels. It's interesting, there are quite a number of people who have head injuries and who end up homeless because their functioning has been affected, and there's not enough support if they don't have a good family to look after them. We had one lad and his dog, and he used to sleep with the dog, the dog was black and white, and the lad was enuretic. And one night some new red sheets had come in, and after a night in the new sheets the dog was black and red, and so we had to shove them in the shower together to get Mitsy black and white again.

The Community has paid people on the periphery, for example a temporary secretary or someone to do some PR, but nobody within the Community was paid. The volunteers get pocket-money – in 1967 it was £1 per week – which is comparable to what the residents get on social security. But the Community provided for you: there were second-hand clothes; and there was tobacco, that was a great source of currency in itself really, everyone had a tobacco allowance. And if you didn't smoke you had 50p or something to cover the tobacco that you would have had. It's not that everything was held in common, the idea was that you lived in voluntary poverty.

The Community has always done what would be called street work now, going out every night, taking food and clothing to people, and keeping contact. The idea is not so much to give people charity and food but to actually maintain long-term relationships with people who are still on the street. In many ways the Community's attitude is very Buddhist in that it's to do with deep compassion, and being with people, and sharing what is possible.

Anton believed that his motivation and the motivation for the Community should not be forgotten so all the houses had a Crucifix but that was the end of it. There was no proselytisation in any way although spiritual things would come up. The Community believed it should identify with social issues, particularly to do with poverty. The midday meal in the Community was always soup as a conscious and deliberate identification with the poor. For many years the Community had no money, it was living hand-to-mouth. We got tea from one of the warehouses. As the tea-chests were winched up the front of the warehouse they would bang against the wall, and you'd get little trickles of fine tea dust that would land on the pavement and build up. People from the Community would go and scoop the tea up. And we used to go round the markets and pick up the bruised fruit and veg in the gutters because there was so little money. Anton always thought that the best combination to go to Covent

Garden market was a monk in a habit and a girl in a mini-skirt. They would go around and ask people if they had any stuff they wanted to get rid of. The Community lived like that, so having soup was not just purely to identify with the poor, it was our own poverty as well.

The Community has a strong base of supporters who have been very loyal for a very long time. They provide the Community with money, often small amounts, so the Community's income has increased considerably. Some of the income is from rents paid by residents with Housing Benefit but the Community has always been very modest in the amount that it has asked for rent.

I did enjoy it. There wasn't any part of you that wasn't used, apart from the fact that at times you got too tired even to read. I think that was the great thing about the Community: you're living in that sort of situation where even today anybody who comes in, whether they're a resident or a worker, has the opportunity to get involved in anything that appeals to them. So they get to explore their own competency in those areas and can end up with a huge range of experience. Many of the volunteers and ex-residents went on into other areas of life seeding both new and old organisations with the Community's ideas.

Anton and my marriage was difficult. And for a whole variety of reasons it became more difficult. As I said, Anton was twenty-five years older than I was and although we had been told we couldn't have children, we had Luke four years after we were married. I felt that I needed to have a bit more space with Luke and that Anton's expectations of me were not always compatible with me being a mother. By then I was just that much older, I'd been in the Community for four years, and I had more confidence in my own opinions about things. Anton had become enormously jealous and possessive for no reason, and I couldn't go anywhere. So life became impossible. Then Anton's mother became very ill, and I felt that I couldn't leave him while all of that was going on. And so I stayed until after she died, and then left him about six months later in 1975.

I eventually met somebody else and went with him to Wales. And then in 1978 I realised that Anton was seriously ill. He had contracted malaria during the war, and he also had a blood condition that he was very vague about but he would get wiped out from time to time. Also he was I think a manic depressive, and he would have periods of terrible depression that might last for two or three months where everything fell apart and he couldn't sustain interest in the

90

Community. Then he would come out of that and he would start fizzing and popping with more ideas than anybody could keep up with. I mean, he wanted to get fleets of buses, mobile night shelters going around the place, or use Portakabins on building sites. I mean he had really good visions of how you could do things and work with people, a real lateral thinker. So I came back to St. Joe's and I stayed there to bully him to go to the doctor. The relationship that I had in Wales was coming to an end. My loyalty was really to Anton. I wasn't not living with him because I didn't love him but because I couldn't. He was the father of my child, and one of the things that we discussed before we married was the fact that because he was much older than I was and might die first, part of my commitment was not just to him but to continue to look after the Community. So I felt that I should stay and hold the community together while Anton got better. And then he died.

Everything was left in turmoil because had we known he was going to die ... well, there wasn't the opportunity to discuss the sorts of things that you would have. There was closure in terms of our relationship but there was no clear path for the Community. His underlying ideas are very clear but I'm sure if he had known that he was going to die so soon there's a great deal that we would have wanted to talk through. I had already developed ME while I was living in Wales although I didn't know that's what it was. Living in the Community under those circumstances and in the aftermath of Anton's death meant that I wasn't making a good fist of it. I stopped some very odd people from coming in at a time when the Community was vulnerable, and I managed to give the committee time to get to grips with the whole situation. I was around the Community for another year, and was on the management committee until the mid-Eighties when I became very ill, and couldn't really continue.

I was born Marie-Therese Ann McQuade in 1948 in a little ex-mining village called Carfin in the west of Scotland, about fifteen miles east of Glasgow.

Carfin was a very singular village. The priest as a young man had employed the out-of-work miners to dig and delve a piece of land which the Church owned and he turned it into – for want of a better phrase – a religious Disneyland. This site was quite extensive. He collaborated with a Belgian sculptor, and the people in the village would raise money, and every so often a whole new set of sculptures would be acquired and a whole new tableau would be erected. In the entranceway there's a replica of the site where Our Lady of Lourdes appeared with a life-size statue of the Virgin Mary, and Bernadette kneeling at the bottom of a little stream. And on the other side there's a rose garden with a statue of St. Thérèse of Lisieux which is why I'm called Marie-Thérèse. There's a wonderful bronze sculpture of the Crucifixion and beautiful marble sculptures of all sorts of shrines to St. Margaret of Scotland, to Christ the King, to St. Anne. There was a shallow lake with a little island in it with a beautiful statue of the Virgin Mary with the Christ Child in her arms. And a lovely setting with St. Francis preaching to the birds. Even the mainline train between Edinburgh and Glasgow made a little halt at the village to bring pilgrims. One of the greatest things that could happen to you if you were little girl or a little boy was to be chosen to throw fresh flower petals under the feet of the Blessed Sacrament as it was carried round the gravel paths. And torchlight processions. And thousands and thousands of people. So I grew up in this fantasy world that was absolutely real.

My parents were second cousins. Their grandfathers were brothers and both my grandmothers were called Kate Dillon. My father started off in the Post Office although he had been one of a group of boys who had made it right through high school. His friends went on and became teachers and one became a Cardinal. But because his father had died, my father had to leave school and work to support his mother. My father met my mother when he was doing his training in the RAF just outside Newcastle where she lived with her parents. Because their parents were cousins he visited. My mother was the youngest of about six and my father and she walked out while he was there, and they corresponded while he was away during the war. When he came back they got married on August the 4th 1947. I was born on May the 9th 1948, so it was very, very finely judged. I'm the eldest. I've got three brothers, and my sister is the youngest. My mother also fostered babies until I was about sixteen so there was always a new baby in the house.

We lived on a little estate in a two-bedroomed house with quite a decent-sized garden. There were my parents and the five children and foster babies. So things were fairly cramped. We were very fortunate because the village was completely surrounded by farmland, so as children we were much freer because there weren't the fears that people have now about children being abducted. I was fascinated by natural history so the house was always filled with baby birds at nesting time and jars of caterpillars falling over the pantry in the summer. There was a derelict siding to an abandoned heavy engineering works and you could go through the fence and there was an old steam train permanently rusted to the rails, and the actual rail itself was wonderful because it was filled with orchids, and I remember botanising along there when I was about ten. So as a child a lot of my life was very free.

My parents were very heavily involved in the life of the village, it was very much a co-operative place and they would have helped anybody. I remember, I must have been about twelve, and there was an old guy who was a tramp wandering outside and he obviously wasn't very well, and my parents weren't in. I didn't even think about there being anything wrong, I just asked him to come into the house. And he wouldn't come in past the hall so I pulled a chair out for him to sit on, and I made him a cup of tea and a sandwich and then he wandered off. I told my parents and it wasn't an issue, it was such an accepted thing that my mother was always enormously hospitable. Once she brought home a couple of nuns she had met on the bus and they came and stayed and slept on the floor. She worked in the Post Office and she was always interested in people, particularly foreigners. Somebody with a strange accent would talk to her, and the next thing you knew they would be dossing on the floor for a night or two.

I went to school in the village to begin with, and then to grammar school in Hamilton which is about four miles away. I was a fairly typical rebellious teenager I suppose, and if anything odd happened in the school they used to come looking for me.

In my teens there was also quite an influential figure, not just for me but for many people, a priest called Father Giarchi who was a wonderfully romantic Scots Italian, very slender, incredible-looking with huge dark round liquid eyes and dark hair, and it was known that he had a bad back and had to wear a surgical corset, so this made him a martyr as well. He did youth missions and he would come to a place and be there for two weeks – a week with the boys, a week with the girls. He knew quite a lot of people in the pop world – Jimmy Saville was a friend of his – so at the end of his mission there would usually be a big dance with some pop group. But the main thing was that he talked about things that nobody else talked about. I had talks with him about my feelings and he encouraged me or he listened to me patiently at any rate. I wasn't a very holy girl at all, I was one of the few in my group who, as soon as I got to sixteen, decided I had to find out what it was all about, doing all of that teenage stuff, telling your parents you're going to one place and going somewhere else. I did feel very constrained by the whole Catholic guilt trip. I wanted to hitchhike round the world. I'm sure if I had I would have probably ended up barefoot and pregnant in Marrakech or maybe not even as far as that.

Instead I joined the Civil Service. I worked in the local office of Ministry of Pensions and National Insurance, now the Department of Health and Social Security. I didn't want to go to university. Careers guidance didn't exist. There was a little room with some leaflets, and if you were really keen you could go and ask somebody to find the key, unlock the door, and you could have a look at the leaflets. The main pressure on you at school was to teach. One of my friends is convinced they were short of Catholic teachers so that was why they didn't give us any other options, but I think it was the poverty of their imagination. Catholics had been very much discriminated against and there were very few options even then to get beyond a very low level, even in something like the Civil Service in Scotland because of the Orange Lodge. So I was really ripe to move as soon as I could.

After about a year I went to Edinburgh with my brother for the 1967 Festival. The Simon Community was having a sleep-in and a fast on the pavement in Princes Street and I was just smitten. I mean, here was everything that I believed in being put into practice. I was nineteen. I had a couple of weeks' holiday due so I went and spent them in the night shelter in Edinburgh which was just one huge room that took as many people as could walk, crawl, stagger in the door at night. It was the most basic level of care with people sleeping where they could on what they could. There were some blankets and some mattresses but they weren't very salubrious.

There was a little back room where the workers slept during the day. The Catholic chaplain of Edinburgh University, Father Anthony Ross, a Dominican, had helped to set up this project and was very much the mentor of it, but the place ran itself to a large extent. There were workers who had come from London and who had been through the Community and this was what I wanted to do. This was living my life as I believed I should be living it. I decided I had to join the Simon Community nationally, so I came down to London and met Anton. I joined in October 1967 and we were married in December.

After Anton died in 1978 it became very difficult to live in the Community. I had gone out one evening to see some friends and had left Luke sleeping. I could hear this terrible noise as I came near the house. I thought it was somebody freaking out but actually it was Luke, aged six, trying to get out the front door and people were holding him back. I thought, this is not right. He hadn't known his father very well but he was obviously affected by his death. The house was not a good environment to bring up children where we were sharing a very small three-bedded room with a young woman with obsessive compulsive disorder, and a budgie. I applied to the local authority which did consider me homeless and gave me a very nice flat at the bottom of Malden Road just by Luke's school. It meant that when Luke was at school I could be in the Community during the day, and we would eat there when he came in from school at night and then we would go back to the flat. But I became more and more ill and I couldn't manage to function, and then my brother turned up. He had worked in Simon when he was younger and then became a social worker so he took over at the Community which was a great relief for me.

This would be 1979. As I got better I got involved with the Women's Workshop, which was being set up by Camden Council. I was still involved with the Community on the management committee and helping out round the edges, but I was working part-time mainly with the Women's Workshop which offered facilities for women and which ran an after-school club, advice sessions and all sorts of classes for women, you know the psyche-yourself-up-to-be-a-strong-woman sort of thing. Then I was offered a job by somebody who had worked in the Community and who was up in Yorkshire running a project helping kids deemed to have no future, teaching them skills. I went up there, but that wasn't a success. I just got very ill again with the ME, but this time I did become very depressed. I was in Yorkshire for a year exactly. I thought if it is depression I knew one excellent psychiatrist on the south coast so I moved down to Hastings, which is where Anton's mother had been based, and got involved with a similar project to the Women's Workshop, again part-time and as a volunteer.

Once Anton died I qualified for the state Widowed Mother's

Allowance which was non-means-tested. This was very good, not that I earned very much, a few pounds a week here and there. The Community had applied for an *Open Door* programme so we made our own film with them. Out of that, *Open Door* asked me if I would sit on their consultative committee. So once a quarter I would go and it used to come in handy for the bills. I would get expenses and twenty-five quid and it always seemed to coincide with my electricity bill and phone bill coming in. There was not much slack anywhere.

About a month before I went up to Yorkshire I met Julian, the man to whom I'm now married, but I thought although this relationship does look very promising I can't change my plans because I haven't known him for long enough. So all this time Julian and I had been having our relationship, firstly trotting up and down to Yorkshire and then up and down to Hastings. The depression slowly lifted, and apart from one or two little episodes in the next year or two, I've never been depressed like that again. Julian and I married in 1983. He was a lawyer. He subsequently retired and now we live in Wales in a big family estate with lots of forestry. He does that, and I help with some of it. I've done some studying, modules for degree courses, so I'm stacking up credits but with no clear end in view at the moment.

It's difficult for me not to do things, and as I've got better I've got more and more involved with the Simon Community again because I feel very keenly the promise that I made to Anton. It's what I believe in, I still believe the Community is one of the cleanest things that I know of, it's the least tainted sort of structure. That's not to say that it hasn't had terrible things happen but it has managed to retain its independence and a great deal of clarity of vision.

It was the bad apple

Tim Cook
Alcohol Recovery Project

I always remember the bad apple story. I remember one of the men telling me that a group of them – all crude spirit drinkers – had been begging outside the Old Vic theatre, and a man had come out of the theatre in a very smart suit and was about to get into his car, a super-duper chauffeur-driven car. One of the group gave this man a sob story and was given a pound or two, and as the man drove off he said, 'Oh, God! what a fool he was.' And the bloke who used to tell this story said, 'Well, he's the fool, is he? Driving off in his car while you're standing here with no shoes on in the pouring rain?' They could be quite realistic about the position they were in, and if they started to say, 'Oh, you know, I fooled him' it would be countered with, 'Oh well, who are you kidding? Look at the state you're in mate.' There were a lot of stories like that around. On the other hand they had the capacity to deny reality. I remember one man died after a terrible bout of crude spirit drinking, and they literally sat round and said, 'Oh, he always used to get those apples off the market, it must have been a bad apple that killed him.' I mean they wouldn't face up to the fact that it was really very heavy crude spirit drinking that killed him. So they were always torn about their drinking, not wanting to really face up to it, coupled with a knowledge of the reality of their situation compared to the people going to the theatre and going off in their cars.

IN THE EARLY 1960s Griffith Edwards, a psychiatrist at the Maudsley Hospital, became concerned that there was very little in the way of provision for what were then called the Skid Row alcoholics, crude spirit drinkers who were usually men in their forties, living on the street. Following a report looking at various issues concerning homeless discharged prisoners, Griffith Edwards formed a steering group and persuaded the Home Office that money should be made available for a two-year experiment to see what could be done in a hostel for homeless Skid Row drunkenness offenders. The terms used were synonymous really: habitual drunken offender, Skid Row alcoholic, homeless alcoholic, and so on and so forth. I was working at the time in Blundeston Prison as a welfare officer, in the days when prison welfare was still voluntary society driven, and I had become very interested in alcoholics who were in prison. I saw a job advertised to be a warden of Rathcoole House, which was technically the Alcohol Recovery Project (ARP), near Clapham North tube station in London. It was one of these job ads that just talked about an exciting, challenging opportunity – which means only fools should apply. I've never actually been told but I suspect there were probably only one or two applicants, because most of the jobs I got in my early life, I was the only applicant or one of two or three.

Anyway I was offered the job, and started towards the end of April 1966. I lived in Rathcoole House and began to think about who we were going to admit and how we were going to run it. The aim was always to focus solely on men who had as many as thirty or more convictions for drunkenness and who were homeless crude spirit drinkers; and to create a therapeutic community by involving the residents. Before we opened our doors it had all been wonderful getting the place ready, with marvellous ideas flying around and systems being put in place. The systems were more organisational systems than systems of treatment. We agreed for example that the local GP, Dr Benno Pollak, would give each resident about an hour's thorough medical examination; and a psychiatric interview would be done by a registrar from the Maudsley; and there would be a weekly group meeting with the psychiatrist. We had policies about what happened if they drank, which at that time was, if you drank you left; how we were to manage the meals; what the cleaning system was going to be; the kind of records we were going to keep; what the rules were about pressing residents to get work; the links with the Probation Service. They were not complex systems but they were all in place. It's no good trying to think out what you're going to do once you've got your first resident. In that sense it was a lesson I learnt, so when I later worked for the City Parochial Foundation and people were starting projects I could say, don't think that you can have one or two young kids coming to the youth club and then you work out what you're going to do when violence erupts; you've got to have all that sorted out beforehand.

The first man who came, Manchester Fred he was known as, I

think he came on the May Bank Holiday, and I remember Griffith Edwards saying to me, 'The minute you take in your first resident, everything will change.' And he was right. We quickly filled up, and soon had nine or ten men, it was only men in those days. One's life was never the same again. It was astonishingly exciting. And it was hard work and the long hours were unbelievable. When I look back I think, well, how did you do it? But you do things when you're – what was I? I was twenty-eight – in good health, and energetic. I think if you had not had a lot of energy and had been prone to coughs and colds and headaches, you wouldn't have survived, there's no question about that, you really were dependent a lot upon good health. I can remember Griffith Edwards saying to me, 'Well I won't be in till midnight, but if you want to ring me, we can discuss it,' and you would do that without hesitation. None of this time off in lieu, or my shift ends at whatever. I mean, you did 'work.' I put work in quotes because it was just your life really, I mean just phenomenal hours. Absolutely extraordinary.

Apart from me there was a young Community Service Volunteer also living in who came a month or two after I got there, so that I could have a day off. And we took in without question the hard core Skid Row alcoholics, crude spirit drinkers; they were the hard end of the group. And of course many of them knew each other so they really became a sort of drinking school that wasn't drinking! This had its pluses but it also had its minuses. There was a lot of collusion when people did behave badly or went drinking.

No one knew what these men were really like. They were all extremely interesting people. When sober, very few had any serious psychiatric problems at all. They were quote, perfectly normal, unquote. The GP, for example, was keen to work with the hostel because he thought he would discover extraordinary sorts of illnesses, but in fact he said, once they'd sobered up they were remarkably healthy; although they'd had terrible accidents happen to them. He said it was quite a different kind of patient for him, but he didn't discover wonderful new or long-since-forgotten illnesses. He said they were all in quite good shape because to sleep out in the colder winters of those days, you had to be quite fit. Those first six months until Christmas were just vivid and dramatic, I learnt a lot, and I think I was operating by the seat of my pants, just having to absorb so much knowledge about the way the men thought or behaved, whether it was appropriate to have the no-drinking rule and so on.

We'd kept quite a steady group, and we were rather pleased with ourselves. Several men had stayed sober and in work the whole time. In those days people could still get jobs, so I can hardly think of anybody who didn't get a job, some quite quickly: working in the parks, working in the markets, factory work, hotel kitchen portering.

And then by Christmas Day 1966, eight months after opening, the house was totally empty. They had all disappeared drinking. I think we had nine or ten men in the hostel and within a three-day period they all just disappeared and failed to come back. We had mounds of food. I'll never forget finding the very green sausage rolls about a fortnight later because nobody had eaten them. And that really required a substantial pause for thought. We had to recognise that the kind of men we were taking in were not suddenly going to say, 'Well thank you very much, yes I've always wanted to stop drinking, I will now do so.' We were dealing with men who were certainly almost all over forty – the younger drinker on the street was almost unheard of then – so they were a tough, difficult group. And that Christmas was really something! We hit the buffers at that point. We had not anticipated that Christmas is a boozy time for everybody, the whole atmosphere as you walked down the road, in the pubs and everywhere booze was coming out of every nook and crevice. I was not someone who, at any stage in my life whether Christmas or New Year, got really boozed up, so in that sense I hadn't realised quite the pull that it had. I mean these were guys who drank all the year, so Christmas was only an excuse.

I knew where they went drinking, there were hordes round the Elephant & Castle, some went to Waterloo Station and others to the gardens in front of the Old Vic. Many an evening and night I spent in places like that. We decided that we would go looking for them after Christmas and bring them back because the sooner they were back the less damage would be done to them. Of the missing nine or ten we probably got four or five of them. I remember bringing two of them back in a car one night off Waterloo Station. One or two others drifted back, and then we started again.

After that Christmas we made the residents' meetings rather more serious in content; we discussed with them individually, more openly, the problems and – temptation is too mild a word – the addiction really. We decided we'd have an Alcoholics Anonymous meeting in the house one evening a week, and some did quite well out of that. I remember one man who came after that Christmas. He got a job the same day he arrived, and he really latched on to the AA meetings, and he just never drank again. For some, AA was critical. We involved a man I'd known in Blundeston Prison, a right character and an alcoholic who had stayed sober after Blundeston. He was very much into AA, and he helped get it going in the hostel so we began to pull in support from recovered alcoholics. Some of the men were hostile to AA and didn't want it, but some found it supportive and helpful. We just tried everything we could to strengthen their resolve to stop drinking. But it was a monumental task.

I remember one man called Beery, and no one ever thought he would stop drinking. He got a job road sweeping, and he said to the psychiatrist one evening, 'Look, I've been here six months, I've got a job, I've saved up, I've bought a bicycle; what do I do now?' And to some extent there's no answer to that. In fact he went drinking a few days after that, and he died. The men always used to say, if you'd been sober a long time, and then suddenly went drinking again, particularly the stuff they drank, it had a worse impact on you. I suspect some of that was myth, but anyway the fact is he did die, I think he choked on his vomit if I recall. But he summed it up very well: I've done all that you asked of me, I've done all that I hoped to do; now what? Two or three got married. We always used to say of the ones who'd never married, if only they could find a good woman; but the ones who had married said, 'If it wasn't for the wife I wouldn't have gone drinking.'

What was interesting for me and why I was excited by the work was that a number of us working in various hostels in South London used to meet quite regularly with Dr Griffith Edwards to discuss cases, and how we could better deal with problems, and better tackle behaviour in the hostel as well as the wider policy issues like what are the lessons to be learnt from this? In 1968 the Home Office set up the Habitual Drunken Offenders Working Party which I was on with Griffith Edwards. We were keeping records at the time as part of the research being done on the hostel by two psychologists, so there was an intellectual and analytic element which was very attractive to me, as well as the sheer business of keeping the hostel clean, trying to keep the men sober, referring them to the doctor, claiming them back from Waterloo Station or whatever. That was the bedrock really I think, the excitement of trying to tackle something new.

One would hesitate to say that ARP was unique, but it was new. There was a lot going on in America around Skid Row alcoholics, they'd been working at it perhaps five or six years before us, and it reassured us that no one had yet found the key that we were somehow blithely ignoring, or were unaware of. The alcoholics remained a group who were not easy to help. But, yes, the excitement was, you were in on the ground floor of a project, which is always exciting. It was a project that was tackling – as did so many Sixties things – something that had not been systematically tackled before, and certainly not been written up and researched. The problem was addressed seriously, I think that was the key, and that interested me because I knew I couldn't get all my satisfaction just out of endless discussions with men who were drunk and therefore incredibly boring!

The word 'addiction' didn't really surface at all until the Sixties. Just taking the addiction world I lived in there was Rathcoole, Giles House for alcoholics, Phoenix House for drug users, the Community Drug Project up in Camberwell, and there was our – ARP's – own development in 1969 with the shop fronts. The shop fronts were walk-in centres for homeless alcoholics interested in trying to stop drinking; a way of reaching out to them.

Then there was the Simon Community. I remember Anton Wallich-Clifford, its founder, coming to see me at Rathcoole with a monkey on his shoulder, and a bevy of very beautiful women. The Simon Community dealt with homeless drinkers, and they ran houses which, well certainly the ones I visited, were much, much more tolerant than we were. In my memory they certainly didn't have rules about drinking and not drinking; and the physical conditions at the hostels were pretty grim. It's quite a spiritual movement in a way, Simon Community, and everyone was on the same level, there were no such things as staff and residents. And indeed I remember, I think it was Tommy, saying that he had been in one of the Simon hostels in Battersea, and – typical Tommy, very scathing about the workers and volunteers – I remember him saying, 'Just because they say 'fuck' and roll their own cigarettes, doesn't mean they know what it's about.' Simon was not highly regarded by the men we had, but I know there were men who took one look at us and ran, and who preferred Simon. So it's not good or better or worse, it's just very different. The history of the Simon Community is important, but in the early days it was slightly eccentric I have to say.

I mean just in one little patch around addiction there was an extraordinary amount going on, and funding was not too difficult; I'm not saying it fell off trees by any means but it wasn't too difficult, it was pre-Lottery. And then you look at everything else that went on: the rediscovery of poverty, the development of disability organisations, rights and responsibilities emerging as issues, advocacy, homelessness with government ministers going out on soup runs – there was an enormous amount of activity. I recently listed all of the terms which started to appear in the voluntary sector world at that time. A lot started in the 1960s like advocacy, addiction, counselling, women's aid, battered wives, community transport, community development – community this that and the other figured a great deal – race relations, black history, free schools, welfare rights, carers, mediation, disability, social housing to name just a few. It was an explosion both of activity and of thinking, and of opportunities for people like me who wanted to be involved in some way. It was a sea-change for the voluntary sector, there's no question about that, absolutely no question. And it's encouraging that so much of what started then has continued, and has developed, and the funding has been found, and much of it's statutory now, compared with those days, and that's remarkable. It was easier, partly because there were a lot of things that had not been tackled at all, and homelessness certainly hadn't. When Griffith Edwards and I went to the City Parochial Foundation in late 1968 to get money for the ARP, we had a very vigorous conversation for two hours, and when we put in a proposal we got a big grant.

The funders were not hassling you for business plans and outcomes. But now it is, 'Well where's your business plan?' The equation used to be much neater and simpler. I'm not saying that there shouldn't be any discussion about outcomes and business plans but I think for people who want just to start something today, and thank goodness people still do, it is harder.

A typical day at ARP began between seven and eight o'clock. The men used to get their own breakfast, but I was usually up and around. I had a room on the ground floor as you went in. All the rest of them had bedrooms above. The first issue would be, whether the men should get up or not, that was an interesting issue. I took the view that they shouldn't be pressured into work, and that if they stayed in bed and were sober and it took them quite a long time, weeks and weeks if necessary, that this may be their way of trying to sort things out. Now this created some interesting problems, because the blokes who were going to work were not too happy that others stayed in bed. I remember a man called Patrick, I'll never forget him. He hardly got up except to eat for six months, and then he suddenly got up and got a job on Clapham Common as a park keeper, and certainly ten years later he was still sober. When he came to us Patrick could hardly utter a word, was incredibly inarticulate; by the time he left you couldn't stop him talking. And if someone had said, 'Why?' I wouldn't have had a clue. I think we must all be careful of attributing wonderful cures, or thinking what we're doing is marvellous. Some of it is you're in the right place at the right time.

And another man I remember, Tony, funny how these names come back, who was a great failure. He only drank crude spirits, and was a cinema addict. He would stay in bed, then he would disappear for the afternoon and go to the cinema. And the first time I put any pressure on him to go and get a job, he just disappeared drinking and never came back.

So the day would start in the early morning with breakfast. Then I would make or take umpteen phone calls and receive letters referring people, arrange doctor's appointments for new people, get them to see the psychiatrist, write up the records, possibly go off to Spring Hill Prison. It was an open prison where a lot of the drunks were in the fresh air with the Prison Service believing this was doing them a lot of good, what a load of cobblers. But anyway, we went out there, and I would interview a few. And you went through this dance of, 'Well do you really want to stop drinking?' 'Oh yes, absolutely.' They'd give you a load of great stories. And they would all swear that this is it, I never want to drink again. I'd say, 'Well you've been arrested seventy times for drunkenness; why now?' 'Oh this is it.' Unless we were full, I think we took almost everyone we interviewed. The vast majority of referrals were from the Inner London Probation Service and they sent very poor quality letters of referral on the whole, partly because this was a group the Probation Service didn't deal with much. I remember one man, Bernie, who did incredibly well – and thirty-three years later I am still in touch with him. The probation report from Cambridge said this bloke was pathetic and hopeless – 'an inadequate psychopath' – but he might be worth a try. Now, we had to take him blind, because I wasn't able to get to see him for some reason, and he arrived, and he was a great success. For all the careful assessing you do, sometimes you think you might as well stick a pin in and take them on a random allocation basis, you'd probably do just as well. So there was the administration, there'd be a meeting perhaps at the Institute of Psychiatry or the Addiction Research Unit, and then having to be back at the house as the men came back from work, talking with them about how had they got on, having the evening meal, and chatting about this that and the other.

We had a cook, Mrs Smith, who used to produce vast quantities of good solid food and who was quite an important person, she was there for many years. Once a week there would be the house meeting. Occasionally if someone hadn't come back, I'd wait up but if he arrived back drunk we didn't allow him in. I would usually take them to the Camberwell Reception Centre run by the DHSS, which has long since been closed. Some men would refuse to go there, and they would wander off into the night. Once I remember I took two and they said they'd rather be left in the car park in Camberwell. I left them there to sleep, and I thought, crikey! they'll fall asleep and the first lorry that comes in in the morning will run them over. So I got up very early and went down to see them, and they couldn't even remember that I'd taken them there or anything. I was worried and they'd slept like logs. That was a lesson for me, that I worried often a lot more about them than they worried about themselves. The men used to say, 'Look, we've slept out, you don't have to bother, we aren't going to die on the streets.' They understood their way of life a lot better than I did.

Certainly before the famous Christmas I did have them back if they were drunk but then we began to be a bit more thoughtful about it, mainly because in a sense you were giving men a double message. You were saying, you're here to stop drinking, but you were also saying, if you do drink it doesn't really matter because you can come straight back. If the man had been there six months sober and working hard and slipped as they would call it, we would tend to be more willing in the house discussion to let him come back. Someone who had been at the house three days and just gone off, I think the men took the view, he's just here to get his giro and all the benefits he can and he would disappear. Often men who had only been there two or three days, you didn't see again anyway, although I have to say there were not that many. The majority on the whole stayed for several months and got jobs before moving on to other hostels.

Perhaps at an earlier time in their lives the men might have been in the forces or in work, but for a long long time they had been in and out of prison just because of their drunkenness. Most of them got very short sentences, ten to twenty-eight days for non-payment of fines a lot of them. It was all in and out, in and out. Some crimes were slightly more serious, petty theft or stealing a bicycle, stealing money from a news vendor. They would all describe themselves as extremely honest and it was just the drink that caused them those problems.

They were drinking meths mainly, after-shave, antifreeze, boot polish melted down. I'll never forget Eddie who had left the hostel and he came back to see me at my home, and asked could he go up to the bathroom and wash, and when he came down, he seemed very happy: he had drunk all my after-shave! I always laugh about that. So they would do anything to get the stuff. I think that's largely gone now, certainly the people I know now working in the homeless agencies with drinkers say that these cans of strong brew have replaced all that.

They'd got hooked on alcohol quite early on. I remember Tommy describing how he used to go and collect beer in a milk bucket for his granny and he always used to have a few sips on the way back, and that's how he started. Tommy was an interesting character and a very nice bloke indeed. He came from St. Helen's and my wife got to know him very well because she comes from that part of the world. He stayed sober, then broke out and then came back and never drank again; he got a job in the parks and married. I think he died of cancer, but certainly the last twenty years of his life were sane and sensible. But he was interesting, and characterised something about the men. He was very judgmental about anyone who didn't quite fit his way of drinking. What I used to find was, if I suggested we took a twenty-two-year-old, say, into the hostel – which we never did because it would have been a disaster to have a twenty-two-year-old with that group – they all said, well he couldn't possibly be an alcoholic. Their idea was unless you'd done what we've done, you can't be an alcoholic. So they were very rejecting of anyone who didn't quite fit their pattern; if you hadn't drunk crude spirits, oh he's not an alcoholic, he only drinks beer. They defined the problem as it affected them, they were not willing to expand their horizons in that sense. And Tommy was absolutely like that, in drink as boring and as sentimental as you can possibly get. That was the other thing you see, I mean the idea you could try and talk sense with them when they were drunk. They were boring, boring and would go on for hours and hours and hours. Their paths to Rathcoole were many and various, and they'd got there somehow, from St. Helen's, from Ireland, from Scotland, they'd come to London for work or to escape pressures, wherever they were. There was a lot of division between the Scots and the Irish in the hostel. It wasn't that they abused each other, but they were quite disparaging of each other. They're tough, quite unforgiving of themselves and often of others.

I remember George who was probably the most difficult man we ever had in the hostel in terms of upsetting every single person in it, but he stayed sober so there was not much we could do about it. He used to exasperate me beyond belief, and I remember going to discuss him with Griffith Edwards once, and I clearly was not being as objective about George as I ought to have been in fairness, but I remember Griffith saying to me, 'Well tell me, what do you think it's like to be George? How do you think George sees the world?' He used to do that with us, we'd present impossible characters who were driving us mad in the hostel, and he would say, I can hear him now, 'Well tell me what you think, what do you think it's like to be George?' And I struggled with that for ten or fifteen minutes, and I was different from then on with George, and could deal with the men who were hostile to him. Because he absolutely was a military man, a martinet and he would complain about the state everyone had left the kitchen in, and he was just prickly and obsessively tidy and clean, and in a hostel for alcoholics being obsessively tidy and clean is not easy. But he stayed sober, and moved into a flat eventually.

In 1967 we started another hostel because there were a number of men who were doing quite well, and we thought they ought to move on from Rathcoole. I got married in 1967 so my wife and I went to live in the other hostel, and the Community Service Volunteer stayed on in Rathcoole. So we were then running two hostels. And then we got some flats. By the time 1969 came, we had got a block of flats and two hostels, and there were just two staff, and so that was quite busy.

I left ARP in the autumn of 1974 after about nine years altogether. I was exhausted, the project was developing well, and I thought I couldn't do much more. I worked it out, the number of groups I had attended in the houses over the nine years were hundreds, and I thought, I can't sit through any more of these again. I was aware also that I'd spent from 1962, the best part of thirteen years doing nothing but hostels and prisoners and alcoholism, and that somewhere out there, there was a slightly bigger world I ought to be thinking about, or learning something about. I thought the social policy course at Brunel with a particular interest in the voluntary sector would give me the break I needed. I got a very substantial grant from the Department of Health and Social Security. Weird days. I remember, I just filled in a form and within a fortnight they gave me the grant, paid all my fees and a maintenance allowance because I was married with two children. It was as much as I had been earning. I still feel guilty about it to this day in a way, but it was just a period when you got money like that. So I left in a state of exhaustion and with a real need to broaden my field and perspectives.

I was born 25th of April 1938 in Leicester. My father was also born and brought up in Leicester. His father was certainly a drunk, an alcoholic, but an Edwardian-style gentleman drunk. My father was an only child and very, very intelligent but it wasn't so easy to go to university in those days so he ended up in business. I think his dream was to have been a university lecturer of some sort, but instead he spent all his life in business working in the hosiery trade in Leicester. He was away in the war, so from the age of three I don't think I saw him between 1941 and 1946. My mother originally came from Stoke-on-Trent, and after I was born she certainly didn't go out to work. She's now ninety – my father died in 1992 – and she spent all her life bringing us up. I was the first and my brother is three years younger than I am, and my sister is nine years younger.

There was nobody on my father's side at all. I saw a lot of my mother's parents, but her two brothers we only saw from time to time.

In 1946 we moved to a village, Barrow upon Soar, just outside Loughborough. I went to the village primary and then to Loughborough Grammar School from 1949 to 1957. I loved school, and I took to it like a duck to water, couldn't wait for the term to start. But it was wonderful only because I was reasonably intelligent, and grammar schools were actually very good if you were bright, but if you weren't, they were poor.

I was very lucky with my peer group at school. There were seven or eight of us who just got on very well and I'm still in touch with them. My school was all boys, although there was a girls' school, and we used to go on hiking holidays in the Lake District together, so there was a mixed group, but it was outside school. And a whole group of us practically lived in each other's houses, particularly during the holidays. We all went on to university, and quite a number of us ultimately into what you might call public services. Interesting, because careers advice at school was non-existent, absolutely non-existent.

Loughborough in the Fifties must have been one of the least exciting places on God's earth. We were all desperate to leave it. The first coffee bar opened in Loughborough when we were sixteen or seventeen, and we'd sit for hours over frothy coffee, it seems naïve now. Trying to explain to one's children today that the first coffee bar was a great moment, and so was the first Indian restaurant, I mean they just look at you as if you have come from the Moon. We spent a lot of time just talking. I don't think we were political in the way the Sixties became political. We certainly used to talk a lot about the nuclear threat, and nuclear weapons. A close friend of mine, Peter Preston who went on to become Editor of *The Guardian*, and I went to the meetings when our MP, Anthony Nutting, resigned over Suez. But I wouldn't regard us as a politically mature group. Social issues we certainly discussed. Here we were in middle-class Loughborough at a grammar school and we were unsure as to what we could contribute, but of our group, one went into journalism, one became a director of housing, I went into public welfare, another went into education, one went into the church, several went into teaching, one went into the Prison Service. Out of a not obviously politicised group, only one went into industry. My father regarded that as appalling. We used to go on walks in the summer with my father and have long arguments about capitalism and how dreadful business was, and he'd say, well without a wealth base what are you going to do. He was always appalled at how grammar schools and others rather disparaged business, and he was absolutely right in that, he was well ahead of his time. He said that at his school, which was a grammar school in Leicester, as soon as anybody said they wanted to go into business the school lost interest, and it was only the academic and the non-commercial sector that interested them.

I went to Cambridge and did law. When I qualified, I decided I didn't really want to do this. I'd spent my whole life up till then wanting to be a barrister, I think fuelled by rather dramatic presentations on the radio of great criminal cases and thought, this sounds fantastic: public speaking and debate and arguments and drama. But the nearer I got to seeing what the law was like then and the rather conservative atmosphere of the Inns of Court, I suddenly decided I didn't want to do this. And I've never regretted that decision for one single moment. At graduation one of the law dons told me that there was a job going at Sheffield University, i.e. they were desperate. So I thought, this lets me off the hook for a bit. So from 1960 to 1961 I went to Sheffield which I thoroughly enjoyed. I think I was a good lecturer, but doing research wasn't for me at all. I had completed the Bar exams, and I saw a course advertised, first of its kind, in criminology at the Institute of Criminology back at Cambridge, and I thought, that sounds interesting. Why I thought that I do not know, but somewhere deep down I was moving towards thinking about the people who were at the receiving end of criminal law. I did that. That was 1961 to 1962.

In February of 1962, a friend – with whom I am still in touch – showed me an advertisement in *The Observer* for assistant warden at Norman House, hostel for ex-prisoners in London. I applied. Again I suspect I was the only applicant because I got a telegram saying, 'Please come for an interview.' You don't normally telegraph applicants; well they don't have telegrams these days. And that's really where all my voluntary sector work began, and I've stayed with it ever since.

I arrived at Norman House on the Monday, having been best man at Pete Preston's wedding up in Blackpool, a really glorious, rather grand wedding with top hat and tails, that was on the Saturday. Norman House was a big North London house, a hostel for homeless ex-prisoners, the first real after-care hostel of its kind. I began the first month sharing a room with a couple of the men. And again the hours were just indescribable. Norman House was like Rathcoole except they weren't alcoholics, although there was a core group who had serious drink problems. That really opened my eyes because I had had a very easy life. Frankly, all my life's been easy in one sense, I make no bones about that. I'd done well at school and on to university, and in those days you could get any job you liked practically. I got a job that no one wanted, but nonetheless it was still a job. So suddenly you end up, as I did at Norman House, with men who had come from children's homes, and really very damaged backgrounds, showing very curious behaviour, many of them. And the prison system, how inappropriate that was, and what the hell were some of those men doing in prison? So again you were working these long hours, and you were tired but you were never exhausted, you kept going. I learned a great deal from the men and from people like Mervyn Turner and the warden at the time, David Garland, about the inappropriateness of the prison system; men who had got long sentences with no representation of any sort. You're only talking thirty, forty years ago, but it was in the Dark Ages, a lot of it. So again you had all that stimulus of saying, crikey! we should do something about all this. You had opportunities because there were a lot of interesting visitors from the court, QCs and judges and others who used to come to open evenings that one got to talk to. It was, a modern phrase that I wouldn't have used at the time, a mind-blowing experience.

I'd read a lot on the criminology course so it was fascinating to have done all the theory, and to think, well this doesn't fit. So one became quite iconoclastic possibly about some of the theoretical side of criminology and very angry about a court and a prison system that really wasn't able to take any account of – or appear not to be able to take any account of – individual needs. The alternatives for many of the men who were homeless and who came to Norman House were the large lodging houses with dormitories of 100. We used to visit the lodging houses because we tried to get digs for the men when they felt they wanted to move on from Norman House. The digs those days were 'no coloureds, no Irish, no dogs.' There were some real eye-openers for me from little old Loughborough. In university, however much you went to societies and you heard interesting talks it was a very cocooned world. On my day off from Norman House I used to go to four films in a day with an old school friend who was working in a youth club. He and I used to try and get the same day off, and we'd find ourselves in obscure cinemas out in the middle of nowhere seeing Swedish masterpieces by Ingmar Bergman, us and three people in the cinema. They were great times.

A marvellous man called Tony Parker used to visit Norman House quite regularly, and while I was there he wrote a book called *The Unknown Citizen* which was his second major book, about one of the residents of Norman House, and I got to know him very well. He put me on to my second job. A new prison had opened near Lowestoft called Blundeston to take preventive detainees who were on the whole rather inadequate men who had got lots of convictions and who had been given sentences of from five to fourteen years preventive detention. Preventive detention was essentially a sentence they were given more for what they'd done in the past than for their actual offence at the time. Blundeston needed a welfare officer. I'd been at Norman House about nineteen or twenty months by then, and I didn't know whether to move or not. And Tony Parker said to me – it was a typical Tony comment – 'You're not sure whether to do it or not? Well, could you bear anyone else to do it?' And I thought, well no I couldn't actually. And it was a wicked thing to say, he knew me very well. So I applied. There were four applicants, I do know that, because I happen to know two of them. Anyway, I got that, and I went to work at Blundeston for two years. And this is one's luck, I've always worked with extraordinarily interesting people, and the governor there was a man called Eric Towndrow, who was a genius in my view, and he wanted to create Blundeston as near to a therapeutic community as possible. Some of the officers didn't like it and some did. Although it was a secure prison and the men were in for quite a long time, there was no doubt that there were men there who changed, and who never went back to prison. I got to know a lot of them, and over the years stayed in touch. I still hear from one at Christmas, thirty years later. But Eric Towndrow really opened my eyes to ways of dealing with and responding to people. Again one could do anything. We started a volunteer scheme, we organised coaches for families so they could visit because it was a typical, bloody 'wonderful prison in a lovely setting' but impossible to get to for families, certainly from places like Liverpool. There were a whole lot of things we did: Alcoholics Anonymous, Gamblers Anonymous, all those things were started in the prison, and it was vibrant. Again the hours were very long, and I was the only welfare officer and there were 300 men. And then there was an escape from Wormwood Scrubs I think, and the Mountbatten Report came in and everything clamped down.

I had become interested in the question of whether the prisoners who were in Alcoholics Anonymous would be able to continue their efforts when they were on the outside. Will it hold? For some it did, and for others it didn't. But it was a problem you could start to get to grips with, and that just interested me. So when I saw the advertisement for Alcohol Recovery Project I applied.

One of the girls from my school days who had been part of our 'group' was in London. I didn't know, but my mother met her mother, and her mother said Gill is in London, and I think Tim is; this is her number, she'd love to hear from him. So I rang her, and she said, 'Well come for supper,' and one of the girls who shared a flat with her, Margaret, was there, and the rest is history. Margaret and I married and lived in one of the ARP hostels for a couple of years. She was teaching, and then we had a daughter. Miranda was born in 1968, and then we moved and lived literally a few hundred yards away from the hostel. We had two children, Miranda and then Alastair.

When I was at Brunel after ARP I decided that I wasn't going to go back to the alcoholic world. I didn't quite know what I was fitted for really. I'd done the hostel work, and I'd run the ARP for nine years. We were living in south London and I was keen not to move because the children were at primary school. A job came up in Cambridge House Settlement in Camberwell, and I thought, well that's interesting, that's broader, there were literacy projects, community work and so on, and I applied for that job and got it. I stayed there two and a half years, and although I worked hard, and I think I gave it my all, it never had quite the excitement that all the other jobs had.

In the summer of 1977, Sally England, who had worked with me in ARP, sent me a note saying, 'Have you seen the Family Service Unit director's job advertised? Would you be interested?' It just shows you, advertising is a curious business because you don't always see it, and you rely on others. Anyway, Sally drew my attention to it. And I applied to FSU as director – they'd had a year without a director – and I got that job. I had a great time for eight years, that was again really just enormously hard work, and very different. It was national, units all over the country, a very interesting organisation, difficult, but some first-rate work going on. Challenged you in every conceivable fibre of your being. There were a few dark days, but not many, and certainly in total it was a great great experience.

I'm a disaster for your book I think, I've had no training. I'd run ARP, and by the time I left I had about a dozen staff or so, and certainly at Cambridge House, there was some management, but I had no management training as such. I've always had a great willingness – and I think it starts with Norman House – to listen, and I've never been one given to certainties, I've always been a bit, 'well on the one hand and on the other.' A good friend of mine says that my favourite saying is, 'Well things are a bit more complicated than that,' when people come up to you with neat solutions, so I've always been willing to hold my nerve and keep the various balls in the air until it seems right. Certainly the consensual Quaker-based ethos of FSU suited me very well I think, because I was not given to *ex cathedra* statements, right, we're all going to do that. I enjoyed the consultation and wrestling with the different issues and I appreciated the quality of the front-line work, which again, like the hostel work was really hard and tough. I myself wasn't doing it, but other people were. And I learnt a great deal about management *en route*. There were very few major management crises or traumas while I was there but there were some interesting policy debates. Again funding was not too difficult, we were blessed by that. And like all the jobs I've had, you end up having learnt an enormous amount, and certainly I've been very conscious of that, hoping that I've contributed equally.

When I was interviewed at FSU they said, 'How long would you serve?' I said, well certainly five years, but probably no more than ten, because I'd like to do one last job. I was always hoping I could retire at sixty. And I must have mentioned at some point the City Parochial Foundation from whom I'd got grants over the years in all my jobs, and knew it well. I think a colleague Harry Marsh said, 'I see they're advertising the clerkship for the City Parochial Foundation, and wasn't Tim interested in that job?' So Harry very nobly drew my attention to it, and I'd got two days to get an application in. This was early 1985. And this is the one job where I know I wasn't the only applicant, there were rather more on this occasion, but anyway, I was offered that job, and I didn't hesitate. I started there in October 1985, and retired in April 1998.

About two days after I had got the job at City Parochial Foundation, Bryan Woods who was then the Clerk rang me and said, 'Can you come and talk?' It was after the abolition of the Greater London Council, and the Trust for London was to be created. There was going to be a £10 million endowment from the Department of the Environment for a whole new trust which would be part of the CPF, and I thought this would be great because this would be something that I'm not inheriting. So that was good, we got that up and running by 1988. The whole funding scene in London was changed quite significantly, and we had very good relationships with the London Borough Grants Committee, and there were big new funders coming on stream like Lloyds TSB and

Esme Fairbairn Charitable Trust, the Lottery, and so that was again a moving world. The Trust for London gave us a chance to really think about what we would do with this new resource, and how could you make it different from the CPF. There were issues about funding, monitoring, evaluation, assessment, all those kinds of things which I wrote and talked about towards the end of my time, and indeed still do. Again it was hard work. When I went to the Foundation it was quite leisurely really, 9.45 to 5.00 were the hours, and Margaret said, 'It's about time you had a job like that.' By the time I left, the hours were astronomic. So I realise there's something in me as well. No, in fairness it wouldn't have been easy to have kept that kind of leisured life.

Retirement age was sixty. They asked if I wanted to stay on but I decided no, partly because I'd done twelve years, and I thought that's long enough. But also I thought, if I stay on and I don't like the way things are going or we have a disagreement, well then, by letting me stay on, they're doing me a favour in a way because it was quite clear in the contract, I was to go at sixty. So, they're being generous by offering me another couple of years, but supposing things happen at home, then what do I do? Suddenly give three months' notice? This way, I'm retiring, they've got plenty of time because my successor had to give six months' notice where he was. So I thought, no, let's go while I'm still sane and healthy. Thinking back to Norman House in 1962, it had been a long haul, not all one's holidays taken and so on, that's just the way, no complaint about that. The pension had worked out quite reasonably, it wasn't gargantuan but it was good, none of this problem that youngsters have these days about no pension schemes and buying your own pension and all that. And I thought, well there were things I still wanted to do. And I have never regretted it or any part of my life, not for one second.

What an amazing time to be involved in this sort of politics

David Bull
Child Poverty Action Group (CPAG)

The intellectual and political challenge for our generation in the first part of the sixties was about poverty and the low take-up of welfare benefits. This was immensely exciting, very challenging to the received wisdom, and I think for several of my generation of young academics in Social Policy it gave us a campaign that we could legitimately carry on in the classrooms.

There had been no way of measuring family poverty until Peter Townsend and Brian Abel Smith took the Family Expenditure surveys and used them as a database to study families as a unit which resulted in The Poor and the Poorest, 1965. Hitherto, all you had was taxation information but this was a hopeless way of measuring the family. You needed something which measured families by size, which the Family Expenditure survey did. Nobody had ever thought of using it before. This was the genius, if you like, of Peter Townsend, Brian Abel Smith and Dorothy Wedderburn. So that was one thing. The second thing was the argument that you had to tackle child poverty by using a universal benefit, that is by increasing family allowances, and that doing it through the means test was a hopeless way of tackling family poverty. That argument grows of course in the late 1960s as we start to get all the figures that Tony Lynes, the first secretary of Child Poverty Action Group, was producing in the early issues of CPAG's publication, Poverty: the low take-up of rent rebates, free welfare foods, then free school meals. A lot of this information was gained through very clever planting of Parliamentary Questions at which Tony was excellent.

Survey after survey from Peter Townsend's The Family Life of Old People in 1957 to Audrey Harvey's Fabian Pamphlet, Casualties of the Welfare State, in 1960 had pointed to the poverty of old people who did not claim their National Assistance entitlements. These findings were later confirmed by government enquiries but Tony Lynes was breaking new ground, in those early issues of Poverty, by demonstrating the low take-up by families.

CPAG WAS FORMED in 1965 without any branches; it wasn't a grassroots organisation at all. One of the misconceptions about CPAG is that it started out as a welfare rights organisation, and of course it didn't. It started out as a national campaign on the single platform of family allowances. So, you start off with Tony Lynes working out of Skepper House near Euston Station, virtually on his own, plus a secretary. Tony didn't want branches; that was going to be extra work. And also of course CPAG thought, like good Fabians, that a Labour Government was bound to listen and treble the family allowance overnight. I was lucky enough from the start to be co-opted on to the committee and stayed on it for almost thirty years.

I was teaching evening classes for the Extra Mural Department of Manchester University, and I knew that I had two or three health visitors in the group, and that the notion of child poverty appealed to them. I had no resources except two dozen Fabian pamphlets, copies of *New Society* and CPAG's little 1966 pamphlet, *Family Poverty*. It was just such a stimulating document and it was priced sixpence old money.

In 1967 I was doing research on old age so I was invited to become a member of the committee of what was then called the National Association for the Care of Old People. I used to come down to Euston early enough to nip into Skepper House, where CPAG was based, to say hello to Tony, have a cup of tea, and put the current CPAG literature in my bag and then toddle off over to this much posher charity in Regent's Park that was paying my fare from Manchester.

CPAG soon moved to Macklin Street in Covent Garden where we were all crammed into one tiny room in an attic. There were two little rooms, Tony's office and the secretary's office. I mean Macklin Street was unbelievable. You had to walk up smelly staircases where they had cat boxes on the stairs because there was a rehabilitation scheme for drug addicts downstairs, for which Lord Longford was the great patron. I remember the committee meeting at which Frank Field reported that he'd had a word with Lord Longford about the cat litter on the stairs! You can just imagine this being reported to committee.

But you felt that you were at the hub of things. CPAG seemed much more relevant than being involved in the Labour Party which

I'd joined in 1967, where meetings were just full of putting down these pointless resolutions with such earnestness, as if it was actually going to go anywhere. Even if you'd never studied the system of compositing at party conferences, I think you soon realised, or I soon realised, that I was doing something very remote, whereas doing something at CPAG was so much more immediate than being involved in a political party. I mean maybe it was just because it was London, but somehow you felt that if you decided something at CPAG the Minister would know about it. Frank Field – who succeeded Tony Lynes in 1969 – advocated the principle of WJM Mackenzie, the political scientist, that getting something into a newspaper is most important. If you write to the Minister, all right, we're told the post bag is significant, but they've got to have a lot of letters on the same point; whereas if you get two inches in a newspaper the politicians don't know how many people believe that. This was Mackenzie's principle.

Rosalind Brooke, our first lawyer, together with Frank Field and Peter Townsend wrote CPAG's first pamphlet which was the catalyst for Frank Field to get money to set up a Citizens' Rights Office, a second-tier office for advising the advisers. Audrey Harvey was the first director of that.

There is a story that CPAG didn't have a bank account for a while because it saw itself as being a short-term pressure group. I mean it was almost that degree of naivety. The first branch was formed in Liverpool. When I said we must have a branch in Manchester, Tony said, 'Well really, I cycle over to the House and listen to a debate in the afternoon, then I come back here and write a press release, then I cycle up Fleet Street distributing it, and that's really all we need to do. Why do you need branches?' I swear that's not a parody of what he said. Eventually we persuaded Tony because we were selling the literature in Manchester and three of us – Peter Wedge, Paul Wilding and I – were already giving talks on behalf of CPAG. We formed the branch in late July 1967.

At that point Gordon-Walker, Minister of Social Security, made some outrageous announcement about family allowances and free school meals. Forming our branch coincided with that awful package in which an increase in family allowances was 'balanced' by a 50 per cent increase in the cost of school meals and welfare milk. Tony had shown me how to issue a press release about the forming of the branch, and then they asked me to go into Granada TV to talk about it, and also say something about the Gordon-Walker announcement. We might as well have camped there, we were in Granada and BBC North-West so much. You know, those young TV reporters like Mike Mackay at the BBC and Chris Kelly at Granada, and some of the radio reporters like John Humphrys on loan from BBC Liverpool relied on us not only to supply both the background statistics and the individual stories but also to find families willing to be interviewed. My first interview was recorded and I came back to the university and the porter in the lodge in Dover Street had a little television set and I watched myself, and I was swaying from side to side. I knew then that you don't conduct an interview in front of a camera unless you hold on to the sides of the chair to stop yourself swaying! So that was the first lesson. But it was just so easy. One night I remember meeting Mike Mackay at the studio door. He was running in, 'Oh David, I've not prepared any questions.' And I said, 'I knew you wouldn't. Here are three.' 'Oh bless you.' I'm not kidding!

You soon learned what a two and a half minute live interview was like, and you knew how to answer a question ending on a point that almost obliged the interviewer to come in with the next question that you wanted. I remember being told, 'David, we've got a new interviewer tonight, treat her gently, you know, look after her. David, I'd like you to meet Joan Bakewell.' And yes, this sounds big-headed but it was so important to the development of our branch. In those days both sides, BBC as well as ITV would pay us a fee. The BBC packed it in first. The Manchester branch of CPAG was very well off because we made so much out of television and radio, and every fee was paid to CPAG.

We tried to appeal to an audience whether we were talking to The Mothers' Union, for instance, or backwoodsmen in the Labour Party. The James Callaghan mentality was out there – that old-fashioned view that men's wages were the solution to family poverty. Trade unions didn't like the idea of paying for other men's kids or for irresponsible men who were having more kids than they should have, or, perish the thought, for men who weren't working. So the unions were very difficult audiences.

Once CPAG got going Tony began to get letters from people asking for help, and I don't just mean, 'Can you send me some money?' but, 'Can you advise me on my benefits?' These questions inevitably forced Tony into a sort of advisory role. And we too were very conscious that if you start saying things in the local newspapers about how outrageous it is that 65 per cent of people aren't claiming this benefit, then people who think they should be getting that benefit write to you to ask you to help them get it. The Government was planning a general entitlement campaign, and when they launched it in March 1968 it was in conjunction with an anti-scrounger campaign. Brian Abel Smith, as a government adviser, knew that the two were going to come together. I remember the CPAG Committee meeting at Macklin Street when he stopped by to tip us off! We discussed what we were going to do to ensure that the entitlement campaign took off. When the Government issued in July 1968 the leaflet called *The Short Step*, we felt that the Government wasn't going to do an adequate publicity job. We needed to do something so we decided to talk to all our local radio contacts. We had fifty-seven local authorities and thirty-seven local newspapers in our Greater Manchester catchment area, so we had a job on to alert them all to this campaign.

At that meeting of the CPAG national executive, Louis Minster from the Oxford branch said that in Oxford they were thinking of taking out information stalls to council estates. I thought this sounded rather a good idea worth pinching. And shortly after this, in June 1968, we had a brainstorming evening at the Manchester branch. It was my first experience of a brainstormer, and I remember this vividly.

I tossed in, as one of the suggestions, that we should have welfare rights stalls. And that took off. Nick Bond, from the Family Service Unit which was big in our branch, suggested that rather than go out onto the estates, we should do it in the inner-city.

We picked Ardwick market area and put up a table outside the market, and another table further up the road. So we were ready in July 1968 to do something in conjunction with the entitlement campaign. We had the local newspapers down there and got a bit of publicity. Whether we'd got police permission to set up on the pavements, God only knows, but we set up on the pavements. It was a windy July day, so somebody went into the market to get some heavy potatoes. We had all these benefits leaflets, each weighed down with a huge potato. And of course this attracted attention, having a stall with nothing on it but a load of papers and potatoes. We also had one person with a sandwich board who drummed up custom by walking up and down the pavement. One of our members, a social worker from Rochdale, very arty guy, designed the sandwich boards with huge lettering. The picture on the boards was of a bloke with a sports car and a bimbo on his arm, and it said, 'Even he may not be getting his rights'. This was outrageous, but of course quite eye-catching. We were obviously making it up as we went along. There were no rules on how to run a welfare rights stall. I mean ours was a pioneer effort. Later on our branch of CPAG was explicitly involved in getting Manchester to become the first local authority to appoint a welfare rights officer.

We had a dilemma that Child Poverty Action Group was the wrong name for a rights campaign. As Tony said, it is a pretty strange name to put on the stall, because you didn't want to say to people, 'Are you in poverty?' You wanted to say to people, 'Do you have unclaimed benefits?' And you couldn't do that with the poverty logo. CPAG was the right name for a campaign to shock people about poverty, but now we needed a different sort of campaign which was about getting the public to recognise that people who might not be seen to be in poverty had entitlements they were not claiming.

This presented two difficulties, one was with the claimants, and the other was with the media. I always remember one of the first people who we followed up from our stall in Ardwick was a refuse collector living in Beswick, and I wrote to him and said I'd go and do a home visit. But when I got there his wife was very upset because of course the headed paper said Child Poverty Action Group, and she said, 'I don't want to have anything to do with them because of this word 'Poverty'. It's nothing to do with me.' And I remember the husband sitting there saying, 'But I like this word 'Action'.' So the wife left the discussion, and he stuck it and we discussed whatever his benefits were. I remember that that crystallised for me CPAG's difficulties. If you wanted to demonstrate poverty – on TV, radio or whatever – you picked as examples families who might be desperately poor. If you wanted to pick the ideal family to demonstrate a rights story, then you picked somebody who didn't perceive themselves in poverty and weren't perceived by others to be in poverty, but who nevertheless had entitlements – ideally a family with a waged income, who nevertheless qualified for a means-tested benefit or two. Free school meals were a good example, where a working parent might be entitled to free meals for, say, one of his or her three children. So you were trying to pitch for two very different types of need. And you were also dealing with some of the people in the media who were too thick to see the difference.

I pointed out the stages involved in helping someone get their benefits. I suggested there was a twelve-point continuum between what I called 'passive advice' going right through to committed advocacy. In Manchester, CPAG hadn't thought through that we could become advocates, and we hadn't even thought of making demands on the government departments who were denying people their welfare rights. We would only ring up and say, 'Can you sort it out?' Now that is some way away from ringing up and saying, 'This person needs so-and-so.' That came much later. In fact, from the first welfare rights stall in 1968 none of us went with a claimant to an appeal until July 1970.

Our local MP was Alf Morris in Manchester Wythenshawe. His agent used to come by because I was in the Labour Party and say, 'Do Alf a favour, sort this case out.' The family had appealed against a refusal of benefit, and they'd gone to their MP for help with the appeal, so I went and represented them at the appeal hearing. That was in the morning, and our secretary was at a meeting in the afternoon with the regional officer, Geoff Speight, from Supplementary Benefits. Our secretary rang me, 'Geoff was most upset to think you went to appeal; he said, 'What was David doing going to appeal? If he'd rung me, I'd have sorted it in five minutes'.' It was largely true that you could get satisfaction out of ringing our regional office so that you didn't need to go to appeal. So doing an appeal to oblige your MP was a very strange way of getting into that world of advocacy.

In the 1960s we weren't writing the sort of letters to the local social security office that we began to do in the early 1970s where you would write in and say specifically we would like the following clothing which was listed in a document called BO40. Frank Field revealed the nature of the BO40 in *The Guardian* on, I think it was Guy Fawkes Day 1971. The BO40 was in the 'A' code which was actually covered by the Official Secrets Act and so knowledge of its contents caused a huge shift in the way we behaved. We could now say to people, 'Are you getting these things?' which of course the Supplementary Benefits Commission objected to, because we were using it as a checklist for clothing and bedding. What they disliked was that the BO40 said every man should have – was it two shirts, three pairs of underpants, et cetera.

We found that when you sat down with a claimant and calculated what they needed even in 1972 it could amount to £200 worth of items. You knew that if you put this claim in, you would probably get £40 worth; if you went for an appeal they'd double it. You knew you would never get the lot because an appeal tribunal would be too scared to give the lot. It was just a gradual bargaining process.

In contrast to the aggressive behaviour of the Claimants' Union, our style at CPAG made us more acceptable. Obviously we weren't pussy-footing around like the Citizens Advice Bureaux, which was of course the ultimate non-threatening advice service, but there were exceptions to this such as the regional organiser of the CAB service in our area. She was very aggressive, saying, 'We've got to get into doing more of this, because' – and I quote her verbatim – 'every Tom, Dick and Harry is doing it.' Yes, everybody was getting into the world of welfare rights by the 1970s but of course our style was effective because we used to publicise our results.

We managed to get one decision which upset the Supplementary Benefits Commission so much that they mentioned it in their annual report. It was when we managed to get an exceptional needs payment for a heavy goods vehicle licence. I wrote it up as a success story in *The Guardian* called 'Driving a Hard Bargain'. An advice service worker in Liverpool read about this and wrote to me; I sent him a ten-page summary of my submission which I'd printed up as a teaching aid, and he used the same argument in Liverpool. So we were creating what I called 'quasi-precedents'. Because we were just going to a first-tier tribunal the decisions didn't create legal precedents, of course, but we could cause ripples by publicising them in publications like *The Guardian, Legal Action Group Bulletin* et cetera. We also offered *Social Work Today* a column on their clients' possible entitlements. We must have run 'For Your Client's Benefit' for many years.

There was a dilemma for CPAG in that we were promoting the uptake of benefits yet we were in principle campaigning against their existence. We were saying that means testing is pernicious: most of these means tests could be abolished if family allowances were raised to an adequate level. I say most, because I think the sloppy version which I never fell for and I think CPAG by and large avoided, was saying that all means testing can be abolished. As Della Nevitt used to say very well, you can't really do away with rent rebates and rate rebates unless you posit some universal housing allowance, and how do you get a universal housing allowance? Some things have to be means-tested. But if you're campaigning against means-tested school meals and education maintenance allowances and such huge dependence on supplementary benefit, all of which could be got rid of by increasing pensions and family allowances, then to be running around putting a lot of energy into promoting the uptake of those benefits was potentially a contradiction. So if you are working with individual families and helping them claim their benefits, you must be able to use those families' stories to help expose how many people are let down by means tests. We could intellectually and politically justify what we were doing, provided we went on to use our welfare rights approach to get back to the original aim which was universal benefits.

I came to Bristol University in 1970 as a Lecturer in Social Administration. I was very lucky because with Roy Parker as Head of the joint Social Administration and Social Work Department, I was able to introduce into the social work side a welfare rights placement. So you did a term's placement on a welfare rights project, as well as doing a stint on a welfare rights stall. This all liaised in with CPAG because I had about three students a year and they would take on CPAG's cases. By now we weren't afraid of taking on cases because we actually had a supply of social work students to do the work. If we didn't have enough cases I would write an angry letter to the *Bristol Evening Post* about people not getting enough benefits and how we'd like to help them, and then of course I'd get letters to give to the students to follow up. I would train the students to take the cases to tribunal, and they would co-represent with me, and eventually represent on their own. So we were actually training representatives. And this was all given the blessing of the department.

I was born on the 30th of July 1939 at 17 Tournament Road, Salisbury, a council house, with Nurse Morris coming round the corner to deliver me. My grandparents' council house was next door, and my parents got their house in 1935 when they were moved out of slum clearance in the centre of Salisbury. I recently taped my father telling me how he fiddled his way onto the council waiting list.

They were pokey little houses, but they had big gardens. We had chickens in ours. I remember the kids standing there while Dad and others led an evening of rat killing in the chicken run at the bottom of the garden. At the bottom of Grandad's garden was this air raid shelter which Dad and Granddad had built. It was awful; I hated going down there especially if you had to go and get some potatoes, because it smelt – it was so damp. We never once went there during an air raid – it was always just get under the table. During the war Salisbury was on the edge; obviously we weren't getting the pounding that Southampton got. The fascinating thing was that we had two land girls, and this is bizarre that it should have happened, because here we were in a two-up-two-down council house with a pokey kitchen and a bathroom where you had to boil up a copper and ladle the water into the bath. I asked my mother about this and she said that a billeting officer came, knocking on these two-bedroomed council house doors, asking the housewives. 'Who would you billet here?' And my mum opted for land girls, so she had two land girls at a time sleeping in a double bed in one bedroom, and my sister and I, though I have no memory of this, obviously had to sleep in my parents' bedroom until the end of the war, by which time I was six and my sister – my only sibling – was five. You have your kids sleeping in your bedroom like this for that long in order to have these few pennyworth of rents that the Ministry of War or the Ministry of Agriculture, whichever, paid you for billeting these land girls.

Dad was born in 1911 on a gypsy encampment in the New Forest, one of eight, and his father was a farrier. Most of his sisters were hawkers like their mother before, selling old clothes in Salisbury market, and both of his brothers were bricklayers like him. My father cycled huge distances to find employment as a bricklayer. Talking to him about bricklaying in the 1930s is like reading Tressell's *The Ragged Trousered Philanthropists*: the boss or somebody coming along and counting how many bricks you've laid. It made him desperate: you look after number one, because if number one hasn't laid 200 bricks come half-past five, you're fired. He had no collective attitudes about the workplace at all I think; it was a brutal place. The other thing that rings bells for me is David Storey's play *The Contractor*. They're putting up the tent and sending the guy for the rubber nails and all the mickey-taking. That was the only sort of collective camaraderie that I experienced when working on a building site with my dad and my uncle on Saturday mornings. The desperately wicked, vicious mickey-taking: you know, wrapping a piece of electric cable around the bike wheel of a young labourer who was so thick that he thought it meant that his bike was electrified and he walked home, six miles or whatever. And the huge mirth that this caused. I found it brutal, and it was only when I watched *The Contractor* that I felt, God! I've been there. I was all right because I was one of the bright people who could understand some of these awful practical jokes that were played.

Dad probably never joined anything in his life apart from whichever football teams he played for as a young man, and he's totally without religion. The things I envied him for most were his football medals. Having played in two six-a-side finals when I was eighteen coming nineteen, and not got a medal, it rankled that I had to wait until I was forty-five to win some medals. I've still got them upstairs. They're my pride and joy. So he never joined anything, he didn't join a trade union, he was very very anti trade unions.

My mother was one of five, and she was religious. The church was at the centre of everything, and I was a huge joiner: the Cubs, the Scouts, the youth club. The vicar was a tremendous father-figure and very easy to relate to. You basically didn't have to mind too much if he grabbed your balls because as long as you didn't encourage him he probably wouldn't do it again. I ran the Scouts football team, we cycled miles just to arrange a game. My parents didn't have a phone until I was gone forty. So you cycled, ten miles to another village to arrange a football match, then you had to cycle and play the damn thing. I was a good salesman, I sold more tickets than anybody else for the church pantomime, and of course my prize was that the vicar took me to Bournemouth to the pantomime there. He probably didn't try to touch me up that day, and I doubt if any of us told our parents that we thought he was a little bit suspect because you could laugh it off.

I took the eleven-plus late because – would you believe it – I'd had a nervous breakdown. I'd become obsessed with making up games of football to be played by ninety-two teams that I'd found in my comics and put into leagues. The general view was that this gave me a nervous breakdown. But I thought it was good to get your nervous breakdown over at ten, and then be mentally stable for the rest of your life! So I went off to Bishop Wordsworth Grammar School in 1950, great, learning mathematics with an amazing man who was very inspirational, and only partly because he had a Southampton season ticket. He was superb, and when I changed schools I didn't learn any new maths for fifteen months because we were so advanced. But we had a very strange headmaster, FC Happold, who used to write books about citizenship, which we had to read. He had an idea that English history and geography should all be taught by the same master, and unfortunately we had William Golding, who didn't teach us anything because he never bothered to stand up and teach. He would read, and say, 'I'm afraid I'm very busy today. Read any English book you've got.' Various biographies of Golding I think have got it wrong. We all called him 'Scruff' because he had such an awful beard. But he never taught us anything. Bishop Wordsworth was an amazingly interesting school for a working-class kid to go to; there were only about two or three of us per class.

Then we moved because my father joined his brother as a bricklayer by the river Blackwater. Dad decided he couldn't fiddle his way to get a council house and he'd have to buy. He just borrowed to get a £1400 house in Camberley. Everybody had cash in that family, stashed away. Sold his car and we used my uncle's builder's van if we went anywhere. So we had some means of transport while Dad was paying back his sisters all the cash he had borrowed to buy our first owner-occupied house. By then I was going to Frimley and Camberley Grammar School which was very fifth-rate. What was it an American observer of our education system said? Our education is first-rate for the first-rate and fifth-rate for the second-rate. Well this was a fifth-rate maintained grammar school in which I was always in the top three. That was no effort. It was assumed by my mother that I would go into the building trade like my dad, but that I wouldn't get my hands dirty the way he had, and so obviously I had to be a draughtsman. She assumed that because I could trace brilliantly and draw pretty well and did rather well at 'O' level Art, I obviously had to be a draughtsman. I remember going to talk to the Head about going on to Guildford Technical College, where my sister would go to do shorthand and typing a year later.

I assumed I'd go to Guildford Tech but the Head said, 'Whereabouts are you in class?' And I said, 'Third.' 'Right, well if you're third,' he said, 'the year that you entered, 300 people would have sat the exam, so you are one in a hundred, and one in a hundred should go to university.' So I went home and said the headmaster says I should stay on and go to university. The first question I remember being asked, probably by my mother, was, 'What's the difference between a university and a college?' And I couldn't answer that question. I went to university in 1958.

I went to Exeter when I took Sociology because they were short of males, and so I became a Sociology student by gender discrimination, which was my first, and possibly only, experience of positive discrimination working totally in my favour. I got a 2:1.

I became political in my second year when we had to debate the respective merits of the grammar school and the comprehensive school. As somebody who had thought he had done rather well out of being a grammar school boy, I thought the only side to speak for was the grammar school side, but that was already taken up by a bloke called Turner, so I had to read up the comprehensive side and debate that. That was one of the most significant experiences of being converted by what I had read, based on just one chapter in the book by Halsey and Gardiner and Co. But it opened my eyes to the fact that a meritocracy didn't work. I'd read Michael Young's book *The Rise of the Meritocracy* when I was in the sixth form, thanks to a history mistress who got very excited about it. The slogan, 'IQ plus effort equals merit,' which was on the front of the little paperback of *The Rise of the Meritocracy*, I had found very persuasive. However what I read subsequently in 1960 demonstrated that this didn't work, and there were all sorts of built-in reasons why the eleven-plus was failing working-class kids. This made me political overnight.

In my final year I did some survey work. We were asked to go and do some knocking on doors for some one at a London university. I found that fascinating, knocking on somebody's door, walking in and asking them questions. Could there be a finer life than this? I found out that some of my peers in that final Sociology year were working on a housing survey for Professor Donnison. So I went and asked Peter Fletcher, Professor Donnison's man in Exeter, if I could work on his survey, and he took me on, and I became his protégé eventually working for him full-time for two years.

I spent two years interviewing people who lived in tied cottages in the Tiverton Rural District of Devon, asking them about the experience of renting from your boss: lose your job, lose your home. I also carved out my own little piece of research on the District Council's first group of nine sheltered bungalows. I was allowed to interview all the applicants about why they were applying, and then to go back and interview the nine residents about how the experience compared with their expectations. I wrote my first article which was based on this work.

I talked to the Head of Department about applying for a job at Essex with this new young professor called Peter Townsend. I always remember him saying, 'Such an arrogant self-centred man,' and later in the interview, I was taken aback when he said, 'But maybe you should apply, you have a lot in common.'

This is bound to sound smug, but the only cause that I committed myself to was CPAG and there was never any time in my life to take on another one. I did join the local Labour Party but it was by accident! My wife and I had moved into our first owner-occupied home in South Manchester on the northern edge of the Wythenshawe constituency in 1967, and this infuriating estate agent wouldn't come and take his board down. So I decided that I wasn't going to take it down for him, but I would annoy him since he was a staunch member of the local Conservative Party by putting Labour election posters on it. And then the bugger would come and take it down. Which worked, of course. But that meant I had to find out where the local Labour ward office was to get some posters. I found out where the local ward secretary was, went round, and within two months was vice-chairman of the ward. I mean, that is how Labour Party politics worked. And yes, let's face it, there were a lot of people in their forties and fifties running that very small ward party, and suddenly they had somebody of twenty-eight who knew a thing or two, and I was the young protégé, would I like to become a magistrate, all sorts of things, can we put your name forward? I got a bit involved but my wife, Flo, didn't.

It was apparent that after six years of marriage my wife and I needed to find a way of separating because we'd not been really living a very full marriage. We'd got married in '64. Philip Larkin said that sex began in 1963; well, it didn't for me, sex began when you got married. We were probably the last of that sort of generation. We still get on great, my ex-wife and I, if we're talking about our shared sense of humour, and our appallingly sardonic view of everybody around, starting with her mother, but that wasn't really the basis for a marriage. However, it did mean that in Manchester during those years I was married to her, Flo put a lot of energy into CPAG as its secretary. But we led very different social lives; she spent a lot of time at night clubs which I couldn't stand.

The three things I had going for me, as an anti-poverty campaigner, was that I was in a marriage where it suited both of us to be together for dinner, and then night after night she would go to a night club until the early hours of the morning, and I would work. We had no social life together really, so I had no demands. I used to work in the big bay window at the front of the house, working there exposed for everybody to see me till two, three in the morning. There was a retired Education Welfare Officer two doors away who approached me one day and said, he hoped I didn't mind him saying so, but wasn't I working too hard? The second thing was that I was in a university department where I could just give as much time as I liked to CPAG. Our branch secretary used to joke that we had the advantage in Manchester because David spends four-fifths of his time working for CPAG and a fifth for the university. And thirdly, having joined CPAG, I had committed myself to that cause. I did pay £2 a year to Shelter, but didn't ever devote any time to it. I later got appointed by Bristol University to the management committee of the CAB, and I joined the committee of a local housing association again through the university. But basically I never did any voluntary work other than CPAG.

In 1985, when I was forty-six, it occurred to me that I could start adding another string to my bow by becoming a barrister. That was a long haul and when you had done it in order to be a social security tribunal chairman, you then needed to have five years 'standing'. This meant five years sitting around forgetting anything I'd ever learnt, which didn't matter because none of it was remotely relevant to being a social security tribunal chairman. Roughly at that time I took an early retirement package, and I think a month later I got the notification that I'd been appointed to chair tribunals.

I edited two books on football in 1992 and 1994, which made over £10,000 for CPAG. I just wrote a lot of cheeky letters to possible contributors and many of them said 'yes'. I even got John Major for the first book, called *We'll Support You Even More*. *The Times* were launching a new version of their Saturday newspaper and they wanted an excerpt from John Major's chapter for the front page. I mean, me ringing up *The Times* and selling John Major's chapter for £600 was absolutely wonderful for CPAG. I suppose I'm doing things in reverse because I'm now doing less charitable work than I did while I was working. I took a form of early retirement – I prefer to call it premature pension – at fifty-seven and a half. I suppose the contradiction in my life is that I've been a dilettante academically, I've shifted interests a lot, and have never settled enough and never finished the sole-authored book that I needed to write – unless you count the football biography published in the second year of my 'retirement'. I've flitted from interest to interest and priority to priority whereas, in my voluntary sector and political commitment, I was totally dedicated and never switched. So all my dilettantism was professional rather than political or voluntary.

I was in the natural way of trying to put something right that was wrong, see

Joe Kenyon
Claimants & Unemployed Workers Union

I had loads of enemies. You don't make friends with the kind of work I've done, not in official quarters. You make enemies.

At fourteen I was writing letters for people or filling in the sickness forms for them. They knew I could write, and it looked good because I had copperplate handwriting. And it was at fourteen when I first took on the local parish council on behalf of a homeless family, and earned the wrath of the local parish councillors for exposing their favouritism and nepotism. I was naively innocent and this woman she came to me and said she couldn't get a house. She was living in lodgings in a very small terrace house similar to ours with a living room which had flags on the floor, and the kitchen had been concreted. There were two bedrooms. And in this house where she lived there were the tenants – a man, his wife and three kids – in the big room and then in the small room lodged this woman and her husband and two children sleeping on a straw mattress. They used to have straw mats in those days, absolute breeding ground for fleas and bugs. And in the room where she was – she showed me – there were even bugs in the walls. She tried to get a house from the Council but they wouldn't let her have one and yet she had evidence that councillors' friends and neighbours were being given these new council houses. In all the houses in that village they just had the one tap in the kitchen, no hot water or anything like that. Well in the council houses that started to be built in 1927 they had two taps, hot water and cold water, and they had a bathroom and a bath. I mean they were very modern so naturally everybody wanted these council houses just for the convenience of having hot water and a bath, see. And even pit bosses who had good houses except that they'd only got the one cold water tap, they were given council houses but she couldn't get one even though she was lodging.

So I'd got all this information from her and I wrote it down and I sent it off to the parish clerk exposing and naming them all: councillor so-and-so's son got a house, his nephew only got married a week ago and he's gone into a new council house. They used to have the parish meetings in the infants school in the village and this woman went to the meeting and she had my letter read out by the parish clerk. And after the meeting was over two of the councillors came out and pulled this woman up and said, 'I bet thou's been to a lawyer hasn't thou.' She said, 'No I haven't.' They said, 'Well thou hasn't writ that letter.' She says, 'No I haven't, Joey Kenyon has written it.' And they hated my guts forever after that.

I WAS BORN on 27th July 1915 in Carlton which was part of the West Riding. It wasn't Barnsley then, just a small pit village. Had two pits in it. I had three brothers and three sisters, one sister was older than me and the rest were younger. My dad was in the army when I was born but he was shortly discharged because he got caught in some gas. When he was well enough he worked in pits.

I started school at five. But I used to have long periods off school because I'd nothing to wear you know. The only clothing I ever had during my school days was a pair of slippers, pair of stockings, one pair of trousers, one shirt and one jersey. Never had a coat or an overcoat or a raincoat. I did have a cap but I won it in marbles. I had a fountain pen which I got for so many marbles and this is how I used to survive. And many a time when I was at school I had no interest in lessons, and I hadn't been able to take part in the games because I had this pain from being hungry. And occasionally head teacher has taken me to his house and given me breakfast because he could see I'd had nothing to eat. When I was feeling good I could work better. But I was good in any case at writing.

I remember as a ragged ass nipper, my mother gave me a note to take up to the big house which was other side of the village. It was called The Ridings. It stood in about half acre of ground with an eight foot wall all the way round it. Sometimes we used to go past it and we could hear dogs barking. So my mother gave me a note to go to this house one day and off I went. And aware of the dogs, I opened the gate a little bit slowly to have a look round to see if I could see the dogs. I couldn't. So I went up the drive and then the dogs came out barking and one of them jumped up and flattened me against the wall holding me with its paws and breathing into me face. I was only short; well I'm short now. And I can remember its hot breath on me face as it growled and panted. But somehow I managed to get to the door where the bell was and pull it. And the maid came and she shifted the dogs and then I gave her the note and she disappeared and I stood there for about ten minutes and waited. She came back with a parcel and off I went home with the parcel and my mother opened it and there were some cakes and one or two other fancy things, and there was a pair of white slippers which fitted me, a pair of trousers in a tiny black and white check, a cricket shirt and very pale blue jersey. And I remember screaming at my mother, 'Oh you've sent me begging.' And I ran out of the house across the fields and then I got tired and a bit scared and decided to come home. And I got home at about 10:00 o'clock at night and my mother had been crying. So I put those clothes on and they fitted me perfectly, and I went off to school in them and I felt marvellous. And I often wonder now about kids that's brought up rotten and not looked after and not dressed properly, whether or not that affects their ability to learn their lessons at school. I know it made me feel better.

When my sister was fourteen and I was eleven or twelve, she left home to go into service in Leeds. Most working class girls at that time – there was mostly only work for men in pit villages – used to get jobs in service in Leeds or other places where people could afford servants. At that time my dad was in sanatorium in Maidstone in Kent because of his chest. My mother had a voucher for 7/6d a week from the parish relief and that was to keep her, me and the four younger kids. Across the voucher was stamped 'not to be used to buy alcohol or tobacco' as though we could afford to buy alcohol or tobacco out of that much money! But it was there, it was an offence for you to spend money on cigarettes or drink if you were getting parish relief. And she also got five shillings a week from Pit Benevolent Fund. I used to go there on a Monday to collect it. That went to pay the rent which was 4/6d a week. Out of this 7/6d we had to all live, buy food, clothes and whatever which was about a shilling a day for the family. So my mother took in laundry but then some spiteful neighbour reported that she was doing washing and the parish relief people came along to see her. I remember her crying after they'd been and they stopped her money but they had to restore it because there was no way we could live. But she was taken to court and fined £3.00 and the sound of those magistrates lecturing people for working, earning a little bit extra – and it still happens today – I'll never forget it. How the hell they thought she was going to pay the fine, I don't know. Because of this trouble of my mother having to go to court, my dad discharged himself from the sanatorium and came home.

And the next thing that happened was furniture started to disappear from the house. I asked my mother, 'What's our sofa doing in the neighbour's house?' And she said, 'Oh mind your own business.' Then I asked why sideboard was in somebody else's house. And all the furniture – we hadn't much: we had a sofa, we had a sideboard and we had a table and some rugs in front of the fire – which were worth keeping got moved out because we knew that she couldn't pay the fine. The bailiffs had been instructed to collect the furniture so naturally my dad had the furniture moved. It is same sort of thing I've used many times since for people on strike or people on Social Security who have had bailiffs come. I helped to get rid of it, move it out and then just leave some odd bits of wood and furniture for when the bailiff came. And I remember that bailiff coming and he took the beds except the mattresses, apparently there was some law that they must leave you something to sleep on. We'd only got two mattresses anyway. I sometimes wonder how they managed in those days.

That was around the time of the 1926 general strike. And you read histories about that strike and about miners suffering but it was one of the best times of my life because we had two meals every day. We had a lunch and we had tea which is something we never got before. I can remember we used to go up to the soup kitchen and I could smell bloody tea brewing and there used to be a crowd waiting for the door to open, shouting and kicking and falling out. But at least we had a good dinner, well what we thought was a good dinner anyway. I don't suppose you'd think much of it now, whatever it was there were always some potatoes and vegetables. Sometimes we had corn beef sandwiches, sometimes we had an apple and orange, sometimes a banana – things which we could never have bought at home. So we were actually better off and not only me but lots of other kids were better off in the strike. What we saw developing that summer was a new sort of community relationship within the villages around. They each had comic bands with blokes with combs, bazookas or the odd drum and concertina. And they used to have competitions between the comic bands. I had my own comic band and I used to lead mine with a melodeon. I'd had one given, an old one, and I'd learned to play it on my own. And the other kids had bazookas and we used to march around singing:

I'm the man for mixing mortar,
Five and twenty bob's a quarter,
I'm the man for mixing mortar
In a barber's shop.

They had ladies' cricket teams in each village. I remember my mother used to play in the cricket team and they had got to the final which was in the local park near us, and I can remember her and one or two other women in the house laughing and joking because they were all going to wear men's pyjamas in the cricket match. Where the hell they got the 'jamas from I don't know because I'd never seen any 'jamas in my life. And they were laughing and roaring and after the game they put a tea on for the cricket players.

When I first started work at the coal pits as a lad of fourteen, I walked in and said, 'I'm starting work this morning.' And the manager, he says, 'Aye.' So he told a great big hefty lad, 'Take him out to doors, he's going door-trapping.' So he took me up to doors and we got to the other side of doors on account of air-flow you see, and he says, 'Here thou is and I keep the door shut all the time except when tubs is coming.' So when the tubs came I had to pull the door open and when they'd gone through I had to shut it again. And off he went and I was locked in that little room and I was frightened to death to be honest. There was not much light and there was only a flat stone in the room. From what I could see this other lad, the other door-trapper, used to sit on it because there was a mound between your feet where they used to spit tobacco. The tobacco collected and grew to a mound of dust. I thought, I'm not sitting on that so somehow I lifted about a dozen sleepers and made myself a nice cosy seat. I used to sit there and read. In fact I read some of Ruskin's works while I was sat there door-trapping.

One day I'm busy reading and Joe Hughes comes up on the scene, creeps up cussing and shouting, 'What the hell are you doing?' And he got a wee stick and I thought he's going to wallop me with it, so I went for him head first, sent him flying, broke his stick, knocked his lamp out and he was cussing me in Welsh because he was a bloody Welshman, see. Then he took my lamp and left me in the dark. Well, that didn't stop me from working because I had tied a piece of rope onto the door handle and I used to pull it open when the tubs came through and I'd give the door a kick to shut it. When I got out of pit at half past one the lampman says, 'Manager has got to see you.' I went along to the manager's office and he says, 'Now then, what's this about you assaulting Mr Hughes and he also says you've broke his lamp and you've broke his stick.' I said, 'He was worrying me with stick, and I'm not letting nobody hit me with a stick, see.' He says, 'If it weren't for your family depends on your wages you'd get the sack. I'll let you keep your job but I won't match the fee tomorrow.' Well, that ends the story except in 1945 one Saturday I was going to town and I called into Walkley Arms and I ordered a pint and heard a voice say, 'That's young Kenyon, in't it?' I says, 'Aye.' He says, 'Can thou remember when you was in the office for assaulting Joe Hughes? I was sat in back at door listening. I pissed myself, and when you'd gone manager said let him keep his bloody settee!'

My father was killed in June 1938. He was in pit yard getting some coal and a wagon hit him and broke his spine. They wheeled him to hospital in a wheelbarrow, and he died next day. And that's what got me to start studying mine safety. I made the Coal Board managers' lives a hell by quoting every bloody mines act and regulation. Every time there was a breach of rules or regulations the job stopped. I stopped it. Those men would do anything I asked them. Once we asked for a rota system to be installed because under-managers were putting favourites on. First we brought it up at Union and they had a meeting with the Coal Board which said, 'No we're not having a rota system; we're not letting men run pit and decide who's going to be set on or off.' I said to them, 'We are in a rota system and it's starting in the morning.' And I told men, 'When you get to pit, go down pit, have your lamps right and then sit down, don't shift.' So they all sat there and under-manager says, 'What's up?' I said, 'We want a rota system and we're not shifting till we get one.' They got manager out of his bed and he came rushing to pit. He says, 'What's up?' I said, 'We want a rota system and we're not shifting.' So he gave way.

While I was in the Army I met Rene on one of my home leaves. I'd got a date with her sister-in-law and she wanted me to make a foursome up. So I fetched a mate to take Rene out but he didn't turn up. And what I remember about her was when we were standing near this lamp on our own, I saw her eyes, black eyes she had. And

I fell in love straight away with her. And she had a natural brown complexion as if she were sun-tanned and she use to look ravishing when she put her make-up on. People used to think is she Italian or Maltese, no she's English. I went back into Army off my leave still thinking about her, and then I got hit by a landmine and I was in hospital for four months. I came out of the Army in 1942 and I got a job in Sheffield, learning turning and I kept thinking of her. I thought she lived at Shafton so I kept going into pubs there thinking I'd see her and I did that for six months. And then I got a job in security in Shaddock where they were making radar sets. And it was Wakes Week, so I had a week's holiday and I went up to pubs again and I saw her mother-in-law. She said 'Rene's away now, you know. She got married and he died, he got killed at Singapore. And she's living in Doncaster because she can't manage on the money, so she's got a job in a tank factory. But she's coming tomorrow.' So I says, 'Right, I'm coming up tomorrow.' And I went up the following day and the tables were full but there was a chair empty at side of Rene. She admitted later she had kept that chair knowing I was coming up. I sat down and then asked her to marry me. Straight away. Those were the first words I said to her, 'Will you marry me?' She didn't know what to say at first. I went back to Shaddock on Monday and got a furnished house that day and sent her a telegram and said I was fetching her on Friday. And I went and fetched her on Friday. We got married and we've lived together happily ever since. She already had a son then we had one together.

After the war we came back to Barnsley. I had to come out of the pits in 1959 because of my chest. But I'd done about twenty different postal courses so then I was organiser-tutor for the National Council of Labour Colleges for six years till TUC took over. I couldn't get on with them, they kept pulling me up because I wanted to introduce socialism into subjects.

I then went to work for Equity as organiser. But the Legal Department complained about me because I was putting them out of work. You see what happened was I used to go in and settle disputes there and then. One was when an agent in Doncaster phoned me up and says, 'I want to know if you'll come over to club at Barnby Dunn just outside Doncaster. I've got an act here, they're booked for £4,000 and the club manager has cancelled them and told them not to come in.' I said, 'Are they on contract?' and he says, 'Yes.' I says, 'Are they members of Equity?' and he says, 'Yes.' And I says, 'Right,

I'll see you at the club at eight o'clock.' And I went up to Barnby Dunn club, and we went in and and I asked for the boss of the club, the manager. And he took me in his office and I says, 'Now then, I want £4,000 off you, you're in breach of contract.' 'Well I can't afford it now, things is getting tight.' 'You've got a contract here and you've given them less than required notice to cancel it. Consequently they need paying. And if you don't pay, nobody else will work in this club, I'll see to that.' And so he paid up. He had booked another act at £2,000 and he said, 'Will they work now?' And I said, 'No. You've paid them off, this is damages. You have to employ them. If you don't, you'll have them to pay as bloody well.' Well I reported this to Equity, thinking I might get a medal. I got a bollocking, 'You've no right to go settling disputes like that.' I says, 'Oh, you're wanting me to write to the Legal Department, then they'll write back, and they'll write back again. I've had three or four cases and now they've settled, and they've been writing letters for the last five years. I know how to delay claims by writing letters. I'm an expert at that you know.'

I finally left Equity the following year because I'd been invited to open a club in Sunderland, boilermaker's club. I remember once I took Rene with me. When we got in the club we went and sat down and there was a magician's act on called Tony and Tanya. And Tanya took off her dressing gown and sat down on my knee and put her arms round me and planted a big kiss on me. 'This is my best man.' Rene was always suspicious after that. Because you could have had loads of women, but I wouldn't. And I says, 'You know very well I'd never bother with anybody like that. But if it's making you unhappy, I'll pack it in.' And I jacked it in.

Well, I knew I wasn't going to get a job again because I were blacklisted by Barnsley Labour Party you see. So I thought I'll start a bloody union, a union for claimants and unemployed workers. I mean I was already doing the work. I wrote a leaflet asking for holidays with pay for the unemployed. And that's what hit the media. I put down a good sound reason why they should have payment for a week's holiday if they'd been unemployed for over a year. I said it would help to restore their dignity and their energy and their ambition if they had a holiday. Every newspaper was bloody ringing in.

After that it all happened very fast. Branches of the Claimants and Unemployed Workers Union sprang up in main cities throughout the UK. Each branch decided how they wanted to operate. There were no rules and regulations. We had a newsletter or pennysheet I used to call them. We would write them and duplicate them and send them around the country. Some branches paid subscriptions but the work was all voluntary. Once I got invited to do twelve programmes for Look North, BBC Leeds. I said, 'Send me a cheque but make it out to Claimants and Unemployed Workers Union.'

One man wrote to me from St Austell in Cornwall about being refused social security and he'd been a postman for twenty-nine years. He sent me a five pence postal order – I've still got that postal order as a matter of fact because it got lost in a closet and I came across it a few years ago – and said he'd packed the job up but he wouldn't give a reason, said it was embarrassing. I thought, he's sent his sub and I've accepted it so I'll have to go down and do his appeal. I hitchhiked to St Austell the day before, and on one lorry I got going down to Bristol this fellow was telling me that he was going to have to give up his job because he suffered from haemorrhoids a lot, driving a lot. I thought, that's it, that's my answer. So when I got to the Appeal Tribunal I said the reason the postman didn't like explaining why he gave up the job was because he's got piles. He rides a bike, I don't know how many miles a day, I think it's around twenty miles, and the last thing you want is something wrong with your rear end if you're on a bike. So we won his appeal. 'That's funny,' he said, 'how did you know I had piles?' I says, 'I didn't.' Anyway, I wouldn't undertake an appeal in Cornwall again because it was half the bloody week had gone by the time I got home.

Years ago a widow from Petersfield wrote to me saying that in 1940 her husband bought some shares in the Mexican Railways so Social Security wouldn't give her any money. So I phoned the Social Security officer up and told him that she's got no money and those shares are useless, they're no good. I said if you want them you can have them, and they agreed to pay her. And then I had this colonel from Harrogate, he wrote to me. He'd been rich, he used to have his own airplane before the war, and during the war he had been on Eisenhower's staff. And he'd lost his investments and he was on supplementary benefit getting £19 a week, paying £22 per week for bed and breakfast in a hotel in Harrogate. He knew he could get grants so he went up for a grant for some clothing and they gave him £2 for a pair of trousers. And I finally finished up getting his pension increased by £37 a week, and a clothing grant. I said, 'I bet you wouldn't have bloody spoken to me if you'd met me in the 1950s, would you?' 'Actually,' he said, 'this is the best education I've had in my life.'

What you've got to be careful of is people like this woman who wrote to me from Harrogate and asked me to meet her because Social Security wouldn't give her a rent allowance or any supplementary benefit, so all she'd got was this tiny pension. She took me to the flat where she lived, see, and I went in. Floors were bare, tiny green card table and a chair which she used to sit and eat at. She had one cup, one saucer, one saucepan, one frying pan, and she'd got sheets of newspaper stuck together to make blankets for the bed and covers for the chair. Now that's a horrible story isn't it? When I ferreted it out, she was worth £76,000 in investments and cash in the bank. So you can't go charging in. I got to know her and said, 'Go and spend some money on this bloody house. Buy yourself a television set and buy yourself some bloody teeth so you can eat properly.' She'd no teeth in. And she'd been an English teacher in a private school.

I was over to Stockbridge when the steel men were on strike, and I was showing them how to get their benefit. That was 1970. And I went to talk to shop stewards in this pub. It was full and I explained to them what benefits they were entitled to. And one lad says, 'What if you're single – can you get benefits?' I says, 'Well if you're paying rent or you've got a mortgage or other responsibilities.' He says, 'Well I've been down and they've refused me.' I says, 'Come on then let's have a demonstration.' And I took him down to Social Security and the young manager there, you could see he was bloody terrified from the start. And he took me into his office and I explained they'd refused this man a payment. He kept bobbing up and going out. I expect he was phoning for advice, you see. One time he bobbed up and a girl came in with a cup of coffee just as he was going out. And I thought, I'll have that. Drank his bloody coffee and when he came back I said, 'I drank your cup because it was no good letting it go cold.' So he says, 'Yes I can pay him.'

I was in South Shields once and a bloke came up to me and says, 'I've read your leaflet, but I've got a job on a ship and I have to be in Harwich by six o'clock in the morning, and I've no fare and nowt to go down in and they've refused to help me. Dole office has refused and social's refused.' So I said come on, and got on the telephone and phoned the manager, and he says come on in then, and we went to see him. He says 'You that man from Barnsley? Aye, I've heard about you.' He took us in his office and fetches a cup of tea and I tell him, 'You won't forget there's a fellow here and he's got a job on a ship and he's to be in Harwich. That means he has to leave Newcastle by latest two o'clock, and it's getting on for twelve now.' Anyway, he gave him a grant for shoes, for his fare, shirt, tie, a suit. And I says, 'Seeing he's got all this he'll need something to put it all in.' So next thing we had a hold-all and off he went.

We started a branch at York, and then we went to Liverpool and started a good branch there. Well, I don't know how many places I visited, you know, at least sixty or seventy different towns. We had a meeting at Bradford, we had a good union at Bradford and a good secretary, an ex-shop steward. And then the different left-wing groups attached themselves to us and started to break it all up. Students from Bradford and Birmingham came in one night to this meeting and started talking about the Trotskyists, Marxist economics and they broke that up eventually. They broke that up at York did students. They broke that up at Liverpool did students. They broke it up in Birmingham and set up alternatives. Students had read something and all at once they wanted to change the world in five minutes you see. And they hadn't a clue what we were about. And then they'd go in and be abusive in Social Security offices as well, which I never was. I've a way of putting people down without being abusive, like drinking their coffee.

They attacked me for creating a personality cult. They obviously did not know how the media worked. The media didn't want to write about everybody, they wanted to write about a person and exploit it. The media exploited me but I didn't mind because it was good advertising. I got letters from people asking me if they could start a union and I went to nearly every town in Britain I should think and to Scotland and one in Belfast. I got letters from America and from New Zealand and Australia as well.

Michael Young got me onto the National Consumer Council. They didn't want me on but he insisted. And I was on for two years, 1975 to 1977. I enjoyed it. The others on the Council got £13 I think for attending but I didn't because I was on Income Support – it would go straight to social security but I wasn't bothered because I liked it you see. Once the others were grumbling about paying tax. I says, 'Pay tax? I keep – I think it was £2 then you could earn, stopped out of my pay – so don't start talking about income tax and you're all on salaries. It's just pocket money to you.' Just before reappointments came up we had Roy Hattersley at a meeting and he was talking about wage freeze coming up, and I said, 'Why don't you bring a price freeze in?' 'It's easy,' he says 'to put a wage freeze on but it's difficult to put a price freeze on.' 'You know why?' I said. 'No,' he says, 'why?' 'Because you've neither the bollocks nor the brains to get on with it.' I was off Council week after. And Michael Young resigned. He invited me to Dartington Hall to talk to people there, rich people, about poverty. And I had women crying when I described the way people lived. They were bloody weeping. And one lad said to me, 'I'll have a word with my father when I go home, I didn't know there were people like that in this country.' The world's lovely to them, lots of pocket money, lots of hobbies and a full garage of cars and motor bikes.

In 1975 or 1976 the European Commission President invited me to lunch one day and he said we've decided to give you for the Claimants Union £15,000 a year for seven years to help you develop. And Barbara Castle vetoed it. She bloody vetoed it saying we don't allow funding for private organisations. And then she set up the welfare rights organisations in local councils which they've got now.

The Claimants Union is practically non-existent now. There's a man down near Cambridge, he does a bit. I send him stuff. There's one in Liverpool, there's some down in Cornwall, not many. One in Portsmouth. There's a lot of them that's died. But some Claimants Unions turned themselves into other organisations to get funding. They are getting funded by the local authority, so they have to have different names see. There's one in Sheffield it used to be a Claimant's Union, and one at Camden I think.

In the 1980s I went on a BBC programme with Austen Mitchell debating with Lord Addison about Workfare. And they took a vote at the beginning and there were 76 per cent in favour of Workfare and about 15 per cent against it. Austen Mitchell asked me and somebody from the Low Pay Unit to go in as witnesses. Lord Addison had this economist from Liverpool and he put his case with this economist quoting benefit rates. She says, 'I know they're right because I've checked and double checked them.' And they were all wrong – she said single payment for a man on the dole was £47 a week, it wasn't it was only £27. Later on Austen called me in as witness and I says, 'She's checked and double checked these figures but you don't have to check these figures, the correct figures are in this government leaflet.' And I read them out. Lord Addison didn't know what to say, didn't know what to do. And when the programme was over the producer for Any Questions said, 'Will you come on Any Questions? We've listened to that, we thought you were brilliant because you smashed Lord Addison down. He's supposed to be leading adviser to Tory Government on economics and you beat him, you really thrashed him.' When Austen Mitchell introduced me it was a bad introduction, made it appear I was living it up on the dole. So I thought if I'm going to win this vote I've got to change their opinions. So I put it on about working in the pit and having this bad chest, and having to come out, and I pulled all the sympathy you see. And when I went to hospitality room Addison says, 'You're a rascal you.' I said, 'If I was sitting in the House of Lords getting £25 a day, I would be a rascal.' So he kept away from me.

I'm interested to see what happens to this lot, New Labour they call themselves. I'm still a bit dubious. Whiz kids start off with a bang and then they go rotten. But I liked him – Blair – in the election. I want to see now what they'll do regarding the ordinary person. I've got to wait now because since Rene died I'm torn between the problem of living and dying. You know, I want to live and I want to die.

The public threw their generosity at us

Roy Green
Community Transport

When I moved to Smethwick in 1965 the people who came to assist me were Community Transport. I needed help because I have Still's disease, it is actually juvenile rheumatoid arthritis. I got it when I was two. It's a rare disease which affects the legs. Occasionally it affects the arms, sometimes the eyes, but very rarely affects all three – until it got to me. I was totally blind by the time I was two. I have no sight whatsoever. You may have seen all my braille books so you would have put two and two together.

My walking obviously is limited, my arms are very limited. These days I can't lift a teacup to my mouth with my left hand, so what I do is support it with my right hand. It is a bloody nuisance but not much more than that. It hasn't stopped me doing anything. I've been all over the world, and I do a great deal.

I also have Sjögren's syndrome, another bloody nuisance to be honest because what happens is my mouth slowly goes drier and drier. I'm talking reasonably well at the moment because I've just washed my mouth out but I keep a cup of tea here because I desperately need the fluid.

BRYAN SCRIVENER WAS the founder of Community Transport and started it up in 1964 with his wife Dorothy. Bryan was a car mechanic and driving instructor, and Dorothy was head of the mental health section of Social Services in Birmingham.

She and Brian noticed that there were quantities of furniture which people were throwing out in posh places like Solihull. Perfectly good stuff, but you know it doesn't quite fit the image dear! So Bryan decided to take the furniture to people who really needed it, and then eventually he and Dorothy with Maurice Powell started moving furniture on a larger scale. Maurice did a bit of furniture lifting but he wasn't actually the physical man, he was a solicitor and did all the paperwork.

Originally Bryan used his own vehicle – I think a long wheelbase Land Rover – but then some of the other volunteers had their own vehicles so we had a number of Land Rovers of one sort and another. And of course Rovers are very good for carrying things as well as people. Bryan was a member of the Land Rover Club, and Rover came on board, liking the sound of this group, and gave them a forward-control Land Rover, that's what Bryan calls it. It was designed as a troop carrier for desert warfare, two and three-quarter tons I think. We needed something which was just under three tons, the rule being you had to be twenty-five I think to drive anything over three tons.

Community Transport finally acquired a warehouse at 25 Bristol Road, Birmingham which had been Dale Forty's, a very famous piano firm in the Midlands which no longer exists. Anyway, Bryan and Maurice moved me into my flat in Smethwick. Bryan never misses an opportunity: he got me a telephone within ten days of meeting me and he said, 'Would you like to take on transport manager?' And I said, 'Well, we'll try it, try anything once.' So I then worked as transport manager with the group. We designed a braille map which we produced with my brailling equipment. So there I was in the office with the braille map. The records were all in braille, and we used to bring the office records and my home records up to date every night. Bryan would ring me from the office. Bear in mind in those days you put your ten pence in and you could talk for as long as you wanted, it was quite cheap. And we took about an hour and a half to bring the records up to date every night. I did that for about six years.

I think Bryan would now be considered as dyslexic. He can't spell and he can't write, but he can speak very well. Bryan is a real joy. The reason he started Community Transport was because he liked playing around with lorries, he loved it. I mean half the time he'd be under a bloody lorry. 'Bryan, the Bishop of Birmingham's on the phone.' 'Oh, hang on, I'll just come out from under this lorry.'

Bryan was doing all the day-to-day administration and I was simply telling the vans where to go, which for a person who's blind isn't bad going. I've still got that map upstairs, it is about five feet across stuck on a piece of hardboard. And we got little braille symbols, like AG would be for Acocks Green which is a local area.

It's got raised lines for the main roads and little labels for the other roads. I've got a knowledge of all the arterial roads going out of Birmingham – it's like spokes of a wheel – and I can give you the names of all of them, all round. So suppose there was a call in Selly Oak, another one in Northfield, another one in Longbridge, I knew these were off the Bristol Road, so I knew those would be put together. If there was somebody in Aston, in Witton, in Erdington, in Kingstanding, in Sutton Coldfield, they would go to the north of Birmingham. I didn't have to know every single little road because of course the drivers would have their A-Z maps.

It's quite funny because taxi drivers bring me home and I direct them here, and when they put my wheelchair onto the road and help me out of the taxi they suddenly realise, 'Oh, are you a bit short-sighted?' I say, 'No, I'm totally blind.' 'Well, you've just directed me all the way from... How did you do that?' They really do get quite uptight about it. But if I tell them I'm totally blind before I start, there's no way they'd take me. I've had taxi drivers turn to someone else and say, 'Where's he going?'

We used police cadets as volunteers for two reasons. One, they were likely to be relatively honest and socially aware, and two, most important, they could drive. The police cadets were really good. We applied to various forces asking them to second cadets as drivers. Now bear in mind drivers were hard to come by. And volunteers of seventeen to twenty years old who were the sort of people we were picking up on, weren't capable of driving in those days. I mean this was 1965. But police cadets were taught to drive. They had to drive. Community Service Volunteers also sent us a lot of young helpers. Remember that Community Transport at that time was entirely voluntary, they had no paid staff at all; Bryan, Dorothy, Maurice and myself worked absolutely free. And I quite often worked till two in the morning.

In November 1965 at nine o'clock at night we were at the office on the Bristol Road when we heard this noise. Somebody knocked on the door and said, 'You're on fire at the back.' The place was in flames. So I threw myself across the table to reach the telephone, dialled 999 and said to the fire service, 'Fire!' 'We're on our way. Get out.' So, I slammed the phone down and tried to get out. Now, with my difficulties that was a problem. I had to climb over one of the vehicles which was outside, and two minutes later the place collapsed. Bryan soon arrived himself and said, 'The one thing that got me about you, you were so bloody calm.' I said, 'What else was I supposed to do?' Anyway, Bryan and a police cadet grabbed our three vehicles and drove them clear of the building.

We lost absolutely everything, the whole place had gone up, it was made entirely of timber. It didn't survive. All the records and everything went up in flames. We had collected furniture and mattresses, they didn't half burn. Of course nowadays Social Security give people money to buy mattresses. In those days they accepted second-hand mattresses. How many fleas there were in that place I wouldn't want to judge. The terrible thing was that not only our place went up, but Bryan and Dorothy were living in the flat above it. They could not get back in, they lost absolutely everything.

During the fire the Lord Mayor of Birmingham who lived nearby drove past in his mayoral car, and stopped. 'What's going on here?' Bryan collared him and said, 'Well it's actually Community Transport.' And from then on we got a lot of support from the mayoral rooms.

In Varna Road – the vice area of Birmingham – there was a place called the Balsall Heath Association, an association set up to provide assistance to people within the area. It ran youth clubs, children's clubs and mothers' clubs and other activities as well as advice sessions. We knew the person who was head of it, and she said 'Well, if you've got nowhere to go, come to Varna Road.' So we moved into the premises of the Balsall Heath Association which was basically a large family house, and it became the offices and storage place for Community Transport.

The person who was running the Balsall Heath Association left soon afterwards and Bryan and I took over – sitting in opposite desks. I learnt a great deal of how to run things from Bryan. I learnt for instance that if you make a list of all the telephone calls you're supposed to make instead of trying to remember them all, you might actually get most of them done! We'd been just a tin-pot organisation that took people's furniture, and took it to people who needed it. Now Bryan was running the Balsall Heath Association as well as Community Transport.

The *Birmingham Post* got interested in us because of the fire. A couple of days before Christmas 1966 the *Post* published an article about a family who were living in an attic in very bad conditions, and the article went on to say that Community Transport was distributing furniture but unfortunately was very short of furniture to give.

Within two days we had, I calculated, something like 300 calls offering furniture. Suddenly the public threw their generosity at us: beds, wardrobes, carpets, cookers, chairs and tables poured in.

It wasn't just individuals who gave us furniture. Field's had a great big warehouse full of second-hand furniture taken in part exchange for new items. Bryan said, 'There's furniture as far as the eye can see. I've never seen so much furniture in my life. And they want us to clear it.' I said, 'Where the hell do you think we're going to put it?' I mean there was no way we could store all the stuff. We thought the newspaper article might bring in a dozen or so offers because it was coming up to Christmas. But hundreds! In the next couple of years if ever a three-piece suite was required we knew who had a permanent supply. We made an arrangement with Field's. 'Look, we haven't got the storage space; you've got this great warehouse, can we come and pick stuff up as we want it?' And they agreed which was absolutely amazing because we had all that furniture, and most of it was really good quality.

Anywhere there was a transport need, Community Transport provided it. For instance, if organisations such as Shelter wanted anything moved we'd do that. If they wanted a family moved, we moved them; if they wanted a display stand moved to somewhere else, we moved it; there were people that needed moving and they couldn't afford to, we used to move them.

So eventually Community Transport was offering personnel transport, and that became very popular. We hadn't got the restrictions that we have now and we had not got the laws relating to disability so Community Transport used to take all sorts of people. It started off with the Scouts who gave us an Army lorry but then we started to take old people, young disabled people, children's groups, all sorts of people. We'd take them wherever they wanted to go, even went abroad occasionally. There was great competition between the volunteer police cadets to be the one who did the driving abroad! Meanwhile I got a paid job on a newspaper and of course that meant that life became a little more difficult, because I worked from three o'clock in the afternoon to two in the morning at the *Birmingham Post*. I was a copy-taker and wrote feature articles, and did the odd bit of by-lining, little articles. And so I had to do the work at Community Transport in the morning up till three in the afternoon. Fortunately I didn't require much sleep.

In approximately 1970 Community Transport decided to

centralise so someone else took over doing the transport and I became press representative, partly because of my newspaper experience. I stopped doing that in about 1973 and moved back onto the committee as one of the users, and then got involved in collecting. Although we didn't charge for the service we asked for donations to cover the cost, that was all we were allowed to do. We weren't officially allowed to do that to be honest, but nobody ever questioned it. And I was actually taken on to ring Social Services and DHSS and places like that, and say, 'Look you haven't given us our twenty quid for those thirty-five jobs we did.' We found that they were very bad payers. They wanted a service for nothing you see. 'But you're volunteers.' 'Well yes, but you could go to the commercials.' 'Perhaps we will pay then.' Because it would cost them twenty times as much to go to a commercial firm.

I suppose I was with Community Transport till about 1980, something like that. I was asked back to the national get-together about five years ago. I occasionally make contact with our local Community Transport, but am no longer involved in the group.

In the late 1970s Community Transport needed a good administrator. National Westminster Bank was paring down its staff, and in those days they didn't say, OK, nice day, on yer bike. They made staff available to voluntary organisations. We applied and got Norman Williams who was a tremendously good organiser. The one disadvantage, Norman lived in Manchester, so eventually the centre moved to Manchester.

To jump forward a little bit, the irony of this is, some years later Norman got an MBE on the basis that he started Community Transport. Bryan said to me a couple of months ago, 'People have said that I should feel miffed about this; to be honest it doesn't bother me that much.' But I think it is so unfair, because as I've just demonstrated Bryan started the whole thing, was there for twelve, fourteen years, and he kept the place going. After twelve or fourteen years of Community Transport he moved on. He and Dorothy went to live in Wales, and he became a monk in the Eastern Orthodox Church. He's got his own little cell, it's a retreat. Dorothy is a painter and has written one or two books. Bryan, he's so gentle, he's so loveable. I've seen him stand there, be hit by someone, and he just gently cries and says, 'Well why do you want to hit me?' He's an absolutely amazing man.

Community Transport has now expanded out of all proportion.

Dial-a-Ride and Ring-and-Ride came from Community Transport. Tower Hamlets and Hackney and other places have all started their own community transports, and some of them have got together. So there has been a sort of, if you like, co-development of organisations.

It's rather on the Sheldrake model. Rupert Sheldrake's thing was that if you solve the problem here and now, then it will make it more likely that the problem will be solved in other places in the world. The ethos is that this problem has already been solved, so therefore it's become an easier problem to deal with. Anyone who solves it makes it easier for the next person. That's the way it is.

I was born in 1937 in Quinton in Birmingham. I was running down a gully when I was about eighteen months old I think – no one's ever told me this – but I remember hitting a lamppost. Now you don't normally run into lampposts if you can see. I can remember being carried into the house and a damp cloth being put on my head, so I must then have lost my sight. By the time I was five I was in hospital, and I never came out till I was twelve. It wasn't like it is now when you go home for weekends even when you're very seriously ill. In those days you didn't. I didn't get a proper education. I learnt braille when I was seven. There was a big department store called Grey's, and Edward Grey's daughter, Hilda, used to teach blind children on a voluntary basis. She taught me a bit of poetry which I still love, and she introduced me to books. I was an insatiable reader and read extremely fast.

I didn't really know my brother and sister although they did visit me a couple of times. It's one hell of a long way away by bus. I was in Bromsgrove, and they were in Smethwick which must be what, twenty miles. Aunts occasionally visited but not frequently. So really there was no family life.

I did a bit of music on my own. At the hospital there was a harmonica group, but they didn't teach me because I was the youngest child in the ward. I started playing the harmonica, not brilliantly but it was better than the rest of them. Then I was given the opportunity to apply to Worcester College which is the top college for blind boys in the country. The women went to Chorleywood. Apparently I passed easily but they said, 'Hang on, you can't walk.' That has something to do with education? So I didn't get in.

I went to Condover Hall, a school which had recently started for 'blindness and other handicaps.' Notice the terminology. We do not talk about 'the handicapped' these days, we talk about disabilities or people with disabilities. 'Handicapped' is pejorative, like spastic and cripple. Anyway, I went to this school for blindness and other handicaps, and I was the only person with an IQ above 100; most of them had got an IQ very much lower than that, most of them couldn't dress or bath themselves, couldn't wipe their own bottoms even. Their disability had resulted from some kind of brain damage. That doesn't mean that if you can't wipe your own bottom you're necessarily stupid, but most of them were. The school didn't know what the hell to do with me. I mean I read every book in the library. I am a sponge, an ineffable sponge, and I can take information in at an enormous rate. Even my very close friends who are highly intelligent themselves are somewhat befuddled at the speed. This is not a boast, it's just a fact. I read a book and I can bring it straight back to mind. I stayed at Condover Hall till I was sixteen. I loved it there because I was like a very big fish in a very small pond. I then went to Harborne to learn basket-making for eighteen months. Because handicrafts is what blind people do, isn't it?

I had learnt to type, simply by somebody saying what the letters were. Somebody presented me with a reconditioned typewriter but it worked well. I had actually heard somebody say, QWERTY, YUIOP, ASDFGHJKL and so on, and that was the keyboard. They only said it once and it just stuck. I decided – this was the first time I'd ever decided something for myself – sod this for a game of soldiers, I will never be a basket maker. With a friend I actually started a firm making stools but we ran out of friends to sell them to. I mean I didn't know anything about advertising and selling in those days. Then I decided that I was going to get to the Royal National College, Royal Normal College it was called then. The principal came down and liked me and decided to take me on, and I learnt shorthand and typing.

I also did music. I was going to take my LGSM, Licentiate Guildhall School of Music, but unfortunately Eric Hunt, the musical director, dropped dead and the person who took over from him did not think that people who were doing the commercial course for typing should be doing music anyway. I was going to get an extra year to do just music, and he simply said, 'No, not having you,' That was that, bang. So I then went to work at the British Cycle

Corporation, and after three or four years 7,000 of us were declared redundant. I tried, I think, for something like a couple of hundred jobs, and every time I tried for one they said, 'Oh, isn't that brilliant, you do languages? Oh you do shorthand? Oh good gracious me! Oh how wonderful! We haven't had a male secretary but you sound so good. Oh you're blind. I'm sorry, unfortunately the job has just gone.'

At the same time I was looking for a place of my own. I was then twenty-four or twenty-five and like all young people I couldn't stand living with my family any longer. I'd gone to live with my grandmother. I'd only spent holidays with her in the past, so then I could tolerate it. My grandmother said to me some years later, 'You know, I'm so glad that you didn't have to go and play an accordion on the corner of a street.' I thought, sod me, with a brain like mine? I ask you. During this time broadcast language courses had accompanying booklets and each one was produced in braille by the Royal National Institute for the Blind. I did Starting Spanish and Brush Up Your French. Then the BBC did Russian, so I did that. Then they did German, and I did that. And then they did Italian, and I did that. And eventually I took O levels in all of them, all at the same time, all in the same year. I don't think I got them all but I got three I think. I went to the Institute of Linguists classes at Birmingham University and got my Associate of the Institute of Linguists in London, the only blind person ever to have done that. For the record, I actually speak seven languages.

A friend of mine in the DHSS asked me go to a school with him to learn Punjabi. He left after about six weeks, and at the end of the year everyone else was writing sentences in the language, I was writing essays. And the headmaster came to hand me back my fee for the year! I then went off to the Birmingham School of Music, which is now the Birmingham Conservatoire, and got my LGSM, my Licentiate, in Piano.

While I was at the Royal National College there were various clubs and one of them was a radio club for building radios and transmitting. And later on while I was in Varna Road I decided that I would get qualified. I've now got an A licence which is the top licence for radio transmission. That is my station behind you, I can transmit all over the world with that.

I heard on radio one day some people talking about this chap who spoke fifteen languages and who was a member of Mensa. I thought, a member of who? So I got the information, and they sent me the home test and I did it with a friend of mine reading it to me, but we did it absolutely strictly to the rules, no extra time, no concessions. The only thing was I couldn't actually do the visual questions but with only three-quarters of the test I came out above the level. So I joined Mensa and I've been a member for thirty years.

While I was at Community Transport I went to work for the *Birmingham Post* where I was for seven years. Typing at speed was what you did on a newspaper because obviously people ringing from Jerusalem or New York was costing money, so you type very fast. I had always enjoyed speed; I can't drive a car so I drove a typewriter. Anyway I eventually took part in the British typing championships and came third. And as far as I know I'm the only blind person ever to have taken part in it, and I was the only man that year.

The joy of my life was receiving my PhD from Birmingham University which had previously rejected me for a degree course. The OU which I joined in 1976 did wonderfully with me, they were really good, a wonderful system, the Open University. I've now got five degrees so for somebody who can't possibly take a degree because I'm too disabled, I haven't done badly. My PhD was in relationships, disability and sexuality. You see the whole point is, as they often say, disabled people don't do it dear; they don't and if they could, they shouldn't. In actual fact, I have to say that disabled people can and do, although I can't say they're at it like rabbits; they are just exactly the same as everyone else.

I'm now a lecturer at the University of Central England. I teach care staff how to treat disabled people. I won't embarrass you by telling you the things I have to sort out with them, but it's an ongoing job. My attitude is that of course disabled people are sexual, and you have to recognise that fact. I constantly say if you've got somebody helpless on a bed and he says, 'Can I see your bum?' all she has to say is no. Or yes if she wants to. It isn't a big deal. Able-bodied people tend to see disabled people as though they shouldn't have feelings.

My wife was a bit younger than me, and looked very young, and people thought she was my daughter when we met, it was quite funny. She became ill, and we parted after about eight years. The least said about that the better I think. Having a family meant that I was normal. I only had one biological child who died. And I now have Ann who I think of as a daughter and who is around a lot of the time, she's lovely.

I love sculpture and I'm getting museums to accept that sculptures really are to be felt. I mean I can appreciate they don't want everybody touching the sculptures but you know, it's really not going to do any harm. I've rung the British Museum and asked if there were any sculpture exhibitions I could have a look at? And when I explained the position the head of education said, 'Yes, yes we'd love you to come and look at our things' So I went to see an exhibition of Egyptian sculpture with Ann. It was absolutely beautiful. I was looking at this rather lovely goddess who was wearing a skirt but only just. And she'd got her arms up above her head. And suddenly Ann disappeared. When I moved away she came back and I said, 'Where have you been?' She said, 'I'm not standing by you while you feel that.'

Another thing that happened on that trip, the head of education who was absolutely brilliant, was pointing things out, feel just here, that sort of thing. And I'd been looking at all these statues, and we'd finished and everybody had gone, they were clearly going to close the place, and Ann and the head of education went to find somebody to lead us out of the building. So the place was deserted except for me and the warden. She came over and said, 'You were clearly enjoying those statues, it was lovely to watch you. Mind you, everything's not stone.' And she put my hand on her arm and said, 'That's not stone for instance. That's real.' And then she took my hand and put it on her bottom, and said, 'That's real as well.' Wasn't it beautiful. I thought, my goodness, why isn't the rest of the world like that?

Touching – It's the only form of looking I have.

You thought that a really great society was going to come out of all of this

Peter Kandler
North Kensington Law Centre

Much as I hate that disgusting newspaper, the best headline was in the Sun which said 'Poor Law in a Butcher's Shop'. North Kensington Neighbourhood Law Centre opened its doors on 17th July 1970, but of course we were working towards it during the Sixties. It was a converted butcher's shop we were in – not very converted then – it still had a hole in the roof as we couldn't afford to do much.

North Kensington was like the worst kind of experience you can think of in South America because the people were disenfranchised. There had been a Tory Council in Kensington for 100 or 150 years – will be for the next 1,000 years. The local people had no say because they were in the poor area of the borough, and the Tories didn't care. There were all sorts of political groups in North Kensington like the Vietnam Solidarity Group, and it was a very very exciting time. Of course in the Sixties we on the Left believed we were going to win, and although we didn't win we can't have taken away from us the fact that we had those feelings then and we were achieving things. All over the world people were making revolutions, or doing something about the poverty in which they lived, and it was a very optimistic time.

MY INVOLVEMENT WITH the Law Centre started partly as a result of my experience in New Left and in community work. New Left was a Marxist-Socialist organisation half in and half out of the Labour Party. I got involved in it in the early Sixties, and people like Stuart Hall and EJ Hobsbawm and Edward Thompson – they all became professors – were the leading figures. I learnt my politics in the basement of the Partisan coffee bar in Soho for which New Left used to have a lease. We tried to make the trade union movement aware of the bad conditions its members were living in but they weren't interested so in the early 1960s we set up an experiment in community work in Notting Hill, North Kensington. We built up some local organisations and then we, the middle class, had other things to do and left, and all the organisations collapsed. The next time we came was in about 1966 and this time it wasn't a New Left project. A group of us set up something called the Notting Hill Community Workshop which was an offshoot of CND, and we rented a slum house in St. Ervans Road for £12 a year from a woman who bought the house for our purposes. This time we made a permanent commitment to stay in the area and a number of us ended up living in the area. I was on the management committee of the Community Workshop, and we employed two full-time workers; the idea was to give sufficient information and self-confidence to local people to enable them to start doing things for themselves.

As part of the Notting Hill Community Workshop we set up the 1967 Summer Project where people from all over the country, mainly students, came to help. I ran three legal advice points – cycling from one to the other – and it confirmed my belief that legal advice is useless because it has no teeth. I am told – but I don't remember – that I wrote an article for the Nottingham Community Workshop bulletin about the idea of law centres. Anyway, a group of us started talking about law centres and we got together a steering group. Michael Zander came back from the States with ideas picked up there on law centres, and the Society of Labour Lawyers published a pamphlet called *Justice Rules* supporting the idea. The Society of Conservative Lawyers published a similar pamphlet based on the expansion of Citizens Advice Bureaux. Labour lost the 1970 election so we decided to go ahead and try and raise money ourselves from charities. Tony Gifford who was Lord Gifford then and is now a QC was involved, and it was a great help having a lord traipsing round the charities. Eventually we managed to raise £4,000 which was a reasonable sum of money in those days, from the City Parochial Fund and Pilgrim Trust, and we decided to risk starting. There was me as the first worker and an articled clerk, James Saunders, and a secretary-cum-receptionist. The management committee was the original steering group. So that's how the North Kensington Law Centre started. We had fairly massive publicity in the press and telly and on the radio, and in the first two weeks we saw 300 people. We got visits from a Welsh farmer and somebody from Manchester. And we got a phone call from the Isle of Wight asking us to be in Portsmouth County Court next morning.

We couldn't afford to do much about the premises. As it was a butcher's shop it had a very big window for displaying the meat with the slab inside, and tiles on the walls and hooks on the walls where the meat was hung. We had the meat safe which was only converted to a room fifteen years later because it took a lot of work to rip everything out and make it an ordinary room. Upstairs there were just a couple of dingy rooms. When James Saunders became homeless for a short period of time he slept in his office on the top floor where there was still a hole in the roof so he had to put an umbrella over the bed to stop the rain coming onto him.

The majority of the clientele came from the streets and roads nearest to the law centre as all law centre research shows. We got people coming from within a few miles radius, mainly West Indian and white working class, very few middle-class people. We did have a rough-and-ready means test which meant that we didn't act for people with a reasonable amount of money. The newer waves of immigrants didn't come in till after that, that is Moroccan, Spanish, Portuguese. The people suffering most were in the slum areas because that was Rachman territory, and Rachman's successors were just as bad.

The age range was from teenagers – because crime was involved as well – to any age. But the older people didn't come in for a very long time because they were very suspicious of us: firstly we were a free service, and secondly none of us dressed in suits. My son always used to say when he saw me putting on a suit for court, 'Dad is putting on his court suit.' And I remember one very funny story where a very posh solicitor from somewhere like Lincoln's Inn rang me up and said he had a poor client who was a tenant, and would I give her some advice. In those days landlords' solicitors knew very little landlord and tenant law because they didn't need to know it as they'd never been challenged. I said, 'Well she's got to understand that we don't have an appointment system and she may have to wait an hour or two as there's a crowd in the waiting room.' I was dressed casually and I hadn't bothered to shave that day. And this taxi drew up and a woman in a fur coat swept in and said, 'Where's the solicitor?' I said I was a solicitor and I explained to her that she would have to wait quite a long time as there were five people before her. Without saying a word she swept out again and as she got into the taxi she pointed at me and I only heard the words, 'And that's the solicitor,' and off went the taxi.

I remember the first time the law centre appeared in the County Court there was a real racist, fascist judge. This first appearance was me applying for a black woman to set judgement aside on a possession summons on the grounds that she had never been served with a summons. Now, landlords were allowed to get away with murder in those days because tenants were hardly ever represented, and of course most of them didn't understand what was going on. When I had to call my client to give evidence the first question the judge asked her was, 'How long have you been in this country?' I said, 'With the greatest respect, your honour, I don't see the relevance.'

The second question was, 'Are you on social security, and if so how long have you been on social security?' So we had a row, and in the middle of the row he passed me a note which said, 'You've still got your tie on underneath your tabs.' So I snatched my tie off and put it in my pocket. I asked for the application and signed it myself and handed it back. And after all this he said to the landlord's lawyers, 'Well I can't oppose this application, I have to grant it,' and he set the judgement aside.

The magistrates court appearances run one into another. I remember once I went unshaven, in my casual clothes and apologised to the magistrate who said, 'Well I know you are very busy, Mr Kandler.' In those days if you didn't dress properly the magistrate would probably say, 'I cannot see you Mr Kandler.' That was the favourite phrase in those days. Things have changed a lot since law centres.

I have all sorts of memories. One of the things I used to do – if a tenant was illegally evicted – was to get an iron bar and break the door down and put them back in. And I would call the police to stand by in case there was a breach of the peace. After all, tenants are entitled to go back in if they've been illegally evicted. So when the Central Office of Information came round and said they wanted to do a film on the law centre, I said, 'Well what about this idea?' and they said, 'Oh no, we can't do that, because that would show there's bad housing in London, and this film is going all round the world.' I said, 'No film.' They went off and talked to the Home Office and they came back with smiles and said, 'The Home Office said grudgingly that they didn't have anything against you so we can do it.' So this film of me breaking down a door went off to Australia, Canada and all sorts of places.

We were swamped with volunteers – barristers and solicitors –

because of the publicity. It was pre-Thatcher and there was full employment so we had to open in the evenings and sometimes at weekends. And of course, unlike the middle class, the working class had much greater difficulty in taking time off to do things like seeing lawyers. We would have a crime evening, an employment evening, housing evening and we ran a 24-hour service as well.

Luckily James Saunders, my articled clerk, was brilliant because the only training he got was from 1st May when the Law Centre actually started from my flat in Ladbroke Grove until 17th July when it opened in the butcher's shop. Once the Law Centre opened we got so swamped I had very little opportunity to give him any further training. He always says that he learnt everything about criminal law from me but nothing about organisation. I had no idea of organisation. About three weeks after opening somebody said, 'What about record cards?' I said, 'What are they?' So we started off in a real muddle but we managed to straighten it out eventually.

It was great. I didn't notice getting tired at all. The hours were ten, twelve, fourteen, sixteen hours a day, just depended really. However, I got married at the same time and because we didn't see very much of each other that probably contributed to our break-up ten years later. My son was born on the evening of the first AGM.

We started to get a bit more money in so the staff gradually grew, and after three or four years there were probably about nine or ten of us. The first thing we had to do, which I hadn't thought about, was to get a bookkeeper before I got struck off for not having proper accounts! And then we got a second accounts person and they both helped with the administration. We also got Pam Ditton, the first woman solicitor in the Law Centre, and she was a good organiser as well. The organisation still wasn't very good, you know. They always joke at the law centre that there are still files lying around with my reference on them that have never been billed. So we just gradually learnt. I couldn't teach people about organisation, I just never thought about it. We never had any negligence actions or anything against us, a complete fluke I should think, but we didn't really overlook things at all. And in those days civil work was easier because there weren't all these very tight time limits. No doubt some clients suffered from us being slow but that was a disease common to all solicitors.

Later we decided to collectivise but collectives can be good, bad or indifferent, just like hierarchies. It wasn't a real collective because when I lost my temper it was more effective than anyone else losing their temper. Although I theoretically believed in it, it was very tough in practice, negotiating from being director of the Law Centre to being equal. If we had started off as a collective it would have been different, but it just wasn't possible the way we started with people joining over a period of time. So the collective only really took off after I left.

I'll tell you a funny story, although it's jumping a little bit ahead. In 1974 we were going broke for the second or third time, but we thought we were really going to have to close then, because of course the Royal Borough of Kensington and Chelsea showed no interest in us. And since it had an unbroken record of interfering with anything it helped anyway, I wasn't very keen when the management committee decided to write for money. Sir Mawby Crofton wrote back and said, 'We will lend you money' – God knows at what rate of interest and how we could have repaid it – 'not give you money, if Kandler resigns from the staff and O'Malley and Perry resign from the management committee.' They were two left-wingers on the management committee who were particular friends of mine. I published the correspondence in the national press and we raised £12,000 – it was a hell of a lot of money then – from private individuals, and that enabled us to survive until Labour won in 1974. Elwyn-Jones then became Lord Chancellor and he bailed us out. We've received government money ever since in one form or another, one of the few law centres which does.

I was a sort of travelling salesman for law centres so that meant even longer hours. When you're the first it gives you a buzz, it keeps you going. The day after my son was born I had to go up to Leicester University to give a talk about law centres out of which grew the Law Centres Working Group. This is now the Law Centres Federation. I had to persuade the law centres that it was in their interest to have a central organisation to protect them. Now the Law Centres Federations is quite a strong organisation, and it's just got half a million from the Lottery. We were the first law centre, the second was Brent in 1971. Although to be fair to Brent they had been trying to set up a law centre before us but we got the money first.

So it was a fairly exhilarating experience but we had enemies. The Royal Borough of Kensington and Chelsea was a particular enemy because you see, one of the things we were doing was getting the tenants of the Royal Borough to sue them for disrepair and of course that had hardly ever been done before, so that was great fun. I'll never forget when the Tories of the Royal Borough and their wives decided to meet the poor. There was a meeting in All Saints Church Hall in the middle of the poor part of North Kensington, and the poor decided to get their revenge by locking them in all night. The police were called of course, but the police could see into the church hall and could see nobody was being harmed, and in fact people got very merry and there was a bit of striptease and all sorts of things I'm told. I wasn't there and I didn't know about it. The police quite rightly waited until about 6 o'clock in the morning when everyone got thoroughly bored and the door was opened and everybody left. There were no arrests, the police behaved very sensibly. The Tories were absolutely livid with the police and said they should have crashed in and rescued everybody. I gave an interview to the *Kensington Post* in which I said that the real villains of North Kensington were not the police but the Tory councillors because if they did proper renovation and repair and provided social amenities, there would be a lot less crime in the area. And ever since then they've decided – nothing will shift them even though it's now nearly thirty years later – that I was the one who organised this lock-in. I always say to them, to my great regret I had nothing to do with it.

Our other main enemy was the West London Law Society. Like most private solicitors they were completely against any idea of a public legal service because they thought they were going to lose all their work. So the West London Law Society was almost entirely obstructive but luckily for us Charles Wegg-Prosser who was a member of the Labour Party and the Society of Labour Lawyers and on the Law Society Committee, was also our treasurer, and he together with Muir Hunter protected us.

Then of course the landlords and the police hated us at that time because I was really the first solicitor in this country ever to go to a police station regularly. In spite of all our boasts about our great legal system and how it's better than any other in the world, we had no rights to have a solicitor in the police station until ironically Thatcher of all people brought in the Police and Criminal Evidence Act in 1984. Many a swearing match I had with the coppers on the desk who would be really obstructive while they tried to beat up or get confessions from clients before I could get in. I had no right to go in, and they had no right to see a solicitor. Of course my regulars began to know, they just said, 'We're not saying anything until you let our solicitor in.' Probably they could hear me shouting out the front. But in fact the police hated James, my articled clerk, even more than they hated me. One of our inquiry agents who was an ex-copper heard two coppers in the police canteen talking about getting James down a dark alley and beating him up.

On the whole we had the press and television on our side which as you know is very important. I deliberately sold the Law Centre in terms of a liberal experiment, not a socialist experiment, and I got criticised for this by some of my socialist friends. We were a wonderful source of stories to the media. For example, the *News of the World* which used to be a half-decent newspaper used to have a landlord and tenants page, and I got a few free meals out of the journalists. In those days they got the perks, lunches – they don't now – and I would tell them stories about vicious landlords, and they would put them all in the *News of the World*. And so we survived. Once the law centres had taken off and local authorities helped to fund most of them, they began to spread round the country. So we managed to conquer our enemies.

I was born in Fulham, London on 12th June 1935. My grandparents came here from Odessa and Riga in 1900, my mother's parents from Odessa and my father's from Latvia.

My father's father was a bespoke tailor. And my father was the only son and the oldest child of six or seven. Academically he was far brighter than me but instead of going to university he started off as office boy and ended up as managing director of his own firm in his fifties. We lived with his parents in a big house in Munster Road in Fulham with the tailor shop at the front of the house. I was there during the war. It was great fun listening to the bombs and having to sleep under the table, and going to air-raid shelters and not going to school. I quite enjoyed the war really. I remember an uncle who was in the Army coming back from India, and I remember the smell of his uniform and the polish on his boots.

My father was a chartered ship broker. He was a middle man between the cargo owners and the ship owners. He was the first Jew allowed on the Baltic Exchange after the war. And he played tennis for Middlesex. He didn't have much of a sense of humour but he cared for his kids. My mother was an East End girl and left school at fourteen. I always assumed – male chauvinist piggery – that the set of Dickens and Wells that I've got were my father's; I only learnt after she died that they were my mother's. She could play the piano but of course never developed because she became a housewife and a mother and that was it. My father, because of anti-Semitism, wasn't put on the board of directors of the firm he helped to build up so friends persuaded him to take a gamble in his fifties and to start his own firm which he did. He didn't start to make money luckily for me until I went to university which I think was a good thing as I learnt a lot about comparative poverty. We were always tenants. Once we had a mad landlady who used to harass my mother so I threw my bike at her one day and hit her with it. I was about fifteen and she took out a summons for assault against me in the magistrates court. I had to go up to my father's solicitors, some big City firm, and agree to write a letter of apology to get the summons withdrawn. I never forgave landlords for that, never. I could have had several convictions as a juvenile if they'd had a juvenile court in those days: criminal damage, theft of flowers from front gardens which I used to sell on street corners, etc.

When we moved to Willesden I went to Willesden Grammar School as was, which was a local tough working-class school. My parents' plan was for me to leave school at sixteen and become articled to a solicitor because in those days you could do five-year articles. Thank goodness I failed so many exams that they had to put me in the sixth form. I got distinctions in history, English and English literature and failed miserably at everything else. The school and my parents said, 'There's nothing for it, you'd better go to university.' What sort of person I would have turned out if I had left school at sixteen, I really don't know. I was lucky to go to the London School of Economics where you get a broad experience and education. I suppose it was lucky my parents bullied me into doing law rather than history which is what I always wanted to do. I don't think I was academically bright enough to have succeeded in history. I have a sister who is six years younger than me. My parents took her away from the French Lycée, which is still a posh school, and sent her to Pitmans in order to be able to afford to send me to university.

When I went for my interview at LSE I still only had my three distinctions at O level. I went up a narrow, winding staircase into a book-lined study and there was this tall, distinguished professor with a shock of grey hair. He was Professor, I think it's Sir David Hughes Parry, QC, with about six lines of letters after his name. He looked over the top of his glasses at me, 'How on earth with a record like yours do you expect to get a law degree?' A very reasonable question actually. I was on my fifth attempt at maths and fourth attempt at Latin for A level. I've always been good at interviews and I said with a judicious mixture of truth and lies, I said, 'If I like something, then I'm good at it.' And that was the truth. The lie was that I liked law. 'Well,' he said, 'if by some miracle you get Latin and maths this Christmas then you can come in the summer.'

When the results came out at Christmas half the school was waiting outside by the notice-board applauding me as I walked up to get the results because I had actually passed maths and Latin. I failed economics but I still got in. Then I failed constitutional law in my first year at LSE and had to retake it in the summer; I failed the whole of my second year and retook it; and then I scraped through my third year. In order to qualify as a solicitor I had to take the Law Society exams but when it came to finals, I failed bookkeeping and trust accounts twice. The Law Society said they had never known someone with a law degree get such bad results. I said, it's easy if you don't do any work. I went off to Spain for two or three months waiting for my second result, intending to learn Spanish to go to Cuba. Never learned Spanish. And I got a telegram saying, 'Regret failed Mobern.' Mobern was, I thought, some qualification on failing but in those days a three word telegram was very cheap, and Mobern was a combination of two friends of mine, Morris and Bernstein. I came back to find I had passed in all the subjects but they had failed me because I hadn't got the total aggregate mark. So I had to take it a third time. I didn't qualify until 1963. My parents of course were in despair. They were good Jewish parents in the sense they wanted their son to be a professional, and there was I, when I finally passed, giving up law and working for the Campaign for Nuclear Disarmament. I left home at the same time, and lived in a bedsit in Hampstead. Then I had a series of strokes of luck.

But to go back a bit: I was very very shy. When I was in my first year at LSE my mother said, 'I've made an appointment for you to see a psychiatrist.' I was about to tell her to fuck off because that was something weird Americans did in those days. But then I thought, no no, it's quite sensible. My mother knowing nothing about this sort of thing had seen a big advert on the Underground which said, 'For blushing, stammering, shyness, see me,' and the 'me' was Ramon Wings. He could have been a complete charlatan of course, but in fact he wasn't. Although it cost a pound or two literally, which was much more money in those days, it wasn't a rip-off. And we had a chat for a couple of hours and he said, 'Look,' he said, 'Come to my classes once a month for a year.' And the classes were full of people who blushed, stammered and were shy, whatever. And for the first time in my life I realised it wasn't a crime to blush. I would blush when I got on the Tube train. And I still blush occasionally in court and everyone looks at me very puzzled but occasionally it suddenly happens for no reason at all. However, a long time went by before I slept with a woman. It was while I was at CND, and this woman was doing voluntary typing and she took me home and took me to bed. I was about her fiftieth bloke, and since she was only 21 she got bored with me and chucked me over after six months, which was very distressing at the time. There was a woman in the office below CND who asked me why I was so miserable, and she was older than me, and I told her, and she took me home. And she taught me a great deal. So I had those strokes of luck.

At the time I was offered a job as London Regional Organiser for CND, my mother rang up in despair. 'I accidentally opened a letter addressed to you,' said she lying. 'It's a circular from the Society of Labour Lawyers, and firms of solicitors are advertising so they must be socialist,' she said desperately as a Tory. So I rang up a guy called Raymond Pollard – the firm was called Pollard, Stallibrass & George Martin in Victoria – and the advert was for conveyancing and probate. I said, 'I don't like conveyancing or probate.' And he said, 'Come and have a talk anyway.' And we had a long talk about revolution. He hadn't advertised the job but he offered me the job as assistant solicitor for the trade union he acted for, which was the ACTT, the film technicians' trade union. So I went back into law. That was very lucky. And the other thing was finding the Partisan coffee bar. For me it was like a curtain being lifted on society, and that's how I got politically involved through New Left and through the Labour Party. I got back into law which was probably a good thing in the end, and became very active politically in doing community work in North Kensington. To some extent you were making your own luck but to some extent you need the luck, and it was luck that pushed me in various directions.

By the end of the 1960s I'd been doing a lot of political and community work, and I was really exhausted so I wrote to friends, Nicole in Paris and Senta in Bonn, and asked if they could put me up for a couple of weeks. And although Nicole wrote back and said yes, by then Senta had already rung up and said yes, so I went to Bonn rather than Paris. And we got married. Actually my family was very good about it because Senta is German and not Jewish, and it was only twenty-five years after the end of the war, and the truth about the Holocaust was still coming out. It helped that my father-in-law was the German Ambassador to Ghana and was tall and good-looking and a nice guy who was also a progressive. I expected problems, which I wouldn't have taken any notice of, but there weren't any. I think my parents were so relieved I had reached the age of thirty-five and was getting married, that they were quite happy about it. So we got married in 1969 and Leo was born in October 1970.

In the Sixties I lived in a collective house which again was a good experience for me, because I met so many more people than I would have done if I had lived by myself or with one other person. Our political guru at that time in the Sixties was a guy called Jim Garst who came from the Mid-West in America, had been in the Communist Party and on the losing side in the AFL-CIO battles of the Forties. He came here on the run from McCarthy. And there were two mathematicians in the house who were rather frightening because they both had IQs of 170 and are now professors. We were all involved in the local Labour Party and we ran the local ward. That was a great experience. When Senta and I got married John and Jan O'Malley suggested that we form another collective house which we did. We lived in Lancaster Road in the middle of the poorer part of North Kensington for about ten years. John's sister was the fifth person. John and Jan had three kids, we had one kid, so the kids were brought up together. But as I say I was working fourteen, sixteen hours a day, sometimes seven days a week, and enjoying every minute of it. Although Senta knew all this was going to happen it didn't really give us a great amount of time to form a relationship, and then Leo arrived. We were also hit by women's liberation. While I theoretically agreed with the ideas of women's liberation I had been brought up traditionally to expect a woman to provide my meals, pipe and slippers, and I was working sixteen hours a day as well. Neither Senta nor I knew how to cope with the new ideas, or how to adjust emotionally to them, and I couldn't cook which made it worse. My mother would never allow me to cook and then I just hadn't learnt in spite of living in a collective in the Sixties. My punishment was having to do all the washing up. I'm very good at washing up for sixteen people. So our marriage really stuttered and finally the light went out in a sort of gradual way, there wasn't a big blow-up; there didn't seem to be anything left. Well that's a summary of it; it was of course both better and worse than that.

I stayed with the North Kensington Law Centre about nine years. Being active in the area and living in it is a great strain when people know where you live and know where you go to the laundrette and all the rest of it. We – the O'Malleys, Senta and I – decided we would move. We moved to Clapham and bought another collective house there, and I went from North Ken to Balham Law Centre and spent about eighteen months at Balham Law Centre.

Most of my time at Balham wasn't doing case work, it was political fighting against the awful Wandsworth Tory Council who decided they were going to close all the law centres down. And we won that battle. Then after ten years of marriage we separated, and I was worried about my son who was very upset at the separation. I wanted to earn more money to give a decent amount of maintenance, and I was very tired, so I went back into private practice. I think in different circumstances...

I ended up joining a firm in Brixton, which will remain nameless, and I spent about eighteen months there. It was appalling. And then a mutual friend put me together again with James Saunders, my first articled clerk at North Kensington Law Centre. James was running a fairly big criminal firm, and so we became partners until I set up my own firm at the age of fifty. Funnily enough I was repeating my father's pattern. It was a big risk, because there was I, fifty, with no money, no savings. James' firm was not making enough money really to support three partners so we had a perfectly friendly split-up. James let me take with me my first fifty cases and gave me all the furniture. I found a shop in the Golborne Road, which is my patch, just down the road from the Law Centre. It was the idea of Jane Mendelssohn who was my secretary at Saunders that I should do this, and she came with me and became a managing clerk, and the firm has developed and is reasonably successful. A lot of my old clients came back to me – it wasn't like a young person starting in a new area – so people assume the firm is much older than it is. While I get a great deal of enjoyment out of it, in terms of the future I don't care what happens to the firm really except for the workers, because I reckon having been part of the start of the law centres is enough for me.

Unjustly refused

Michael Dummett
Joint Council for the Welfare of Immigrants (JCWI)

I became very aware of racism and very hostile to it, and learnt how very difficult it was to escape racism in the United States in the 1950s. I had received a Commonwealth Fund Fellowship to study for a year at Berkeley in California, and I arrived just after Emmett Till, a young boy from Chicago whose family lived in the South, was murdered, lynched. He was lynched for looking impertinently at a white woman. So that was the first thing that hit me when I got to the United States.

While we were in the US the bus boycott started in Montgomery, Alabama. And we used to get the weekly edition of the Manchester Guardian as it then was which included a series of articles by Alistair Cooke. I felt that these articles about black Americans, two about Montgomery in particular, were slanted against the black people, and he described Martin Luther King as a pretty smooth operator. Later on, Alistair Cooke wrote how he had always supported moderates like Martin Luther King, but at that time his support was not obvious. I wrote a letter to the Guardian complaining about these articles, and Alastair Hetherington, the then foreign editor who later became the editor, replied, 'We are more inclined to trust our reporters on the spot than someone living in California.' So I devoted my three months vacation in the summer of 1956 to getting to know the black community of the United States.

I went to Chicago and stayed with a black friend on the south side where I heard Billie Holiday – I'm probably the only person in Oxford who has heard Billie Holiday in the flesh – singing in a little bar, and it was wonderful. I went to New York and to Montgomery and to New Orleans and to Nashville, Tennessee all the time staying with black people. At that time segregation was in full force throughout the South, notices saying, 'Coloured Only', 'Whites Only' everywhere. Even in Montgomery I went with my black friends to buy a quarter of whiskey or something, at a liquor store, and there was an actual chain down the middle of the shop: white people that side, black people that side. So I stood on the righthand side with my friends, and got to the counter and was told, 'Can't serve you here'. So I stepped over the chain and bought the whiskey and stepped back.

In Montgomery the bus boycott was still in full swing. I went to a meeting addressed by Martin Luther King who was beginning to be known but he was still only the leader of the bus boycott and had no national organisation as yet. And so I met him and we talked in particular about these articles by Alistair Cooke. Martin Luther King said he hadn't found anything so vile in any of the Southern press, and would I try and correct them? So I said I would try. I did what investigation I could, and came to the conclusion that Alistair Cooke probably had never stirred outside his hotel. He had met the mayor, he met the manager of the bus company, he met the police chief. 'Vivid eyewitness descriptions: a description of a street in the black part of town' didn't correspond to anything on the ground at all.

IN THE 1960s I was very much involved with CARD, the Campaign Against Racial Discrimination. It had a considerable standing with the general public but inside CARD there were constant squabbles, worse than squabbles. CARD had been conceived as an organisation of organisations. Although it had some local groups of its own, it mainly relied on its various affiliated bodies, particularly what were called immigrant organisations. However, a number of these organisations had disaffiliated so that by 1967 several of us both inside and outside CARD were very unhappy. I had talked about this to people such as Vishnu Sharma who was actually employed by CARD, he was the national organiser or some such title. He has since died. He was a very good friend of mine, and a lifelong member of the Communist Party, and a very strong influence in the Southall Indian Workers Association which was affiliated to CARD. Another was Tassaduq Ahmed who represented, well actually they were Bengali, but they were then called Pakistani organisations. And various others, one of whom was Joe Hunt who represented the West Indian Standing Conference which had affiliated to CARD and then disaffiliated. We were a very small group of people, some in CARD and some outside it, all dismayed by these constant quarrels within CARD which we thought made the organisation much less effective than it could have been. We decided one reason for the quarrels which rent CARD was that it tried to take on racism over too wide a front, that it concerned itself with every manifestation of racism and racial discrimination. After all it was called Campaign Against Racial Discrimination. However, this was bound to have the effect of throwing up practical and ideological differences between members of such varied backgrounds which in turn disrupted the planning of strategy. We thought the way to get cooperation between these very diverse organisations – I mean they were diverse culturally, politically, even racially after all – was to concentrate on a narrow sector where ideological differences wouldn't affect the work. We decided that the one issue to concentrate on was immigration. I had become aware from acting for the local group in Oxford which was affiliated to CARD that a lot of people were being wrongly refused entry to Britain. At that time there wasn't any system of entry vouchers, people just arrived at the airport and were sent straight back if refused entry, and they were very often refused.

The case that my wife, Ann, was most proud of was one in which a young boy was refused entry to Britain and sent back on the ground that there wasn't adequate accommodation for him. She went to battle. It turned out that what had happened was that the Immigration Officer had rung up the police in the area where the boy was going to stay and the police had said, 'Oh, sixteen people are already staying in that house.' The policeman had been to the house when a lot of relatives had assembled for the funeral of one member of the family. So there weren't sixteen people living there, but just because a policeman said there were, back goes the boy. It took months to unearth that fact. There was a very high rate of refusal, but the system was such that if you made representations, if you rang up the Immigration Officer and said, 'I wish to make representations on behalf of so-and-so,' they would not send them back straight away but would give you time to put a case.

It was a very haphazard thing. On behalf of CARD I had set up this little network at Heathrow of people who would ring me up when they heard of cases. Then I'd have to get on the telephone straight away and wait for about three-quarters of an hour before I could get through to the Immigration Officer to say I want to make representations, and then I had to rush to Heathrow. A lot of other organisations scattered over the country had been acting similarly when they heard from any of their members that some relative had been refused entry. But it was a very hit and miss business. I saw a lot of people who had been unjustly refused, but there were many more no one heard about. So we thought if we got all the so-called immigrant organisations both inside and outside CARD to join together, we could then deal much more efficiently with these cases. However, we didn't want to deal with casework only, we also wanted an organisation which campaigned solely on immigration laws, not on anything else to do with racial discrimination. So that was the plan we made. And then, during the summer of 1967, Vishnu Sharma and I toured the country. We never penetrated Scotland but we went round almost the whole of England, visiting local organisations saying, 'We're going to set this up, will you come to the founding meeting?' A large number were quite enthusiastic and promised to come. The founding meeting was held in September 1967 in the Dominion Cinema in Southall which was owned by the Indian Workers Association. So we had a splendid place for the meeting, and something like 170 organisations came. Some people there argued for it to be a new CARD in effect, even a rival to CARD. Those proposals of course were the exact opposite to our strategy so we resisted and set up an entirely new organisation. We planned a constitution which put immigration as its central concern but also made it possible for the new organisation – the Joint Council for the Welfare of Immigrants – to take an interest in other matters concerned with race. I was elected Vice-Chairman.

We managed to get the Home Office to agree to give us a small office at Heathrow Airport, and we appointed our first salaried worker to be based there. This enabled him to cope much more quickly than I had been able to do when I was relying on our informal network. I'm afraid that after three months he retired, shattered by all the emotional stress of dealing with these cases. Of course some people were admitted to the country, but it's really a matter of how many were refused. I think a very substantial number. The first Chairman of JCWI was Frank Bailey, a West Indian, and he personally took charge and spent his days at the office at Heathrow.

JCWI has continued to exist for thirty-three years. Even though some people have become discontented with its name I think the initials are so well known that it would be a great pity to change. The reason for the name, which was suggested by Tassaduq Ahmed was this: quite unknown to us, our founding meeting took place I think a few days after the publication of the report by the Wilson Committee. Sir Geoffrey Wilson headed the committee that the Government had set up to inquire into whether there should be some sort of tribunal to hear immigration cases. The committee then discussed whether there should be legal representation, and it argued that it wasn't necessary to have actual lawyers but that appellants ought to have some kind of representation, and they should be represented by organisations concerned with the 'welfare of immigrants.' That's the phrase it used. So that was why we decided to call ourselves the Joint Council for the Welfare of Immigrants, because it echoed Sir Geoffrey Wilson's report. As soon as JCWI had been set up we wrote to the Home Office saying that we have formed exactly such an organisation. The Home Office was not at all pleased because the Wilson report went on to say that if the organisations concerned with the welfare of immigrants did not voluntarily set up representation arrangements for appellants, perhaps the Home Office could arrange to do so. What Sir Geoffrey hoped was that representation would be done voluntarily, and we had just done it. I mean, we couldn't have done it without months of preparation, so the timing was extremely fortunate.

But the Home Office wouldn't have that; they replied that what the Wilson committee recommended was that the Home Office should take the responsibility for forming a joint body. Absolutely untrue, but they agreed to have JCWI represented at a meeting to which they had summoned six other organisations to discuss the formation of a body to collaborate on representing appellants in immigration cases. Of these other six organisations three were affiliated to JCWI – CARD, the then National Council of Civil Liberties and the National Council for Commonwealth Immigrants – plus three unaffiliated organisations including the then National Council for Social Service. After a lot of argument it was accepted that JCWI should have greater representation than any of the others on the grounds that we represented this vast number of other organisations. Then, just as that body was about to be launched, Callaghan announced that there was after all no need for appeal hearings and hence no need for representation.

I never did casework once JCWI was set up. I mean I'd done an awful lot of casework, acting for our local branch of CARD in Oxford, but once JCWI got an office at Heathrow I thought, OK, I don't need to do that any more. JCWI had practically no money of course. I'm not sure how many of the affiliated organisations paid their membership fees but we had some donations, and in the first year we survived from month to month. We were paying a salary to our first worker before Frank Bailey, the Chairman, took over the office and of course we had the usual costs of postage, telephone et cetera.

We had no headquarters at the beginning, we used to meet in the office of the London Council for Social Service which was very supportive, not only did they give us their office to meet in, they seconded Mary Dines whose salary was being paid by them while she worked for JCWI. She's a dynamo, absolute dynamo, I've never come across anyone with such a capacity for work. She threw herself heartily into this. She became the mainstay – too weak a word – of JCWI. And then the government introduced a system of entry certificates, so that ended the necessity for having an office at Heathrow because people were being refused entry at the point of origin rather than at the airport. Because we had to make appeals and represent their cases, we got an office in Toynbee Hall in the East End of London. That was the first office JCWI had of its own. I don't know if we paid rent, I can't remember.

The Home Office reconvened meetings on the Wilson recommendations in I think 1969. You know what it is, trying to remember years. I had become Chairman of JCWI so I went along to the first meeting, and in accordance with JCWI policy, objected to the presence of the Community Relations Council on the ground that it was not a voluntary organisation and that it was actually responsible to the Government. We were not supported so there was nothing we could do but pull out, and we did. The remaining organisations then set up UKIAS, United Kingdom Immigration Advisory Service, which the Home Office funded.

JCWI never had any Home Office funding. In the early stages we assumed that we would be Government funded but at some point, and I can't tell you exactly when, we took a very firm policy decision that we were never going to take any money from the Government. I have a strong belief in that. The thing is, if you do take money sooner or later the strings, which may not be obvious at first, will be twitched and you will be told, you can't do that. By that time you've become reliant on the money. I think that's what happens to a lot of organisations. In the early Seventies when I was still Chairman, two very nice civil servants, I can't remember from what Ministry they were, had heard of JCWI and wanted to give us some money, and I think they were perfectly genuine. They said that we were doing a very important job, but by that time we had our policy in place.

We applied constant pressure for amelioration of the immigration laws. We issued leaflets and reports but the campaigning work, as far as influencing public policy was concerned, had been a complete failure. I can't say that we had any direct enemies of the organisation as such. Of course, the atmosphere still is hostile to immigration which has now been transferred to hostility towards asylum seekers. The Government deliberately blurred the distinction between immigrants and asylum seekers by talking about illegal immigrants and bogus asylum seekers. So the general atmosphere was always one that was hostile to our aim, but I can't say that actual hostility towards the organisation was ever manifested. Although we've had more than one office where unidentified people or groups smashed the windows and daubed paint on the walls.

Then there was the famous 1968 Immigration Act which barred our citizens coming here from East Africa. JCWI was the first to make a response. Marches have now become so usual no one takes any notice of them, but then I think they were less usual and did have some impact. We organised a march. JCWI wasn't very old at that time, but we had all these affiliated organisations. We organised a march against that Act which had been rushed through Parliament very quickly. We got a substantial number of people from all over the country to come and march down Whitehall. And there were people at the side jeering at us and saying, 'Wogs go home' and all that sort of stuff. CARD never dared, they had had some public demonstrations but they never dared to try and organise a mass march. JCWI did, and although we didn't get the Government to repeal the Act we had an impressive turnout.

Enoch Powell took the opportunity of the passing of the 1968 Immigration Act to make his 'rivers of blood' speech which of course was very bad throughout the country, as I'm sure you know. The intensity of racism greatly increased when he made this speech and later ones. Asian women were spat at while they stood at bus stops, and there were I think three actual murders in the street. It was very difficult for the Government, or the Opposition for that matter, to say that what he was saying was untrue. They just said, 'It's absolutely essential to keep these people out.' Well why was it essential to keep them out? The Government hadn't said why it was essential, they just said it's essential, we've got to rush this Bill through to stop them coming in. Heath never said when he sacked Powell from the shadow Cabinet that the substance of the speech was wrong, just that its language was wrong.

JCWI has never had much in the way of allies. I mean now there are quite a lot of organisations devoted to asylum seekers, and we're on good terms with them and cooperate with them, but for years we didn't really have any allies. I'll tell you one thing that always disappointed me very much. I believed that by setting up JCWI and making it a success we would stimulate people to do similar things in other sectors. The one I most regret which was never taken up was the police. I think there ought to have been something comparable to JCWI about police behaviour and brutality, to use the cliché. It never happened, and I don't know why it didn't happen. I thought that once they see that this strategy works people will apply it in other sectors, but they never did. So that's been a great disappointment to me. JCWI couldn't take up these other issues because we could only just struggle to do what we had set ourselves to do.

I have been with JCWI since its foundation. I was Chairman and then I became just a member of the executive committee, and I went on doing that for many years but for some years I've been a trustee. So I still have a connection with it, and so has my wife, Ann.

There's no doubt in my mind that JCWI's major achievement has been the help that we've given to individuals. Helping individuals and representing them before adjudicators provided the central basis for our analysis of what was going on.

I was born in June 1925 in Devonshire Terrace near Regents Park, London.

My father was a businessman. He started his own business dealing in silk and then he switched to rayon when artificial silk came in although he never abandoned silks completely. After the war nylon became the thing but I don't think he ever dealt in that. My father came from a line of yeomen farmers in Devonshire, he was brought up as a Congregationalist. His father was the first one of the line to leave Devonshire and go into business. When he retired my grandfather returned to Devonshire so my father was brought up there.

My mother's family was called Eardley-Wilmot, that was her maiden name. I don't know a lot about them, I think they were a line of squires, that kind of people. My grandfather died when I was about six. He had been head of the Forestry Service in India, so my mother was born and brought up there. My grandfather had been knighted, he was Sir Sainthill Eardley-Wilmot, and I've got some of the books he wrote: *The Life of a Tiger*, *The Life of an Elephant*, *Leaves*

175

from the Indian Forest. They are illustrated by photographs taken by my grandmother, and line drawings by my mother who must have been quite young when she drew them. My grandmother lived a very long time as a widow in Henley, where my grandfather had retired. She had a very nice house just by the bridge as you come out of Henley, going towards London. You entered it from the street and went downstairs, a two-storey house, downstairs there was a lawn leading right down to the river. A most beautiful house, I liked it very much. I was at boarding school and I remember one holiday, we actually stayed there; I think the idea was to get away from the bombing, and my poor father had to travel up to London. There was only a branch line and of course the trains were constantly cancelled and late. But mostly I knew it from visits which we made quite frequently to see my grandmother who lived there with just one faithful servant called Daisy. Daisy always addressed my grandmother as 'your Ladyship' or 'my Lady.'

My mother didn't keep up her drawing and she didn't keep up her music. We never had a piano although she had learnt to play. I think she was quite good because she had gone to Germany and studied music a bit there. All given up. She developed this enthusiasm, which I can't share at all, for breeding Alsatian dogs so we always had a kennel of Alsatian dogs, and she took them to shows and won prizes and that really absorbed her recreational time I suppose. I think it was a great pity she gave up both drawing and music for those wretched dogs.

I'm the only child of that marriage; my father had been married before, divorced, and had two sons and a daughter. My parents kept moving. I mean it was quite ridiculous actually. My father of course had an office in London, he had to go there every day, and so we lived for some time in London, and then they would get fed up with London and move to the country after a few years. And then my father got fed up with travelling up to London so we moved back to London.

As it happens, my very first memory is – very odd to have this but it's very vivid in my mind – standing at the window on the first day after we had moved to the country near Epsom from London. I remember standing at the window and remembering the journey the previous day. I don't remember the journey, I remember remembering the journey, it's strange, but anyway, that's how it was.

At one point we were in Kensington – but it wasn't our own house, we were being put up by some friends – two doors down from Christopher Isherwood. I had read some of the Auden and Isherwood plays, and I liked them very much. A parcel was misdelivered to our house, a parcel for him, so I took it round and took the opportunity to have a short chat. This must have been just before the war, because Auden and Isherwood together went to the United States in the summer of 1939. So I must have been about twelve. There was a long period during the war when we lived in what were called service flats in Pembridge Gardens, Notting Hill. One day, about a year or two ago, I was taking a bus from Oxford, and I had decided to get off at Notting Hill as I had a bit of time to spare. I thought, I'll go and look at that place, it was called Vincent House, and I looked inside, and it was exactly the same. Amazing!

Every year we went on a family holiday together, almost always to Brittany, near the seaside. I used to enjoy that very much. My father was very keen on golf, and when I was older he induced me to play. I always hated the game but I never told him. Have you ever played golf? It's very very boring. My father was also very keen on skating, we used to go to a rink in Bayswater. And that I did enjoy a great deal, and actually got quite good at it and learnt to do figure skating and dancing.

Politics played a very large part in my upbringing which was during the time leading up to the war. Both my parents were very strongly aware of the menace of fascism. My mother supported the Labour Party, my father had always been active in the Liberal Party, part of his Devonshire heritage I think. They talked politics all the time.

From the age of eight onwards I was at boarding school called Sandroyd which was then near Cobham. I did very well scholastically but I was absolutely miserable there, I didn't like any of the boys and they didn't like me. And then I got a scholarship and went to Winchester. That was quite different, I was very happy there.

My father realised perfectly clearly that I was not cut out to be a businessman. I mean the business would have been bankrupt within a year if I had taken it over. I went into the Army when I was eighteen in 1943, and came out in 1947. So I spent two years in the Army during the war, two years after the war. I went into the Artillery, I was a Gunner. I was selected to go to one of those War Office Selection Boards to determine whether I should become an officer or not, and I failed dismally. I quite liked the Gunners as a regiment because I was learning to become a specialist, plotting trajectories. I don't know how interesting it would have been on the battlefield, but it was quite interesting in training. I had no idea why but I found myself transferred to a place in Bedford where I spent six months with a heterogeneous group of people, some from the Army, some from the Navy, some civilians from the Foreign Office, and all that happened was that we were taught Japanese eight hours a day. We weren't taught to speak, we were taught to read and write. I knew 2,000 characters by the time I had finished there. And then I found myself in this place which called itself Wireless Experimental Section about five miles outside Delhi. It had nothing to do with the wireless, that was just bluff. It was a place for intercepting messages sent by the Japanese forces, which we decoded and translated. And I can't tell you how boring that was. When the war came to a horrible end with the atomic bombs, everyone in the Wireless Experimental Centre was sent away to Karachi except for those few who knew either Russian or Chinese who remained there and started spying on our allies.

So I was sent to Karachi, and we were all given the option to sign up to serve for another two years. If you signed, you became an officer, and you translated or interpreted for Japanese war crimes trials. I thought it would be a horrible job to do, so I was sent to Malaya to join a field security section. It wasn't at all like being in the Army. You were sent out in ones or twos to different parts of the area trying to track down people who had worked for the Allies during the Japanese occupation so that they got some kind of reward; and reporting on the economic situation and political activity.

Towards the end of my time there, I learnt a lot about racism. The military government came to an end, the colonial government was reinstated, and the British came back. Now a lot of them had genuinely suffered badly, they had been in Japanese prisoner-of-war jails, but they came back with the idea that everything was going to be as it had been for them before the war. Before the war the colonial government rested on the idea of British prestige in particular, and European in general. For example, before the war – I don't know whether it was a law or just a rule – no European could stay in Malaya who didn't earn more than a certain amount, because if you didn't earn more than a certain amount you wouldn't be able to keep up the style of life that helped to maintain the prestige of the white man's life. And the usual thing, they had clubs to which no Malay or Chinese was admitted. They came back and they tried to behave in the old way. So I really learnt what racism was from these attempts to maintain attitudes of racial superiority. Of course, nothing could be the same as it had been before the war. The British just ran from Malaya, they simply ran. The Civil Service – all the British – left and gave no instructions or support to their Malay or Chinese subordinates as to what to do when the Japanese arrived. Any prestige they may have had was shattered by that. It was a disaster. I was in contact mostly with people living there – Malay, Indian and Chinese people – and when I came across the colonial attitude I resented it deeply, it seemed to me a horrible way to behave towards other people. So I left Malaya with a very strong feeling against racism.

I got demobilised just in time to come up to Oxford in October 1947. I had a history scholarship which I had obtained before I left school, and I certainly planned to go to university; I just didn't know when that would be. If there had been no war and I had gone straight up to Oxford from school I would have read history. While in the Army I had got a bit interested in philosophy, I'd read a little bit in a very rambling way, Whitehead, Maritain, a few things. Politics, economics and philosophy I thought must be interesting, so I opted for PPE. And having done that, I became absolutely captured by philosophy.

I got my degree in 1950, a first. I hadn't made up my mind what I wanted to do with my life. I had worked for something like three weeks on the *Glasgow Herald*, I don't remember how that came about but I did, just to see if I liked journalism. I then applied for a job teaching philosophy at the University of Birmingham as a temporary lecturer just for one year. I shudder to think how bad my lectures must have been. I'd never lectured to anybody before on anything, and I had no idea how to do it. I do remember a moment of blind panic when I was just outside the door and I was about to walk in to give my first lecture. I also took the Civil Service exam. It's quite different now, but in those days you could get into the Civil Service essentially by writing examination papers. You also had an interview, on which I did rather badly. Anyway I got in, having written six philosophy papers, and one paper in political theory but I never went into the Civil Service because of All Souls.

All Souls is a very strange institution because it has only Fellows and no students, graduate or undergraduate. It elects two Fellows by examination every year. So I sat the All Souls examination. I don't remember why I decided to do this but I was lucky enough to be elected. There I was, a Junior Fellow of All Souls. And that had a catastrophic effect on my life in Birmingham because at All Souls there's a rule that you have in your first year to spend so many nights sleeping in the college, and that meant I had to cram my teaching at Birmingham into a few days and then rush back to All Souls to do nothing in particular except sleep. So when my year at Birmingham had come to an end, I breathed an enormous sigh of relief.

I've been at Oxford ever since although I used to go quite often to American universities to do a term's teaching or more. As I've already described, the first time I went, it wasn't to teach. I had gone to Berkeley in California, chiefly for the purposes of learning mathematical logic. I had got very interested in mathematics and its philosophy. I wanted when I was a junior fellow at All Souls to read mathematics, take a degree in mathematics but the Warden was a very authoritative character and he forbade me to do that on the ground that if I failed to get a First it would lower the prestige of the College. So I just got someone to give me some tutorials in mathematics without taking a degree. I wanted to learn about mathematical logic but it was hardly done in Oxford then, now there's quite a flourishing school but then it was despised both by mathematicians and by philosophers.

I taught several times at Stanford University in California and I got involved a bit in civil rights. There was a good friend of mine called John Howard who is black, and he later said that he and I constituted the civil rights movement at Stanford. We both joined CORE, Congress on Racial Equality, and we went and picketed various places. So I got involved in that kind of action in California. In 1964 when I came back to the UK my wife and I thought we really ought to be doing something here. I'm sure we should have got involved much earlier, but anyway, we didn't.

I had the idea of trying to set up a CORE-type group here in Oxford, and so I started going round and meeting various people. And then I discovered that Evan Luard, at one time Labour MP for Oxford had had the same idea, so we joined forces and set up the Oxford Committee for Racial Integration, OCRI as everyone called it. Later they changed the name to Oxford Committee for Community Relations. Well, it's a pity; the name OCRI was suggested by one of our founder members who was a West Indian from the university, and we picked the word 'integration' because then it was the slogan of the American civil rights movement, and we wanted that resonance. Later the word became degraded by people like Alec Douglas-Home who used it to mean assimilation: 'the trouble with them is that they won't integrate'. People were amazing, they complained of women wearing saris or shalwars, and if you said to them, 'Look, if you went to India, you wouldn't put on a sari, would you?' they answered, 'No of course I wouldn't.' They couldn't see the analogy, they simply could not see the analogy.

I'd seen how CORE operated in America, and how the bus boycott was organised and I realised if you want to stop something you must get together and stop it. We were quite successful actually in that first year with two companies in Oxford, Morris and Pressed Steel. If you worked there you were the aristocracy of manual labour, I mean they paid far more than anybody else and they employed an enormous number of people. But each of them discriminated in different ways. When we started there wasn't any law against racial discrimination and so Morris would only employ black people in the cleansing department sweeping floors and nothing else. Pressed Steel was different, they didn't discriminate against Afro-Caribbeans, to use the modern term, but they wouldn't employ any Asians at all. We managed to get both those policies overturned. Although there was no law against racial discrimination neither company wanted it to be known that they discriminated, they didn't want headlines in the local paper. We had some cooperation from the manager of the employment exchange who actually arranged a meeting between several of us and representatives of Pressed Steel. In the case of Morris we had a lot of help from the union because the Transport & General Workers Union man there was a member of OCRI, and when appealed to Morris were willing to cooperate. So that was quite a triumph.

When we were in process of setting OCRI up, we had a visit from a representative of the National Council for Commonwealth Immigrants, and she was very much concerned with local groups which she classified as either liaison committees or campaign committees. Liaison committees were to be supported by the NCCI so as to get Government money, whereas campaign committees were not. We had to choose whether or not to accept their conditions for becoming a liaison committee and thereby becoming eligible for a grant, and we did just that. As a liaison committee we were affiliated to the Campaign Against Racial Discrimination. That was how I got involved. I happened to be sent as a deputy to CARD, and once I got involved with CARD I didn't have much time to work for the local OCRI group.

I was elected Reader in the philosophy of mathematics in 1962. With one other person who was then lecturer in mathematical logic, we managed to set up a new honours school in both mathematics and philosophy for undergraduates. What we did essentially was to take the pure mathematics part of the mathematics syllabus and stick philosophy in. So that's one of the things that most pleases me, having started that school because I believe that that's a very good education. I was thirteen years Reader in philosophy of mathematics, and I resigned from that in 1975. Then I was lucky enough to be elected a Senior Research Fellow at All Souls, and held that position for only four years when I was elected to the Chair, Wykeham Chair of Logic.

Ann and I met in the university, she was at Somerville. We married in 1951, so I have been married for 49 years. Ann has published several books, her first a marvellous book called *A Portrait of English Racism*. And then later, she collaborated with a lawyer on *Subjects, Citizens, Aliens and Others*, which is a book in a series meant for lawyers, but I think it's of interest to many people besides lawyers. And there have been other books as well.

I now realise I was very naïve and didn't go about things the right way, but I wanted to fulfil my promise to Martin Luther King to put right the reports of Alistair Cooke. First, I tried to get the *Guardian* to accept an article on the subject and they wouldn't. So then I thought I'll try the radio. At that time there was a practice of having philosophers speak on the radio, and a man from the BBC came and asked if I would do such a programme. I said, 'I will if you let me speak on the subject of racism also.' I gave him a copy of my proposed talk, and I never heard from him. He turned up again one day, having obviously completely forgotten. I was so furious I more or less drove him from the door. For that reason I never gave a talk on philosophy for the BBC. I never was able to put the record straight as I had promised Dr King I would.

We were the welfare branch of the alternative society

Caroline Coon
Release

I was in love with a Jamaican musician. Then, to my despair, he was imprisoned for being in possession of marijuana. I was visiting him in prison, and tried through the appeals process to get his two and a half year sentence quashed. So, in 1967, as well as being in my first year of a fine art degree course at Central St Martins School of Art and Design, I was also working with lawyers on his case.

THE HIPPY REVOLUTION was beginning to make an impact and causing the establishment to go shock-horror. A magazine called *Black Dwarf* had just started. It was leftist, Marxist, anti-government, anti-police. One of my tutors at art school was Derek Boshier who was best mates with Clive Goodwin, the editor of *Black Dwarf*. Tariq Ali and Sheila Rowbotham were involved with the paper too. Then Mick Jagger was arrested – you remember, for returning to England with pills he had bought legally in Italy? Word got out that the *News of the World* was publishing a lurid character assassination of Mick, this hero of our 'disgusting' generation.

Clive Goodwin rang me – he knew I was involved in a drugs case myself – and he asked me to help him organise a demonstration. We started ringing everyone we knew, telling them to be outside the *News of the World* the next evening, a Saturday night. I guess three or four hundred people turned up. Our aim was to stop the *News of the World* distributing the paper. It was the first demonstration I'd ever helped organise. We all lay down in Fleet Street blocking the distribution lorries. Of course, we were eventually moved on by the police. We marched past Downing Street and up Whitehall and at four o'clock in the morning I was sitting on the steps of Eros in Piccadilly chatting to people like you do at demonstrations. We had what I now recognise as post-demonstration sadness, that has-it-made-any-difference feeling you get after you've put a huge amount of effort into a march. The youth I was chatting to was Rufus Harris and he said he knew other people who felt the same way about the drug laws. He told me his sister knew John 'Hoppy' Hopkins and that there was to be an underground meeting to discuss what to do about the sudden increase in drug arrests. Hoppy, who organised the Notting Hill Free School, had been arrested and imprisoned for marijuana. Rufus took me to this meeting, and further meetings were organised. Something had to be done. Not only had Mick Jagger been picked off, but other young people were literally disappearing off the streets. Nobody knew where they'd gone. Doors were being kicked down at two o'clock in the morning and the police would barge in.

The third meeting I remember was really big – twenty or thirty people – at Joe Boyd's basement flat off Westbourne Grove. He was one of a group of Americans who had come to Europe to avoid the Vietnam War, and he had started a record company. This meeting was quite a gathering of those of us who were later to be recognised as the vanguard and leaders of the underground. Jim Haines was there, and Michael X and Colin MacInnes. It was agreed that what was needed was an organisation which could advise people about what to do when they got busted. The others at the meeting had started their careers and were already organising the underground so nobody had the time to actually do it, so I said I would. I came up with the name Release inspired by the fact that I was trying to get my friend released from prison. As a matter of fact, at this time I was deeply distressed and angry because my views on justice had been utterly shattered by seeing what a working class black person went through in the British 'justice' system. With my class background I had been conditioned to assume that our legal system was absolutely fair old boy, incorruptible, the best in the world. And in court with my friend I had seen that it was not. I was beginning to get the hang of the law, and knew that Legal Aid wasn't working. Release set out to do something about it.

We knew that Release had to be a 24-hour service. Young people were relatively safe during the day; being busted at night was the most acute emergency. So we couldn't be just a nine to five organisation. We raised some start-up money. And I had my art school grant. I had an extra phone put into the studio in my basement flat on the outskirts of Notting Hill, and I employed a secretary. I'm dyslexic. I'm much better now but then I couldn't write letters which you could pass to officialdom. And since we were going to put out lots of leaflets and information, I had to have someone who was my literate right hand. Rufus Harris was also there.

What Rufus and I knew we had to do was inform people of their rights. For me, Release was not about drugs *per se*. At this point in my life I'd never taken drugs. I didn't drink, I didn't smoke cigarettes, I had not smoked pot. For me Release was essentially about civil liberties, legal rights, and what we now call human rights. I felt people needed to know what to do when they were arrested: you don't have to be pressured into a 'confession', you don't have to make a statement before you've seen a solicitor, what the police claim to be illegal drugs must be confirmed with analysis, you are legally entitled to a telephone call, etc. One of the first practical things we did at Release was put out a know-your-rights Release Bust Card. We had thousands printed to distribute free of charge.

At the same time Steve Abrams was raising money from the Beatles and other famous people to publish the first *Times* advertisement saying that the laws against marijuana were 'immoral in principle and unworkable in practice'. Steve was also organising the first Legalise Pot Rally in Hyde Park. The rally was on one of those brilliant 1960s Peace and Love sunny summer days. The Beatles 'All You Need Is Love' single had just been released. As everyone converged on Hyde Park Rufus and I gave out the Release Bust Cards. That day was like the official birth of Release. Hundreds of people not only got our 24-hour telephone number but a card telling them their rights. And then Alan Ginsburg began to recite poetry and sing with his squeeze box. The police stepped in to stop him because it was illegal to play instruments in the park. I pointed out it was not illegal to sing! So Alan continued to read his poetry and chant 'ohmmmmmm'. Richard Neville was there – he'd just arrived from Australia – and he was giving out the first London edition of *OZ*. At the end of that incredible day I went back to my studio and immediately the phone started ringing, and ringing and ringing.

Release opened at 9.00 am promptly and closed at 10ish, and from then on the 24-hour emergency telephone service cut in. At night we needed a person to be at the end of the phone and someone else to go to police stations. So we had this incredible rota of

volunteers, doctors, solicitors on night call. One of the reasons I
knew it was possible to run a 24-hour emergency telephone service
was because before Release I'd used the Samaritans 24-hour
emergency help line. Chad Varah, the founder of the Samaritans in
1953, was one of my heroes.

We were the first youth organisation which was really an
alternative social service run by young people for young people.
Although Release was set up ostensibly to advise people on their
legal rights in relation to drug laws, young people came to us with all
their problems: running away from home, pregnancy, homelessness.
We were inundated. The first thing I had to do was find and select a
group of lawyers with the ability and will to act radically and
challenge the social and legal *status quo*. We also needed doctors.
Within a few months we had a nucleus of great young professionals
to help us. Hundreds of young people came to us with shocking
stories of police corruption: 'they kicked the doors of the flat down
and they stole my drugs and they walked out with my money.' Many
people, even George Harrison, were ringing up and saying, truthfully,
'I was planted'. We also had men coming to us who I found
potentially dangerous, freaky and quite difficult to deal with. One of
the reasons why Rufus Harris was so essential was although he was
actually quite a shy and passive person he wasn't at all fazed by
aggressive and distressed street people and heroin addicts. I took on
the more public role of explaining what we were about.

I knew that to start something like Release I had to go to the top.
I thought that one of the reasons why police and prisons were
behaving illegally and obstructively was because the people at the
top didn't know what was going on. I thought all I had to do was tell
them the facts, and word would go down the line and the corruption
and misbehaviour would stop. For a start, I went to see the head of
Scotland Yard and the person in charge of prisons at the Home
Office.

At Scotland Yard I was handed over to the head of public
relations. There he was behind his desk scowling. It was for me a
classic moment. I realised that the establishment had assumed Rufus
and I were the stereotype of what they considered 'disgusting'
hippies: smelly, barefooted, working class ne're-do-wells! Well, of
course, I walked up to Mr PR's desk, put out my hand, introduced
myself and said, 'How do you do'. Mr PR leapt to his feet and said
'Oh, oh, oh, good gracious me, ah, Miss Coon! Would you like a

glass of sherry?' It was very funny. This is where my class was an advantage. It gave me the Queen's English voice of authority, a poise and manner which got my foot in the door with leaders of the establishment, and was a protection against quite a lot of sleazy sexist male behaviour. I informed Scotland Yard that Release would be insisting that anyone who was arrested was treated fairly and within the rules. We were also writing up detailed case histories and keeping records.

The press began ringing us for information and stories. At first, because of my horror of publicity – I had all these upper class pretensions to unlearn – I was saying, 'No' to the press. I said to Rufus, 'Let's wait a few months until we have some facts and statistics before we talk to the press.' I think this helped to make us, despite our youth, a credible, serious organisation. In 1968 we moved from my studio into a proper office in Princedale Road, Notting Hill. There was a substantial underground scene developing, a mass counter culture, an alternative society with a growing network of shops with cutting-edge alternative clothes, independent record companies, alternative magazines, alternative entertainment venues. Instead of classical music and alcohol there was rock and roll and drugs like cannabis. And we were the welfare branch of this alternative society.

At almost the first hippy underground gig I went to, I saw several people who were what became known as 'bad tripping' on LSD. People knew I was from Release, and they brought their bad-tripping friends to me. A lot of vulnerable young people could become very distressed under the influence of drugs. The effect of drugs can be to strip away self control, will power and confidence and allow expression of all kinds of repressed feelings. We decided that the Release team would be present with doctors and lawyers at alternative society gigs like Middle Earth, Implosion and festivals like Bath and the Isle of Wight. It was especially important to organise 'trip tents', a calm quiet place where people could sit with their friends and a Release volunteer while bad trips passed. Psychiatrists who had been trained to treat alcohol dependence were beginning to learn how to treat people dependent on drugs. People were beginning to read RD Laing. At Release we were particularly interested in what was happening within the family, what was being unrecognised, denied and suppressed which might cause young people to become distressed enough to block their pain with narcotic drugs. We were asking: what is the cause of drug addiction, and what can we do when an addict comes to us for help? Right from the start I knew it was quite wrong to brand as criminals people who were dependent on drugs.

Release was costing an enormous amount of money for, among other things, office rent, phone bills, stationery and the wages of the Release staff who were not volunteers as well as for the fines and legal costs of people who were busted. At a general meeting of underground leaders I presented the plan for part of the cost of Release to be met by 6p for every ticket sold at underground all-nighter events. This was agreed, and it really helped. It was like the alternative society's community tax.

Although there was never enough money and although we were all broke, the Release office was very bright and funky, threadbare but lovely. We had psychedelic posters on the wall, political posters, information. We were on two floors. A creaky little staircase. A private counselling room, a general reception room, and the library. The young librarians' important job was to get in all the most up-to-date research papers on drugs from the medical journals, international reports, references in newspapers, etcetera. The reception room was an open space where Rufus had his desk on one side and across it his secretary, and I had my desk on the other side with my secretary, and on sofas and chairs sat volunteers and people who had come for help. Part of our function was as a drop-in day centre. We were getting people coming to us from all over the country and from abroad; hippies, young people, even the police dropped in. And very quickly I realised we had to have one unbreakable rule in the Release office for everyone: no drugs.

There were young people who were no more a threat to society in terms of their drug use than were people drinking champagne and smoking cigars. But we had to ensure that the small but important percentage of young people who had become addicts were not only treated properly by the police but that they received the social, psychological and medical attention they needed. The people who needed our help most were the 10 per cent of the population vulnerable to drug dependency, a dependency which leads to acute distress, illness and an inability to engage in society or work. Addiction to alcohol and drugs is an illness not a crime. Sending drug addicts to prison is not only immoral but useless. Group therapy for all kinds of psychological distress was becoming best practice in Britain and America. Two key people in the Release story are George and Ann Mully. Ann became the main Release doctor, and moderated the twice weekly evening group therapy sessions.

By 1969, the arrest and imprisonment of young people accused of violating the Dangerous Drugs Act of 1965 was one of Britain's most urgent social problems. When Brian Jones of the Rolling Stones was busted for the second time and it looked as though he would go to prison we, the leaders of the underground, organised another demonstration. At my studio a group of us made over one hundred fake joints. The next afternoon we marched up and down Kings Road smoking these 'joints', chanting 'Free Brian Jones'. The police were at the demo almost before we were but they couldn't do anything because it was a peaceful demonstration. Then the police decided that we could only walk on one side of the pavement. Suddenly there was a flare-up because somebody had stepped across the invisible police line. The police rushed in. Steve Abrahms, Suzy Creamcheese, Chris Jagger and Jeff Dexter were arrested and thrown into the back of a Black Maria. As the doors slammed I banged on the van shouting, 'Don't worry, I'll be at the police station'. And then I was thrown into the Black Maria, too. For the first time I witnessed a uniformed police officer beating someone up. People who had come to Release told me that they had been beaten up by the police, and I found it incredible so I'm glad I saw it. At the police station I was charged with breach of the peace and damaging a Black Maria to the value of £1. At court I was given a conditional discharge but the magistrate said that I was also to pay £10 costs. I said to the magistrate 'It's all very well to arrest me, but I'm certainly not going to pay you the cost of arresting me!' The magistrate, somewhat taken aback, said he'd give me two weeks to come to my senses, and if I then still refused to pay the court costs he would send me to prison for two weeks. Right, I thought, I've been advising people what to do when they are arrested and sent to prison, this is an opportunity to see inside Holloway Prison. So I refused to pay the £10 costs. When the police turned up at my front door to take me to prison I had my toothbrush and toothpaste ready. I didn't do the full two weeks because a television presenter paid the costs and got me out of prison to do a TV interview. But three days inside was enough to get an idea of what prison is like.

After two years work at Release, Rufus and I wrote and published *The Release Report: On Drugs Offenders and The Law* (Sphere Books

1969). The report was an analysis of the detailed records of all our cases since 1967 with emphasis on corrupt police procedure. In the week of the report's publication I was invited to Scotland Yard for what I thought was a routine liaison meeting about teenage runaways. Instead I was escorted to a plush office on Scotland Yard's top floor. There I was confronted by a phalanx of top brass including Commissioner Sir John Waldron, Deputy Commissioner Robert Mark and Birmingham's Sir Derek Capper. I was informed that Scotland Yard had read the Release report, and that I must withdraw it immediately. Further, because the allegations about police procedure and corruption were entirely false, I would have to make a public apology. I refused. Once I got back to the office I immediately telephoned Bing Spear at the Home Office. I complained to him that since I had just given evidence to the Wootton Committee on *Drug Dependence* and I was about to give evidence to the Deedes Committee on *Powers of Arrest and Search in Relation to Drug Offences* what had happened amounted to intimidation by the police of a Government witness. I thought the powers-that-be would back off.

However, when the Release report was due on sale we discovered that no shops had it in stock. We contacted our publisher, Anthony Chetham. He refused to take our calls. Eventually we were tipped off by a sympathiser that the book had been 'remaindered for pulping'. Rufus and I quickly raised the money to buy the whole print run and we sold the report from the Release office. For the Release report to have been stopped before it even reached book shops meant that police and Government had threatened the publisher with the Official Solicitor. Today it is easy to forget to what extent in the 1960s the truth about drugs, racism and police corruption was vigorously censored.

One of the most important things we did at Release in the 1960s was to inform young people of the difference between soft drugs and heroin. Thereby we helped prevent a heroin epidemic. Today because American and European Governments brandish false War On Drugs rhetoric while stubbornly refusing to control drugs in an educated rational way, there is an explosion of heroin use and young people are needlessly dying.

Right from the first moment I volunteered to run Release I thought someone else would step in and I could carry on with my painting career. No one did so I carried on, perhaps because I could do the job well. However when I spoke at conferences beside Mr

Professor this and that I felt I wasn't making enough of an impact, lacking any qualifications myself and being a girl. To be more effective I decided I had to get a degree so in 1970 I left Release to go full time to Brunel University to read Psychology, Sociology and Economics. During this time Release went bankrupt. In 1971 I had to drop my studies to go back to Release to raise money and put things together again. Except for one's own personal conviction, there was very little reward. That the establishment was hostile was to be expected, but the Left and counterculture was hostile too to the very idea of leaders. My position was, and is, that someone, with the consent of the group, has to be a spokesperson. Spokesperson or leader is simply a practical organisational mechanism and essential for conveying aims and ideals through various media to a wider public.

By the time I left Release we had fifteen paid staff with over twenty volunteers. We were paid a bare minimum but everyone worked incredibly hard. At first Rufus got £5 which was then raised to £8. And before I was paid £5, I was paid nothing because as main spokesperson I was on the radio or TV every other week so I got by on media fees. It didn't enter my head that I should be paid for what I was doing. I hadn't yet learned to contradict my upbringing. I thought it was a right and honourable obligation to do charity work.

There has been this sexist critique of me that the only reason the media paid any attention to Release was because I was a 'dolly bird'. I've always confronted this sexism. Like recently, I did an interview with a journalist who said to me, 'Didn't you get noticed in the 1960s just because you were beautiful?' And I replied what sexist nonsense! Because in fact in the 1960s we were surrounded by the most beautiful, decorative, glamorous men – Tariq Ali, Richard Neville, David Hockney, Michael English, David Bailey, Martin Sharp, Malcolm X, Stuart Hall – and these men's achievements weren't repeatedly reduced to mere physical appearance, to their young bodies, beautiful hair and velvet trousers. As a feminist I believed, as I still do, that women have the right to be as decorative and attractive as men.

Oh but most of the time life was magnificent. I was young, loving life, loving! It was marvellous to be with a group of people who were optimistic about changing society for the better. And Rufus and I really supported each other. When things got on top of me and if I was too down to go to the office, Rufus would cover for me. And if it got too much for him, he could take time out too. The splendid happy moments at Release were as a supportive surrogate family helping other people. On the other hand the very miserable moments were when every week we were not able to stop young people from going to prison. We did our best to stop it. But sometimes there was nothing we could do. I found the fact that Government was so ready to punish and imprison young people quite unbearable – and I still do.

I was born in London on 23rd March 1945. I was brought up on a typical Kent dairy farm, with fruit and hops too. Father was one of the first farmers to introduce mechanisation – vining machines – into the hop fields. When I was five I remember my father panicking because the Cockney hop pickers down from London had gone on strike over the loss of their jobs.

My mother was born with a hole in her heart. She was married at sixteen and when at seventeen, she was pregnant with her first child, her doctors thought giving birth would kill her. I grew up knowing I'd had an older brother, Roland, who had been terminated. When my mother was pregnant a second time she kept it a secret until it was too late for her doctors to intervene, and she gave birth to me. It was only as a result of surgery developed during the Second World War that she was able to have the hole in her heart successfully operated on.

I was the oldest surviving child but whenever I was asked how many children there were in our family I would say five. My five brothers: Richard, William, Charles, Henry and Stewart. Only recently did it dawn on me, hold on a second, there were six children in our family! I think, because I was a girl, I wasn't counted. I didn't count myself. Now I have two surviving brothers. My three youngest brothers died of infantile muscular atrophy, a genetically inherited muscle wasting disease. I have not had children, nor have I ever been married.

My parents were born in the south of England. My father's parents divorced when he was very young. He had a distressing childhood, not being his mother's favourite child. My mother was the child of my grandfather's mistress, and for a time he ran a ménage à trois. My mother grew up not really knowing who her parents were. My grandmother covered up the fact that she had three children from two men to whom she was not married by running a nursery school for the children of absent diplomats. So my mother blended in with all the other children.

My mother and father strenuously covered up their unconventional childhood and parentage. My father was the kind of man who would joke, 'I was beaten as a child and it never did me any harm.' I remember my mother confiding family secrets to me when I was very little. Nanny would dress us children up for tea and we'd go and say hello to our parents before we went to bed. The times I saw my mother most was sitting at her dressing room table as she dressed for dinner. I can remember the smell of her perfume and her beautiful clothes. She would tell these intimate stories of her life and the family history as if she was offering an excuse or an explanation for certain things that were happening. My mother would say, 'Your father is trying to do better for you than the way he was brought up.'

My father inherited a huge amount of money from his family with which he bought a lot of land from my mother's family. This enabled him to act the country squire. In fact his money came from 'trade'. His grandfather was born working-class, an extraordinary man who became chairman of the Prudential Insurance Company. We had beautiful land, servants, a chauffeur. The house was like a typical manor in a village with a village green and church. We had a mill on the property with a mill stream and lakes. We had ornamental ducks and peacocks.

My mother's parents lived just up the drive in a little cottage on the land my father bought from them. My grandfather, whose father had been a Mayor of Bristol, was the archetypal Victorian patriarch. He believed that women were second-rate, only fit for breeding. In her youth my mother was a talented artist but she was only allowed it as a hobby. Neither my grandmother nor my mother were allowed to work for money. My grandmother was really a very talented musician who, on my grandfather's say so, gave up the violin. She doted on him. He was twenty years older than her. When he had all his teeth out and false teeth, she had all her teeth out and false teeth too.

I think my parents were really happy when they were teaching us as children. We went sailing, gliding, my father loved shooting and fishing. There's nothing in the world that children could do that my parents didn't take us to: the circus, museums, art galleries, the cinema, the ballet. On the farm we were expected to know the names of every blade of grass, every flower, every tree. We were also expected to know the names of all the cattle. Actually, that became one of the problems. I would go away to boarding school and the cattle and the calves would grow so going around the farm became a terror because the calf I could name in the Easter holidays by summer was unrecognisable.

Right from the start I felt that my parents disliked me. They colluded in my punishments. My mother would decide I had done something wrong and order me to 'wait outside your father's study'. And when my father came home he would eventually take me inside the study and beat me. That happened quite frequently. It was ritualised. I won't go into detail. Being sent away to boarding school at five seemed to me to be an extension of my parents' system of punishment. They suggested that when I learned to be good they would love me. When I was fourteen my mother told me that I would never be a great artist because all great artists had one man shows by the time they were my age. And I believed that. In a way I was lucky to be told when I was eighteen that because I was so bad and such a disappointment to my parents I was disinherited. At that age you aren't exactly thinking of your inheritance but from then on I was psychologically and materially free to challenge my parents – their behaviour and beliefs – in a way that my brothers for the sake of their expected inheritance of land and money never could.

At five my parents sent me to boarding school. In fact it was to a wonderful Russian ballet school, the Legat Ballet School, in Tunbridge Wells founded and run by Madame Nicholiva Legat. The teachers absolutely loved us children. They taught us meticulously and in a way which maximised talent. So in contrast to my thwarted and unhappy grandmother and mother, at the Legat Ballet School I was encouraged by the fine example of what women could do as artists.

Madame Legat had a huge bronze Buddha in her sitting room. She admired Indian culture. We did yoga every morning before breakfast. When you learn something at that age you never forget it. Yoga taught me how to relax. Given that my upbringing turned me into a highly strung person, this was really useful. Since then I've used yoga technique to counter anxiety – you know, lying flat on the floor letting stress flood out of your body.

One evening I remember being asked to do the Bluebird solo from Sleeping Beauty. I was so terrified of being inadequate I froze. When Madame demanded I start I just sat down in floods of tears. She asked me to her room. I don't remember what exactly I told her but she understood because she wrote a letter to my parents asking them to stop beating me. Now I realise what a heroic intervention that was for a teacher. She risked losing me as a pupil and with me her fees. Which is what happened – my parents took me away. I was ten.

I was then sent to Sadlers Wells – later called the Royal Ballet School – which at first didn't have boarding facilities so I was put in digs at Barons Court, a short walk from the school. At Mrs Temple's digs there were four or five of us children and a nanny. The others used to go home at weekends and often I didn't so I would walk from Olympia down Exhibition Road and I would haunt the Science Museum and the Victoria & Albert Museum with my sketchbook and draw and have a wonderful time.

By the time I was ten I could hardly read or write because we didn't have academic lessons at Legat. At first when I went to the Royal Ballet School I had detention every week in every subject except art until I got a group of friends together to make sure I got the minimum marks to avoid detention. When I was fifteen the headmistress said I shouldn't bother to take my O levels – probably they were afraid of any failures – but I insisted. Although I couldn't spell I've always trusted my intelligence so I took my O levels and passed five.

I absolutely loved school but by the time I was fifteen, I knew I was going to grow too tall for ballet. Lady Agnew, headmistress of the Royal Ballet School, wrote to my parents to say that after my O levels I should go on to art school but my parents warned me they were going to stop paying for my education and that I must earn my own living. When I left school and came home I didn't know what was going to happen. The house was silent and I was standing in the hall not knowing what to do when my mother appeared, hysterically shouting, 'I can't stand you in the house, get out!' And in an effort to please her I did get out. I just didn't know how to say, 'Oh stop being silly Mother' and march upstairs. I was afraid of confronting her and so I just said, 'Yes, OK', and I got myself back to London. I turned up on the doorstep of a friend of my mother's who had a boutique in Knightsbridge and asked if I could work for her, and she agreed. The problem was that the only adults I knew were friends of my parents who told them that I was in London because I was a bad rebellious girl. One family I stayed with received a letter from my mother urging them to stop me scrounging off them. Very soon I found myself a bedsit.

It was a question of what can I do to earn a living and carry on my education? First of all, add a couple of years to my age because people don't employ sixteen-year old girls. I did a modelling course and began modelling for Norman Hartnell. I got my A level art at night school and then did my Art Pre-Dip at Northampton School of Art. I wasn't eligible for a grant because my parents were too wealthy. My parents also refused to help my brothers through university. By the time I got to Central School of Art at 21 I got a grant because by then I had earned my living for four years and was therefore eligible for Mature Student Grant status. Part of my ability to run Release was because, despite my class, I had been on the streets; I knew what it was like to be poor and without adult support.

I do regret dropping out of college and university. In 1967 I left Central School of Art because of my work at Release, and then in 1971 I left Brunel because I had to take care of Release's financial crisis. It took me six months to raise the money to put Release back on track again and then I was too embarrassed to explain to the university why I had missed so much. I began writing. I wanted to record what had happened at Release and – with my by now developed feminist politics – to describe what had happened to me as a woman in the 1960s. Then, because I was a 'leader of youth culture', the editor of *Melody Maker* asked me to write about pop music. I was interested in counter culture dynamics and how young people would react to what had happened to the Peace and Love generation. By the early 1970s, 1960s rock and roll heros like Elton John, David Bowie and the Rolling Stones had gone establishment and corporate. I predicted a reaction. It was thrilling to be there to write about and photograph the punk rock movement as it emerged with bands like the Sex Pistols, the Clash and the Slits – the next generation's Hate and War reaction to authoritarian government, Peace and Love hippies and psychedelia.

Slowly, after Release, I put my life as an artist back on track. I paint in my studio from 5.00am to 5.00pm every day. I learned how to be chronically impecunious. I'm a feminist in my life and in my art, I have continued to be a political activist, especially in campaigning for the end of prohibition.

My body chemistry does not dispose me to getting that much enjoyment out of drugs. I just get horribly sick and incapacitated. But I love a little bit of everything occasionally – especially pot. Not to mention a little bit of champagne. I smoke less than ten cigarettes a week. I've only had three trips of acid in my life, and they were terrible. On a trip all my conscious will-power, optimism and happiness is stripped away and I am a child again, raw, in a nightmare of acute distress. On the other hand that I survived those bad trips was very educational. They helped me understand who I am. I realised that psychological pain and distress of itself doesn't kill – that I could survive and pass on through to the safe side. It is my conscious will-power which overrides my childhood conditioning that I am a useless, unlovable, ugly person.

I have never felt comfortable giving either a joint or even a glass of alcohol to anyone under twenty-one. I know only too well that it's not the drug that is the danger – the danger is not knowing the young person, a young person who has yet to know and understand themselves, and they might be vulnerable to addiction. And no, although drugs can be important to social life, I do not think drugs are much help to creativity. Most great art be it writing, music or painting has been created without or despite drugs.

It has only been in the last ten years or so that I can talk about the 1960s without crying. I would cry because not only was it a very happy time, but it was a terrible time too. I was dealing with my family, the Release work load, my own career. My ideals about how society should work were being shattered daily in interactions with the real world Establishment.

You can't deny a woman developing on her own

Elizabeth Rawlinson
Prisoners' Wives Service

Once I said to a prisoner's wife, 'Why were you so welcoming when I first came to see you?' And she said, 'Don't be so stupid. I was so lonely, I was on my own with two children under five, I had no money, I couldn't go out, I had no friends, and I was just pleased to make a cup of coffee for somebody else. It was as simple as that.' And that's what I used to quote to volunteers who wanted to do visiting.

It's so simple, the people are so lonely that anybody visiting them is a change of scene if nothing else. Even if you're not telling them what they want to hear, or not being the sort of person they want to see. I have to accept that my families would refer to me as their posh friend because I haven't got an East End accent. Only once a woman slammed the door in my face, and that was because she had a man in the bedroom. Otherwise it was great.

SYLVIA CHANCELLOR, LADY Chancellor, had a charlady who came weeping to her one day and said her husband had been sent down for fraud. So Sylvia went to Tom Sargant who was secretary of Justice, a legal group helping men who they thought had been wrongly convicted. He put Sylvia in touch with an articulate middle class woman whose husband had been convicted and sent to prison, and who had found that she couldn't get any help anywhere. Together she and Sylvia set up in St. Botolph's Church in 1963 a centre for any prisoner's family that wanted to come. They had expected people to come to the East End of London, but people don't when they're in the situation of not having any money and not knowing what to do. In fact Sylvia and the other woman parted company because Sylvia decided that a visiting service was what was needed. Sylvia Chancellor was a remarkable woman, she was gifted and a member of the aristocracy so she did have entrée to things which normal people don't have. And it was she who got the Prisoners' Wives Service going.

I appeared on the scene when my husband and I moved from Reigate in Surrey to Blackheath in London. I had tried various things while I was in Reigate: I had chaired the committee of an old people's home; I had been on the school board of my children's junior school; and I had tried various voluntary things, and none of them had given me satisfaction. I am absolutely certain that if you want to volunteer for something, you've got to enjoy what you are doing and feel a certain satisfaction.

So I felt this was a time to review things. I had made a friend of a woman who was a volunteer attached to a girls' Borstal in Reigate, and she talked about the work and I went with her to the Borstal several times and I was really interested. So when I got to London I got in touch with the Probation Service and asked if there was any voluntary work that I could do, and they said, well come on one of our courses, which I did. This was at a time when there were volunteers working for the Probation Service.

While I was on the course the Probation Service said to Sylvia Chancellor, 'We think we've got somebody who you would be interested in.' So she came and interviewed me in Blackheath. This was in 1966 and I was given my first family to visit.

I just turned up on the doorstep in Bethnal Green and said who I was. This woman's husband, aged 40, had been committed to Brixton for three months – all the early cases we had were very short sentences. She had an eighteen-month-old baby. She had a gas fire on hire purchase so I contacted the North Thames Gas Board by phone and they agreed to defer hire purchase payments on the receipt of a letter. She had a TV on hire and we agreed to pay six weeks with the remainder to wait for her husband's return.

We used to have awful trouble with the National Assistance Board. And what I used to do I remember was, instead of dealing with things myself I used to take the prisoner's wife to the National Assistance Board. I'd explain to her not to get angry, not to get fussed, not to get worried, but to be kind to the person on the other side of the counter, and say thank you and say how helpful they had been and to notice the different attention they would get using middle-class manipulation. It worked, they really did find that they got help much easier than when they threw the chairs about and shouted and made a commotion. Prisoners' wives were very badly dealt with; they were not seen as a one-parent family, they were seen as having a husband, and the husband was in prison but not supporting them. So they only got the minimum allowance, a very small allowance. We were always fighting with the National Assistance Board.

That was my first family, and I got hooked. I realised that here was somebody who had benefited to a certain extent by my being there, and that I had enjoyed meeting her and talking to her and seeing her family. So I was getting something out of it. In fact I reckoned I always got more out of Prisoners' Wives Service than I ever put into it. It was as simple as that.

The Probation Service had seconded a young probation officer, Carol Martin, to work part-time with the half a dozen volunteer visitors. She had a desk in the probation office where we would ring her, and leave a message for her to ring us. She also used to chase us up. When we had done a visit she would then come back to us to find out what had happened, and to give us any help that we needed. I think most of the time it concerned practical things. Carol advised us who to get hold of because we didn't know who to contact, what charities would help, where to get second-hand clothes and second-hand furniture, and that sort of thing.

The work was largely practical, to sort out the immediate problems. Some of the wives I went to visit didn't even know their husband was in prison. Quite a lot of them had no idea. They were waiting for their husband to come home that night and he didn't turn up, he hadn't told them that he was going to court because he was ashamed, he was hoping to get off. They were supposed to be informed by the police; the police would come and knock on the door or shout up at the window, 'Your old man's gone down the nick'. And it was really humiliating for them. In those early days we worked on this so that somebody would go and tell the wife quickly and confidentially.

Most of our referrals came direct from the Prison Welfare Officers. A man would come into prison and be distressed about what he had left at home, say his wife was waiting for him and she didn't know. The idea then was for us to get round there as quickly as possible to let her know what had happened but not to do more than just the practical things. Of course that was all that we were any good at, sorting out the immediate problems. We had no training of any proper kind.

Sylvia Chancellor wanted us to visit more wives and so she discouraged us from doing more than a one-off visit. Carol, rightly as a probation officer, wanted us to give each wife ongoing support. She admired Sylvia enormously but Carol had difficulty putting her point, and it was quite some time before we started to do ongoing visiting. Eventually we tried to go on for the whole term of the man's imprisonment unless the woman didn't want us any more. I actually see a woman still, I don't visit but she visits me. Her husband went down for about eighteen years, and her children are now grown up, very settled, she's got grandchildren.

I was looking this morning at my early notebooks, and there was one woman in October 1966 who was disabled with multiple sclerosis. She was in a small house in Brixton and she managed to drag herself up the stairs. Her husband was sent down and she had nobody to do her shopping for her or anything like that. I did in fact actually get a solicitor involved in her problem, and the man did get early release on welfare grounds to look after her. I felt that was a great achievement which gave me a great fillip. If one could do something like that one really felt that one had been helpful. And of course I could help her with shopping and visiting her husband in prison. That was another terrible difficulty as she had a wheelchair. We got him moved to a prison near her home, and we got her transport costs from the National Assistance Board which was very unusual at that time.

We campaigned for payment of fares. That was the first big national campaign we took up. We were of course based in London and dealing only with London families, but that was the first national issue that we took up, and I remember going with Sylvia to the Houses of Parliament to see an assistant to the Home Secretary. Wives got fares once a month to the prison but more and more men were being moved out – the London prisons were full of remand prisoners and short-term prisoners – and so the wives had longer and longer journeys. Suddenly in the late 1960s the prison governors started to grant second visits. We maintained that all visits should be paid for because it wasn't fair to expect the wife to pay for it out of her National Assistance money, and that the men got very agitated if their wives didn't visit, they thought that they were carrying on with somebody else. If they were going to give the visits, we said that they should give the wherewithal to pay for them. So we campaigned and now they do cover the cost of the visits including, I believe, the remand visits which are daily.

We never had men volunteering for us in the early days mainly because the husbands in prison would be so anxious about a man visiting their wife particularly in a voluntary capacity. They're suspicious enough anyhow so that wasn't viable really.

We decided that we couldn't cope with dealing with women prisoners whose husbands' needs were very very different from prisoners' wives. The family situation of women prisoners was much more catered for. The husbands of the women prisoners were at that time getting help from the proper people who were trying to see that the children were looked after and going to school and all the rest of it. But we did visit and give advice and help to gay partners when their partner was in prison. This was much later when gaydom was more accepted.

We tried to have staff meetings, usually in a room at the Probation Service headquarters. It was always very disappointing. I think a lot of voluntary organisations find that people who lead busy lives don't want to go out to evening meetings. Later when I was more involved, Carol Martin and I used to arrange groups of visitors in areas of London where we would meet in one person's house. We were very isolated working on our own. I still think volunteers should realise that they need support, that they can't do things well just on their own. We instigated training sessions where we'd have various people coming to talk: a prison officer, a prison governor, a magistrate, a social worker and obviously a probation officer. We also had somebody who dealt with depression which was the most difficult thing for a volunteer to deal with because you can get dragged into their depression rather than being able to help them out of it.

Between 1968 and 1970 I wasn't doing any visiting because my husband's work moved to Bristol and I came down with him. When I came back to London Sylvia, who was into her eighties by then, said, 'Look, you ought to come onto the committee as my heir-apparent, and you ought to take this over because I am too old. I can't go on with it any longer'. And I did so reluctantly because I had never liked committee work. I said well, I'm prepared to take on the administrative role, still and always as a volunteer, but I'm not prepared to take on fundraising which was a thing I hate. I must be in a hands-on situation. And so she kept on with the fundraising for quite a long time.

I remember when the Mountbatten report – *Report of the Enquiry into Prison Escapes and Security, HMSO 1966* – came out about the state of things in prison. Sylvia went to see Lord Mountbatten, and he put a long paragraph into his report about the fate of prisoners' families and what should be done but it was never implemented, it was just the security of the prisons that was looked at and dealt with. Sylvia knew so many people. It was much more difficult for me when I took over because I had no influence with anybody. I lacked a lot of self confidence because I could see how Sylvia could deal with things and I couldn't. She had a lot of people – probation officers, prison welfare officers, etcetera – who loved to be in contact with her and who she used to have round for cocktails at her Knightsbridge flat overlooking Hyde Park. And they thought she was wonderful. Good for her, she successfully manipulated them.

I was advised to go and talk to the women's groups of churches in London to recruit potential visitors, and I think I went to every one. I really made no impression on them at all and I came to the conclusion that people go to church for their own needs, not because they want to actually help other people, and that's fine but that's not where you find volunteers. Except the Seventh-Day Adventists who are immensely involved in helping people in their locality were very good. Methodists are good, but not very imaginative in the sense that they can't see why people can't manage, why they get into this terrible state of poverty. They used to collect toys for Christmas for our families, and I had to explain to them that we didn't want broken toys, teddy bears which had no limbs, that we didn't want our families to have things which were cast-offs from other people. We wanted good toys and not to denigrate the families because our families shouldn't be treated like that.

I think our disappointments were when we were working hard to get improvements and changes made and they were refused, mainly by Government. To a certain extent I found that the first two years of a Government in office were the times to get changes. After that they're looking forward to the next election, and prisoners and families do not come as a high priority because they're not very popular with the electorate. You shouldn't ever try and get changes made just before an election. I remember thinking we'd been successful in getting a place for families to wait at the Old Bailey where they could say goodbye and try to find out where their husbands were being taken. I don't know whether it's changed or not but they would be standing outside in the street, just a little group of unhappy people waiting for the court to finish sitting. It might go on until half-past five, sometimes six o'clock and then they were allowed to go and see their relations in the cells under the court. Well we didn't get a room for the families. Security I think was the excuse.

The Prisoners' Wives Service always remained a London organisation until I took on the administrative role. I thought there should be groups in other places, and various people had encouraged me to think this. I thought of PWS more as a city organisation than a rural one, because it was too difficult to organise properly in a rural area. I wrote to all the senior probation officers in every town, and I went to see any who were willing to see me. Without exception they were all enthusiastic but they wanted us to set up the organisation in their area. And I said, this really is not on, we haven't got the resources, we cannot do it. We can give support but what you need to do is to find one person who is prepared to take on the job of setting it up. We will then support this person, give them all the expertise that we have managed to gather but it must be someone in your own area because that person will know who to go to for funding, who to approach for help of all kinds. We don't know it from London, and we can't do it for you. In fact I had very few results. One or two probation officers did set up something of their own run by the Probation Office.

We never were run by the Probation Office, and that was the strength of PWS: we were independent. And this was purely because of the strength of the original committee which said these families are not criminals, and they are not the responsibility of the Probation Service. We want to be able to see them in confidence and not have to report back about things which they don't want told. The committee stuck out for independence and won.

The Probation Service's aim was to work with the men in prison so they sometimes criticised the PWS for being a divisive organisation. I had a senior probation officer in east London say to me once, 'You know you're all wrong. Here are two inadequate people who have struggled along together, and you are trying to make one person more adequate.' That made me shudder. And I think probation officers always hope that the man can go home and be welcomed by his wife, and although all will not be hunky-dory, it will be on the same uneven keel as it was before. Because finding accommodation for a man coming out of prison is a very difficult problem for the Probation Service.

You can't deny a woman developing on her own. I had a woman who lived on a terrible council estate in north London and she started a boys' club for teenagers. She was so creative. Whenever there was a street party she used to make costumes out of paper and things, not only for her children but for other children too. Then she got a job in a nursery school, and eventually took a training and worked as a teacher in a nursery school. No, you can't deny a woman developing on her own.

The name was changed in the 1990s to Prisoners' Families and Friends Service because it was never just wives; it was mothers, it was grandmothers, sometimes it was partners, it was friends.

My mother was the youngest of a family of ten, and her two eldest sisters brought her up. She was very uncontrolled and demonstrated her individuality – when she was eleven years old – by pawning a gold bracelet and going up to London and spending the day there. She was, as a mother, great fun. She was the first person to wear a divided skirt to bicycle round the village. She was always inventing things for us to do. My father was a clergyman and she was very unlike a clergyman's wife. She disapproved strongly of the Mothers' Union because they wouldn't let divorcees join so she set up groups of wives who were not the most respectable in the parish.

My mother always voted Labour, and I was brought up to think, to be a non-believer, that you queried everything, that you disliked snobbery. Certainly I've never voted Conservative. The only good thing I've said about the Conservatives is that if you wanted something done when they were in opposition you were more likely to get it done than if you asked the Labour people. The Labour people have too many other things which they are involved in so that on the whole prisons don't come very high. But if you can get a good, kind Conservative, you can wring their hearts with what happens to prisoners' families.

My father was a very quiet, very studious man. He was Scottish but we don't know when he was born. It was an Army family, all his brothers and his father were in the Army. He didn't go into the army because he had a deformed leg, probably from infantile paralysis when he was quite young. His mother was a Quaker and wanted him to go into the Church so he did. I never was quite sure whether it was a vocation for him or whether there was nothing else. My father went to Oxford and was the youngest student of his year, got a degree in history. He was a member of the Society of Antiquaries and he did a lot of research. For days on end he would go into a silence when he was living with someone he was researching into. My parents were very different.

My twin brother and I were born in 1919. For a lot of my growing up time we had two maiden ladies living in our house. The first one was my mother's sister who never married, and because she had no other home she came and lived with us as a pg, paying guest. Clergymen weren't paid very well at that time. The other one was a woman, Aunt Violet, who lived in the village where my mother and father were married. She was, well a typical old maid I suppose you would say. She was the sort who always wore her handbag on a long string round her neck, between her bosom. She was a Brown Owl in the parish. She was totally hopeless but terribly terribly kind, and terribly worthy, terribly churchy. When she left us she went to Tunbridge Wells because she fell in undying love, she must have been in her fifties, with the vicar of the parish there, and he allowed her to scrub the sacristy out. She even pursued him out to British Honduras, where he went as a missionary and she went after him but came back again. Poor Aunt Violet.

When I was four we moved to Worcestershire, where my father took on the parish of the Wych which is between Great Malvern and Little Malvern. There we had a governess who came to the house and who taught us – my older brother, us twins and a younger sister – plus some other children in the neighbourhood. Then she set up her own school which was a about a mile and a half away, and we used to walk to her school every day until we were eight. We then went to day school until we were thirteen and we all won scholarships to boarding schools. I went to a school called St. Cuthbert's just outside Bournemouth which then moved to Kent. I was a typical schoolgirl, pretty uninteresting. I did well academically. I became head girl eventually and I did enjoy it.

I was the least bright of us four children, I consider. After I finished school I went to St. Andrews University which I chose because my father being Scottish we always had our holidays in Scotland, and my headmistress was also Scottish. Because I was a scholarship child at St Cuthbert's I suppose that everybody assumed that I would go on for higher education. My sister and my brothers all went to universities and I suppose my parents expected it. I was going to get an arts degree but I hadn't done any significant Latin and I was useless at grammar, and that was a compulsory subject for an arts degree so I changed over to science which was much more in my line.

When I finished university, the war had come. I was twenty. I joined up in 1940, went into the WAAF, into Fighter Command where I became what was known as a plotter. You pushed things about on a table when the aeroplanes were coming in from Germany to bomb Britain. When I went into the WAAF I was very left-wing, and refused to have a commission but then after I had been working in Fighter Command for some time they offered me a commission in meteorology, and I said, no thank you. So I was offered a commission in Intelligence and I was sent to Bletchley Park, Station X, which was the most boring place I've ever been. There's a terrific amount of guff written about it now but it was extremely lonely. It was interesting while you were working but otherwise you were alone because you were all billeted out – there was no accommodation for people at Station X – so you were on your own in the evenings. We worked a shift system. I was coding and deciphering, dealing mostly with the information being sent out to the various generals and to Winston Churchill. In fact members of the section I was in were sent with Churchill when he went to Russia and elsewhere because he always had to know what was going on. It was then about 1944, I was there when the end of the war came, 1945.

I met Owen at a 21st birthday party in Nottingham when I was a plotter, but I didn't marry him until 1944. And when I was pregnant in 1946 I came out of the Women's Auxiliary Air Force. For the first three years our home was a prefab in Lutterworth where Owen was working with Frank Whittle on the first jet engines. We had this little box of a home. They were all new, beautiful and provided by the Council. It cost us 12s 6d a week, I think, in rent and rates. The thing I most remember about our home was the terrible condensation. The prefabs were built of aluminium so if you had tins of any kind they went rusty, and you couldn't bear to put your hand on the outside wall of the house in hot weather, because it got so hot. We had to make a garden, and we were the only people who had a lawn. Everybody else grew vegetables; we had a few vegetables but we insisted on having a flower garden. We were the only people who had a car, we were the only people who had a telephone, we were one of the few people who had a refrigerator. It always made me feel very ashamed. We got this house because we both got points for the number of years that we had been in the forces. And our points added up to more than other people's so we were very lucky.

I had my first child in Lutterworth in a little cottage hospital. I had two children with fifteen months between them. We decided we'd have two and that we'd get them over with quickly and there weren't nappies for too long. When the children were one and two years old we moved down to Reigate because Owen was offered a job in the research and development organisation at Redhill Aerodrome.

I never was very adventuresome. Except for the army I have never, I am ashamed to say, worked for money. I was committed to the children really through to their adolescence. At that stage I did various voluntary things until Owen got a job with Esso in east London. We moved to Blackheath because he could get there through the Blackwall Tunnel. We bought a very nice Georgian house on the heath which was practically derelict. Remember the old Brooks advertisements in the newspapers for houses? This one said, 'Innocent of modernisation since 1794'. And we rushed to see it and it was really beautiful, but in the most awful state.

This would have been about 1963. I was forty-four. And that was when I started to get involved with the Prisoners' Wives Service. That was my life. I think it took over pretty well 24 hours a day.

Can you stand on it?

Gwyneth Maysey
Consumer Advice Centres

I shall never forget – we still use the term in our house now, 'Can you stand on it?' – a fairly elderly lady came into the centre wanting to buy a new gas cooker. I went through all the functions and features and timers, and she said, 'That's all very well dear, but can you stand on it?' And I looked at her, and I said, 'I really don't know; why would you want to stand on it?' And she said, 'Well, my kitchen clock is above the cooker, and for the last twenty-five years I have been standing on the cooker to wind the clock.' So I had to go away and find out what the cooker was made of and whether it was actually steel. We did have some bizarre questions.

YOU KNOW IT'S over thirty years ago. A lot has happened in between. It was my first job, my first proper job. I hope I can remember. I'd left university in the summer of 1969, and I did a couple of vac jobs, and then I decided the time had come to get myself a proper job. My degree was in music, I didn't want to teach that, and I couldn't think really what else I wanted to do. I said to my father, 'I want to work with people and I want to earn at least £1,000 a year.' And he laughed and said, 'Who's going to pay you that?' I enrolled with a graduate agency, and told them much the same, and about four or five days later they phoned me and said, 'There's this job come up with the Consumers' Association, the *Which?* people, and you seem to have the right kind of background, would you like to go for an interview?' So I went for the interview and they offered me the job. I didn't really know what was involved because I think the Consumers' Association, CA, was still working it out for themselves at that stage. It was their second pilot consumer advice centre; they had already done one pilot in East Croydon in 1968.

What CA was trying to do was to look at a way of reaching people of the socio-economic group which I think it's probably fair to say were not *Which?* readers, with a view to giving them pre-shopping advice. That was the original intention. Meanwhile the Citizens Advice Bureaux had been dealing with consumers' complaints since the beginning of the war, i.e. problems when something had gone wrong with the purchase. We moved more into complaints later on. People probably thought, well if they helped with advice beforehand, perhaps they can help me afterwards.

I was employed by CA to work in the shop premises they had leased for use as a consumer advice centre. It was in Kentish Town in the London borough of Camden. There were four of us working there, all in our twenties. We were given training in how to interview and a lot of background knowledge on products, and a little bit of training in kitchen planning as well. At the same time we were trying to stock the centre with various items which we begged and borrowed from retailers and manufacturers. We had a shop window which was quite radical for an advice centre in those days. We used to put consumer items in the shop window and place questions next to them to catch people's eye as they were walking past in order to get them into the centre. We had stands with vacuum cleaners on, and we would switch them on so that people could actually try the relative suction power of an upright versus a cylinder. So it was very hands-on in that sense.

In 1969 we just opened the doors rather than having a big formal opening because the idea of a consumer advice centre was still very experimental. I think CA had taken out the lease for six months only, it certainly wasn't regarded as a permanent event. We got quite a lot of coverage from local papers like the Ham & High. And people started to come in.

There wasn't a huge amount of admin. We did have to fill out interview sheets and questionnaires about enquirers. It was a very reactive service: the minute anybody walked through the door – whatever you were doing – you stopped and you went to see to them. Which seems to be quite a novel idea now! We were also trying to work out which information retrieval system to use. We had a thing called Kalamazoo, did you ever hear of Kalamazoo? Like the original computer, a sort of juggle-box where each card had cut-out pieces on it to represent a different feature, and you put pins that looked like knitting needles through this box, and the cards which had the cut-outs in the right place got held by the pin, and you took them out. It was a pretty primitive form of sorting and retrieving which of the 130 cookers or whatever on the market met the different criteria of each consumer. It seems unbelievable to think that it was only thirty years ago. Besides the *Which?* reports on the performance of different makes of product, we also had huge books with pages and pages of various products on the market. They were mainly the sort of white goods that people would spend quite a lot of money on, second only to buying a property or a car. For a lot of the people whom we were trying to reach of course it would have been one of their biggest outlays, because they probably wouldn't have owned a car, and were in rented accommodation. So the idea of actually spending quite a lot of their disposable income on a washing-machine or a cooker or a fridge meant a big outlay, and really we were trying to help them to make a more informed choice. That was the intention behind the centre.

We had big reference books like Benn's Hardware for people who were trying to find stockists of something or a spare part for something. In addition to brief enquiries about where to buy things, we also did an awful lot of interviews with people who wanted advice on the best buys for a specific product. And then you would actually go and sit down with them in one of the interview cubicles and you could be there for a good hour, no trouble. You did the interview using checklists for each of the products, a kind of aide memoire listing points we needed to cover on each item. The checklist also helped us to make a note of what the interviewee wanted as we went through. So initially we would try and go through the whole checklist say, for a washing machine, and talk to them about the kind of washing that they did, the number of children they had, type of job the husband had, whether they were at home all day to do the wash, whether they needed to do it when they came in from work. We would discuss with them the constraints of a limited space. It was amazing the number of people who wouldn't have thought about, for instance, buying a top-loading washing-machine which had to be put under a work surface. So it was very much to do with lifestyle and not just to do with the product itself. You would then write up your report at the end of the interview and what your recommendations had been.

We worked Tuesday to Saturday in those days. Our weekend was Sunday and Monday, because we thought it was actually quite important to be open on a Saturday when people weren't at work, but likely to be going out to spend large amounts of money. We worked until six o'clock on Saturday evenings, and I don't ever remember begrudging it. So, yes there was a buzz. What I was trying to do was dissociate it from the buzz I got actually just from working in my first job, and I mean I was wholeheartedly into it, definitely, loved it, loved it. I used to wake up in the morning facing a new day, I mean it was just great, lovely. But you do get older and more cynical, I'm afraid, about work.

We certainly knew we were being innovative. There was a buzz around it. We did have a lot of fun because we got a lot of attention from the media, the national and consumer press as well as the local press. Also I got interviewed for consumer type programmes, or for consumer slots in other programmes.

As a pilot project we were supposed to shut at the end of three or six months but there was a campaign to keep the place open, and eventually we were there for about two and a half years. The campaign was started by a few of the people who had actually used the centre and didn't want to see it go. People wrote to the local paper and said it's really valuable and we ought to hang on to it, and, it did become a cause célèbre locally. Eventually the Consumers' Association decided to bow to local pressure, and they kept it open, taking a longer-term view that this was the prototype. It was the only one in the UK, and that was all very well for people who lived in Camden but not much good for anybody else. CA started a process of trying to persuade local authorities around the country to set up similar advice centres in their own vicinity. So we did have an enormous number of VIP visits; chairmen of various local authority committees and chief officers and others came to find out what we did. And of course the CA Council members would call in, unannounced and unrecognised! I remember the first time that happened – we didn't get caught twice – we actually cut out pictures of all of the CA Council members and stuck them behind the loo doors! But we came a cropper when the Chairman of the CA Council at the time, who happened to be female, called in at the centre. She asked to use our facilities before leaving, and we couldn't really say no, but she came out grinning, and she just thought it was very funny.

I would have to say that there were more callers in socio-economic groups A, B and C1 than we wanted. I mean we were forever trying to find a different pitch to reach people for whom, had they made a shopping mistake, it would have been a worse disaster because of the amount of money involved. I remember dealing with one guy who definitely was a C to D, quite a wide boy, and he wanted to know about freezers, about big chest freezers, and when I started digging about the quantity and the type of produce that he was going to keep in there, it became patently obvious that it was not going to be one-pound packs of peas. He was talking about half-sides of beef and lamb and when pressed on the regularity with which he and his wife would be stocking up the freezer, it also became fairly obvious that it rather depended whether the lorry off the back of which they fell had come by that week. We also had people mainly from Hampstead who had heard about the service and almost camped out. They would walk in and say, 'We're having a new kitchen fitted and we want to buy these things,' and an interview even on one item could take nearly an hour. We all got terribly used to drinking our coffee cold.

Mainly women came in but there were substantial numbers of men as well. Lots of the men came in with their wives, and I think that that may be a reflection again of a different kind of era where the man was much more the breadwinner and therefore wanted to see where the money was going.

We had our regulars. There was a tramp who lived in Kentish Town, and partly because we were quite nice to him and it was warm, he used to come in quite frequently and we had to develop systems for dealing with him. If you were on the desk and you got caught with laddie, then somebody else would give it five minutes and then go to the back of the centre and ring you and you would say, 'Oh I'm ever so sorry, I've got to go and do an interview now,' and he would shuffle out.

If people were passing the door they might put their head in and say, 'Oh, thank you, I did actually go and buy the ... but I couldn't get it at that price, so I had to pay...' And people would write in and say, 'I didn't actually like the one that we finally settled on when I saw it, but I knew enough about it by then to choose what I wanted, and I'm delighted.' I mean it's probably one of the most enjoyable jobs I've ever done, just actually trying to help people, and having them write afterwards.

Consumer advice was very political in the sense that the local authorities which the Consumers' Association were managing to interest in this concept were almost exclusively Labour-controlled. Labour authorities like Greater Manchester Council and West Midlands, and some of the Scottish authorities, and Lambeth and

Hackney and Haringey in London took up consumer advice with enthusiasm. By the end of two and a half years CA had actually persuaded enough local authorities to set up consumer advice centres themselves, so they decided that that was it. By then they had persuaded Camden to run the Kentish Town centre themselves. So, we as CA-employed staff actually moved out but it didn't shut as a consumer advice centre.

We were the practical face of the theory. And I was definitely committed. I became converted to the idea that there was information around and that people actually needed help to find it, because it would help them to make a more informed choice than had been possible beforehand. And consumerism really has permeated the rest of my career, considering it was something that I got into accidentally.

Both my parents came from Cardiganshire in West Wales. My father came from a big family and there frankly wasn't enough work and enough money to keep all the children at home, so my father opted to come to London, and worked with an uncle of his who had a dairy business in Kensal Rise. My mother came up when she was about eighteen. She went to friends of the family who had a chemist shop just on the edge of the West End somewhere, and she worked there and lived in because you wouldn't have let an eighteen-year-old girl come to London and live on her own then. Although they went to different chapels, my parents met at or around Lyons Corner House at Marble Arch where the London Welsh youth used to go after chapel on a Sunday night. And they were married within about six or seven months of meeting each other.

I was born in a nursing home in Highgate in September 1947 which I understand was quite a posh thing to have done at that time. My parents were married at the beginning of the war, in October 1939, partly because they thought that my father might be called up. In the event he was rejected on medical grounds because he had a bad heart. So he stayed in London through the whole of the war, did firewatching, and he and my mother ran a grocery and dairy business, which is what all Welshmen did when they came up from Wales. I understood from my mother much later – because they're Welsh Presbyterian so one didn't talk about all sorts of things at home – that they had wanted children right from when they got married but they'd been married eight years before I came along. My father was over the moon and I think partly because of that, and the fact that they were comfortably off – I mean they worked very hard but they weren't short of money – nothing was good enough for my mother. So I was born and bred in London. My mother had some fertility treatment in order to have my brother two and a half years later which must have been very early on in the development of fertility treatment. There's only two of us, Gwyneth Margaret Jones is my full name and my brother is Brynmor Llewelyn Jones. Both my parents were Welsh-speaking at home, so my brother and I grew up having learnt Welsh.

My father used to get up at about half-past three in the morning and he used to do milk rounds, did four of those before breakfast. My mother opened the shop at half-past seven in the morning to catch people on their way to work because we were directly opposite the tube station, and they shut the shop at seven o'clock at night. And when they shut the shop they would start cleaning down all the surfaces. I remember as a child helping my father to bag up rice and sugar into pound bags, and watching him bone bacon at half-past eight, nine o'clock at night, huge sacks of it, hand-boning it. I remember counting the hours they each did in a good week, a 93-hour week. It was hard work. They had Thursday afternoons off when the shop was shut, and they opened just two hours on a Sunday morning, and then Sunday afternoon we used to go off to Sunday School and Sunday evening we went to Welsh chapel in London. It was quite a strict upbringing.

We used to spend the summer with the family that was still down in Wales. My parents took us down so we would be there for the whole of the summer holidays. It was great for city kids. As a result, we probably knew quite a lot of our relatives better than many children do because we spent such a long time with them.

I went to a state school which was just around the corner from home, a five minutes' walk, until I was eleven, and during that time I had started to play the piano, and shown quite a lot of aptitude. I got a scholarship to the Guildhall to be taught there on Saturdays but I never actually took it up, because my parents sent me to boarding school at eleven. I've discovered since from Mum that it was partially to do with the music and partially to do with the fact that they recognised that I was growing up and that they were tied to the shop all the hours that God gave, and I think they were a bit worried about the extent to which they were going to be able to keep an eye on me. So I was sent to a boarding school in Ashford which I was quite happy about. It was called then the Welsh Girls' School but subsequently became St. David's. Strong Welsh connections, quite a small school, second tier public school, but with a very strong music tradition which was one of the reasons I went there. I was away at boarding school until just before I was eighteen. I was a bit of a rebel at school.

I had been pursuing my piano with singing as a second subject, and I had passed my final exam grades by the time I was fourteen, and as far as I was concerned, piano was going to be it. My parents wanted me to go to university to read English because they thought that a degree would be a lot more use to me than a music qualification but I wanted to go to the Royal Academy. I have to say retrospectively they were absolutely right. We effected the good old-fashioned British compromise, and so I ended up going to Reading University because it was one of the very few at that time that actually offered a practical music course for a BA Hons. So something like five-eighths of my finals marks were actually for performance. That was how we got round that one. I ended up with what they wanted, which was a BA Hons. Mus., and I ended up doing what I wanted to do, making music rather than writing about it all the time.

By my second year in the university I recognised that I wasn't good enough to pursue a career in music. When I came out I thought, well what do I do with it? And of course, you didn't get very much careers advice in those days – well it didn't exist – and the best advice you would get was to teach. And I thought, no I actually love music too much to go into a secondary school in London where it would be treated as a Friday afternoon lesson. And also I have to be honest and say, when I came out of university I did want something else, I wanted a break. I couldn't even listen to a pop song without analysing the chord sequences automatically. So I went and worked for an American entrepreneur called Sam who was about as wide as he was high, and smoked big fat cigars, and he sold everything from cosmetics to swimming pools. I arrived there in Kew and I didn't have any shorthand, and I didn't know how to operate a switchboard. At the beginning I was scribbling like mad, and then I suddenly thought, hang on, this is letter number two. And it was either you owe us money or we owe you money and we can't pay it, or where are the goods. So I just used to take down the name and address and write 1, 2 or 3 in the middle of the page, and go away and write what I thought was a perfectly respectable business letter, and put it in front of Sam to sign. After a couple of days, he said, 'This ain't what I dictated.' And I said, 'No, because I don't take shorthand.' He said, 'Oh, this is great, this is real English.' So we got on fine after that, but after six weeks I thought this is going to drive me mad, I can't do this forever. I enrolled at the graduate agency, and then got the offer of the job at the Consumers' Association.

This was the 1960s but when you have come out of university and you're twenty, twenty-one, you don't actually register that the Swinging Sixties are happening. I do remember going to Biba's, and wearing very, very short skirts and white boots and having asymmetrical hair and all the rest of it, but actually when you read what other people were up to in the Sixties you think, I wasn't there, that wasn't me.

I had met my husband-to-be through the London Welsh, just before I'd gone to university, and we married soon after I got my degree. But then in 1976 I left him, we didn't have any children. I just walked out one morning. I thought, no, I'm living a lie. We've got absolutely nothing in common apart from the fact that we're Welsh. After the Kentish Town Consumer Advice Centre I was invited to go back to CA and design the first training course for the first teams of consumer advisers around the country. From there I went to the Research and Development unit in Lambeth, which was a very small and select group that really serviced the various borough departments, and particularly the head of Trading Standards. When my boss got promoted I was offered the job of head of Research and Development, but I made no secret of the fact that the job that I actually wanted to do in Lambeth was managing their consumer advice centres. They had three shop-front centres, one in Lambeth Walk, one in Brixton and one in Streatham, and they also had a mobile unit that used to travel around the borough. I remember being away on holiday, I got back and the head of Trading Standards phoned me at home and he said, 'Right, as of next Monday you are the principal for the Consumer Advice Centres. And if asked, you went through a very long and gruelling interview to get it.' And so I ran Lambeth Consumer Advice Centres for about four years. Terrific job. Horribly pressurised, but great. We were dealing with something like 150,000 presenting problems per annum. As the years went on each one of those problems actually involved more and more time to resolve it. The average number of times we had to see a person about their problem when we started was something like 2.4 times per problem presented and by the time we had finished it was about 5.7, 5.8 times. By then pre-shopping advice had become a very small part of the work. Most of it was complaints in spades, about everything and anything – building works, second-hand cars, shoes, etcetera. We got an agreement from the Council that they would not be immune from complaints about Council services and us trying to get things done. It was an incredibly busy time and I put all my energy and time into working, although I did marry again at that time. And it was a terrific team of people. We had such a lot of fun, and worked really hard. I was in Lambeth between 1976 and 1984. At the same time I and a few others started up the Institute of Consumer Advisers so I was one of the founder members of that.

After Lambeth I went to the Electricity Consumers' Council which was a policy-making body representing the consumer to the industry. I was there from 1984 to about 1989 part-time because my elder daughter was born in 1985. I had just about got back to working full-time when I found I was pregnant with Anna, and she was born at the beginning of 1989. I had a nearly-four-year-old and a brand new baby, and I decided that as I had to work full-time, I would need to work somewhere closer than the Electricity Consumer Council which was in Tottenham Court Road. So I looked around, and I was very lucky in that Lewisham, which is the borough that we live in, were looking for a service development manager in the Building Works Division. I was in the post six weeks when the job of head of building works came up. After eighteen months of acting up I was appointed General Manager of Lewisham's Building Works Division. That was a super job, and it was only eight minutes down the road. Even though I was still working long hours, it did mean that while the children were small I could just disappear to watch a school concert or attend parents' day, and then go back to work again. It was ideal from that point of view. This was between 1989 and 1994. Then I became a victim of redundancy. Unfortunately because of the pressures of compulsory competitive tendering which had been introduced into local authorities, it became pretty obvious that it's exceedingly difficult to run what is effectively a cut-throat commercial operation within a socially responsible environment. I'll just give you a very simple example. As a Council we employed our own workmen, which meant that if there wasn't much work coming through we still paid them a guaranteed sum. The people we were competing against did not. If they had a job on, they'd go down to the local pub and they would recruit people, and the minute the job was finished they would leave them back down the pub. So we were actually up against the sort of black market end of contracting. The Council decided that the way to try and retain all of the services in-house was to amalgamate our direct labour organisation with the highways and refuse organisation. I was out of work for about five or six months I think. And then got the job that I currently have, with the Office of the Rail Regulator.

My husband who I married in 1982 shed me in 1994. I was left with a five-year-old and a nine-year-old. And an imperative to work full-time. So, a very difficult period. I didn't want him to go. It was a huge shock. It was standard stuff, you know, a new model, trade-in. He does his best by the children, he's bought somewhere only about two or three miles away, and has them every other weekend.

It's a very strange sensation, spending a whole evening talking about yourself. Because one doesn't do it very often.

You've made the mud churn

Muriel Hackett
Newcastle Consumer Group

I'm not good on dates. I tell you, I forget, you do at eighty-five you know.
Our consumer group got set up in the early 1960s. I saw an advertisement
in the local evening paper saying the Consumers' Association were
calling a meeting in Newcastle. I went and it was well attended. They
sent excellent speakers up from London who talked about how consumers
had very few rights at the time. How could you protest about shoddy
goods or poor services? The Consumers' Association wanted grass roots
groups to set up – to take up local issues as the Consumers' Association
was taking up issues nationally. Out of that meeting several local people
called another meeting and I went to that as well. I suppose at that point
we were the people who were buying into the idea.

I WASN'T ON the committee of the Newcastle group at first, I was
on the periphery. Then the committee wanted help sorting out their
questionnaires on local consumer issues and so I offered to help.
And after that I was in. I did an awful lot of work following up the
returned questionnaires and getting the answers, a lot of collating.
We had some very difficult times. We were completely amateur, we
made the most awful mistakes. Well we didn't understand the
technique of questionnaire design for surveys. We had none of us
done it before so we asked the sort of questions that got voluminous
answers which we didn't want. And then of course we were afraid to
say the wrong thing in print, and everything got rather watered-
down for that reason. Gradually – when I say gradually, I mean it
was over months rather than weeks – one or two semi-professionals
joined us, and they very quickly refined the questions we sent out.

We discussed the goods and services that we felt needed
investigation. One of the most shocking surveys we did was on
cleanliness in hairdressers, and one woman latched on to it like a
leech, she sent us pages and pages and pages which we couldn't
possibly publish. And then we lost that member because she was so

upset that all this work she had put in had not come to anything. That was where we went wrong you see. You have to pose the question with very careful wording which I was fairly used to with setting examination papers in my job. But it wasn't sufficient. We had to learn, and we learned the hard way.

Another questionnaire was on shrinkage in curtain materials, and I did that entirely alone. We soon learned that you've really got to tackle a small field, haven't you, to begin with. We got information from over seventy or so members about their experience with curtains. And shrinkage in curtain material at that particular time was very bad. You see curtains were only just getting back into production after the war and there weren't yet any synthetic materials. Curtains could shrink up to eight inches you know, it's hardly believable. But this was the sort of thing that prompted us to say, well things ought to be getting better now. As a result of our survey, we wrote to the curtain department of local department stores, and finally Hedley's, the soap works who are now Proctor & Gamble, sent their home economist who was very receptive and we became quite involved with her.

We did lots of other surveys, don't ask me what all of them were now. I threw every one of those consumer magazines into the skip when I moved here, you just cannot keep everything.

After the first few meetings, the committee met in the university common room. That was central for the Metro and the bus, and there was parking in the evenings. There would be about six or seven committee members. So I got to know people, a different set of people. And we had a little party at Christmas but we were not a social gathering, we were a more serious gathering. We met mostly once a month in the evening because most of us were working people. There was an awful lot of discussing and chewing over of questions. What we failed to do at the very beginning was to get focused, I can see it now but you couldn't see it then, and we waffled round the point. Well once John Beskerby arrived – he was an academic at the University of Newcastle – he sorted our points out for us; and there was no question about it, he did his homework, and things tightened up and became more interesting altogether really. Gradually members changed in that they all became more professional in their approach, and we learned to get more focused. For example, when we did children's shoes, were we going to stick to sizing or quality, or two or three features?

We published the results of our surveys in our little magazine which was then just typewritten sheets. It was all very very amateur. And then we became a little more professional with our hand-outs, our magazines. And somewhere along the line the Consumers' Association offered us facilities in a room in London, and there began to be a bit of toing and froing. Then the National Federation of Consumer Groups started up in 1963. It started in Birmingham because the secretary, Janet Upwood, lived there. She began to do a little bit of coordinating between the groups. By the way we were the third. First there was Brighton and Oxford, that's right.

I was asked to do four minutes on the local radio about the work of the group, which I did and then of course realised where you go wrong in the way you put the thing over. I mean I put our work over beautifully, but the radio wanted more chattiness! We also talked to women's and other groups. We got known and we were free; I think we asked for expenses. We addressed all sorts of meetings, and, you know, the old men in the audience would be sitting on the front row nice and warm and comfortable, and were all asleep! We never had big meetings like Women's Institutes did. But we did have one big meeting with the local Chamber of Trade. They were not at all sure what we were about generally. We were absolutely scared stiff. Dorothy Craig, who by the way is now one of the higher ups in the National Federation of Consumer Groups and I went, and I said, 'I'll take the history part, I'm on firm ground there, and you take the working part.' So I went in and I said to the man behind the screen, 'This is another lamb to the slaughter you know. We've offered ourselves up on a plate.' They were very nice to us but they were very suspicious, and it took us a long time to convince them that we weren't a society against the retail trade, that we were a society which was trying to improve circumstances to their advantage as well as to the customers'. That's the only large meeting that I remember addressing.

A lot of people had a grouch about consumer matters and they brought it to our group meetings and to public meetings, and nothing was going to stop them from telling the whole story. And we had to say very firmly at the beginning – and it wasn't easy – we cannot deal with individual complaints but we can tell you how to go about it in the correct way. And this was generally what happened. But you couldn't stop them once they had started, and the whole meeting was bored stiff of course. You had to tell people that you first complained to the shop which sold the goods to you, not to the manufacturer. Basic facts, very basic, like that. The Small Claims Court procedure came later on. People found it hard to go about a complaint properly. And by the time you had educated one lot, you had got to start on the next lot. That was a big part of the work.

We teamed up with the Consumers' Association to get consumerism into schools. I was in a strong position because I had home economics students in my classes at teacher training college, and they could spread the word a bit. It didn't work at first, and I could see why, because the teachers had no idea of what consumerism was at all. But one lecturer in the college who wasn't a member of the consumer group did help on the nutrition side. On one occasion at Christmas we got children in one school counting the number of peanuts that you got in a packet in order to work out how much the peanuts actually cost. You got fifty-six in this one, and twenty-seven in another, etcetera. These were ten-year-olds, they were not sophisticated but we got a lovely survey out of that.

Then there was the socks survey which we did at a convent home for children. The idea was to test the effect of wear and tear on children's socks. We bought six pairs of socks and asked six children to rotate these socks which had to be washed every night over a two-week period. We did a similar survey on T-shirts with six little boys, all roughly the same size. And of course, when the surveys were completed, the socks and the T-shirts would have changed from this size to that size as a result of the nightly washing. I made the arrangements but my students did the actual surveys, and then they wrote up their own results. And we published photographs in one of our magazines. So we did get into schools and we did get requests from teachers, but it didn't really catch on.

We also took stalls at exhibitions, and put up displays in the public libraries. So we did work hard.

I think my interest just grew. Apart from my teaching work and a bit of social life, I did nothing but work for the consumers' group. My work with the group came and went. It was a bit tidal. I would say I put in less than half a day a week say, three hours in the evening or two in the afternoon, plus a lot of phone-calling.

The group was changing all the time because people retired and people died. And then as new people came in, new ideas came in. The odd enthusiasts. But otherwise it was a hard core. Probably we had about ninety members, I think we never quite got up to the hundred. What I liked the best was organising, but I'm not one to stick my neck out. If I agreed with an idea I would take it up, but the idea probably didn't come from me.

I went to the national conferences if I had friends nearby, kill two birds. I wouldn't have said the national conferences were fun but they were very interesting, and we met people we had only heard about. We were amateurs of the lowest order.

A question that's been asked a lot of course in the last six or so years is – is there a role for consumer groups today? There are still issues that need tackling but I mean quite a lot has been done, things like shrinkage in curtain materials. Alongside the Consumers' Association we fought hard for food labelling, for information on cans, fireproofing of night-dresses, and that sort of thing. We acted as a movement altogether. When a son of a friend of mine joined the Office of Fair Trading the first job he got was to go and look at all the women's nighties in the shops to see if they had an inflammability warning. So that was one good result of our work.

There's much less impetus in the consumer group now. And our group is certainly held together by a smaller dedicated few than it was. They're probably down to about six stalwarts now. I wouldn't know how many members in all as I've moved from Newcastle down here to Kent.

Asking me these questions you've made the mud churn. It hasn't been churned for some time.

My date of birth is 16th March 1913. I'm so used to saying it to doctors. My name then was Jones. I was born in Liverpool where my father was in charge of a bonded warehouse and we lived in a village called Eastham in the Wirral.

On my father's side of the family, I come from a line of cattle feed merchants in Liverpool, and on my mother's side four generations of tailors, which we knew nothing about until my niece and I started to probe. My mother was a tailoress. Her father had died when she was fourteen and she was the eldest of four. There were not the social security benefits of course that there are now, so her mother started up a little grocer's shop in her front parlour. She got my mother apprenticed at fourteen to a dressmaker.

In 1916 when I was three my father, with money from a well-off aunt, gave up his job and started up as a grocer in a little village in the Wirral. Father always said he was a grocery and provision merchant, a provision merchant was on a higher level than the grocer. And my mother, well she would be occupied with her family. You didn't have domestic help in those days, and it was a biggish house. Very convenient I realise now. Father used to go to town on the ferry, and this village was where the Liverpool ferry came in, it's not there now. The house and the bottom floor at the front had been made into the shop, and one end of that had been made into the Post Office. And we actually lived at the back of the shop, and above it there were two huge attics, lovely play rooms they were. There were two of us, my brother was four years older. It was a very happy childhood.

Everybody came to the Post Office and I met everybody. Apparently I was a chatty child. Our village was small, it had the parish church and we joined in everything. We always went out as a family. On Sunday we went for a walk with my father in his bowler hat, and my brother's dog Heidi, and me dressed up in my best, horribly dressed. There's a photograph just in the hall which you can look at on the way out of me when I was three, dressed in that heavy gros grain. There was no nylon then of course, it was silk. That photo is actually one of my first memories – and my father away at the war you see, and my mother very thin.

My mother and father had taken a great dislike to the school master and his sister who ran the village school in a very heavy-handed way, so they refused to let me go to school. Another of my early memories is my mother having great arguments with the School Board man because I didn't go to school till I was seven when the bus came to the village. Then I could go from door to door to the convent school; I'm not a Catholic by the way. It was very, very poor. I mean the nuns were awfully nice and we were taught good manners, but I didn't know which number you took from the other. I only went to the convent for a short time because it was obviously not good, so I was then sent to the big council school and there were sixty in the class. And yet that teacher took the trouble to come and sit beside me and show me how to do subtraction.

At eleven I won a scholarship and went to West Kirby. I loved it, absolutely loved it, I was there six years. Oh it was everything a school should be, a girl's school of course, an academic school. I joined in everything. I left home on my bicycle shortly before eight and got the eight o'clock train to West Kirby. The train would pick girls up all along the local line, and then we walked in twos, very precisely, to school. It just fitted me. I made good friends, friends that I still have today.

After school most of my friends went to Liverpool University, but I don't know why, I seemed to have a conscience that I ought to start earning, so I went to college in Peterborough which was only a two-year training. It was a general course but I took history and needlework mainly.

After college, it was in the bad times you know, 1931, and getting a job was a major goal. I was one of the lucky ones. I got a job immediately in Birmingham. But some of my colleagues applied for twenty, thirty jobs before they got one. I was teaching in one of these huge redbrick schools in a very bad part of Birmingham. They were large classes, and I was very lost. I remember feeling terribly little. But I was lucky again, very lucky, because through the recommendations of my junior school head teacher I got a job at the local school in Port Sunlight and went back to live at home, so I was made. Port Sunlight is a lovely village. It was Lord Leverhulme's paternalistic set-up. Most of the children lived in the village, therefore there was no trouble over poverty so the children came to the school from stable backgrounds and did very well.

After six years at the school I married a Tyneside man. That's how I came to live in Newcastle. I met him in 1933 on holiday after I left college, we corresponded, and then it sort of developed. We married in 1940 which was a year after the war began, and life was a rather uncertain business. He was an accountant. He was very keen on the Royal Naval Voluntary Reserve and became an officer early on. Then I left off teaching, well you had to in those days you see. If you were married you were out, there was no question of that. And we had an ordinary little semi, they were tremendously cheap because Newcastle was a dangerous area. And eventually he was sent to Sunderland at the harbour, and then he went to London to the Admiralty as a paymaster.

We lived in Notting Hill Gate in Pembridge Gardens in a one-room service flat. I got to know the middle of London quite well. I used to walk from Notting Hill Gate through Kensington Gardens, Green Park, down to the Admiralty to meet my husband for lunch. But that didn't last very long because of course you had to register and within days I was conscripted to teach. Teachers were conscripted at that time.

The school which was in Parsons Green was most amusing because these children had been evacuated during the phoney war when there was very little bombing. Nothing happened, so they all came back, and everything was disorganised. I got the class of, I suppose they would be eleven or twelve-year-olds who had all been fished off the streets. There had been a bit of bombing and our school, one of these huge redbrick efforts, had been bombed, and they were opening one classroom at a time. As soon as they got enough children for another class they got the workmen in to repair the next classroom. I remember so distinctly, I went in with one of the workmen after he had unlocked the door and every book in every cupboard had slid out onto the floor. And then the women came in and cleaned up and the next lot of children were sorted out and put in. But they were delightful, those children. I enjoyed them very much. And you taught on what bits of paper you could find in the cupboards. I was there only a matter of six or seven months.

And then my husband was called up. He was given a ship, and we came home to Newcastle. As soon as I got home I had to register for work again, and I was then sent to a boys' school but only just round the corner, I could cycle to it. At that time you went where you were sent, literally. My husband was sent to a ship in the north of Scotland, and eventually he was in the Navy. We were married in 1940 and he was killed in 1942. They were torpedoed. His ship had been out to Cape Town, heaven knows why, and his sister lived in Cape Town. So we got news through the family, which you wouldn't have got from the ship as it would have been censored. I was at home in Newcastle of course and I stayed home, and I went on teaching. Well there was nothing else you could do, they wouldn't let you stop.

I had to make a new life really. I went back to be with my mother who was ill but I still had to keep myself. I still had to teach, so I travelled back and forth to Newcastle. I was at the boys' school six years or so. After mother had gone into a home it began to dawn on me that this was no use, that it wasn't what I wanted in my life. I saw an advertisement where you could add another year to your two-year training and make your course into a three-year course, which wasn't quite a degree course but it was still accepted by the universities. I was only teaching part-time, and part-time even with a pension didn't leave much money over. This was the point at which I felt I wanted to do this one for me. And that's when I went to college, Radbrooke College in Shrewsbury where I got a certificate in Home Economics. I had let my house in Newcastle in the meantime, furnished, to two colleagues, because I had to earn some money as I didn't get paid while I was doing this course.

And again I was lucky, very lucky, because at the end of the course I got a job. A friend of mine at Radbrooke College wanted to work in the country, and she got a job at Denman College outside Reading, and then for some reason which I've quite forgotten she wasn't able to take it up and she said to me, 'Well why don't you have a go?' The subject was Rural Domestic Economy and the idea was to teach women the skills to be a country housewife. I worked with a most delightful woman called Miss Doris Cumming who made quite a name for herself in being one of the first women to be boss in the dairy and in cheese-making. You know, women had lowly positions whereas she was one of the first to get a higher position, and she ran this place. Oh it was fascinating, I loved it. You met so many different types of people. Nothing was normal. You did your work in the evening and you were off in the daytime. We used to drive in the moonlight to all the kitchens of the big houses where the Women's Institutes had their meetings. And then we used to have groups of women come into the centre for the day and they enjoyed themselves. There were modern kitchens and we had goats and we had hens, and we did all the things that a country housewife in the normal way would have done.

I dealt with the goats, you'd never believe it but I did. And we used to have some amusing times. Our pair of goats had two kids and one was a billy. Have you dealt with a billy-goat? It gaggles. You know they have slit eyes, goats, and the eyes close up. We had to dispose of these two goats because we only needed two goats, not four goats. One of them, the billy, was sold to a rural school as their goat, the school goat. And the nanny was sold to some other people in the same area, and we had to deliver them, so we removed the seat from the back of the car and tied the goats to the front seats, and my colleague drove and I sat beside her, this wretched billy who was behind me spent the whole of the time licking my neck. And Doris said, 'Don't stop him, he's quiet.'

I didn't want to leave. But on the other hand I wanted to go home. Some friends of mine in Newcastle had seen a job advertised at the Girls' Public Day School Trust in Newcastle, and I went there part-time. I was there six years, and enjoyed it very much.

After that I trained teachers for twenty years at Northern Counties Teacher Training College and I loved it. It was a very famous college, established around 1890. It was mainly cookery, needlework, household management as well as hotel catering. I specialised in needlework. But then the college changed to general education and we began to take men. I wasn't enjoying what I was doing any more, and there was jockeying for position in the college. Before, we had always worked together. Even the cleaners valued themselves as a part of the college, and then you see the men came in, male students, and male lecturers, and it became very different. The standard of the Home Economics course was very high, but the standard of the general course was very very much below ours. So I retired about a year before I was sixty. Since then time has absolutely flown by.

I've only been here in Kent a matter of months, to be near my nieces. I drove down here from Newcastle with Brindle my dog, but I took three days over it. I've built that conservatory since I moved here; it is nice, I'm very pleased with it. In the summer I can potter without the wind if you know what I mean.

There is always an intolerant minority

Allan Horsfall
Campaign for Homosexual Equality (CHE)

There was an imperative fear around safety and security and therefore, if you wanted to keep safe, you had anonymous sex. If you got caught for doing something naughty in a public lavatory or a back street, it was a matter for the magistrates court, a fine of £5 or £20 or £25. Curiously the law seemed to view public gay sex as less serious than gay sex in private!

The way that a lot of people came into conflict with the law before 1967, was when one person fell foul of the police who would raid his house, find his address book, his diaries, go through his correspondence. They might find forty names, and then they would go from house to house saying, 'We've got a confession from Jones, we've got a confession from Smith; no good you remaining silent, we know all about you,' which was all untrue of course, but that's the way they used to break men down. So you got into trouble for having your name in other people's address book or if you wrote a letter or told people where you worked, you were a hostage to fortune.

If the police got a whole group of people from an address book, it was regarded as a ring. Then they decided who was the ringleader, and he was the one who invariably went to jail for the longest time in order to set an example. There was a big witch-hunt in Bolton as late as 1963, six years after Wolfenden was published, and the age range there was from eighteen up to about fifty-four. The police picked as ring-leader a 24-year-old lad just because he knew most of the others, and he went to jail for eighteen months. This was with no involvement with toilets or public soliciting, it was entirely private consensual, no threes and fours, all couples. One of the men committed suicide, one was struck off by the General Nursing Council and a lot of the others lost their jobs, and that's the way it used to go. I suppose the biggest case was in Altrincham. That was in about 1936 which involved twenty-nine men, and it gave

Altrincham a name which it kept for years and years as Britain's capital
of sodomy. All the jokes in the pubs for years afterwards were along the
lines of if you drop half a crown in Altrincham, for God's sake don't try
to pick it up.

CHE, THE CAMPAIGN for Homosexual Equality, started under the
name of the North-Western Homosexual Law Reform Committee
because the work that was being done by the Homosexual Law
Reform Society was seen as purely London based, driven by the
Hampstead set. It became clear to me that homosexual law reform
wasn't making any progress in the provinces. The trendsetters may
well have been in London, but the blokes overwhelmingly were not
in London.

The North-Western Homosexual Law Reform Committee was set
up in 1964 in order to progress in the provinces the
recommendations of Wolfenden whose terms of reference were
concerned with prostitution and male homosexuality. The
Committee happened to be located in Manchester; it wouldn't have
mattered if it had been Bristol or Newcastle, it just had to be
somewhere away from London so that people could see that we
could push homosexual law reform forward in the provinces without
the sky falling in.

I had no intention of setting up the North-Western Committee. I
had been pressing Anthony Grey, secretary of the Homosexual Law
Reform Society in London, for a long time to set up local groups in
order to put pressure on their local MPs. But the Committee was
dreadfully frightened of anybody putting a step wrong. I think
Anthony Grey was the first gay secretary they had, and they were
very apprehensive about appointing him. His qualifications for
doing the job were not in doubt, but the dangers of employing a gay
man was something that frightened them badly. In the end they
decided they would appoint him although he did the job under an
assumed name, his real name was Edgar Wright. In the Society's
view the work had to be done by do-gooders rather than the victims
of the law. When the Wolfenden Report came out, the *Daily Express*
ran a leading article the morning afterwards saying to the
Government, 'Don't listen to the pleas of perverts.' And I think the
Homosexual Law Reform Society felt that if their work was seen as
the pleas of 'perverts', it would harm the cause. Although, pre-1967
the North-Western Homosexual Law Reform Committee didn't

advertise itself as gay, we certainly never denied it. In fact, although I had to talk to the press and write to the press, deal with reporters, I was never asked until long after the law had been changed whether I was gay.

A lot of the fear in Parliament came from the miners' MPs. I was working for the National Coal Board at that time, and living in a house that belonged to the Coal Board in the middle of Atherton, a mining village on the south Lancashire coal field. The North-Western Homosexual Law Reform Committee used to meet in the boardroom of the Manchester Diocesan Board for Social Responsibility. The chairman of the Board, Ted Wickham who was the Bishop of Middleton, said that if we used his boardroom as our address he would be in serious trouble with the right wing of his Church. And I thought it would not be a good thing to use a box number. In the end I got our Committeee notepaper printed with my address, which was a Coal Board house, and we launched our first leaflet, 10,000 copies, and sent it around to social workers, gay groups, a mailing list from the Board of Social Responsibility, and to the press of course. The local press sent along their cub reporter and I thought, they're doing this to wind him up, poor lad. But anyway I talked to him, and they ran a front-page feature with a banner headline over eight columns. And I thought, well all hell is going to break loose now. Not a murmur. No letters opposing it, no hostility from neighbours, not much at work. I thought, well this really can't be as controversial as people are trying to make out. So we put more leaflets out, inviting people to sign that they would support us. And one of the first to come back was from Alan Fitch – not gay – who was MP for Wigan and who was sponsored by the National Union of Mineworkers. And I thought, well this is a catch, this is just what we want. We made Alan Fitch Vice-President right away so we had a voice in the House of Commons. At one point Denis Skinner, MP for Bolsolver, wrote in the *New Statesman*, 'Well yes, reform might be very admirable, but no way will it go down in my constituency with the miners.' So I wrote to the *New Statesman* and said, 'Well I'm publishing from the middle of a mining village, and I find it all right, I don't know what Skinner's on about.' So it was clear that opposition to reform wasn't due to homophobia, it was fear of losing votes. We were never a large organisation, but because MPs could see we were working in the provinces and that it was going down all right, I think it gave them confidence.

The North-Western Homosexual Law Reform Committee continued until the law was changed in 1967, ten years after the Wolfenden Report. For all we knew, once Wolfenden was implemented we would disband. But we quickly realised that there were other things to do. Wolfenden had been watered down by what I call wrecking amendments, amendments that make an Act entirely unworkable. The two main objects of the Wolfenden committee were to get the police out of peoples' bedrooms; and to ensure that people who had consenting adult relationships were not subject to blackmail. But what the wrecking amendment to the 1967 Sexual Offences Act did – contrary to Wolfenden – was to say that it shall remain an offence if more than two people take part or are present, and that it will be an offence under all circumstances to have any sex in a public lavatory. Well, I am not necessarily in favour of public lavatories, but public lavatories had become institutionalised by an oppressed part of the population before the law was changed. I argued in a letter to the *Guardian* in the early Sixties that if the Wolfenden Report was implemented then lavatory sex would disappear, but I was wrong. Although the legal repression had gone, the social repression remained.

The North-Western Homosexual Law Reform Committee was re-named first of all the Committee for Homosexual Equality, and then we decided that Committee didn't sound sharp enough, so we changed it to Campaign. The objects of CHE were to remove the restrictive clauses in the 1967 Sexual Offences Act which had departed from Wolfenden; to set up some sort of social organisation for gays who were isolated; and to provide support for gays who continued to get into trouble.

We tried to set up a social organisation by establishing a separate company that belonged to CHE called Esquire Clubs Limited. That sounded about right without using 'gay' or 'homosexual'. We talked to breweries about funding but they wouldn't touch it at that time, they wanted full collateral which we couldn't find. We talked to chief constables to see what attitude they would take, and by and large they were pretty good. They said that they wouldn't stand in the way if we kept in touch with them. We almost got there in Burnley, we had lined up a lease on old assembly rooms in the centre of the town, and it was within days of being signed. We had enough money, and willing hands to do it up ourselves and make it work but some one leaked it to BBC Radio Blackburn. Then about two days before we were due to sign the lease all hell broke loose. The church were after us, even the local doctors formed a committee to oppose it. We held a public meeting to try to explain our plans in Burnley Public Library in the town centre, and it was packed, priests getting up and bringing down hell fire on us, councillors, everyone. Ray Gosling took the chair. The police were so fearful of violence that they made teddy boys take their boots off outside and leave them on the lawn, so there was a line of boots on the lawn with lads going into the meeting in bare feet. Michael Steed who was once President of the Liberal Party said it was the greatest meeting he'd ever been to. But we got disheartened about trying to set up the Esquire Clubs which we wound up, and CHE remained as a campaigning group.

The blocking of the Esquire Clubs enterprise meant that the development of gay clubs was left to commercial interests who were only interested in areas of dense population and who were prepared to proceed – and, initially, to operate – clandestinely. We have consequently seen the emergence of a gay club scene which is city-based, expensive, late-night oriented and with a strong emphasis on youth and fitness. The consequence of that is that the old, the poor and the unattractive are excluded as also, if they live outside the cities, are those without private transport. I suspect that these make up the majority of men who seek partners in public lavatories. I also have little doubt that the people who worked so hard to prevent the formation of gay clubs in the small towns are also the ones who are forever fulminating against gay cottaging!

CHE also set up Friend which was for gay people who needed to be supported or advised or counselled. Friend eventually became an organisation in its own right. It did a lot of good work.

I was secretary of CHE until we got sufficiently financially secure to employ a secretary with a small staff. Then I became Chairman. Membership was 5000 at its peak. CHE's office moved from Manchester to London, and that's when I ceased to be Chairman and became President. The structure was the central office and local groups, and that went on until well into the Eighties. At first the whole national membership was allowed to form itself into local groups, but after a time people were allowed to join the local group without subscribing to the central office. This weakened central office financially of course. Nowadays, the local groups seem to have either gone their own way or disappeared.

CHE got to its peak about the time of the Sheffield conference in the mid-Seventies, but then it began to lose its sharp edge as a campaigning group. However, it was and is still consulted a great deal by the media. And of course things change. A couple of lads went to America which resulted in the formation of the Gay Liberation Front (GLF) here, and people began to look upon CHE as being too formal, too structured, too much bureaucracy.

We didn't have any formal relationship with the Gay and Lesbian Switchboard, nor with any other groups. There's always been this dichotomy, not about ends but about means. It exists today, the difference between Stonewall and Outrage! Stonewall is a parliamentary lobbying organisation, and Outrage! is an organisation which waves placards and climbs into the pulpit during the Archbishop of Canterbury's sermon. And each thinks the other is doing the wrong thing. Outrage! thinks Stonewall's too slow, and Stonewall thinks Outrage! is too provocative.

I don't think the national or local press ever dealt with CHE editorially. There were letters and news reports, but never any editorial comment. For example, we had the big Bolton Seven trial a little while ago, and it all happened because a video was thrown into the laps of the police by somebody with a grudge. The video had been made on separate occasions in separate houses; at no point had the seven men been having sex as a group. The video was mostly of two people having sex, but there was the cameraman which makes more than two people present so that makes the whole thing illegal. They prosecuted them all. I picked it up in the early stages from the local press, and I wrote a letter to the *Guardian* complaining about it before it came to trial, and because of that people like Peter Tatchell of Outrage! and Mark Watson of Stonewall got involved. Then Roger Bolton Productions had the foresight to send a camera crew up before the beginning of the trial without having had a commission for it. This was made into an hour-long documentary called Sex Guys and Videotape which went out on Channel 4. The *Bolton Evening News* ignored it completely. I mean, an hour's programme about that fairly small town on any other subject would have had a page about it. When somebody from Bolton was on the TV programme, Changing Rooms, they put it all in the paper, but they get an hour-long documentary about a trial in the town which has become a cause célèbre, no post-transmission comment at all. That absolutely demonstrates the silent hostility. However, we've had letters in the paper all the time: about Section 28 – that badly drafted piece of legislation in the Local Government Act 1988 which forbids the 'promotion' of homosexuality by local authorities – and the age of consent and that sort of thing. The whole battle is in the letters page.

Society as a whole has become more tolerant. But there is always an intolerant minority which can make life very difficult for you.

I was born in 1927 in a pub in a little village called Laneshaw Bridge on the Lancashire-Yorkshire border. My parents were licensees there but they split up when I was about six months old, and my mother went back to live with her parents in Nelson, the next town along. My mother died of breast cancer when I was six, so I was brought up by my grandparents. I never met my father. He was pointed out to me once in the street in Blackpool. I was walking with a great-uncle who said, 'That's your father you just passed.' I turned round to see him disappear into the distance, and that's the only sight I ever had of him.

My grandmother died in 1942 and my grandfather died two years later so I was left with a guardian, the woman who had been my grandfather's housekeeper after my grandmother died.

Nobody wants to lose their parents, but not having parents was an advantage in that I didn't have a family to embarrass. It gave me freedom to do political things that might have embarrassed a family. That isn't anything I would have desired, but it's a fact.

I don't think I've ever had any doubt about my homosexuality. I did once have a little friendship with a girl which might have got close. It never involved any sex. But my grandfather disapproved of it because she came from a family that was quite rough and ready. And they worried about me – as they used to quaintly say – getting a girl into trouble, they always worried about that. And I found, when I was in my teens, I could take a boy home to sleep, and that was fine, but if you were going out with a girl, there was this worry you see. So I thought, well, let's go the easy way, although it was the way that suited me anyhow. I don't think I had any guilt about it, I didn't think about the law. I didn't have sex with a lot of boys but all the boys that I did have sex with now lead normal married lives, consider themselves to be straight. Most are quite friendly.

I went to Nelson Secondary School which became Nelson Grammar School, and finished there in 1943. I didn't stay on for

School Certificate, not very studious so I got a job. There was a feeling in wartime that you didn't know where you were going; you knew that you'd probably end up in the Forces, you didn't know when or how the war would end, you couldn't visualise a world at peace. I tended not to put a great deal into thoughts about a future career. I worked for about a year for a firm of chartered accountants, and then I got a job with the Ministry of Food, an administrative job connected with emergency food storage. We used to take over factories and fill them with tea and sugar and flour and stuff like that, back-up emergency food supplies.

I was called up in the RAF in 1945 when I was eighteen, served three years based mainly in Germany, came back, struck up a relationship with a man who I met in the RAF Association, and set up house with him in Nelson. I got a job with a paint manufacturing company in Burnley for about three or four years, and then I got the job with the Coal Board in Burnley, where I stayed until they moved the office over to Tyldesley in South Lancashire.

When I was working for the Coal Board in Burnley, I was a Labour councillor in Nelson. I attempted to raise the matter of homosexual law reform in the Labour Party locally to get it going as an internal Labour Party policy issue, hopefully to get it raised at the Labour Party conference. This was 1960 or 1961 following Wolfenden. And I was blocked at every level in the Labour Party. I was quite furious and frustrated because I thought it was due to homophobia, and certainly a bit of it was but I think most of it was fear, they were afraid to be seen to be pushing reform forward but they didn't want to be seen to turn it down. My anger disappeared when I could see that it was fear more than anything that was stopping them. I drifted away from active participation in the Labour Party mainly because I became increasingly involved in gay politics. I mean it was more exciting than the Labour Party. Labour Party meetings are rather dull you know. And it was exciting, you felt that you were getting somewhere.

The first letter I had published demanding homosexual law reform was in 1958, I suppose, but the first letter in the *Guardian* was 1960. It created some anxiety for my partner because he was teaching, and as I was using our joint address it appeared in the papers. The anxiety was not so much that it might bring us to the attention of the police, although that was always a thought, but that it might damage him professionally. After a while I got a little house in Burnley, and although we continued as a partnership, it gave me a separate address so that I could do what I liked without imperilling his career. Then, when I got moved by the Coal Board to Tyldesley I was living at some distance from him, but when he retired he came over to live near to where I live now in Bolton. It was hard for my partner in the beginning when everything was illegal. But when he retired he lost his vulnerability and he became part of the movement. He even became Chairman of CHE for a while.

Since I left the paint firm I've always been in public authorities: Coal Board, Electricity Board, Salford Education Office. And I stayed at Salford until they offered me an early retirement when I was 53, with ten years added increments for a pension. So I thought, well if I work till I'm sixty-five I shall only have gained a year, it's just not worth it, I'll take it, and if I get hard up I can get a part-time job. But I didn't.

I've been retired nearly twenty years. Retired people used to say to me, 'I don't know how I ever found time for work.' I now know what they meant.

Birth control for the unmarried

John McEwan
Brook Advisory Service

When I was a medical student at Cambridge I became interested in progressive education and went to visit AS Neill at Summerhill in Suffolk. I then went to London for my clinical training and Neill said, 'You've got to go and see John Hewetson', a GP in Southwark. John was a member of that group which JB Priestley described in a broadcast as 'the gentle anarchists'. They emerged from loyalties in the Spanish Civil War and became objectors to the war against Germany, 1939 to 1945. John had been in prison a couple of times for sedition, to do with selling Freedom. He got established as a NHS GP in Southwark Bridge Road in 1950 and I first met him there in the October.

We became very close friends. One of the great planks of his clinical platform was birth control. That was very much part of the anarchist philosophy, giving people personal freedom from unwanted fertility, particularly important for women. Eventually, in 1957 I got a practice in Walworth so John and I straddled the Elephant; his surgery on one side and mine on the other in the Walworth Road.

FROM THE VERY first I saw, as John Hewetson did, patients who came in for contraceptive advice, usually after the main surgery was over. They came as 'private patients' but if they ever did pay a fee it was something minimal. And of course we provided birth control for our NHS list patients which was frowned on in those days as we were not supposed to do it. You could supply contraceptives on NHS prescription if you could find a medical reason for it. There always is a medical reason: it's good for health. So there I was following John Hewetson, offering birth control in my general practice which was unusual in the Fifties. And then in 1962 John, already on the executive committee of the North Kensington Family Planning Clinic, introduced me to what was in those days the Walworth Women's Welfare Centre in East Street, an independent charitable foundation whose president was the Duke of Wellington. I became a committee member so was involved in the management rather than the professional side of it. These old-established clinics were affiliated to the Family Planning Association (FPA).

In 1962 most of the thoughtful members of the FPA were eager to provide birth control for unmarried women. Among these was Helen Brook, then director of the Islington Family Planning Clinic. The FPA required a majority vote of their whole National Council to make that change in the FPA's rules. The respectable people from the mainly English shires wouldn't have anything to do with allowing unmarried women in their clinics. They consistently voted this position down, three times at national level.

The first thing that Helen Brook did was to invite unmarried women to come to her Marie Stopes Clinic in Whitfield Street on a certain evening of the week. This soon became three evenings; they just flocked in and the word went round like wildfire. These were mostly students or workers in shops and offices. On the whole they were not well off but from reasonably financed families, mainly middle class. There was still a great lack of provision for working-class people.

The data now show that the age of first intercourse was going down in those days, but the trend began in the Fifties not the Sixties. In the Sixties there was an increase in sexual intercourse in the single mid-teens age group. The effect of this was a rise in unwanted pregnancy. But don't say the Sixties was the beginning of the sexual revolution because it wasn't. That was what Margaret Thatcher said. She liked to think that it was all decadence and the fault of Labour governments and left-wing socialists. But in fact the change in sexual behaviour had started earlier on.

It was soon thought by the Marie Stopes management committee that Helen Brook's clinic sessions for the unmarried were overwhelming their clinic. So with a bit of help from Walworth Women's Welfare Centre Helen found premises next door to the Walworth Clinic, in Dawes Street. I was able to persuade an architect friend to design the interior and take charge of refurbishing the house. Helen had received a donation from John Trusted, a banking colleague of her husband, Robin Brook. John Trusted insisted on anonymity at the time, and he also specified that the organisation should be called 'Brook' centres, a name which could be easily remembered by young people. Helen did not want the clinics to be called after her. She didn't think 'Brook' was her name anyway, it was her husband's name. But she had to; it was a condition of Trusted's gift, which got the whole organisation started. The clinic opened its doors in 1964. It was subsequently opened officially by Lord Brain, later to be President of the Royal College of Physicians, who became first president of Brook Advisory Centres. After a while Helen opened another Brook Advisory Centre in Tottenham Court Road.

There were many in the family planning movement wanting such clinics. So family planners from some of the big cities – Birmingham, Edinburgh, Bristol – saw their opportunity to follow Helen's lead. Pioneers need a framework and Helen supplied this. Soon Brook became represented over a broad national base. Each urban centre, though, remained fiercely independent and so the national organisation had to be a loose type of federation, not easily held together during the first ten to fifteen years.

I've never worked as a clinic doctor in a Brook Clinic, but I have visited many as an observer and adviser. The process varies from branch to branch but counselling has always been on offer. This marks the Brook clinics out particularly from NHS clinics. Sadly, the NHS cannot afford counsellors, but Brook always insists on an allowance for counselling in the grant.

There was a very interesting controversy in the mid-Sixties soon after Brook began. A leading doctor felt that all young unmarried women seeking birth control should spend an hour with a counselling doctor at the first visit. There was a great row and eventually after the adjudication of the President, Helen's practical approach was upheld. The principle was maintained of counselling being available to clients on most occasions if needed, but by no means compulsory. And there were indeed many young people with social problems of all kinds, not just about sex and fertility.

The other distinguishing feature of Brook is the guarantee of confidentiality. Later on Brook was to be the leading agency in a consortium initiated by Alison Hadley, then second-in-command of national Brook. The consortium included the British Medical Association, the Royal College of GPs, FPA and others, in order to declare to the public that any young person had a right to a confidential consultation, and this right should always be respected. This poses difficulties for some professionals where there is sexual abuse of a youngster. Many professionals feel they must disclose without consent, but in Brook clinics staff spend time working with the client and wait for consent before disclosure. If you don't do this young people will just stop coming to the clinics, the abuse goes on in secret and the youngster has nowhere to find help. Brook provides a haven for the young abused person and can help to avoid unwanted pregnancy.

In my own practice I don't think I ever had a time when I felt the need to disclose abusive relationships. In fact I was more often than not impressed with the emotional quality of teenage relationships. Maybe things are different now with drugs and all-night discos and the rest of it. Certainly we have more sexually transmitted infections, but in my heyday of the Sixties I thought the relationships of the young were impressive for their loyalty, steadfastness and intensity. It seemed to be about love in those days; it's rather gone out of the window hasn't it nowadays.

In the mid 1960s I was one of the few doctors around working with the intrauterine device (IUD). I took on some evening sessions in the out-patients department at King's, normally unused at that time of day, for the International Planned Parenthood Federation. I started with one evening a week, soon to become two. My partners fortunately agreed that I could do that. IPPF member doctors were trained and in turn started to train others so the IPPF wanted to pull out. Therefore we had to have a charitable company to run the King's set-up. I went to Helen and to Caroline Woodroffe, then General Secretary. They were pleased to extend their management to King's and so we became a branch of Brook. St Bartholomew's Hospital through their Chairman, Robin Brook, also started a Brook clinic.

I had a seat on the Brook national Board from 1971. In 1984 I was elected Vice-Chairman. Two years later our Chairman, Pauline Crabbe, had to resign for health reasons and I became Chairman in her place, later confirmed at each AGM until 1995. Far too long, but in that time Brook expanded a great deal, a giddy pace of expansion and has now seventeen Centres. Eventually we produced a new constitution which limited the Chairman to two periods of three years.

One of the things I had learnt at King's was that it was extremely difficult if not impossible for the 'official' NHS to run a service like Brook. Brook is like a family. You go there and get a warm welcome; you've got a specially selected person behind the desk and they will be extremely nice to you. There will be coffee and easy chairs. The NHS doesn't run like that. There are plastic chairs or wooden benches, and you might get a receptionist and doctors quite unsuitable for youth work. And then there's what to call it. 'Youth Advisory Clinic' is as near as officialdom gets to an empathetic title whereas: 'Me and me mate's going down to Brook tonight.' It's a brilliant name; Trusted was quite right.

In addition to Brook and the FPA there were PAS (Pregnancy Advisory Service) and BPAS (British Pregnancy Advisory Service). BPAS is a very good set-up and they do sterilisations and vasectomies as well as abortions. Marie Stopes now works similarly. These were the charities which undertook abortion work. Brook never carried out abortions. To do so would have weakened our support within the birth control movement, and opened up our young people's birth control services even more to attack by those who disapprove of abortions.

The main problems for younger teenagers have arisen through court battles about providing services. The results have been confusing for everybody. The Law Lords eventually came up with some conditions for doctors to provide contraceptives to people under sixteen without their parent's knowledge or permission, the so-called Fraser criteria. Very briefly these are that the under sixteen should be able to understand what is happening; that persuasion to inform parents has failed; that the young person will have sex anyway; that without contraceptives their health will suffer; that giving the advice and prescription is in the young person's best interests. This judgement was liberating for doctors, but was difficult to disseminate to the potential users. For a long time young teenagers thought that if they went to a clinic for contraception their parents would be told. Possibly their boy friend might be arrested, and this was a feasible outcome in the UK.

Helen Brook was a great fan of Marie Stopes. One of the chief planks in Marie Stopes' platform was about married love, about sexuality and having good sex especially for women. Helen knew as did Marie Stopes that a key point in this was to relieve the fear of unwanted pregnancy. Helen took the doctrine further. In a more liberated age she did her best to provide birth control for the unmarried, a point that Marie Stopes was very cautious about.

The battle for Brook now is more about getting young people to use the services. It's a much harder battle than getting the services set up in the first place.

I was born on 5 February 1929 in Hove. My father was in the radio business, selling radio receivers wholesale. I have one brother two and a half years older. My father had a rough time in the First World War, having been in the Argyll and Sutherland Highlanders and taking the brunt of the trenches. I think he contracted TB in the trenches, because he was treated for that at the end of the War and for a few years after. He never talked to us about his wartime experiences; I don't think they ever do. He lost his elder brother, also in a Highland Regiment and that was very sad as they had been close. So in a sense he was a bit of a casualty all his life.

My mother qualified as a doctor at the Royal Free Hospital in about 1923 but she didn't practise because she was getting married. So it wasn't until 1940 that she started practising medicine for the first time. And she loved it of course. But the work took its toll on her and she developed high blood pressure and died of a heart attack in 1956.

We had a comfortable life. Sometimes we had a house of our own and sometimes we lived in a comfortable flat. My parents afforded private education for both of us and I went to Sherborne School on a scholarship in 1942 until 1947. I had a successful school career and got a scholarship at Trinity Hall, Cambridge. Extraordinary to be free to live as you wish, more or less, quite a shock to the system, because in a Public School every moment is taken up in some way or another. You have no leisure time really, unless you're cycling out into the country on a Sunday afternoon or something like that. I had a very serious accident at home in December 1947. I crashed into a lamppost on my bike, stupidly carrying a squash racket and it got caught in the steering. I broke my jaw and the base of the skull, and was in hospital for three weeks in Brighton. I think I went back to Cambridge halfway through the Lent term. So that was quite a difficulty. But I managed all right. Got a 2:1 in the Natural Sciences Tripos part 1 in two years, then did a Part 2 in Physiology with Pharmacology which was absolutely marvellous. I enjoyed it so much I thought I might not do medicine but become a physiologist. I think material wisdom shone through, as usual. And particularly I was very impressed by my mother and interested in the things she had to talk about. So I went up to the London Hospital.

Then I did a year to get my registration, house jobs at the London, and then I went into the RAF as a medical officer. I said I wanted to go to Hong Kong so they sent me to the Canal Zone in Egypt! Then there was trouble in Egypt and we were posted to Cyprus, but my time was up. So I managed to escape the RAF in 1956 just before the Suez invasion attempt, a nasty bit of imperialism.

I had to make a career decision then about whether to go into hospital medicine or into general practice. General practice was incredibly primitive in those days. I don't know if you can imagine it. But a GP in a poor district would have a cracked lino floor in the surgery, probably quite a small room, perhaps with a little gas fire, and just about room for a couch, although many GPs didn't have couches because they never examined their patients. And you had this great wodge of records, several thousand records which you hoped had been filed in alphabetical order, but almost inevitably they got lost or mixed up. There were no appointments for patients then and so it was quite lucky if you got the patient's notes when he or she was coming in. If you got the notes at least you knew what medicine to give them, because that's the thing you always wrote down.

I decided that I was going to talk to John Hewetson. He had an extraordinary rapport with patients and he didn't treat them the way other doctors treated their patients, he treated them as friends and they responded accordingly. He also was the visiting Medical Officer at Camberwell Reception Centre for men which used to be known as the Spike. It was written about by George Orwell and others. Eight hundred beds and they just clocked in in the late afternoon and clocked out in the morning. John used to run the medical side which he built up from a very poor service. A lot of the problems of the homeless people in those days were medical: TB, epilepsy, mental illness. And we saw the most amazing diseases. We saw a man with beri-beri which is a vitamin deficiency, and leprosy I remember. It was real textbook stuff that we weren't seeing any more in everyday practice. John did a lot of good work there and I helped him a bit. But he didn't have the resources to give me a partnership so I had to go and help him on some evenings, and work for other doctors on other days, so it was a bit of a confused time.

Eventually I was appointed in 1957 to a practice which nobody else wanted, partly because there were no premises. The widow of the previous doctor was staying on so the premises weren't available for a successor. My first wife and I walked up and down the Walworth Road until we found an empty house. It belonged to the Southwark Labour Party which didn't want it so we rented it. That house later became the national Labour Party HQ. My two children were both born there.

I was very keen on maternity work and I used to have a National Childbirth Trust teacher in the practice once a week. I think there were one or two others who did this but not many. And not in working-class districts on the whole. It was OK, I was glad I did it, but the natural childbirth approach seemed to put an unbearable burden of guilt on people for whom it didn't work very well. I think it's wonderful that husbands are present during labour now and that was just beginning in those days. It was a very good way of knitting the family together.

John Hewetson and I at last ended up with premises together in 1970 at the Elephant and Castle in the GLC-built complex. It's still there, it's still going strong. I was in practice thirty-two years, although I eventually did family planning at King's part-time. It was a very full life but a very interesting one.

I resigned from my general practice at the end of 1989, as I was just trying to do too many things at once. King's offered me nine sessions a week as Consultant in the Department of Obstetrics and Gynaecology so I decided to take it. And I think I made the wrong decision; I should have left King's then because the Thatcher reforms came in, in a big way. The chief executive of King's tried to get rid of my department to save money, which seemed to me a gross mistake as by this time the department was attracting attention, doing good work.

I ended up by having a stroke and luckily it wasn't a big one. I had very good rehabilitation treatment with my physiotherapist daughter's help and got better. I spent the time when I was unable to go to work revising the method of regulating training for family planning doctors and ended up with a more viable scheme with 5-yearly re-certification. We formed a new faculty of the Royal College of Obstetricians and Gynaecologists. Did you know there was a Faculty of Family Planning? Well that's much better than the old way. Doctors can go into family planning now and yes they can end up as consultants. There are now over seventy Consultants. So that's been a success.

Since I retired at sixty-three, I have done quite a lot of medico-legal work because there are failed vasectomies, perforating coils, injections given at the wrong time. And I quite enjoy that. I kept my hand in doing locums for the local family planning department until January 2000; then I thought I should give up while the going was reasonably good.

It was years before we could use the word 'abortion'

Helene Grahame
Pregnancy Advisory Service

At the beginning we were only allowed to advertise pregnancy advice, never abortion. And then the text of every ad – which we were only allowed to place in the small ads sections of publications – had to be scrutinised by the Department of Health and the Code of Advertising Practice. Many of the magazines had an Irish circulation, and if they had accepted an advertisement which offered help with unwanted pregnancy they were stopped at Customs and couldn't be distributed. The same applied to Spain. So the magazines wouldn't take our ads any more. It took us quite a long time to realise that we were still only seeing women who were sent by doctors. Most women didn't want to go to their doctors, we had to reach them directly. And I suddenly thought, where are you forced to look at something? Waiting on a tube platform, or sitting looking at the cards that are overhead inside a tube carriage!

I started nagging London Transport, 'Will you accept this wording?' 'Would you accept that wording?' At that time, and possibly still for all I know, every other sentence in printed material circulated by services providing abortion advice had to say, 'Subject to two doctors' certification' and 'Providing you have legal grounds under the Abortion Act of 1967'. So, it was totally user-unfriendly. One of the things that all these restrictions enabled me to do on behalf of the Pregnancy Advisory Service was to get a lot of press coverage in feature articles and on radio and television. I must have said in countless interviews that we wished we were able to advertise openly so we could reach the women who most needed our help. Advertising agencies had seen or heard what I had said, and two or three agencies got in touch with me and offered help. One in Camden Town, unlike the others, didn't take me out for a plush lunch, they just came to learn about the restrictions and talk it through, and come up with some ideas. They were miles off the mark originally because they didn't understand how there could possibly be such absurd restrictions, but in the end they came up with the slogan we used for years, 'If you're happy being pregnant, fine; if not, phone...' That message seemed to us as clear as we were going to be allowed to get away with. But it took over two years to launch because London Transport still wouldn't accept it. In the end I had a brainwave. The Chairman of London Transport was Kenneth Robinson, who had been a Labour MP and a Minister of Health, and had been one of the sponsors of an early pro-choice Bill. I wrote to him protesting, saying how long this had been going on for and then I told the London Transport advertising department what I was doing, and within a week they agreed to our poster. But there were endless conditions: it had to be a black poster with white writing on it so that it couldn't be defaced; we would not be allowed to select our own sites even if we paid premium rates; and if there was a public riot the posters would have to be taken down at our expense and we would have to pay for the remaining time we had booked. We grabbed at the chance. There was no riot, and only three people ever complained. But I found the posters were displayed on disused bits of the linking tunnels or right at the very end of the platform where almost nobody waited. We had constant rows but finally we got them on the escalators at a premium cost. That worked well because people are stuck on the escalators, and see the posters going down and up.

The advertising campaign in the underground made a very significant difference especially for women working in central London. Copycatting gained us more press publicity. Life, the anti-abortion organisation, had an almost identical poster: same lettering, dark brown instead of black, and it said, 'If you're happy to be pregnant, call...' and then their number. The terrible difference was that the women who phoned them were told they must keep their babies because abortion was so wicked. They often reached PAS fearful, guilty and distraught by their experience of Life.

THE ABORTION ACT was passed in 1967 but didn't become law until 1968. It was a culmination of more than a decade of attempts to change existing legislation to make abortion legal under certain highly defined circumstances.

The concept of a Pregnancy Advisory Service must have begun even before the Act became law. After all the excitement of the victory in Parliament, it wasn't clear how much difference it would make because hospitals would not carry out abortions and many GPs would not discuss abortion. Doctors had every right not to discuss it because there was a conscience clause in the Act which said that family doctors need not give advice on unwanted pregnancy. Something more was going to be needed: some kind of service which would channel women who wanted an abortion through the various stages that the law required to secure the legal right to have an abortion, and which would help women identify the surgeons and the private hospitals or private clinics where the abortions could be carried out. None of these existed. There had been private 'abortionists' for many years but they were rarely available to women who didn't have the right contacts and considerable funds. Realisation dawned that there would be women, maybe hundreds, maybe thousands, all over the country who would satisfy the legal requirements but had nowhere to go. Abortion really was a backstreet affair then. Rich women and women with nous could find their way surreptitiously to Harley Street; women in the East End and the inner cities usually managed to find access to the back streets, to self-styled 'women's friends' who would do abortions for them, and usually very risky ones. So the whole atmosphere around abortion was that it was frightening, it was dangerous and squalid, it was a back-street job.

Early efforts to set up services came from members of the Abortion Law Reform Association. Two very different personalities sharing one goal gathered support: an accountant called Alan Golding, the former treasurer of the ALRA, and Martin Cole who was a lecturer at the University of Aston in Birmingham and who around that time enjoyed a reputation for his very advanced views on sexual relationships and sex education. A relatively small sum of money – around £3,000 – was raised in London from various organisations and individuals who were interested in family planning, abortion and world population issues. The people who took the first practical steps towards setting PAS up in London were three middle-aged family planners – Sylvia Ponsonby, Elizabeth Mitchell and Leah Harvey – who had all been volunteers in a London FPA clinic and members of the ALRA. Then the Birmingham Pregnancy Advisory Service (BPAS) was set up. Nowadays it is one unified organisation called the British Pregnancy Advisory Association with country-wide branches.

But back to the three women, one of them in particular, Sylvia Ponsonby, actually walked the streets of central London looking for premises and she found a little building in Margaret Street, a few yards away from Regent Street, not more than three minutes walk from Oxford Circus. She immediately recognised that this place would be anonymous because there were so many people walking around that nobody would know what you were walking down that street for. So in October or November 1968 she took some rooms in a little rabbit warren of a building with oilclothed semicircular stairs that went up and up and up – five flights! They had a room on the ground floor and a room on the third floor. They sent out a press release the day beforehand – a very cautious press release which I had actually written – saying a new charitable service was being started for women with unwanted pregnancy. If you weren't actually looking for an abortion, you could easily not have understood what it meant. It was years before we could use the word 'abortion', years and years. Sylvia went along to the office to open it up, she had the keys, and she imagined as she travelled to the office that she was going to sit there waiting all day for a phone call to come through, perhaps from journalists. Instead of which she found queues of women all round the corner into Regent Street. It was absolutely amazing.

There was a telephonist who would let the patients in, and then walk them up to the third floor and then come back to answer the phone. They also managed to find one or two sympathetic doctors. They had a psychiatric social worker because the committee believed it was essential to have somebody who would be able to help these frightened women through whatever psychological crises they were facing. That was an essential part of the process. When the women were seen by the social worker they had a long discussion about the alternatives to abortion, and what they really wanted, and whether they were being pressurised in any way by families or boyfriends. Then they went on to see a doctor who took their medical history and gave them an internal examination, and certified they had legal grounds; there had to be two medical signatures to certify that a woman had legal grounds for an abortion under the new Act.

The original doctors were GPs who would work a session or two for PAS, working on, say, Monday morning and Thursday afternoon, or perhaps more than that, perhaps less. They were paid by session at similar rates to family planning doctors. They had been recruited by the FPA's Medical Officer, Dr Sara Abels, a young woman who was passionate about women's rights, and especially passionate about their rights to abortion; she tragically died very young of cancer. As the Senior Medical Officer for the FPA she had access to the names of doctors all over the country who had been interested in or were working in family planning, and who might therefore have been expected to be more sympathetic to abortion than the ordinary run of GPs. She wrote to them all in her capacity as senior FPA doctor, to tell them that PAS would be opening up and she would be interested to know if any family planning doctors were prepared to work there. She got into such difficulties with Caspar Brook, the Director of FPA, for doing so that she only barely hung on to her job. As an individual Caspar Brook was staunchly pro-choice, but at that time he believed the FPA's major objective should be status and respectability. Although the FPA had been in existence since 1932 it still wasn't respectable, and he was fearful that the FPA would never be given a government grant if it was seen to be helping an abortion service. He took the view that nobody on the staff of the FPA could be allowed to be involved with anybody setting up an abortion service. Those of us who chose to had to remain anonymous.

Sylvia Ponsonby and the other two family planners with Alan Golding as their Chairman and two or three other activists including Joan Windley who ran the Marie Stopes clinic formed a management committee. As FPA's Assistant Director I had to be kept in the background, and although journalists knew of my involvement with PAS, they agreed never to quote or name me. True to the tradition of charities, one of the first things the committee did was to collect a group of influential people as patrons to form an advisory board. It included respected psychiatrists and gynaecologists and distinguished lawyers, philosophers and others so that the writing paper and the leaflets could all be headed by this impressive list of names. Respectability was paramount. Sylvia Ponsonby continued her close involvement for many years, probably too long for many of the PAS staff because she insisted on buying the stamps, counting the telephone calls, and keeping the petty cash book, and all the admin jobs she had been used to doing in a local family planning clinic. But by then PAS had grown enormously, and had a large paid staff who thought she was an interfering old woman. But she remained totally dedicated until she died.

The demand for help was such that within a couple of weeks of opening, PAS had to rent more rooms in the building, and over a period of years they took the entire building except for one little basement room where the landlord's bookkeeper sat. It was an incredibly unsuitable building. Women and staff had to go up and down all those stairs, they were dark and they were twisty, and the staff ran up and down them all day. There would be form-filling on one floor, counselling on another, doctors on the top floor, you would have to go down right to the bottom again where people were actually trying to arrange a clinic bed and a date for an abortion. In the early days finding doctors and clinics prepared to accept relatively modest fees, and access to an overnight bed was a daily nightmare.

PAS was very good about communication. Right at the outset it offered extensive written information for women about what would happen to them at PAS, and what to expect if they were referred to a clinic and had an abortion, and what each step would be. I would take the draft leaflets home and rewrite, design and arrange publication. I was one of the people who was constantly called on for advice in those early years. I did a great deal of work for PAS but only in my spare time; I was forbidden any known involvement but eventually I joined the staff, part-time.

The promotion of research was one of the original objectives of PAS. We set up a study of the first 3,000 patients to try and define their characteristics. It was published within a couple of years of starting because it was very important for everyone to understand that women who wanted an abortion were not what we would now call 'slags' or 'slappers'. The study demonstrated for the first time something more than mere anecdotes about the kind of women who were desperate to have an abortion. They could be divided into two groups, women aged 18 to 20, and those over 24. The over-24-year-olds were primarily married women who had had as many children as they wanted – perhaps two or three more than they wanted – or women who had had extramarital affairs, sometimes they were women who had been raped or whose partners had used a split condom. They were housewives and mothers living on small incomes; or in more extreme circumstances had gone off with somebody else for a while and who knew that another pregnancy would be a disaster. And then there were the younger women who had had sexual relationships without using contraception. We found that the use of contraception was very poor, knowledge was very limited; accidents were many, particularly with the condom. Quite often even those women who knew about contraception didn't have it to hand when it was needed. Younger women often thought they couldn't get pregnant the first time they had sex, or they had unprotected sex after a party with somebody they hardly knew. At any rate, the study showed a picture of the many different types of women who were having an unwanted pregnancy and didn't want to carry on with it. It also revealed some of the factors about those who having talked to a counsellor decided not to go ahead with an abortion; sometimes they were under pressure from a boyfriend or from family, but they themselves wanted to carry on with the pregnancy. We also looked closely at the use and knowledge of contraception, which as I say was extremely poor, but it gave some pointers into how much women disliked the diaphragm and condoms, and how many had anxieties about the Pill. At that time there were several Pill scares. Every time a woman who had been taking the Pill died it would be headlined all over the newspapers.

PAS grew extraordinarily quickly. A number of new ideas began to become apparent to the committee at PAS. One of them which was very interesting and unexpected was that there wasn't really a need for medical social workers to do the counselling. At that point the management committee decided that they should find a way of training women who were sympathetic and committed to choice in abortion, who had skills of empathy and listening to take over the counselling role. PAS counsellors played a leading role in the wider development of counselling. While many, perhaps even most women welcomed the opportunity to talk to a counsellor because very often she was the first person that they'd ever talked to openly about abortion, some women were quite resistant and they didn't want to have their way of life, their beliefs and their thoughts scrutinised.

You have no idea of the atmosphere in the early days of the service: the hostile environment, the constant attack, the actual practical difficulties. The NHS simply would not carry out abortions at all in the early years. I can remember going to Margaret Street one evening – it was open in the evenings of course – and there was the weekly crisis about clinic beds. You had maybe, these are figures out of my head, maybe you had forty people who needed to have an abortion that week and you could only call on thirty-two beds because those were the beds agreed for PAS's patients in private clinics. PAS had negotiated the fees and they were substantially below the private sector.

At the same time private clinics around London turned themselves over almost exclusively to abortions and were making huge sums of money, were getting themselves in the national press every day of the week and especially in the Sundays with stories of young girls, particularly foreign girls, French, and Italian mostly. These distraught girls would queue up outside those gracious houses in Weymouth Street and Harley or Wigmore Streets, get their abortions from an abortionist who was performing one after the other, and be left to walk, bleeding, off the operating table. These scandals created the atmosphere in which there were a whole succession of attempts in Parliament to have another go at restricting the law. The climate of opinion was that it was an unsafe, bloody, horrible business which no respectable woman would subject herself to if she valued her life. So, they were very difficult days.

As the demand grew, the doctors and the clinics began to play dirty. If, for example, the gynaecologist who was performing abortions in clinic A went on holiday, and clinic C was being closed to extend its operating theatre, then within minutes the whole of the private abortion sector knew there wouldn't be enough beds and raised their prices. While we would tell women that you're going to have to pay, say, £100 instead of the £200 or £300 that the private clinics normally charged, patients would get to the clinic – and they had to take the money with them – and when they got there they'd find the clinic wanted £300 and they were sent away. Then they would phone PAS and we would actually have to try and give or lend them the extra, and we would have to start angry new negotiations with that clinic. And that changed week by week, even day by day. It was a nightmare, especially as time was of the essence. A delay of a few days could take the woman beyond the legal time limit for abortion, or even in the early years beyond the competence of the gynaecologist.

There seemed to be almost never a day that there wasn't some abortion scandal going on somewhere with front page headlines, and obviously the Government didn't like it. At that stage London was called the 'abortion capital' of the world, and the Department of Health would have done anything to make it different. One of the things the Department did do fairly early on, around 1971, was to ask PAS to set up a special rapid service for women flying in from overseas in search of an abortion. This was largely an attempt to keep foreign women away from taxi touts who would take them to private clinics where the cab drivers would be paid a cash bonus for each woman they took there. The Travellers' Help Unit at London Heathrow Airport came to an agreement with PAS that they would phone us if a woman arrived from abroad and asked for information about an abortion service. PAS would give them an appointment over the telephone and the Travellers' Help Unit would tell them how to get to Margaret Street by tube. The Department of Health asked us to make it a permanent service available for women arriving from abroad. And the Church of England's Board of Social Responsibility also asked us to agree. There was a lot of ethical argument about offering a service to foreigners while there were still women in this country who didn't have any access to an abortion. Although we weren't very keen we decided that since that group of women attracted the most hostile and dangerous publicity for everybody involved in abortion services and were most vulnerable to exploitation, we ought to do it but we couldn't do it at Margaret Street, it was too small. We also reluctantly accepted that women from overseas would have to be top of the queue for beds since they were invariably more advanced in pregnancy and had already booked their return journeys.

In 1972, we rented two floors of a beautiful house in Fitzroy Square to run the special service for women from abroad. At that time I began to work half-time for PAS as Press and Information Officer having left the Family Planning Association. I was often first to arrive and I used to find a very unhappy-looking group of women standing on the pavement. There were area steps down to the basement, and women were queuing up with their luggage, straight from a plane or from a ferry or a train, waiting for the centre to open at half-past nine. For many years those were the women who I met and talked to, frequently to ask them if they would talk to me anonymously about their circumstances especially if I was writing something for a magazine or a newspaper. I think at that particular time nobody was terribly keen to be seen on premises that were offering abortion help, but these women were spectacularly different. They never spoke even though it might be clear to some of them that there were other women from the same country in the waiting-room. We had multilingual counsellors and we tried to do everything to make the atmosphere as friendly and welcoming as possible with flowers and foreign magazines. The Irish women in particular were conspicuous because they went to such extraordinary lengths to be unrecognisable. Coming overnight from County Limerick to a Bloomsbury basement waiting to be counselled about the possibility of an abortion, you wouldn't have thought they would fear being recognised. Nevertheless they would wear scarves up over their mouths and hats pulled down, or headscarves with dark glasses. And because I suppose that the problems of abortion in Ireland got a lot of publicity, I did quite a bit of broadcasting. Usually a doctor and I would be in an English studio, answering questions from an Irish audience, and so I frequently went through patients' case notes to search for cases which would make most impact on Irish listeners. I remember one which was quite extraordinary: she was an Irish nun who had been given home leave for a weekend and walking back to the nunnery across the fields she had been attacked and raped. She was getting towards the end of her childbearing days, but you can imagine the kind of distress and emotion that had been engendered in that nunnery. Well, the convent found the money, and they actually sent her over to us on advice from the Department of Health, and we were able to look after her.

PAS pioneered new kinds of services, like 'lunchtime' or 'quickie' abortions, and attracted great criticism from the pro-life lobby. One day, quite by chance, I came across a report of a study of post-coital contraception by an American researcher. For two years I nagged the management committee of PAS to make it available. And I mean, it took that long. Once we did start post-coital contraception in 1982 the anti-abortion lobby accused us of carrying out illegal and risky abortions. I don't know how many people knew what post-coital meant but today it is a safe and popular method of birth control that can be bought over the counter.

You have no idea of the kinds of problems there were, especially during the short time the organisation became a collective. One of my functions was developing new services at PAS. Once I had suggested a donor insemination service for childless women, and the staff were in a turmoil. Men on the premises, I mean, other than boyfriends and husbands? Men on their own account? Men producing sperm samples? No way! Then when we did eventually start it we offered it to unmarried women and I got many abusive and obscene letters. Right from the very beginning we discovered that donor sperm samples would have to be tested for HIV so during the planning stage we started testing and when we opened up we already had HIV-free donors, so that was a bit of luck.

I stayed at PAS until 1988 when I edited a small book, *Out of the Back Streets*, to celebrate PAS's 21st anniversary. It was a kind of oral history with PAS people, counsellors, doctors and founders recalling their personal memories through the years. I don't know if anyone else found it as fascinating as I did.

———————

I was born in London in 1923. I thought that I was born Helena with an 'a' until I discovered when I came to take exams it was 'Helene' on my birth certificate, but everybody always called me Helen anyway.

My father was a Russian Jew who came to London when he was about fourteen years old. There were pogroms in his part of Russia which is now Lithuania. Or vice versa. He had an older sister in London who had married here, and he was the first of the sons to come over. Although he was still a child he pushed a barrow for a living, but eventually he became a moderately successful businessman and brought his seven brothers and sisters over to this country. My mother was English, a Londoner, though her parents were Polish.

We lived in Stoke Newington which probably still has got some rather grand houses. Ours was a large house. It accommodated in my earlier years both my widowed grandmother and my unmarried aunt until she went off and got married. We always had a maid and a daily, and my mother seemed to do a good deal of work herself. She stayed at home but she was very intelligent. Our family doctor, who was fond of both of us, always said that my mother had a far greater potential than I did. But she was never able to realise it, she was always a wife, a mother and a more than dutiful daughter.

My father was a wholesaler of what used to be called – I don't know if it exists now – Nottingham lace. The business was tablecloths, curtains and towels, and all that kind of household stuff, and it was down in the City. He worked very hard, very hard indeed, long hours. Businessmen then worked six days a week but I always had the impression that the working day was quite leisurely.

I was the elder of two daughters; three years after me my sister, Myra, was born. Both of my parents had lots of siblings, although my maternal grandmother had lost four children out of the eight that she gave birth to. I went to the local primary school in Stoke Newington. They were before the 11-plus but my mother was quite ambitious for her children and she was very supportive. I think my father was ambitious for his daughters in a different way. He wanted them to have a good life, a good income and a loving husband and children but my mother wanted them to be educated. And I was quite lucky, I got a scholarship to North London Collegiate School in Camden Town which was and still is one of the very best girls' day schools in London, and I was there till the war broke out. I must say that once I got there I was a very very little fish in a big pond, there were so many highly intelligent and clever girls there. The school was founded in 1850 by Miss Buss who with Miss Beale were two of the pioneers of women's education. It was very proud of its traditions and its heritage of academic excellence, very committed to higher education, the professions, and I think would have slightly looked down their noses if you wanted to be a secretary though a nurse would have been just about acceptable, or a missionary.

I was evacuated with the school for a few months when war broke out. We were evacuated to Luton, very exciting. We had lessons in a field while they tried to sort out space for us at a local high school. You couldn't live in the school so with my sister and a friend, we were billeted. Teachers and girls went up and down the streets knocking at doors and asking how many the house would accept. Because we were three together we were almost the last to be billeted anywhere, and we had three unsuccessful billets. The first family got rid of us, they said there were too many of us and we were too expensive. The second people were an art teacher and his wife. My older friend and I used to have to do all the housework and the washing before we went to school. One of my jobs was to clean the wife's false teeth. When the school found out why we were always late they moved us. And then just my sister and I went to the home of a young plumber and his wife, on a little working-class estate. One day I had a little difficulty with the plumber who thought I was ripe for the taking. When I told my mother on the telephone she was so aghast that she sent my father on the next train to bring us home again. And within two days they had bought a house in Edgware near the school's new building. So that would have been probably the beginning of 1940, yes.

I came back to be in the sixth and upper sixth in the wonderful old building that North London Collegiate have out at Edgware. I was very good at art, and I was taking art, English and history for what were then Higher Schools. Art took up an enormous amount of time. My mother's younger sister who had lived with us was a commercial artist and extremely well known and successful, so my mother liked to think there was art in the family. I thought I might want to pursue art at St. Martin's. My father was so opposed to the idea of girls having higher education that he said that he wouldn't be convinced that I was serious unless I won a scholarship. And that threw me a bit. I think I knew my art wasn't good enough for that, and anyway, St. Martin's wasn't evacuated. I wanted to leave home more almost than anything else. So I decided to do something that involved history. I sat the scholarship exams for the London School of Economics, which was evacuated to Cambridge, and I got the highest ranking scholarship there, the Leverhulme. The County gave me an extra scholarship and then somebody gave a scholarship for scholarship winners, so I could pay my own fees. I was the first woman in my family to go to university, and it was thought extremely odd.

I went to LSE in 1941. It was wonderful, wonderful. And almost more wonderful was that as a scholarship holder I was one of a group of eight students who Harold Laski had offered to tutor, and that was very exciting. The war was on of course and Professor Laski, who was much admired by President Roosevelt, used to be flown backwards and forwards to Washington, and he would always come back not only with marvellous stories – 'As I said to Franklin on Thursday' – but he would also bring each of us books like *War and Peace* which we couldn't get here. Nothing was particularly distinguished about my time at LSE other than my pleasure at being there, and my problem with the Director for organising mixed-sex fire-watching shifts. I lived in digs on Jesus Green. I've always thought that the only reason that my father allowed me to go to university was that he thought Cambridge would be safer than London during the air raids.

When we finished university women like me were drafted immediately into the highest rank of the Civil Service, the Administrative Service. We were disposed of in different departments, usually in some area of work in which we had neither interest, skills or knowledge. I went straight to Combined Operations where I was one of a team which kept a check on where all the landing forces were for the Second Front. It may sound very glamorous but my part of it certainly wasn't. We produced a weekly publication – quite heavily coded – for the Chief Commanders, Americans, French, and British about the location of every single kind of ship or craft on the Allies' side. It was my responsibility to get it out, and then I went to His Majesty's Stationery Office in Harrow where it was printed. Because of the top secret nature of the material each printer was only allowed to print one page so that they couldn't make any sense out of it. I worked through Sunday, Sunday night, Monday, Monday night, and I came home Tuesday morning, and was due back at work late Tuesday afternoon until Friday. I did this for several months, and then I absolutely collapsed. I had, I suppose what we currently recognise as a very minor breakdown. I was on sick leave for a couple of weeks and I didn't know what I was going to do, so I rang up my old tutor, Harold Laski. He was very indignant about the kind of work that I was doing and how unsuitable it was for somebody who had other skills that might be tapped. He first sent me to see Dame Evelyn Sharp, the senior woman civil servant who was a mandarin-like figure. I was terrified. Then he rang me up and said he had talked to the First Lord of the Admiralty, and they were putting me somewhere more appropriate. They sent me to the Admiralty where I became the gunnery officer responsible for the whole of the landing craft for the Second Front. I know, it was just unbelievable.

About a year later in 1945 I married an accountant I had met before I went to LSE. Jack, my husband, found a flat on the night before we got married when he ran into somebody on Hampstead Heath in the snow who was about to leave a flat in Hampstead to get away from the flying-bombs. So I was able to get out of the Admiralty. Married women could get out of the Forces quicker than anybody else. I didn't know what to do so I advertised in the *New Statesman*, and I got a number of replies, all offering me part-time work. One was from Robert Harling who was the editor of the *Architectural Journal* and also a well-known artist; he commissioned me to write a history of the domestic chair. Simultaneously I was approached by a wealthy Greek carpet manufacturer with offices in the City, who was – this was a time of civil war in Greece – deeply interested in and committed to progressive forces. He wanted somebody to monitor all the Greek political news, and to write letters to the press, mostly the *Spectator* and the *Statesman* and the *Times*. He sent me to the first ever meetings of the United Nations in Church House, Westminster. So I sat through all the first sessions of that with an acute sense of making history. And while I was juggling with that and the history of the domestic chair, I had a third offer from a public relations firm in Great Ormond Street who offered me a half-time job, that was my first experience of public relations. I used to go from the carpet maker to the public relations job, and I did the domestic chair at the weekends. Within two or three months at the PR company I was asked to make way for Alastair Buchan, eldest son of John the writer, who was just back from the war.

I didn't really want to do anything by then, I wanted a breather. But I was prevailed upon to work for my father. He blackmailed me by saying, 'I have no son, I built up this business; I don't want it all to go when I retire.' And reluctantly I fell for it. I was never there full-time, and I never learned the business, he never had any intention of my doing so, and I found it incredibly tedious. He was right, he didn't have an heir, an heir to carry it on. After I had a second child, I didn't stay.

I had two daughters, Jennifer in December 1949 and Judy in June 1952. I was at home for a long time with one exception. I was asked by the Department of Employment to sit on a committee which was set up to look at domestic employment, and examine if it could be transformed from the pre-war slavery or drudgery into something more like a skilled job. And whether it would be possible to provide training which would enable somebody who qualified through that training to work in a hospital, students' hostel or some other institution. Sitting on the committee was to my taste, not because I was a particularly competent housewife but because it was a way of dignifying and improving domestic work in institutional care and I found that worthwhile.

The Department of Employment set up a National Institute of Houseworkers, and I was asked if I would employ one of the very first group of six Caribbean women who were being brought over with a handful of men to see whether the women could be trained to do jobs in homes or hostels, and men on the trains. That was the very first intake of West Indian workers. The Government advanced their fares over here, we paid them a little money and they worked a very short day with a day and a half of formal learning in this new institute.

That was about the only thing that I did while my children were young. When they got within hailing distance of going away to college or university, I began to think about having my own life. I was really spending more of my time with my parents than my own family because during that time my mother had the first of her malignant melanomas and many operations and I decided she was my first priority as her cancer spread. Our family doctor said, 'You're the kind of person who would feel guilty if you hadn't done everything that you possibly could for your parents, and I don't think you could live with that, so hold off a little while.' And I did, probably another couple of years, but by 1965 I thought I really must do something.

I applied for three or four jobs simultaneously and I was interviewed for all of them. I was so muddled about what I wanted to do, I went home and said, 'Whoever offers me a job first, I'm going to take it.' We needed the money anyway. As it happened, it was Sir Theodore Fox, Director of the Family Planning Association, who asked me to start the next day. So I thought, wow! I got £1,004 a year, full-time.

Within a year Caspar Brook had become the Director of FPA having been the whiz-kid of the Consumers' Association. In his first week he sacked the Deputy Director; in the second week he tried to change everybody's working hours, and the entire organisation went on strike. He made his presence known with a vengeance. He didn't care for my boss, the press officer, who was an elderly gin-sodden, divorced barrister, never without a cigarette in her mouth and an exceptionally difficult lady especially when tight. Although I didn't know all this at first, I had a distinct advantage with the media. Because I had two teenage daughters, the media used me not only to outline the Family Planning Association's view of the new methods of contraception but also to talk about how I reacted as a mother of two girls in their teens who could easily get pregnant. Family Planning was a very quickly-developing world and I grew with it.

Incidentally, while I was at the Family Planning Association I was jointly responsible for the pregnant man poster, if you remember that. It was recognised as far back as then that unplanned pregnancy was a major problem, and the Health Education Council had decided to put money into campaigns for contraception. Since I was on the committee, it was the then Director of the HEC and myself who went to brief the advertising agency. Alas, I have no claim to any part in the selection of the agency but it turned out to be Charles Saatchi. It was the pregnant man poster that made Charles Saatchi – it was his idea. I remember looking at dozens of roughs, and choosing that. It said, 'Would you be more careful if it was you who got pregnant?' and showed a dishy young man at least seven months pregnant in a bulging sweater. I remember taking the first rough back to the FPA offices, very excited, showing it to Caspar Brook who said, 'I don't like it, I find it very distasteful. But, you've chosen it, and I've got to take some advice from you, it's your job. God help you if it gets into trouble.' Well it didn't in fact, it just took off all round the world. For 48 hours I sat at my desk broadcasting to worldwide radio programmes.

While I was at the Pregnancy Advisory Service in the 1970s I became interested in public health services. I became Chair of the Camden and Islington Community Health Council from 1980 onwards until I was appointed a member of the Camden Health Authority, which I enjoyed immensely. I worked fantastically hard. Later I became a Mental Health Act Manager and a health service conciliator. I also chair appointments committees for senior medical consultants at several London teaching hospitals, but principally Great Ormond Street. I feel immensely privileged to be able to do something for that magnificent children's hospital.

That's what I do when I don't break my ankle. So I don't take kindly to sitting here doing nothing.

It solved the problem

Dorothy Bennett
National Council for the Single Woman and Her
Dependants

Somebody got in touch with me and told me that there was a meeting in
Commonwealth Avenue off Trafalgar Square. It was one of the first
meetings before we ever became anything. We were just Flora Robson,
the actress, and several other people trying to get it going. Then they had
a wonderful garden party in Kent – everybody talks about the garden
party – but of course I never went because I was a carer by then. I wish
I could remember all these people's names – I can't remember anything
now.

THE NATIONAL COUNCIL for the Single Woman and Her
Dependants was started in 1967 by Mary Webster who was a
Congregational Minister. When she had to give up her job to look
after her parents, she realised the problems that single women
were having with the shortage of money and lack of help. You
had to give up work because you couldn't do both work and
caring. She wrote letters to the press about this and hundreds of
women wrote to her so she started to have meetings and I joined
because I realised this was something I was going to be up against
later on. I felt I ought to help.

Before long we were two branches and then we got it going all
over the country and in Scotland as well. Once we got going as an
association with a national committee we had conferences every
year. Many members had to arrange respite care and they couldn't
always find somebody. I didn't go to conferences until my parents
died, and then I went and helped as much as I could.

Our association's first office was opposite the post office in
Eltham. It was above a shop and you had to go up the back stairs
to get to it. Oh no, we weren't paid. There wasn't any money to
pay us. But you can't do an awful lot if you haven't got an awful
lot of money to throw about. You can't say to somebody it would
be a good idea if you had a holiday in Eastbourne because you've
immediately got to find out how it can be financed. You know
every local church sale had a stall of ours. And when I think of all

the onions I've ever peeled and cooked for them. Oh, pickled onions, marmalade, we did anything that made money. The association started a one-day Christmas holiday. We used a holiday place which was for church people so of course it was closed during Christmas. They opened it up just for single women and their dependants so at least they'd have one Christmassy time. They were waited on and looked after and then they went home again. But they had a Christmas.

Then we got more important and much more well-known so we set up our national office in Victoria so that we'd be nearer the Houses of Parliament. All the MPs who were keen on us could pop in whenever they liked. The Single Woman and Her Dependants got the single woman recognised for income tax. A man could get tax allowance for dependants which a woman couldn't. And we got them made equal. That was the first improvement. Then we got better Social Security with the Attendance Allowance and Invalid Care Allowance. Of course we worked like mad for the Attendance Allowance but then we discovered it was not being used for the care of the person but unfortunately went into granny's purse and she used it for her own use. We discovered that the carer wasn't getting any financial help. That was when we got the Invalid Care Allowance so that the carer got some money.

Of course this new head we've got, she reorganised us completely and now it's called the Carers National Association. She was horrified that we used old envelopes. In the 1980s when the new Director came in, before you knew where you were the head office was blooming with umpteen typewriters, staff and that. Don't ask me where she got her money from. Now we never get asked to raise money for anything. I never add to my subscription when I send it each year. I think to myself, no, she can buy her own machines with somebody else's money.

Some of us didn't want to join the Carers National Association, but we did want to keep together. So any branches which wanted it were allowed to have a Mary Webster Fellowship of their old members. Our fellowship meets in a pub in Bexleyheath and now we're down to six or seven of the original group.

I've got lots of photographs: here's one of the famous garden party and that's Mary Webster, she had a great love of hats. Got none of her in her clericals. And this is one of the twenty-first birthday party of our branch, in 1988. Yes, that's Virginia, the Bottomleys were very good, whatever happened they'd come to everything they could.

I was born in Grays Inn Road, London in 1910. When they got married my parents had one room in grandma's house above the shop. My grandmother had a shoe shop. She sold shoes on the ground floor and the man sat in the basement mending shoes. My father was teaching at a local school, then he had a job in the Post Office and he finished in the Post Office as the Head of Stores.

When I left school at seventeen I decided I'd train as a child's nurse and I trained at a children's nursery in Hoxton. I stayed there for three years but it wasn't really what I wanted to do so I then trained as a hospital nurse. Eventually – during the war – I trained as a radiographer. The hospital I was in got bombed. I can remember helping clear up all the glass; gosh the sound of sweeping that glass and the clacking noise it made!

I got a job at Westminster Hospital as a radiographer. From there I left to run the radiography department at the St George's Hospital near Hyde Park, now the Lanesborough Hotel. Then my father had quite massive stroke which took his speech and his mobility. He couldn't walk, and he lost the use of his right arm and hand.

Well I more or less expected it. My brother and sister-in-law said, 'What are we going to do?' And I said, 'I suppose I'll have to come home and look after him.' 'Oh well,' they said, 'that's all right then.' It solved the problem. It was 1967 so I was fifty-seven. You see, if the son or daughter had married they'd got their own world. A friend of mine cared for her mother and I invited them both to spend Christmas with my parents because they were by themselves. Her sister was married, had her own Christmas to cope with. Like me, she did it all. Sister didn't appear. My friend was much younger than me, too. My brother and his family were in Islington and we didn't see them very often.

Before I became a carer I used to go on holiday to Norway with a friend every so often. I did a trip before father came home from hospital after his stroke. Mother said, 'Get your holiday booked before Father comes home; then you can do it.' I did the coastal trip all the way up Norway. I didn't go away again until I was on my own again.

I was fortunate really because though father couldn't talk after his stroke, he knew what was going on. He knew what he wanted to do. Usually I suppose I got up about half past seven, and I took them their breakfast and then of course they had to be washed. My mother could get up and more or less dress herself with a bit of help. She was crippled with arthritis but she managed well and at first she used to do the cooking. But I did the cooking as well.

The district nurses came to get father up and dressed, and we had a woman who came in a couple of times a week to do the excess cleaning because I had to look after the garden as well as them and the house. Mother must have been one of the first to have a washing machine. So of course that was quite easy. Father did very well in Orpington Hospital. They taught him to write with his left hand but they couldn't get him to speak. What amazed me was that he'd re-write the whole of the *Daily Telegraph* leading article but he would be quite unable to write down what he wanted. He'd want something very much and I'd say, well write it down; but he couldn't. He'd write a letter but he never ever managed to write what he needed.

Really my life was entirely with them. I used to get somebody from the Red Cross or a friend to sit in with them when I went to my committee meetings of the Single Woman and Her Dependants. I was their carer for eleven years. My mother died first and he died a few months later. I couldn't afford to stay in the house I shared with my parents because my pension wasn't as good as it should have been having finished work before retirement age.

And then I bought this house in Shooters Hill, with its beautiful garden. I'd always been used to a garden and gardening. After my parents died I got the wanderlust. I hadn't been free to go out and suddenly I was. If somebody said they were going to visit a garden, or go on a coach outing, I used to say, 'Can I come?'

Raising money has been in our family as long as I can remember. I raised £114.00 for glaucoma by opening my garden last weekend and having everyone in. Six ladies came to make tea and look after everything. Somebody said to me, 'I bought marmalade at your garden party. It was lovely.' 'Well' I said, 'Three fruits, you can make that any time.'

You opened the door

Maureen Nicol
National Housewives Register

The Register certainly worked for me. I have made a lot of good friends. Difficult to put into words really. The Register has been a short-cut for women to meet each other and to lose their sense of isolation when they move to a new place. It's been a meeting ground for women who couldn't find what they wanted in the traditional organisations but still wanted contact with other women and the sort of informal, loose contact that they can get through the Register. At first when I was organiser I had some really heartbreaking letters, people like me really who had moved to areas where they knew not a soul and who were really going round the bend, finding that there was just nobody to talk to. And you really do need to talk, don't you, especially I think when you're a young mother. You need to get away from the position that you've voluntarily put yourself in, you need to be you for a bit, and that's what they were finding they couldn't do. And the Register saved their lives, I mean that's probably exaggeration but that's what one or two of them said. And that was very nice, to feel that you'd really helped in that you had given women a pathway. It was up to them what they did with it, whether they joined the group, how much they put into it, but you had opened the door.

IT STARTED ENTIRELY accidentally in 1960. I had no idea of setting up an organisation. I'd had quite interesting jobs but Brian and I had left our families in the south of England and had made about the third move with two small children – one of whom was quite a small baby – to Eastham on the Wirral on the edge of a very large housing estate. We had no car and there was no public transport. I was pretty isolated really, geographically and mentally. It was quite hard to get to know people on the estate, they were all very much local people who had been on the housing list while in a way we had cheated because we had got the house through Brian's job. They had a family and old neighbour network, and I didn't you see. So for the first few months there I was really fairly miserable, you can imagine, separated from family and friends and job. Obviously in the end you do get to know people one way or another but it takes time, and in my case after a few years we would be off again, moving somewhere else.

And then I read an article in the *Guardian* by Betty Jerman saying that she was in much the same sort of position. She had been a journalist and had had a family, moved out to suburbia, and found that it was quite hard to get to know people of similar interests, liberal-minded people. And this struck such a chord with me that I wrote a letter to *The Guardian*. I'd never written to a paper in my life, and I didn't really think they would publish it, but luckily the Women's Editor at the time was Mary Stott, and she did publish it. My letter said in effect, there must be loads of other women like me feeling mentally isolated, and what a shame we can't get together. And I was not only surprised they published it, but even more surprised at the response: I got several dozen letters which said, what a good idea, go ahead, do something about it.

I thought, my God! How can I? I've got no car. I mean, we didn't even have a telephone, we were really hard up. Anyway I thought about it, and discussed it with Brian, and he said, 'Well, you know, if you don't do it, no one's going to; there's obviously a need.' So, I wrote again to *The Guardian* and said, there seems to be some response; I will set up a register. The idea initially was that there would be a kind of book, a register, of people who were moving or wanting to make contact, and I would just put people in touch. I suppose I had envisaged a response of a few hundred. Well, within about a week I had 400 letters, and the letterbox actually fell off with the postman pushing letters through when we were away. That's how it started. As I say, it was totally accidental.

The letters were all from women who had had a fairly fulfilling job, had children and then their husband's job had taken them away from their friends and family. Some of them were really bubbling over with the idea, 'Oh this is wonderful, what a great idea, yes, what can we do about it?' One or two were suicidal, 'I tramped around the streets looking for somebody to talk to,' or 'I go home and I shut myself in four walls, and I feel they're crowding in on me.' We were so submerged with the home and the children, and getting by, really. I mean we saw nothing of the Swinging Sixties unfortunately. It was more a matter of getting out of the dreary Fifties I suppose.

My first thought was, I've got to spread the load, recruit some of the others to help. So initially I sorted the letters out into regions: south-east, south-west, Midlands, north-east, north-west I think. There were virtually no letters from Scotland, and very few from Wales. Afterwards that changed, and we had many Welsh members for a while anyway. I picked out letters from each area which appeared to be from women who were prepared to do something. So then I wrote to these women and said, 'If I send on the letters in your area, would you be prepared to put people in touch with each other? I'll keep a national record, but you do your area.' And they all agreed, which was great. Most were really very keen on the idea because they tended, I guess, to be the sort of people like me who went to a Women's Institute meeting once – and I was probably unfortunate – when it happened to be the day they were actually talking about jam making! I mean, this is so legendary. And I thought, no.

With every letter that I got I would enter the person's name into the register alphabetically, and I kept that up all the time I was national organiser. Then I'd send the letters on to the appropriate regional organiser. That worked for a short while but then the regional organisers started getting their own publicity, so they would get people writing to them directly, and the whole thing snowballed: the more publicity, the more members; the more members, the more publicity, and so on.

Luckily, I got letters from about half a dozen women within walking distance of me, and that was very nice. I would never have met them otherwise because there was just no common meeting ground. At that time the estate was a desert, there were no shops, schools or anything. And of course playgroups didn't really exist then. First of all I had them round to my house, and we discussed what we should do about the Housewives Register. This was in the very first few weeks. They would come round and help me sort out the letters and stuff envelopes and that kind of thing, yes, they were wonderful.

And then we decided we wanted to stay together as a group, and we started meeting in each other's houses in the day, which was a bit of a disaster because you really couldn't do anything much with kids rampaging around. Very quickly we decided we would meet in the evening as almost every one of us could get away. Again it was always to be in people's houses, never in public halls because we wanted to keep it personal. We didn't want the sort of meeting where you go along and you sit, you listen to a speaker, you clap and then you go home, that wasn't what it was all about. It's been like that ever since, which is nice. We found that as we were developing as a group, the individual contact – which was fine – wasn't enough; we wanted to do things as a group as well.

One of our most successful meetings involved a do-it-yourself art evening. None of us knew anything about painting nor had any experience, but we got hold of some materials and we had an evening when we painted. It was amazing what came out of it, they were really very good, many of them. And everybody enjoyed it. It wasn't an activity that we were going to continue – I did painting afterwards, I took it up again much later on for a while – but just that evening, doing something we had never done before was immensely stimulating. Our group was close to Liverpool where every year there are big art exhibitions so from then on we started going to exhibitions and comparing styles. So that was one of the things we did. What else did we do? Oh golly, all sorts of things. Talked about world government; a lot of the time we tried to do our own research but sometimes if we felt we just didn't know enough or couldn't find out enough, we would invite a speaker. We had somebody from the Citizens Advice Bureau who came to talk to us about the work of the CAB, because again none of us had any experience of that. Sometimes it was a fun evening, we just did something fairly trivial. We weren't trying to be on a high intellectual plane all the time, I mean the idea was friendship and fun as much as intellectual stimulation. That was what it was about.

It was also about emotional support, very much so. And it still is actually. Quite recently, the local group here in Kenilworth had a dinner in somebody's house where three of the women there had either left their husbands or the husband had left them. There was terrific warmth and support for these three women, all upset in different ways. And you just think, women are marvellous at supporting each other emotionally, aren't they?

But back to the early sixties again, we were also reading the current literature. *The Feminine Mystique* of course was a great bible. I don't know that we were rampant feminists really. I think we all felt that we were in a transitional stage. We weren't happy in the way I suppose our mothers mostly were, to be just housewives, but we weren't breaking the bonds, getting back to work. I mean these days we've gone through that barrier haven't we, it's just accepted that as a mother if you want to work, you do somehow. It's not easy but it's possible, and it's accepted now. But at that stage I suppose I felt – and most of my friends felt – that while the kids were small they needed us and we should be there, and that's the way life was.

The Register membership was roughly about two and a half thousand within the first year, which is pretty astonishing isn't it? We got a lot of publicity. We were something new, and a lot of the papers picked up on it, and I guess there wasn't much else going on that summer so they were wanting articles or interviews. That generated more membership, not always the sort we wanted. I did an interview on Woman's Hour, and I don't know whether this is common experience with broadcasters, but a lot of the people that responded to what I was saying – if you want to join a group or you need friendship, get in touch with me – obviously hadn't quite heard what I said, or they had switched on half-way through and they thought it was some kind of marriage club. So that wasn't too fruitful. A lot of women joined by word of mouth, I mean the word gets round in a village that this new organisation has been set up and so Peggy would bring along a friend, and it grew like that. Some of the new area organisers were extremely enterprising. As the regions split into smaller groups they would generate their own publicity like putting out leaflets, and one woman stuck leaflets in prams. And that's how the Register grew. We never actually paid for advertising. Well we didn't have any money for one thing, and for another it would never have occurred to me.

I would have liked to have met the area organisers although I did meet the London organiser, but travelling was very difficult and expensive of course. I would correspond or occasionally phone but we never had any national meetings which was quite good in a way because it meant we never got together and so we never had disagreements at a national level.

I suppose I took on the title of national organiser because that's what I was doing, organising nationally. All the press publicity would quote my name so I was regarded as the one who held it together. The whole idea was that it would be easy for new women moving into an area to get in touch with a national contact in order to be passed on to the nearest local organiser. So that's how it worked.

We never had stated aims and objectives. Our ideas grew organically. For example, very early on I said that we're not going to have any of this nonsense about people doing lots of refreshments. One of the women I'd met had lived in America, and she said that there was an organisation over there which had started out with the same idea as the Register but that they had always served refreshments, and it got more and more competitive, so in the end you got women serving a great banquet, and she said it was just ridiculous. So I said, right, we're having none of that. Tea and coffee and biscuits, that's it, and we've always stuck to that. So whoever is hosting the evening knows that she doesn't have to go to any trouble preparing elaborate refreshments. In fact locally we've got a box with about thirty mugs in it which gets carted round so people don't even have to provide their own crockery. That was one thing, fairly trivial. And another thing is, we never had minutes, we never had elected chairmen, we never had a hierarchy. The idea was for everybody to feel involved. However, each group had to have somebody who was prepared to do the organising, who would draw up a programme from other people's ideas, and would circulate the programme, and would take in any subscriptions. And again, it has stayed like that more or less. Everyone was involved and was expected to host evenings, do research, suggest activities, et cetera.

It was the time of the Campaign for Nuclear Disarmament and we talked about whether we thought the CND movement was worthwhile, whether we should do anything about it, and in fact a few of us went on a march, a big rally that they had in Liverpool. I was really very keen on CND. We had a home-made National Housewives Register banner which we trundled along with our pushchairs, but I felt afterwards this is not a good idea even though I support this particular cause wholeheartedly. But supposing it had been something I didn't approve of, I would be really quite upset. So we must stop doing this, we must stop any activity which involves a group committing itself to one cause or another. Obviously as individuals, fine, yes, do whatever, but not representing the organisation, and again this is something which has stuck.

I didn't have any equipment but quite early on I borrowed a typewriter. It's a bit grim borrowing somebody's typewriter for two and a half years but I did, because I couldn't even afford to buy one then. I didn't have any kind of duplicator so I borrowed one of those too. I started sending out newsletters to the couple of dozen organisers as I couldn't have sent newsletters to all the individual groups because it would have cost so much. I just decided that as we never got together physically we ought to communicate. So I sent out a newsletter saying, this is what's happening nationally, or raising questions such as what do you think about so-and-so, or I don't know how you're all getting on but we found day meetings were hopeless, or I don't think it's a good idea to serve anything other than biscuits at meetings, how do you feel about that? And they would then reply, and, probably correspond with each other as well, and that's how the organisation evolved. Usually people agreed, saw the common sense of it. By the end of the first year I was saying in the newsletter, 'I don't know about you but I'm getting out of pocket, what are we going to do about this? Could we charge some sort of membership fee?' Because we hadn't anything up until then at all. I think we started off with a shilling per person per year which didn't get us very far as you can imagine.

I was tired most of the time that first year, a bit overwhelmed really. Because as I say, I really hadn't intended to do this. On the other hand, it was a tremendously empowering experience. I mean if anyone had told me at the beginning of 1960 that I would find myself on a television programme or in the Woman's Hour studio or writing articles for the *Guardian*, I would have said, you're crazy, me? And I think a lot of the area organisers and group leaders were finding the same thing, that they could do things which they hadn't expected to be able to do. So that was great. You got this feeling, I can do anything if I'm prepared to actually get up and do it. We were wrong of course, you can't do everything. But it was a good experience: it gave you great confidence at a time when most of us had been fairly battered by leaving work and being at home. You do begin to feel a bit zombie-like after a bit. In fact, I've never felt that isolation since which is partly to do with having the Register there. It's been very important in my life and it was wonderful moving back here from Uganda in 1973, and finding an organisation set up, walk in, hello. Great.

Here in Kenilworth there's not just the main group but various sub-groups. There's a very active walking group, I'm a keen member of that; there's a badminton group and a theatre group, and various others. So you can maybe go to a sub-group, even if you're not interested in whatever is going on in the main meeting.

The people who joined the Register were as varied as women anywhere. Some of them were extremely keen to get back to work, very frustrated that they couldn't or they felt that they shouldn't.

Others were perfectly happy to stay at home and possibly do voluntary work. They varied enormously. I mean one of the good things, one of the strong things about the Register is that no one was categorised, no one was told this is the way you should feel or think or do; everyone was allowed to develop individually, and supported in whatever they decided to do. Although it hasn't quite worked out like that we should have been self-destructive, because if you got back to work you found your fulfilment, you made your friends and then you didn't need the Register. In that way we did obviously lose a lot of members because they were too busy, too harassed or whatever to actually attend Register meetings. In practice it's surprising how many stayed, or how many came back after a break because they decided, yes, I would quite like to find out what's going on locally. And in a way that's the Register's strength.

Brian and I moved again in 1963 to Birkenhead. I felt that it would be a good idea to hand the Register on. Things seemed to be going very well, I mean publicity was easy to get, groups were expanding. I think at the back of my mind I knew that while this organisation is needed somehow it will carry on. The day will come perhaps when it isn't necessary any more, and then it will fade away quietly but that hasn't happened yet. And there's always been somebody prepared to take it on; later on it had to be a group of people, because it got too big. So I said in the newsletter three years after the Register had started, now I'm moving again I would really like to hand over, is anybody out there willing to take it on? And God bless her – again I hadn't met her – I literally handed the whole thing over by post to Brenda Price-Jones, all the correspondence together with our capital of about £10, and said, 'Right, it's up to you.' She was in the south in Croydon. And she carried on wonderfully. Soon after that we went abroad and I lost contact with what was going on, but of course the Register carried on. One person took over after another, it's amazing really. I think when Brenda took over she set up a proper registration fee, it wasn't very much but it covered her expenses. We never had a paid organiser, oh for years and years, till very much later.

Originally we called ourselves the Liberal-Minded Housebound Wives Register. Isn't that awful? I suppose we were housebound in some ways but it sounds dreadful really. And obviously that wouldn't do. So again, in the discussion in the newsletter we settled on National Housewives Register and that stayed for a while until

Housewives became a term which people weren't prepared to accept, and then it became National Women's Register. It's interesting, that everything that's happened has grown out of something else; it's all very organic. There's been nobody saying, we will do this, we will do that.

We've been accused of being mainly a middle class group. And I guess there's an element of truth in it really. I talk about being hard up but I was never hard up to the extent where I felt I had to go out and get a cleaning job for instance. If I'd really been that hard up I would have had to do that, and people in that position have not got the time and the energy or the inclination to join the Register. I always hoped that it would be all classes, all colours, all creeds but on the whole it tended to be middle-class people. I myself come from an extremely working-class background. My mother never really understood what the Register was all about. I tried to explain it to her. But she had always known lots of people because they lived in Dartford for fifty, sixty years. She had always been surrounded by family and friends and she was a great chatterer, she could talk for hours about trivial things and really enjoy it. I just couldn't do that. We were sneered at by the tabloids who implied that we were these silly bored middle-class housewives, and why didn't we buckle down. But on the whole most publicity was very sympathetic.

Sometimes I wonder whether the Register is still necessary. It's amazing how active our local group is. Both the women in my family – my daughter and my daughter-in-law – are working, both have got very busy, fulfilling jobs, but they both say, you don't get a chance to talk about other things at work. You're so busy talking about work that you never really get a chance to discuss whatever's going on politically for instance. They've got the same kind of gripes that we had in a way. I mean obviously not the same but they still say, yes, it would be nice to meet different women on a purely friendship basis. My husband often complains that we're sexist. But there's something about getting together with a group of women, and you know whatever's bothering you, somebody in that group is going to understand and have gone through the same kind of experience. Men don't want to talk like this on the whole.

———

I was born in London at the end of 1929 so I'm just about coming up to my 70th birthday which I don't want to think about. My maiden name was Maureen Johnson. Oddly enough my husband and I were both born in the same nursing home in Lewisham in south London three months apart, isn't that a strange coincidence?

My father was a bricklayer and he had been in the First World War. My mother worked in a factory during and just after the war. They met in a factory, packing biscuits.

I think there were about thirteen of them in my father's family. They lived in Greenwich and they were all on the buildings – my father was taken in as an apprentice very early on. My father's story was that his father came in one day when he was just coming up to thirteen, 'Are you still at the school then?' 'Yes Dad.' And his father said, 'No you're not, you're joining me on the buildings on Monday.' And that was it, that was the end of his education. All the family in various ways were just scraping a living. They really had a very hard time, and so did my mother's family where again there were thirteen or fourteen children. Several of them died. They had an old black range, the way those old Victorian houses did, and one of the babies fell into the fire. Terrible. Interestingly enough my grandmother's house was on the site of the Millennium Dome in Greenwich.

My grandfather, my mother's father, worked on the river as a kind of lighterman. A big coal and coke depot was there at that time, big gas works, terrible smell. He was always very ill, he died quite young. My mother's mother had to bring up the family more or less on her own doing whatever she could to get money, mainly cleaning I think. My mother was sent out to service as soon as she left school at thirteen, and hated it so much she ran away and came home crying, so her mother then put her into the biscuit factory.

My parents moved to Dartford in Kent when I must have been about two or three years old. Eventually they took a shop which we moved into and I stayed there until I got married. I had two older brothers and a third brother was born three years after I was. My elder brother was at the grammar school and then he got a job when he was sixteen as a trainee chemist in a paper factory, J & E Hall's. At the outbreak of World War II he went into the Air Force very quickly, not yet nineteen. The next brother joined the Boys Army when he was about fourteen and was a paratrooper by the time he was eighteen. Both were killed, one brother was killed flying in Malta, shot down. The other brother was parachuted into Arnhem and was killed there on the bridge. We got the first telegram in about 1943 when my eldest brother was killed, and then the second telegram came a year later. I was the only one in the house when it arrived and I was so frightened I ran up to my room and shut myself in. I didn't come out for about two days just because I was frightened of my mother breaking down. And we never really talked about it until very much later, and even then not very much. In a way it was too painful. So that really knocked the family for six, you can imagine.

My younger brother got TB in the hip through drinking infected milk. He was taken into hospital at three and a half and didn't come out again until he was about ten, so he was in hospital for a lot of my childhood. We went every Sunday to visit him in that terrible hospital. At that time the regime for TB patients was to put them outside as much as possible, so this poor little scrap would be in a bed on a veranda outside with snow on the ground. Even then I knew it wasn't right.

The shop was a general store but my father ran a greengrocery delivery round as well, and they kept that going until they retired. Then it turned into a charity shop – one of the very early ones actually – and my mother ran that which suited her wonderfully because she was a great gossip, and this was the centre for local gossip.

I had a very disrupted education. Before the war I was at a grim Victorian infant junior school, and I was very unhappy there. My mother made arrangements for me to go to another school which was further into Dartford, but the war broke out in September and they wouldn't take me at the new school because of air-raid precautions, and they wouldn't take me back at the old school. It's unbelievable now, but for two years I didn't go to school at all, which in some ways was wonderful because I had complete freedom. I could do what I liked, I roamed the countryside, and I had a great imaginative life. When the war broke out I was coming up to nine and the only education I had in two years was for a few weeks when I was sent to somebody's house, where the only thing we did was Music and Movement with Miss Driver on the radio. That was it, that was my education. There was no question of going to the grammar school of course so I went to an elementary school. You either left at fourteen or you got a scholarship to the technical college which in fact I did. I discovered while I was at the elementary school that I'd got a gift for debating. I remember – it sticks in my mind even after all these years – the debating society was having a debate on something, I can't even remember what about, and I had to keep a dentist's appointment during this debate. It was something I really wanted to talk about so I hurried to get back and when I came into the class everybody started clapping because I had arrived. Oh it was wonderful. Isn't it funny, remembering that all these years later? Anyway I went to the technical college and did a secretarial course which I didn't much enjoy but it was better than leaving school and working.

By this time I had developed a great love for the theatre, I used to go to any productions I could. So when I left school at sixteen I worked for two theatrical costumiers. The first one was Fox's which is still there in High Holborn, as a very junior person for two years. Then I got a better job as secretary to the director at L & H Nathans which was in Panton Street in a lovely old house; it was an absolute tragedy they tore it down. I thoroughly enjoyed it because while Fox's mainly dressed amateur productions, Nathans was far more professional and dressed productions on the West End stage and a lot of films. Olivier was starting to make films like Henry V for which we were doing all the armour so I saw a lot of well-known actors and actresses. That's as close as I could get to the stage.

I developed on my own really. I mean my parents weren't particularly great readers for instance, but both my brother and I turned out to be. My father was a very intelligent man with absolutely no education at all, and no desire or application to do anything about it really. I always had an awful feeling that he and his like were kind of cannon fodder. He went off to the First World War, went all through that, knew how terrible it was – I mean he had the most ghastly experiences – and yet he let his two sons go off to the Second World War. I can't help feeling if it had been me I would have done anything to stop them going but they both went as soon as they possibly could. I mean it's an awful thing to say, because I loved my father very much, but he was a lazy man really. He was always rushing off down the pub, and he had his mates and his man's world. My mother kept the family together. She was really knocked silly when my brothers were killed. But she survived it, she kept us all going.

My mother's social life was the family and the neighbours. She never joined a political party or went to meetings. I always felt that she half read something, never really grasped what it was about, and didn't then press it any further. How she'd cope with today's technical world I don't know. I mean I'm having a struggle coping with the Internet. She had always wanted a girl but I was a bit of a disappointment because she wanted a pretty girl she could dress up and I wasn't like that. I was a tomboy and wished that I could have been one of my brothers instead. I think she didn't really understand me but she was always very supportive. A very loving woman really.

I have always been passionately interested in politics, reading a lot and hearing my father talk about his life as a boy and his family, they had such a hard life. And it was so obvious they were being exploited yet he really couldn't see it. He was a *Daily Mail* reader all his life, believed every word they said. We used to have the most terrible rows. It was explosive when I was at home, how I stuck it I don't know, and why he didn't kick me out I don't know. So from a very early age I read everything I could. And during the 1945 Election Attlee came to Dartford, and there was a big public meeting and huge enthusiasm. It was wonderful. On my sixteenth birthday I immediately joined the Labour Party and the Labour League of Youth. I've been interested in politics ever since.

I stayed at home until I was married. It never occurred to me to move out. I mean gosh, nowadays it's unheard of, isn't it, to stay at home until you're married. I met my husband, Brian, just before my twentieth birthday at the Labour League of Youth, which was the youth wing of the Labour Party. I had joined the Dartford branch and he joined in Bexleyheath where he was living. His branch came over to one of our meetings and that was it. He said it was because I wore a plunging neckline.

Brian had also left school at sixteen and worked in London in an insurance office before he did his National Service from eighteen to twenty. After that he decided he really wanted to go back into education. He went to a further education college so I only saw him every time he came home. One Christmas, I suppose we were twenty-one, we just said, let's get married. We didn't have any money or anywhere to live, it just happened really, like most things in my life, come to think about it. We were married in 1952 while he was at Ruskin in Oxford, and I think we had about £25 between us. He went on to do PPE at Keble.

At that stage I was busy earning a living, keeping us afloat. I got a job with a market research firm which had offices in Oxford. And I worked there the whole time we were in Oxford until 1956 when he graduated. That was quite good, not as good as working in London, but interesting.

After Oxford he got a job in London with the Coal Board. The only job I could get was working for Kraft Foods in Berkeley Square and that was a bit boring. We stayed in London quite a short time, and then the Coal Board moved him up to the Midlands as a trainee manager. That's when we started the family. Our first child, Simon, was born at the end of 1956 and Sally in the middle of 1959. And then he moved again and we came up to Eastham, and that's when the Register started. Then Brian changed jobs to the Atomic Energy Authority. While there he started teaching evening classes at the local college and decided that he really liked that life. So in 1963 he got a full-time job lecturing in personnel at what was then the Liverpool College of Commerce. That's when we moved to Birkenhead. We went to Uganda in 1967 because he got another job there teaching personnel although he gradually changed to teaching management practice.

I had a most interesting time in Uganda because both the children were at school and we had a house girl so I didn't have to rush home to be there when they got home. Initially I went to work for Mengo, the local Oxfam-financed hospital, which was doing wonderful work with polio victims. Polio was rife with a lot of people with twisted limbs dragging themselves around the streets. In the time we were there they more or less eradicated it through a wonderful immunisation programme financed by the World Health Organisation I think. After a while I found I couldn't go on with the job at the hospital because it was about three miles from where we were living on the campus. I had to rely on lifts to get there and back and quite often I'd get stranded so I had to walk home, and three miles walking in Uganda in the heat is no fun. So I got a job at the university and ended up running the senior staff housing programme, which gave me huge power. It was really fun, I thoroughly enjoyed that. We had a really democratic system of allocating houses on the campus depending on numbers of children and so on, rather than status.

There wasn't a Housewives Register in Uganda, and I guess I didn't feel the need really. I mean, the campus was full of interesting women, and we had a very good social life so I really didn't need it.

It was wonderful being in a totally multiracial society where it was just taken for granted that your neighbour might be black or

Asian or whatever, nobody thought anything about it. It seemed all so simple, and I couldn't understand why race was such an important thing here. Living there it seemed so matter-of-fact and taken for granted. It was wonderful, yes.

We were in Uganda six years. Unfortunately we eventually had to send the children back to England. I think in Sally's class there were something like twenty-eight different nationalities. So it was a very good grounding for them, except that the syllabus was Ugandan-based rather than English-based. They were doing East African geography and history, so their basic knowledge of European history is a bit sketchy. At twelve the only choice was to go to a Ugandan school which was again following a purely Ugandan syllabus, and you know, you really couldn't do that to your children. When Simon was twelve we had to send him back. He's a very gregarious character and he was very happy so that wasn't a problem. But Sally, because she's much more quiet and introverted, really hated boarding school. I realised fairly early on that we were going to have to do something about this, come back to England. This was all at the time of the Idi Amin take-over, and things were getting very unsettled in Uganda. One of Brian's colleagues disappeared, murdered we found out afterwards. Things disintegrated, it was terrible really. Towards the end the vice-chancellor of the university also mysteriously disappeared, never heard of again, and on the campus they were so frightened they wouldn't talk about it. So we said, we're going to have to go. Brian then started applying for jobs and we were able to come back, and we got Sally out of boarding school. She actually ran away while we were still in Uganda. Luckily she didn't get very far. So it was a relief to get back from all points of view.

We returned in 1973. Brian came back to take over the management studies department at what is now Coventry University. An African colleague had come back before us to work in the same college. He got us a rented house, and we looked around and then we bought this place.

Once I got back to Coventry I didn't do any paid work. I thought about it, applied for a job in fact, and then I was quite glad I didn't get it. I thought, this is ridiculous, I don't need the money now. Do what you want to do, girl! I spent the first year or so helping Brian edit a book on industrial relations in Africa, his PhD subject. Then I got a voluntary job with the Citizens Advice Bureau which I did until we went to Hong Kong for five years in 1983 where Brian set up a department of management at the new Hong Kong polytechnic.

When the National Women's Register became a Charitable Trust in 1980 I became one of the original Trustees, and I remained a Trustee until I retired in 1993. So, when I went to Hong Kong I went round visiting the groups there in my role as Trustee. I also worked for the CAB in Hong Kong and for a purely Chinese advice centre. The centre was in the sticks, an area I'd never visited before, absolutely fascinating just to go there.

These days we both do a lot of voluntary work. Brian is very busy with Amnesty International, and I was Chairman of the local WEA branch for quite a while. We run a footpath preservation group locally, we have just published a new local footpath book. It all takes up a surprising amount of time.

He always says he's sorry afterwards

Ellen Malos
Bristol Women's Aid

I remember vividly one woman who came to the Women's Centre, whose husband had left her and then he had come back again, and they had gone down to the pub together and somebody said to him that she had been seen down the pub with some other bloke while he was away. So he had her up against the wall with a knife at her throat. What happened was a social worker brought her to my place, dropped her off. This was about, I don't know, 11 o'clock at night. And the social worker went away and he came back an hour or so later. I'm giving her a cup of coffee and biscuits and whatever; she had one child with her. The social worker said, 'Well it's all right, your husband says he's very sorry, you can go home now.' She said, 'I don't want to go home. He always says he's sorry afterwards. I've had enough. I can't go to my father's because my father has got a bad heart and he turns up there and you know, creates a fuss.' And there was literally nowhere but the room that we had in our own home that she could go to, because this was before the 1977 Homelessness Act when the Women's Aid movement got women written in as being homeless under those circumstances. We felt that this was something that we wanted to take hold of and do something about, that it was about the issues that the Women's Centre was concerned with.

IT STARTED WITH fairness and with workers' rights. I was in the Labour Party and in various radical groups. An organisation called the National Joint Action Committee for Women's Equal Rights had been formed and I got involved in that. One strand of activity related to pay and conditions of work, the more political and economic side of things. In 1969 in Bristol we had a meeting about equal pay which involved the local trades council, and people were very interested.

The second meeting was in a friend's house. She and I were sitting there for about twenty-five minutes and nobody came. So she said, 'Well come on, let's go to the pub.' And I said, 'Well let's wait for five more minutes.' And so we did, and two women came. One of them was Monica Sjoo, a Swedish woman who was an artist. The other one was Pat Van Twest who was also very artistic, and she wrote poetry. So there were the four of us. And we thought that we would carry on having regular meetings. Our group was particularly interested in issues around women's situations and family and single-parent families. Monica was a one-parent, and so was Pat at this stage, so we thought this was something that we should talk about.

And so for quite a while we had these meetings. We used to have alternate meetings: one week it was always a women only meeting, and the alternate week it was more about workers' rights and women in work, a mixed meeting. I suppose it was after the Equal Pay Act was passed in 1969 that there didn't seem to be the same need for the mixed group so that one dwindled, and the other one absolutely blossomed. We were having meetings in different people's houses on different nights of the week depending on who could come. We also had special interest group meetings, so there was a socialist women's group, there was a group which was active on birth control, abortion, contraception, that whole issue. And so it was a very multi-form set-up. Most of the meetings were happening in my place.

And you know, it kind of took over my life.

At that stage John, my husband, and I had a flat with a little box room, and somebody donated a duplicator so the boxroom became the office really. I had two kids at this stage, young ones. And eventually we decided we needed more space for the kids so we deliberately bought a house which had a separate entrance to the basement room so that the women's movement could take place slightly removed from our personal lives, and we wouldn't have people knocking on the door wanting to use the duplicator when we were trying to have lunch and things like that. It's the house that I live in now. So the big basement room with its separate entrance was set up as a women's centre. All of these myriad activities were going on in the basement room, and various overflow meetings were happening up in our front room from time to time as well.

I seemed to be down there every day. My children were very small, my husband was a research physicist and travelled around the world, and worked away from home a lot. I didn't actually have a full-time paid job. I was doing some part-time teaching in a school, and I started doing a few evening classes for the university extramural department. So I was home a lot, and yes, it became my work in a sense.

There was a bed in the basement room, and the husband of one of the women who was involved did some work with Samaritans, so they very often had people who phoned them up and had nowhere to go, and could we make that bed available on an occasional basis? Oh yes, of course we could. To begin with we had various people including couples, but what happened was that more and more the people who were coming were women. They were very often homeless because they had left as a result of domestic violence.

We did all kinds of things, we did pregnancy testing because pregnancy tests then took an awfully long time. When those first early relatively reliable pregnancy testing kits came out, a woman in the group who was a doctor trained us how to use it, and we used to do pregnancy testing twice a week. Women used to come because they wanted to know whether they were pregnant, not necessarily because they didn't want to be pregnant.

A typical week would certainly mean that I would be going downstairs to meetings, say three or four nights a week. The phone would ring and somebody would come in, maybe at 11:00, 12:00 o'clock, 3:00, 4:00 in the morning, and I would go down and give them cups of tea, settle them in, whatever. It did become very much a life, more than a job; I suppose a vocation really for a while. There were vast numbers of people involved, I mean it was a very very large group, and very varied, it was a whole set of groups. I don't think we ever counted our membership, you didn't pay money to join, you just came along, and if you came for more than two or three times, we did a new mailing list and you would get your name on the mailing list. The mailing list must have been something like four or five double-sided pages of A4.

We used to do a newsletter once a month, and at one stage it was myself with two other women, and it would take us probably a day, a couple of afternoons, something like that. We had a network of distributors. We couldn't afford to send it by post at that stage, because we had no money, so we used to actually deliver them all by hand. Because I had a car I could go and drop them off to the various people who were going to distribute them. The newsletter would just let people know what was happening, everything that was going on. It wasn't a discussion newsletter. So we did it for a while, and then would pass it on to another group and they would do it. We also published a journal, a sort of magazine which was called originally *Enough Or Not Enough*, and then it just became known as

Enough. To begin with we used to produce it on a duplicator, and then it started to be printed. I think we did about eight issues, something like that. It's in the Feminist Archive in Bristol, I think they've got all the copies. It contained poetry, articles, sort of agitprop things, political stuff, a real mixture, and drawings and things of that kind as well, so it was more of a general magazine. It had a national circulation at one point in its life. We produced it in the evenings unless there was a meeting going on and then it would be after the meetings ended, so after about ten o'clock.

We developed a rule that women couldn't stay in that basement room beyond Friday evening, because pregnancy testing happened on Saturday morning. I mean there was one occasion when there was a young woman staying there who was very heavily pregnant, kind of lying on the bed while women were coming in for pregnancy tests, so at that point we just said, well we can't keep anyone longer than the weekend, and if we couldn't find somewhere via Social Services or Samaritans or whatever, then sometimes one of the other women would take them into her house for a bit. But that was very hairy because you just didn't quite know how long people might have to stay. But we did that for a while, farming people out to houses of women who had a bit of spare space.

We had several irate partners coming around. We didn't really think about it very much to be honest, because it usually happened at teatime or while I was doing something else, so I just kind of went to the door and said, 'Well, you know, she's not here.' One of the men had managed to somehow get the address via Social Services. And I had one elderly man who stood on the doorstep and gave me the full 19th century line on the fact that he was in charge of the household and his wife was denying him. He said of course he hadn't hit her but she was disagreeing with him about his right to discipline their son, etc, etc. Another husband happened to ring the doorbell as I was chopping up the dinner and I actually went to the door with a knife in my hand. He didn't stay long. But more problematic were phone calls especially if they managed somehow to get my home phone number, which the police had. You could have this guy on the line sobbing his heart out and all of that, for a very very long time, and in a way I felt that you needed to talk him up to a point where you could hang up with the reasonable assurance he wasn't going to ring back and hassle you and harass you. So sometimes they were long conversations, and sometimes they were repeated conversations. And the reason I gave the police my home phone number – we had a separate phone in the Women's Centre by this time – was that it was easier to deal with night-time admissions if I didn't have to go running downstairs every time I heard the phone ring. So I would actually not answer the Women's Centre phone after 11 o'clock at night. But my own phone would ring any hour of the day and night.

The children would be upstairs in bed usually. And my husband was there a fair amount at this stage, he wasn't travelling quite as much as he had been at a slightly earlier point. One of the advantages of course of having it all happening in my house was that I didn't have to go out for my activities, they came to me and a lot of what I did with the refuge was in the daytime. We were members of a babysitting circle as well. My son certainly does show some sense of resentment about the amount of time – well John was politically active as well – that we both spent going to meetings. So he noticed.

When we were doing the pregnancy testing the Society for the Protection of the Unborn Child was just setting itself up, and a rumour went around that we were performing abortions. When we had the National Women's Liberation Conference in Bristol our place was used as a centre for looking after the younger children, and that hit the local papers. Occasionally we would get deepest-down-in-the-well-of-sin type leaflets through the door and stuff like that. Sort of 'jump off the train that's heading to hell', that kind of thing.

This was at the same time as the Chiswick Women's Aid group was set up. The history of the Chiswick set-up is interesting in that what happened was, a relatively sympathetic local authority actually gave a house for a women's centre to the local women's group, which had previously been called the Goldhawk Road Women's Group. Women started coming to that, and talking about the fact that they were afraid to go home. So that was the beginning of it. And Erin Pizzey was a member of that group. So it actually began out of a women's liberation group, but Erin Pizzey's relationship with the women's liberation movement was very difficult, and I think she parted company with feminism as a philosophy. So there was a very difficult history there, and it's been a very difficult history ever since really. The Women's Aid Federation for a long time tried to suppress public signs of disagreement because we felt it wasn't a good way to start a new movement really if it was apparently rowing internally about what it was doing and why it was doing it.

I suppose because Bristol was a smaller place, and because some of us had been involved in various political things before, we somehow managed to hold together a whole disparate set-up without splitting apart. There were different attitudes and we did have arguments but the whole thing held together as a single group with one centre for a very very long time really. And what happened rather than splits was just fragments with people getting dug in to various different kinds of activity.

I think, as a result of the publicity that Erin Pizzey generated for Chiswick, more women were probably being put in touch with us; more women were possibly seeking help who had experienced domestic violence. Local women mostly were coming to us from Samaritans and emergency social services and the hospitals. So the word had got round. We had young women with children who were deeply damaged in various ways, but who were already involved with Social Services. So they had some path into services but no real help with domestic violence because this was before the Homelessness Act. That was at the time, you may remember, when Shelter was in the relatively early stages and campaigning about the use of empty properties. So we went to the Council and said, this is obviously a need; what we've got is clearly inadequate. We were trying to farm people round at friends. We thought, this is something that we ought to do something about. And so we got people to write letters to the Director of Housing and we did this concerted campaign, against a lot of odds, because I mean one of the problems was that it was just when the new local government structure was coming in, so instead of having one authority to deal with, which had control of both housing and social services. Bristol was housing and Avon was social services.

So in fact it took something like two years before we actually got anywhere other than in my basement. And in the meantime we couldn't carry on the way we were, so we were looking for non-local authority premises as well. Finally we set up in a house which was actually owned by a friend of one of the women who was in the group, and he had bought it and it had been trashed by squatters. He was a superstitious person and felt that it had gathered bad vibes and he wanted it to have a good use, to kind of purge it as it were. So he offered us the house. We went in, and the actual staircase and the banisters had been demolished and burnt in the fireplaces, and there was rubbish up to the back windowsills. But we managed with the help of various friends. One friend from London who was a handyman, carpenter and very resourceful person even managed to recycle some old burnt banisters. We were running that, and then Social Services offered us two houses, very tiny, two-up-two-down houses side by side. So we were then managing three houses in very different parts of the city. And at that stage pretty well all of us were women with small kids, giving our time, any time that was available. We negotiated direct rent from the Social Security so that instead of the women getting the rent money, we got it direct, and that was our income except for what we fundraised. So that's really how the Women's Aid Group started in Bristol.

And then because in 1974 the Women's Aid Federation was set up separately from Chiswick Women's Aid we decided to make ourselves part of the Women's Aid Federation, so that's when we changed our name to Bristol Women's Aid. It had been called Women's House Project. But it's run by the Council now, and it's a whole new ball park.

I'm not sure what Bristol Women's Aid's future is, whether it has actually got much of one to be honest. There will be three purpose-built refuges, and possibly four, built by a housing association but it will not be run by Bristol Women's Aid, and I'm not sure even if it's got the tender. I think it has to do with the changes that have taken place and the fact that there is a tension now between offering a service, a feminist-based service based on collectivity and so on, and the kinds of accounting you have to do for local authorities and the degree of professionalisation that has to exist in order to be able to manage the kinds of funding packages that you get. So it is now much more an adjunct to the local authority, rather than an independent service. And I think what happened in Bristol Women's Aid was that those tensions began to create internal problems. So Bristol is going to have refuges, it's going to have a service, but it's not going to be run by Bristol Women's Aid which I find incredibly sad. Maybe Bristol Women's Aid will be able to keep going, a small help-line and maybe a little bit of emergency accommodation. So it's almost as if it's going back to a slightly shrunken version of how it began.

Of course in the meantime a lot of the kinds of women who were very involved would now be working, or if they weren't working they would be under pressure to be. If they were unemployed they would need to spend their time looking for jobs. You can't any longer really easily do the kinds of things that we did in the beginning. Running an unfunded service is much more difficult now I think.

Shelter had been very important for our cause too because Shelter had given local authorities a really bad conscience about empty houses. By the mid-Seventies, the palmy days of state expenditure were already over, and local authorities just simply didn't have the means to use them, so if you could find somebody else to use them for you, it was a way of easing their conscience I think. And it was a creative way of doing things as well really. And by that stage of course the whole notion of refurbishment of old houses rather than knocking them down and building new ones had come up, hadn't it.

So there was a coming together of a whole set of different ideas, yes. The late Sixties and early Seventies is a very underrated period. I mean so many of the ideas that one just takes for granted now were generated then.

———

I was born on the 31st of November 1937 in Ballarat, an old gold-mining town, in Victoria, Australia. My father was Jack Scarlett and my mother was Mabel Ellis.

My father was probably fourth generation Australian, of what we now call Anglo-Celtic background. His great-great-grandfather's whole family had gone from Birmingham in 1843 on the first assisted immigrant ship that went directly to Melbourne, rather than to Sydney, because the local colonists were agitating for much-needed labour. Later they went to the gold fields in Ballarat as greengrocers and then just stayed until people started moving away in the 1950s. My grandmother's family were Scottish and they emigrated to Australia in the early 1850s, so that on my father's side there was quite a long connection with the colony of Victoria.

My mother's father emigrated from London in about 1905. He had problems with his lungs and was told to get out of London, so he went to the Western Australian gold fields for a bit, and then as he had relatives in Ballarat he went there. My grandmother joined him on an assisted immigration scheme as a tailoress because she had worked as a tailoress with the Army & Navy stores in London. Her first job was cutting holes in First World War uniforms where there was blood so that they could be then invisibly repaired and used again. It was she who told me about the Suffragettes chaining themselves to railings. She didn't entirely approve, but that was my first inkling of the women's movement.

My parents were both brought up in Ballarat. My father was the youngest of five and he was his mother's little darling boy. She wanted him to stay on at school and become a schoolteacher but he left when he was fourteen, and went and got himself apprenticed as a painter and decorator, particularly doing stained-glass.

My mother left school I think when she was about thirteen. She did the proficiency test which meant that the brighter working-class children often left school earlier, because if they could pass this then they didn't have to stay until the school-leaving age which was fourteen. She was already going out with my father at that stage, and she actually worked in his aunt's little knitwear shop until she married. Then she gave up work and had five children – I am the eldest – over a longish period of time. She was a very important influence in the sense that she had a real feeling for history, and particularly family history, so she was a tremendous source of stories and she gave you a sense of being very connected with the local neighbourhood. She took us off, sometimes with a couple of our friends in tow, for walks in the bush and that kind of thing. My parents were both very class-conscious, very much Labour supporters, and my father was politically active in some way on the Left after the Second World War. He was invalided out of the army because he was injured in North Africa, and developed asthma.

When my father went to the war my mother was actually very angry, because he had volunteered and told her afterwards I suspect. He was a man with a family so he wouldn't have been conscripted at that stage. She was so angry that he had done it that she just took my sister and me and went off on a gigantic tour to visit everybody she knew in the most far-flung places possible. We got on a train and we went to the far west of New South Wales, where a friend of hers had married a chap who was managing a sheep station, and we went to Sydney, and at some stage we visited Tasmania. So I travelled when I was very young.

When my dad came back from the war he did a correspondence course on surveying and levelling and became a maintenance officer for the state housing commission which built and controlled huge amounts of public housing. He worked in northern Victoria, which was a long way away, and he was quite keen for us to join him. The reason he couldn't really work in Ballarat was because of his asthma.

But my mother never ever found a house that suited us, and it was because she didn't want to leave her mother really, and particularly because her father was a quite violent, aggressive kind of person when he was angry. Not that he ever raised a finger against my grandmother, but the children had quite a brutal upbringing. So, thinking about it later, this whole issue of domestic violence was part of my life. One of the stories my mother used to tell me was about how my grandmother used to take in a neighbour who lived quite a long way across the paddocks, who would come running to her in the middle of the night because her husband was chasing her with an axe because she had told him once too often that he was a drunken sod. My grandmother used to stand there and tell him to go away and go to bed and calm down. Although not consciously, when the issue of domestic violence came along, I think I picked up on it as something that had been around and something that needed to have something done about it and something which made me feel that I was linking myself back into the kind of family that I had come out of.

I went to the local primary school, and then the local high school. I loved school. I didn't like all the teachers but I liked school. I was actually very shy, and I had various physical problems. I had a turned eye and I had to wear glasses. I had a huge raised birthmark on my face, which was potentially malignant so I had to have that taken out. I had to have all my teeth out when I was three because of gum infection, which of course, was just before penicillin. And I suspect this probably had a lot to do with the fact that my father was unemployed for a number of years, and our diet wasn't all that it could have been.

There was a girl, Marion, across the road who was my best friend. Marion went on to the high school and because Marion was going to go to the high school, I think I dug my heels in rather more than I would have done if it had just been me saying, I want to go. My father thought I should go to the girls' secondary school and do commercial subjects, and I didn't want to, I had already decided that. I had some big ideas, you know.

I decided to go to university because I read a book about a mediaeval scholar, and I thought what I wanted to do with my life was to sit in an ivory tower and read books. So given that there was no money and state scholarships were not generous, I went on a teaching studentship, which meant that when I was fourteen I promised that I would work for the state education department of Victoria when I finished. As a result I got bursaries for two years which bought my books and my clothes. Only £50 a year but my mother used to make my clothes anyway. So that made it much more possible for my parents to think in terms of me going on with my education. The university studentship which I had later was paid like a salary, on which I paid income tax from the age of seventeen, but it came with this promise that you would actually become a teacher and work for the education department. So when I didn't do that, my husband, John, and I had to pay back a third of the money plus the whole of the two bursaries. I was sort of bought by my husband really from the state education department of Victoria! John lived in New South Wales and it was a different education department, so I couldn't swap to them. New South Wales couldn't buy me because their studentship was much less generous and they weren't going to pay Victoria more money than it cost them to educate one of their students.

I went to Melbourne University and did English and history, joint honours. University was just amazing. I thought it was incredible. I got very full of myself and went home in the holidays having read Bertrand Russell and sat there saying to my parents, 'Do you know you can't prove that you're really here?' I joined the Communist Party when I was seventeen, no eighteen perhaps. In those days there were not any women's groups, though actually the Communist Party was quite active on women's issues.

I met my husband, John, at an Australian Student Labour Federation conference up in the bush, outside Melbourne. He was more than ten years older than me and was doing a PhD at Sydney University. He had done a science and engineering degree combined, and got a job as an engineer with a company that had defence contracts and they found out about his affiliations and just told him to leave, pack and leave before lunchtime. So he then spent a year or so mowing lawns because it was very hard to get a job with his background. He decided the only thing to do was go back into university. We got married. And then I discovered that there were problems about being married and expecting to go on and work. One of my professors from the history department in Melbourne wrote and told me that there was a job going at the University of New South Wales as a research assistant, and he recommended that I apply for it. So I applied for it, and I had this farcical interview where they were clearly not asking me questions of any substance. I thought, there's something very funny going on here. And then they asked me how I proposed to combine my job, my two jobs. And I said, 'My two jobs?' They said, 'Well yes, being married.' And I said, 'Well I don't regard marriage as a job.' I think whatever hope I had disappeared at that point. And that was it. I enrolled and did my Masters degree in Australian literature externally from Melbourne and to earn some money while I was doing the Masters degree, I worked as a supply teacher being parachuted into various schools when somebody got ill.

We came over to England in 1962 because John was offered a fellowship at Bristol for a year, and have been here ever since. It was John's choice to stay. I mean partly because he wasn't being offered a permanent job in Australia, and because his professor felt that with his political background he could keep him on a temporary position. The professor was a Canadian, fairly right-wing. And John couldn't travel to the United States because they wouldn't let him in. So you know, what options did he really have? I think he saw Bristol as a way out of that sort of trap. And interestingly enough, though we normally talked about a lot of things together, I found out we were staying when colleagues from Sydney University physics department came to some conference in Bristol and they said to John, 'Well would you like to come back for a lectureship?' And he said, 'No.' And I thought, ah! no, hang on... We didn't either of us think we were going to stay forever, but it's just that that's the way it worked out. And by the time we thought of going back, they weren't doing the kind of work that John had started to do, so it was difficult for him to get a job. At that stage I had two small children. I had failed to complete the PhD that I started. His idea was, I do a PhD here and that would be productive for both of us but I got pregnant. I did persevere with the work, but it just became increasingly unviable really. The professor of English thought it was preposterous that I should even attempt it; he didn't say that directly to me but I heard it second-hand and you had people giving you the full-blown child deprivation line. I remember once when we were in somebody's house, having an evening out, and a woman really went for me because I was studying and neglecting my child. So when the women's movement came I was ready for it.

The first women's liberation conference at Ruskin in 1970 was very interesting and very important. There was an enormous range of people there: women in their seventies, women who had been involved in the earlier feminist movement, groups of working-class women, some of them from the trade union movement, some of them not. God knows how they had heard about it. It was very much something that offered a great deal to huge numbers of women really who weren't contented with their lot. I mean it was just a fantastic experience.

We did have consciousness-raising groups although we didn't know that's what they were called in the beginning. And of course there was the whole Housewives Register movement which had started up. It was graduate women largely who were full-time housewives and who got together to discuss ideas and issues. It started off with a letter in the *Guardian* saying, 'Will anyone join me? I'm miserable for not using my brain,' or whatever. In Bristol the Housewives Register invited the Women's Liberation group to speak to them and several of the women at that meeting became very active Women's Liberation Movement members.

I did voluntary work and bits of teaching. I persevered with my degree until after my daughter was born. I had slightly underestimated the extra impact of a second child I think. And so six months after Anna was born I got out all my stuff and sat down. One of the problems was that my PhD subject was 'The Individual and History in the Work of James Joyce and William Faulkner'. By now William Faulkner had died, and the American literary critical industry got busy and several thousand, it seemed, new books came out. I thought most of them were going to be tripe but I was going to have to read them. Up to then I had read everything that was available, I was ready to start writing, and then I had to do all this extra reading. I used to feel physically ill when I sat down to try and do it. I just thought, this is too much for me. So I put it away and got a job teaching part-time, first of all in a boys' school out at Kingswood on the edges of Bristol, and then later in a girls' convent school for a number of years.

And then I did a bit of extramural teaching, evening classes, on 'the family and other topics'. With colleagues I was involved in bringing out a book called *Half a Sky, An Introduction To Women's Studies*. And so I moved back into university life I suppose by a rather sideways route, via the extramural teaching. After a few years I decided that I wanted to put some theory behind what I was doing in the Women's Aid group, to try and understand some of the things

I was having to grapple with like housing policy. So I did a Diploma in Social Administration, a one-year course at Bristol University. And thus I became a social scientist. I worked for a year in the refuge as a paid worker after I graduated, after I got my diploma. And then I thought, no, this isn't really what I want to do with my life, and I did want to have a more theoretical, more intellectual job. In 1981 I got a temporary sessional paid job at Bristol University when somebody was on study leave, at precisely the time the Government was cutting money for the whole social sciences. Around about 1984 or so, I thought, we could start doing domestic violence research at Bristol, and Gill Hague was just about to finish working in the refuge, and so I said, why don't we draw up a research proposal. We drew up a research proposal to look at housing authorities' responses to women seeking help because of domestic violence. And we got a grant. Since then I've had periods of being officially unemployed and signing on, doing bits of part-time teaching, worked amazingly hard for a very long time. Until January of last year I was on temporary contracts, and I've finally got a full-time contract, after my 60th birthday, is this a record? And I then developed rectal cancer and went off on sick leave six months later for six months, and I'm literally just back. So finally I'm coming alive, I've got a real job. It's a bit late actually. It feels a bit late.

I still live in the same house. My husband died four years ago nearly, so the last four years have been personally quite hard. I've done things like having a major car accident and somehow or other you get these periods of one thing after another. So hopefully, but no, I'm not going to say it, because every time I think, right, that's finished, something else happens, so I don't believe disasters only come in threes any more. But luckily I'm well, I mean I haven't got any residual cancer. They keep an eye on me for five years, should be all right.

It was just of the time

Sheila Holiday
Gingerbread

One of the things about being a lone parent is that you just have so little time. I mean even if you don't get on with your husband you can go to the shops for five minutes without taking all the children with you, but you can't when you're separated. Though I have to say I did it a few times, but you see a fire engine going past and you think, 'Oh my God! which direction is it going?'

I NEVER MET Raga Woods. As a single mother with two young boys, she had escaped from an unhappy marriage and was having trouble finding accommodation. She wanted to get together with others in the same situation so she put an announcement in *Time Out* that a support group for single mothers was being set up. She was surprised at the number of responses, to realise there were so many others in her situation. She began holding meetings with single mothers in London in 1969. It is said she got our name from a West London Italian café called the Golden Age of Gingerbread where she was given coffee and cakes on the house when she was really hard up. She then moved off to Spain, and other people took over the organisation and the running of it in January 1970. If Raga hadn't started Gingerbread someone else would have done, I'm sure, because it was just of the time.

The basic aim was to help single parents to manage and cope with all their problems. Gingerbread encouraged people to set up local self-help groups and provided a telephone service to the people who were running the groups. It also gave both single parents and professionals who were working with lone parents a central point to go to. The local groups did the practical day-to-day work, dealing with needs like day care and after-school care which was just awful. And eventually Gingerbread campaigned and set up playgroups or play schools or nursery schools funded by councils.

I used to live in Putney and I had four children. The youngest one was about two weeks old when my husband left in 1970. I must have read somewhere about Gingerbread and I thought, well at least I shall be able to talk to people who are also lone parents, so I joined Gingerbread about six months after it was set up. We used to meet at Judy Chester's house in East Sheen which she shared with a young woman who had a little boy. Judy had been married to a journalist. She was a social worker so she was very good for the group because she knew about the authorities and what they provided and so she was very positive about what you could do when you were on your own. That was very useful. Well, the meetings were interesting really, because basically everyone was learning.

From that group I got on to the national committee. I worked from home for Gingerbread for quite a while, on the telephone advising people about shared accommodation. And that was quite busy but it was a bit dubious, this idea of putting people together for housing. We always said that it was their responsibility but joint occupation can be dodgy. Especially when people are at a really anxious time of their life. I mean, it's not as if most of our members were in the best condition they could be in, and some were in a terrible state. Eventually I took over all the telephone work on the housing side and moved it from sharing accommodation to housing generally.

Later on, it became much more of an information and referral service. We started having talks with Shelter who were at that time reconsidering how they dealt with one-parent families. I think they decided that you don't need to have a special list for one-parents amongst the homeless group because their circumstances are going to bring them to the top of the waiting lists anyway.

We got a national office in the early 1970s, through a grant from the Rowntree Trust in the form of office space plus my wage. This stabilised the organisation. The office was at 9 Poland Street in a building that Rowntree bought and put other organisations in, and they provided the receptionist for the whole building. Friends of the Earth were upstairs. The people in our office used to do all the group work: keeping up contact with the local Gingerbread groups and setting up new groups. At that time – I'm going to show you how far I've fallen now – I could remember every telephone number so I was like the telephone directory for the office. I knew every group telephone number and every contact, every organisation. I still don't know how I did it, and I certainly can't do it now.

Gingerbread got a lot of letters about things that related to lone parents and their children, I dealt with quite a lot of them. We were a sort of Citizens Advice Bureau service. We had a legal adviser so the legal enquiries would go to him; he would give his opinion and I'd write the letter. Originally all the people who wrote to us had a hand-written reply. But eventually it just became too much so we produced a series of information sheets. That was quite sensible because by then many of the questions were repeated, and you could put everything into an information sheet rather than just what they thought they needed to know. But they still had an individual letter as well. I took my turn in running off the leaflets on the Gestetner because everybody did everything. And then there were emotional problems, and social security of course was a huge problem, letters all the time about that, and jobs. It's so extraordinary now, thinking about it, because at the time it didn't seem that there was a career structure or further education for women. So many women who were single parents were advised to go into teacher training because it fitted in with day care, and would then allow them to run home afterwards. I was always very irritated that the only thing that could be suggested was teaching and I resolutely refused to go into it myself. The national committee was producing policy documents to give information to Government about single parents and their needs, information gathered from these letters. In addition we were providing evidence to the Finer Committee which was looking into problems of single-parent families.

After an initial period of being a volunteer, I became Gingerbread's first paid worker – mainly in a counselling role – and I got £20 a week, which was wonderful. I was there for three years. What was so good about Gingerbread was that everyone was equal. The people who were considered to have been the powerhouse of Gingerbread at that time were Gela Day, Clare Jacobs, Judy Chester – all volunteers. And Mimi Ticehurst. With her you knew at some time in the day you were holding yourself with laughter. We were learning about how to set up and organise local groups.

Attitudes generally to single parents were terrible. I think it was good that Gingerbread came along and lifted women, and the other organisation was Erin Pizzey's battered women's refuges – thank God for all that. The National Council for One Parent Families was also very effective.

At that time I think the general public felt there was a division between the different types of one-parent families. The great division was always seen to be between the widows and the others. People felt it was a tragedy that happened to widows through no fault of their own, especially their pension problems, whereas single mothers and divorced people 'got what they deserved.' There was a separate, useful organisation for widows – Cruse – based out at Richmond also with local groups. They had started up much earlier and were well established. We certainly referred people to them.

It was debilitating for lone parents to make endless phone calls in order to find where appropriate help was available. Gingerbread aimed to improve this situation by building up a reliable source of information for their enquiries.

Some of the women out in the country would take a morning's bus ride just to go to a Gingerbread meeting for an hour. That was the only kind of social life a lot of them had, and the only time their children were able to play quite happily with other children and not feel at odds with everyone around them. I think from that point of view Gingerbread really was a very good thing.

Another thing we really had great difficulty with was loneliness, with just being with the children on your own all the time. People are lonely and I think that was why the Gingerbread groups are so important, because even if a single parent can find decent housing, or childcare, or solve this, that and the other problem, you're still on your own, aren't you? I wrote a piece on loneliness and I think it went out as an information sheet.

Gingerbread groups were really able to provide long-term support. For example, some people were almost totally freaked out and Gingerbread groups supported them. I mean, a lot of the time they were an absolute pain to everyone, you think oh not again, not again. And then when all the problems were solved – with proper housing and the children settled – they would turn into some of the nicest people we'd ever met. And that kind of transition I think really was what Gingerbread was about. You know, it's getting back to yourself as a person who can deal with things and then go on and make the kind of life you wanted for yourself really, and that achieved the original aims, to survive and go beyond.

I stopped working with Gingerbread because I knew the job had to become more professional. We were meeting organisations like Shelter and the National Council for One Parent Families as well as Government departments, and we had to be seen as responsible. I think we were responsible but we felt we needed to demonstrate that we were responsible. And when Gingerbread started to hire people for the office, they advertised for people who had degrees, who had a proper cv. In this way Ruth Cohen came to us as our Group Coordinator.

I haven't really had any contact since I left. I think quite a lot of people stayed on in the groups, and became evidence to other people that you could get back to what you call a normal sort of life. They were the evidence of survival. Because a lot of it was pure survival I think, and keeping the children settled. You know, just not collapsing. For the children, it's very difficult I think, because even at its worst for you, you do have a certain amount of control.

I found out that I was actually born on the day and year that Guernica happened, which horrified me; Chernobyl happened on my birthday as well; and Jill Dando was shot on my birthday. So you know I'm not very happy about my actual birthday, yes, I'm in my sixties.

My father worked for Fitzpatrick, the road makers, as an excavator driver, and then he was a soldier in the Second World War. My paternal grandmother was married three times, the first time after being married for nine months her husband caught his bicycle wheel in the tram tracks and he was thrown and died. There were no children from that. The second husband was an engineer I think, and he had an accident and he died. He was my grandfather and they had three children, my father the eldest, and then two girls. The last marriage also produced three children, again two girls and a boy.

It was very, very hard for my grandmother. I remember her saying when my father went out to work for the first time she took a coat of hers to pieces, and God knows how there was enough material because she was so little – only five foot – and she made a suit for my father to go to work in. I mean, it's just incredible isn't it. When my grandfather died his family cut her off because she wasn't what they wanted; she was such a little thing, and they liked stately Edwardian women. She was a wonderful woman, absolutely wonderful. She died when she was ninety-two I think, and the doctor said it was exhaustion. At ninety-two!

My parents had a house in East Ham, east London. During the war it wasn't requisitioned but it was certainly let. All of our furniture went up into the back bedroom. My mother went into the Women's Air Force, my father went to the Army, and my brother and I went to Cornwall. I was three and my brother was seven and the only reason my mother let my brother go was if I went with him so as to keep the children together.

Eventually after a very unhappy billet and then a hostel we went to stay with a couple of women, one, I suppose about forty-ish, and one who was seventeen. And we were there for the rest of the five years. It was just the loveliest time. They had a little house in Cornwall next to the white heaps from the china clay works. It had two bedrooms, toilet and wash house down the end of the garden. Black range in the kitchen. And you didn't use the front room very much because that was for high days and holidays. We lived in this back room and the farmer would come and deliver milk through the window. We just ran in the fields all the time, and over the roads because there was hardly any transport around. Hardly any buses, everyone walked or rode their bikes. And it was just lovely. There was a little school there which I adored, and my best friend went there as well and we broke in a few times so we could play school during the holidays.

I always thought the trauma was coming back to London because it was the difference between green fields, and coming back to pavements and not knowing anyone, and being new in a place even though you should have been familiar with it. We stayed with my grandmother first of all because we couldn't get our house back for a while. I suppose it was difficult for my mother. She was very fierce, because she had been used to having control over her unit of Air Force girls. She never talked about anything. I didn't find out till she had died, when I was going through her stuff, that she had actually been a cook in the Air Force. I mean fancy not knowing that? And about ten years ago I started having dreams about Cornwall. Over the years I've learnt not to ask – I know it's silly for a grown woman – but I don't do it. But I thought I would be brave and ask the woman I'd stayed with in Cornwall – the younger of the two sisters, she's seventy-nine this year – 'Do you know anything about the first place we stayed when we were down there?' And her face was just extraordinary. Never seen anyone look so frightened. And I thought, what's wrong? And so she told me about this woman, the first person we were billeted with, who was a Jehovah's Witness, which was the reason for my brother's untreated impetigo. This was a blessing in disguise, as this was obviously noticed when he went to school, and we were rescued by the billeting officer. Auntie said it was quite a while before I was actually able to eat, and she used to make me a cornflour and water mixture. When I was first told this, I thought, poor child, without thinking of it as me. I think basically that most of my difficulties have come from that. You see I didn't know until ten years ago. And I know I'm upset now, but when I was younger I was the kind of woman who could cry for England, if anything sad happened, pictures, anything. If they still had jobs as professional mourners, I would have been the best in the country, you know. But as soon as I found out about what happened in Cornwall – that earlier neglect – I stopped all of that. It just went. Isn't that incredible? And the constant feeling of despair went also. So I had the worst and best of being evacuated, and thank goodness the best came last.

I came back from Cornwall when I was eight, and then did the 11-plus. I just think it was too early for me as it took me at least another two years to adjust to the return. I went on to the secondary modern in the East End and my brother went to a grammar school. After I finished school I thought, now what am I going to do? I must do something. I didn't want to be round the house all the time. So I thought, at school I'd enjoyed French, I would go and learn French at evening classes. I went to the wrong building. But at this other building they did art classes. So I joined the art classes instead. I did something just about every night of the week there. I decided I'm a group person. Group is what I like because you can go around the edges and you can still have contact with people, and nip in and out as you want to. Groups allow for freedom, equality and companionship – my ideal mixture. Anyway, that was the start. Later, Gingerbread was the second bit of my education, that was the social education really. I was raised as a Methodist and grew up thinking everyone was equal, and that everyone knew that everyone was equal. I was very surprised when in marriage it wasn't so.

Meanwhile, my mother had had this dream that she had wanted to be a comptometer operator. So she put me into that. And I went into an insurance broker's, Hartley Cooper, in Gracechurch Street.

I got married at twenty-two and left the job when I got pregnant three years later. I was married for ten years and at least five years of that I had medicine for depression. I had four children the last being only ten days old when my husband left. I thought I was going to go mad, and would have to be put away. But of course it didn't happen.

The only thing that really happened, I lost my belief in religion totally, it just went like that. You know, it had been such a presence in my childhood so that losing religion took away what had been a kind of unrecognised intermediary thing between me and everything else.

Eventually I had the £20 per week from Gingerbread but I always had money problems. I have to say my husband always paid the mortgage but it was only £10 a week and he never increased it, so the debt of the mortgage went up and up all the time. I had to pay for all the repairs, all the bills. And at one time he cut me down to about £7 a week for four children, three cats and whatever. The thing that kept us going was the Family Allowance. I used to go to Sainsbury's every Saturday morning and I'd buy three bags of flour, margarine, sugar, and I'd come home and I'd make yeast buns, and flapjacks, and rock cakes, enough to go through the week.

The other mothers down at the school did have a sort of social life but I couldn't join in because I had nothing to join in with. So what I did was put everything I had into the children. I tried to make sure that they were able to do as much as they could with their friends so they always knew how to socialise. We had things like free school dinners, different grants and all that sort of thing. They had clothes because I'd always done needlework. Though when I look back at the old photographs of that time, we all look like we're out of a ragbag. Eventually my ex-husband remarried and had another daughter, and she had absolutely everything. She had a musical hairbrush and a musical toothbrush – when we were living on subsistence level.

After I left Gingerbread I went on to do a foundation course at the City Lit. in Holborn, and I did an English degree out at Kingston on Thames which was then a polytechnic. One of the difficulties for me has been, as a one-parent family, that I've been so used to making my own decisions that it's never occurred to me to ask for advice. Silly coming from Gingerbread, but what I should have done was ask for advice about future jobs. When I left college, I thought I'll have a month off with the children at home – it's summer time – before I go and look for a job. I had something like £21 in the bank to last the month. So that plan went out the window. The sub-Post Office down the road wanted someone, so I worked there because the job was close to home and I would see more of the children, but my God! I worked long hours. In fact it was quite a disaster, because the children were on the telephone all the time I was out, and the bills were more than my wages were. I had to have a telephone call box put in.

I then got a job – I'd always liked housing you see – with someone who used to work for Shelter who was setting up his own business buying property for housing associations. For seven months I typed out the same letter every day. I decided that I couldn't stand it any more so I went to the *Architectural Press* which I liked very much, especially the people. Then it was bought out by Robert Maxwell. The funny thing was that Maxwell did a Christmas card each year, and the Christmas card just before he went overboard was of someone skating on thin ice. Eventually I was made redundant.

It took years for my maintenance to get settled and when it did the family were more or less grown up, so I decided to move house. It was actually cheaper then to move from Putney to Wimbledon, so I did. Well of course I didn't know anyone here at all. I looked around, and I saw there was a Friends of Wimbledon Theatre. The theatre had an open day so I went to that, and went to the Friends and said I'd join. And of course then I offered to do things for them. Eventually they invited me onto a committee and I've done that for years working my way from one role to another.

Now the children are living all over the place. The only one who's married is the eldest girl and she's got two little girls, eight and ten. They're lovely. Thank goodness she's got a totally different life to what I had. She wants to give her girls everything, and fortunately she's able to.

You still have to fight tooth and nail

Jean Simkins
Disablement Income Group

*I don't think it's very different for the disabled today. OK, it's improved
in some ways. But you still have to fight tooth and nail, and this still has
to be done by the very people who have the least energy at the end of the
day, those with disabilities and their carers like myself. I would get up at
5 o'clock in the morning. My husband, Geoff, had multiple sclerosis and
I would do three-quarters of an hour's physiotherapy with him in order
for him to maintain any movement at all. I would get the baby ready. I
would take the baby to a nursery at eight o'clock in order to get myself
into the office. My husband had to remain in bed until the district nurse
came to get him up.*

*I then had to pay somebody to look after him after the district nurse
came in which was supposed to be around eleven o'clock. Sometimes she
would come early, which left us with a major problem because he was
definitely not safe left sitting in the wheelchair. Mostly, the helpers
stayed with us quite a long time and they were quite good. But we had
one who was an absolute dead loss and lasted about two days because
after the first day she said, 'Is he all there?', quite audible to Geoff of
course, who had very acute hearing, nothing at all wrong with his
hearing. So I said, 'What makes you ask?' She said, 'He keeps asking me
the time.' 'Well, if you're sitting there, waiting desperately for the only
interest in your life to come back home because before that nothing is
going to happen, you want to know. So you would be inclined to look at
your watch over and over again wouldn't you, if you actually could see
your watch let alone the kitchen clock on the wall.'*

*We had a very good social worker who came round to see us
regularly. On one occasion the question was whether they could give
us any money towards a holiday, and he said, 'I can't, I've tried
every way I can think of and I cannot do anything at all to help you,
you've got too much money coming in.' By this stage I was working
half-time at the Economist, and Geoff was getting his Disability
Allowance. So I said to him, 'What about our outgoings?' 'Oh,' he
said, 'there's no place on the form for that.' We ran a car because if*

we hadn't we couldn't have got anywhere apart from where I could push him in the wheelchair.

I got home about one o'clock as a rule. The person who came in to keep an eye on Geoff usually was the person who also prepared whatever I had already bought and got ready for lunch. When I came in I would put Geoff in the car and we would go down and fetch the babe. We had the afternoon together with the little one until it was time to put her to bed. Then when she had gone to bed, we could eat and have the evening together. I tried to make sure that we never had more than two days when nothing happened because you could visibly see him going down. Boredom was a killer. And so we either had an outing – even if it was only to take him to feed the ducks in the afternoon up at Wanstead Park – or somebody came in.

There were lots of people who were worse off than us because we had the knowledge, and there were so many people who didn't. If we didn't know what we were entitled to we knew how to find out, and we damn well knew how to fight for it. An example of having to fight was the local Council's incontinence laundry service which brought sheets and took them away. The sheets were about 2 foot 6 inches wide, 3 foot if you were lucky, of course they were meant for single beds. The idea that somebody might actually be using a double bed was beyond them. And the sheets were made of a textile equivalent to concrete, which was clearly meant to go through the local Council's laundry services as many times as possible before falling to pieces. How many people's skins had fallen to pieces in the interim, nobody bothered about. And Geoff was only incontinent of urine, but these sheets used to turn up absolutely stained beyond redemption. I got crosser and crosser about this, and we moaned about them but we never got anywhere. So one Christmas I wrapped one of these sheets – I chose the dirtiest, hardest and most unpleasant – in Christmas paper and addressed it to the Director of Social Services who doubtless assumed it was from a grateful client. Inside, in my letter, I said that my husband was a man with a first class degree and a university background at least as good as his own, and I really did not see why he should be expected to sleep on this sort of stuff day in, day out. And please, all I was asking was that this guy should put it on his own bed and sleep on the bloody thing for one night over Christmas. I wasn't asking him for anything else. Whether he ever did sleep on it or not I don't know, but I do know that at the beginning of January the district nurse came and she said, 'I don't know what's happened. We've been complaining to him for years about this laundry

*service, and we're having a big meeting about it this week.' Geoff and I
fell apart laughing.*

*There was no independence, there was no dignity, there was the
assumption all the while that you were on the fiddle, and you weren't
really ill; the fact that you were sitting there in a wheelchair day in, day
out, and you couldn't speak, this was just all part of a plot to get money
out of the Government.*

TWO DISABLED WOMEN, Megan du Boisson and Berit Moore,
were the founders of what became the Disablement Income Group,
DIG. *The Guardian* published a letter signed by both of them in
March 1965 asking for support for the recognition of 'the right of
disabled persons irrespective of the reason for that disablement, to a
pension from the State to enable them to live in a reasonable degree
of independence and dignity in their own homes.' Early on they
organised a rally in Trafalgar Square, and I'm not sure whether that
was the very first public meeting or whether there had been others
before. Tragically Megan du Boisson was killed in a motor accident
on her way to the meeting. She won a *Guardian* award – I'm not sure
whether it was for a piece she wrote about disability and incomes, or
whether it was for actually getting the movement going.

I was working at *The Economist* which is in the West End so I was
pretty close to what was going on. Also, as a Methodist I was going to
the Hinde Street Methodist Church which is just at the back of
Selfridges. The church was and still is enormously active among all
sorts of disadvantaged groups. For example, we did a lot for elderly
people, and both Geoff and I were in their decorating work parties
up to the time when he was no longer able. So I probably heard
about the DIG rally there. We went along to the rally at the back end
of October 1967. I can tie the time down because my daughter was
born in February 1967 and she was a baby sitting up but not
toddling, and at the rally she sat on Geoff's knee. He was of course in
a wheelchair. He was quite strong in the shoulders, and they had got
placards, and it was rainy and windy, and there was another person
in a wheelchair who couldn't hold the placard because of the wind.
But he could hold the baby, so we swapped the baby for a placard!
Geoff held the placard to go down to 10 Downing Street. Trafalgar
Square was pretty full. There were plenty of people in wheelchairs,
many who were semi-ambulant with walking aids, and people who
had got a friend with them because they weren't really safe on their

own. Many blind people were also involved. The demonstration was well organised, and after the rally we all formed up six abreast and went down Whitehall to 10 Downing Street to present a petition. The petition was to improve income for people with disabilities – that was what DIG was all about. And that is why Geoff and I joined because DIG was doing exactly the sort of things that we felt were vitally needed.

The constituency of DIG was, and is, pretty mixed: people with disabilities, carers, and health professionals. DIG's office in the late 1960s was at Toynbee Hall, Whitechapel, London. It was quite small and very crowded. Pat Rock was certainly one of the people there. At that stage she was just a youngster in a wheelchair. I'm not sure if she had polio, but certainly her disability was from very early youth, may have been congenital. But she had a family who took a wonderfully stimulating approach in that she was expected to do the same sort of things that the non-handicapped kids did. She was expected to tidy up after herself and nobody was going to pamper her and make an invalid out of her for which she was always grateful. She had a very good mind, and an enormous slice of obstinacy and determination, which is absolutely essential if you're going to overcome the sort of problems that anybody with a disability like that is faced with. Later she won a Churchill Fellowship and she took herself off to Alberta, Canada to study a scheme where people with physical handicaps used people with mental handicaps as their aides.

I was never employed by DIG but helped out by doing research through my job at the Economist Intelligence Unit. Also in the 1970s I was on the sub-committee of DIG which was responsible for a book called *Whose Benefit?*, and was an *ex-officio* member of their executive committee. The committee met at the House of Commons for eighteen months. One of the people who was on that was Dr Margaret Agerholm. She was involved in all the work that went into revising the DHSS test for the disabled housewives' benefit. The tests and the twelve-page forms had to be experienced to be believed. Margaret Agerholm and I used to go down to the DHSS at the Elephant and Castle regularly where we battled for, oh goodness! I think a couple of years or more, over the revision of the forms. After each meeting we both banged our heads against the wall for some relief.

I remember when Sir Keith Joseph was the Minister in the hot seat at the DHSS, and he was going to speak at a meeting at the University of London Senate House. I went with Geoff and I got my question in. I asked Keith Joseph, had they done the arithmetic on the utter nonsense of a system whereby my husband, who had a deteriorating disease for which there was no cure, was required to present himself every thirteen weeks at the doctor's to prove that he hadn't miraculously recovered, and the doctor was required to waste time on signing that he hadn't miraculously recovered. And if my husband was not able to get down to the doctor's, which for many practical purposes he wouldn't had I not had a car and a will and a lot of muscle power, the doctor would have had to waste time calling on us. It was a waste of time because he was seen by the district nurse every day. Why in God's name could they not either extend the thirteen-week interval, or make the form signable by the district nurse? Actually Sir Keith had handed to me on a plate some wonderful figures. So I was sitting there doing some rapid arithmetic on the side of a page, and I was able to calculate the number of families who benefited from these medical-based benefits and hours of wasted GP time. Of course it came out as a lovely large sum, on the basis of the figures he had just given me, which was something like a quarter of a million people involved. One thing I have always admired about Sir Keith: wherever he went, even in those days, he always had two minions sitting behind him when he was answering questions, and if one couldn't come up with the answer forthwith, the other one was dispatched to go and make sure that it was there for him by the time he got back to the office. DIG had something like four A4 pages of response to my question.

For a very long time I was the only person who put my head on the block with an estimate of the cost of multiple sclerosis to the economy. I did a study for the MS Society on the effect of classifying people as either 'sick' or 'fit' which, as definitions go, is an utter nonsense if you are lifelong disabled. I mean you might be quite capable of winning at the disabled Olympics, which shows that although you are disabled, you're not sick. But there was no place in the legislation in those days for anything other than sick or fit, and if you didn't fall into one or other of those categories you got sweet Fanny. And, this was where a great many people found themselves, especially people with a variable condition, because there was this rule that you go out of qualification for the higher benefit if you try to get back to work. Some people can work for a short time and then can't continue, and this applied to a lot of people with mental conditions as well. One of the issues which has never really been coped with is this question of a partial disability allowance. Apart from those who receive compensation of some sort, most disabled people need more than they get. At that stage I would say DIG wasn't as involved with people with mental handicaps as they were with people with physical handicaps.

DIG's uniqueness was because it concentrated on the financial aspects of disability. Most of the other organisations to do with disability – the MS Society, Polio Fellowship, etcetera – were concerned with advising and buoying up those who had their brand of disability, and researching causes and cures.

DIG worked. It was well organised, we had people who had got the right sort of contacts at the top. We ran the executive meetings in the House of Commons, we had very close links with the MPs Alf Morris, Jack Ashley, and with Lewis Carter-Jones, now retired. Lewis Carter-Jones was very much involved with DIG and he had particular links with the ex-servicemen's organisations. Jack Ashley and Alf Morris were active back-bench fighters for the disability that they knew best, and all the economic implications of disability, not only for the person with the disability but for the whole family.

It's hard to say how much of the improvements for the disabled are down to DIG, because DIG has not been alone in the sense that it's been a general political development. I mean, how far DIG affected Alf Morris and Jack Ashley and how far they affected DIG is something you can never sort out. But DIG was certainly a means of giving more power to the elbow of people like them, and buoying them up when they must have got very tired beating their heads against the political wall, especially when the Tory Government was under Maggie Thatcher and the benefits situation went from bad to worse in many respects. However, I think the need for personal dignity and independence has received at least lip service.

I've had three names: the first one was Pilkington, the second one was Millward, and now it's Simkins. I was born Pilkington in 1934 in Coventry and inherited the Lady Godiva tradition of direct action I think.

My father was a soldier in the First World War, and my mother was a military nurse. They met when my mother came on the ward and discovered that there was a gap between the beds, in other words a bed had disappeared. Now, soldiers are pretty good at nicking most things, but nicking a bed out of a ward in a hospital isn't that easy. A second glance solved the problem. It was my father's bed and it had merely moved itself up and had gone between two other beds in another place in the ward next to his friend. He and this friend had both been in contact with scarlet fever in the trenches, and they were brought out because scarlet fever ran like wildfire. Neither of them actually developed scarlet fever, but because they were stuck in this ward doing nothing, they were just Trouble with a capital T. So that was how my mother met my father. He was a heating engineer but when he came back there were no jobs. Although they wrote to each other incessantly, it was ten years after the war before they finally got together which is why I didn't arrive until my mother was 43. I was the only child.

My mother was one of seven children and she was the one in the family who travelled the furthest; the rest all stayed very firmly rooted in Burton-on-Trent, but my mother got as far as Coventry. However, my parents never did get used to the idea of the modern world and the distances that people travelled. They had heart failure every time I did any trips abroad.

My maternal grandmother, whom I vividly remember, was a wonderful old lady, she lived to be ninety plus. As a girl in a grand house at Foston my grandmother was the lowest form of life, a scullery maid. My grandfather was the gardener about seventeen years older than her, and the housekeeper had her eye on him. But Grandma got there first, which did not go down well so they were both out on their ear.

My father's father was a silversmith in Birmingham. There are several pieces of his work in the Birmingham Museum. My father's mother was a stiff, Victorian lady. I used to go to the house and sit on a horsehair sofa, and didn't dare move a muscle.

Our house in Coventry was near to what I think is still known as Four Ations Corner, that was education, cooperation, damnation and salvation. The library is still there, the Co-op has gone, the pub is still there, and the Methodist church is still there. We went to that church because my mother was a Methodist.

I remember my school days because by this time the war was on. The lower floor of the school had been propped up with thick wooden supports and sandbags in between, so you had these long narrow slots in between sandbags and the wooden supports. And every time the sirens went, which was pretty frequently, you all trooped down and sat on rows of hard planks, accompanied by your gas mask and your chocolate ration in case you got trapped in there. And people were bored. My parents had always read to me and while the teachers were at their wits' end with worry about the bombing, I can remember standing there for hours telling stories. I guess the teachers were terribly distracted, whereas I wasn't. We went out and collected shrapnel after the raids, and we dived into the bunker every time the raids came on, but that was life. I don't remember being terrified or anything.

I went on to do English at university, the Royal Holloway College, London which offered me one of their top scholarships. When I got to the end of the degree course, I was offered the chance to go on and do a higher degree, but I felt that that was not going to get me into the real world. On my 21st birthday I was interviewed by an organisation which gave loans for further training for women, and I borrowed the money from them to do a secretarial course at Miss Hoster's College, on the opposite side of the road from the Museum of Natural History, Kensington. It was a wonderful place. It had about seven postgraduates like me, and the rest of the students were debutantes looking for pin money, and somewhere to put their hangover from the night before. I came out with the minimum required qualifications but no real idea as to what I wanted to do with them. I didn't actually want to be anybody's secretary, and I wasn't qualified to be secretary to anybody terribly good.

When it came to the opportunities that showed up at the time, I and another girl from Miss Hoster's both rather fancied the smell of printer's ink, and there was a job going as secretary at the Economist Intelligence Unit. So we both applied. She had the first interview so she got the job. The lady who was doing personnel work called me into her office afterwards and said, 'We don't have a vacancy, but we will have soon. Would you be prepared to come just as a typist until the vacancy comes up?' I worked as a typist for a very short time, and I think I earned about £770 a year at that stage. I was in the press service section which produced potted versions of the day's issues, very simplified, and which went out weekly to provincial newspapers and to schools.

I got involved with politics after university, and I was an active member of the Liberal Party in Marylebone campaigning for local elections, and also by-elections and I was asked if I would be a parliamentary candidate. I was a Liberal because I had no time at all for the Conservatives; I was essentially a person who wanted change, and all the Conservatives I met wanted to hang on to what they had got, which was fine if you had got anything, but I was more interested in the people who hadn't got anything. But on the other hand I couldn't cope with socialism in the form in which it was then. The constituency that I ended up with was West Ham, and I fought it unsuccessfully twice. I actually moved the date of our wedding for the second election in 1966.

I said I would not fight a constituency which I did not either come from or live in, because you can't possibly know what it's all about really. So I bought a house in Forest Gate with a girl who was a journalist, and later, news editor of the *Church Times*. We took out a mortgage together which wasn't easy at that date. When she went abroad I got somebody else in who has been a great friend ever since. She was upstairs and Geoff and I were downstairs because we could only live on one level. In fact she was au pair to the babe, and sort of second wife as far as Geoff was concerned.

I met Geoff in the late Fifties when he was decorating with the Sunday night group from the Methodist church in Hinde Street, and so was I. But at that stage he was engaged to a nurse from the Midlands, and then she dumped him. He was doing telecommunications research work. When they made the first live Telstar link between here and the States, he was in the laboratories at Goonhilly.

My mother had had a stroke, and I was travelling backwards and forwards to the Midlands every other weekend. Geoff's family lived in Birmingham so he used to give me a lift up to Coventry, drop me off and then pick me up on the way back. At that stage, my parents thought it was lovely till I had to tell them that he had been diagnosed as having MS. I said to them, 'It's the same man. You thought it was great, and now suddenly you don't.' I can understand that it was a terrible disappointment because this was their one child, and my mother was a nurse and she could see there was no future. The day Ruth was born probably did something to alleviate their pain because they had thought there wasn't going to be any family but there she was, an adorable small girl. But I think that was the hardest thing I've ever had to do, was to tell them.

I said to Geoff one night when we were watching Come Dancing on television, 'You know, it's when I hear people like that talking with absolute certainty about how they think they're going to organise their lives, that I wonder what's going to happen to their marriages if they suddenly find that one or other of them has got something like multiple sclerosis.' Because the thing that holds them together is the dancing, and if they suddenly find they can't do that, will they stay together? But we knew before we started exactly what the situation was; we knew we might have only a year or two. The difference between us and my present husband and his wife was that we knew what we were taking on. Geoff's consultant had said to us, 'You realise that you may not have very long?' So we said, 'Yes.' We did. And I asked the consultant, 'Can you tell us whether we can have a family?' And he said, 'I can't tell you. You go away and tell me.' So we went back a few months later and said to him, 'We can tell you!'

But, John Simkins, my present husband and his first wife – he was twenty-one and she was nineteen – had been married six months when she was diagnosed. They were on the receiving end of something which still happens today. The consultant told John about his wife's MS, and John said to him, 'Well when do you want me to bring her in?' He said, 'What for?' 'So you can tell her.' 'Oh no, that's your job.' So John went away and consulted the person he respected most in the world, his father, and his dad said, 'You really can't tell her now when she's so poorly. It's like kicking a man when he's down. Leave it and see how she is.' And of course she got better, and then it was, 'Well you really can't tell her now, because she's fine for the moment, and she might have a relapse if you tell her, you could do her no good.' And this went on for twelve years. One day he came home and walked into a hurricane. She was so angry. She never forgave him. She had been sitting there – by this time she was fairly immobile – watching the television, and she had come to the conclusion that what she had was what they were talking about on the television. So she got herself a taxi and she went down to the local GP's surgery and she said to him, 'Have I got multiple sclerosis?' And he said, 'Yes, of course you've got multiple sclerosis, it's been on your records for years.' He hadn't got the nous not to drop John in it either. 'Well your husband knows all about this.' And she never forgave him, because she said, 'Had I known, we would have made different decisions.' They never had holidays because they were always thinking in terms of saving the money, and that they would do those sorts of things later when the children were off. She missed out on all those things because she didn't know that the time was going to be short. Whereas Geoff and I knew, we packed every damn thing we could into the time. Twice a year we went away somewhere or other by hook or by crook, partly in order to minimise the winter and extend the summer. At the end we used to go to Jersey to a hotel for the disabled.

We lived in Forest Gate for the remainder of Geoff's life, about eight years. He died in January 1974, when he was thirty-four, and Ruth was seven.

I knew the Simkins clan as we were all part of the local MS branch. John Simkins was chairman up to about 1973. I took on the chairmanship of the MS branch once I was on my own because John was spending all his time going to see Marjorie in hospital. So the two families were still very much involved. Marjorie died in May 1975, and by this time there was another organisation that John and I were very much involved with and this was ARMS, Action and Research for Multiple Sclerosis. On 4th July 1975, ARMS had a party for all the people who had been involved in getting it started. On the 6th July John asked me if I would marry him.

In 1981 the then Chief Executive of the Economist Group sent for me, 'I am told that you know a lot about the voluntary sector.' Well of course I did, because I had been involved in DIG and all sorts of other disability organisations ever since the Sixties. Over the years the *Economist* has always been quite generous in terms of charitable giving, but it was totally disorganised. So he wanted it to be rationalised through one central committee. And he said, 'But I want somebody to set it up.' So, that was my new job.

Faith and action

Rachel Carmichael
Leicester Voluntary Workers Bureau

'Are you sick of hearing about young people? Youth clubs in Leicester
urgently need helpers. If you can't beat 'em, join 'em.' That was quite a
good advert for 1969 wasn't it?

AS A MEMBER of the Leicester Ladies Circle, which is the wives of
the Round Tablers, I was sent as a representative to the new Leicester
Council of Social Service and I was elected to the executive committee
in 1966. The committee decided to try to find out what the local
voluntary organisations actually needed. We sent them
questionnaires, and back they came with the answer: we need
volunteers. So I was involved in the discussions which led to the
setting up of a Voluntary Workers Bureau. Our aims for the Bureau
were to recruit as many volunteers as we could, to place them as
appropriately as possible in organisations needing volunteers, and
to identify gaps in provision which might be filled by developing
new projects involving volunteers.

Afterwards, when the Bureau was set up, I said to the general
secretary of the Council of Social Service, 'My youngest child is four,
just starting school, and I could do a morning a week.' Nobody really
knew what a Voluntary Workers Bureau was about but what appealed
to me was doing new things. I'd got four young children, and this
was something that sounded interesting and would fit into my
pattern of life.

Then Anne Swaine came along and joined me. She had just come
into the Council of Social Service office to ask if there was anything
she could do as a volunteer and the general secretary suggested she
work with me at the Voluntary Workers Bureau.

We were I think the third Voluntary Workers Bureau in the
country. There was one in Camden, and one in Manchester, and we
went to visit both of them to see what they did. The building we were
in at 39 London Road has now been demolished. It was very ancient,

very dark and dirty; we didn't have an office of course, we just had to find a desk to interview people. The general secretary of the CSS pretty well had to move out of her office when we wanted to interview somebody. The Citizens Advice Bureau was also there with a very crusty elderly volunteer organiser with whom relations were not very easy. In the same building was the newly started Council for Community Relations which was initially part of the Council for Social Service. We were I think on the third floor, up brown linoleum coated stairs with rubber strips on. The whole thing was very tatty. And quite noisy because it was right on the main road, in a way it was quite a good location because people knew where it was.

The general secretary of the Council for Social Service prepared a booklet called *Are You A Good Neighbour?* which was a sort of volunteer recruitment booklet. People were already coming in sporadically but we then asked them to come in on Wednesday mornings or Friday afternoons, which is when we were available to see them, and sometimes in the evenings because of course some people were in full-time paid work. And then we started to recruit more actively for volunteers. We mostly used the local paper, the *Leicester Mercury*, for which the Women's Page editor wrote occasional articles. We had very little in the way of a budget but we did also start to put in small ads too. Now most weeks the *Leicester Mercury* has at least two whole pages featuring community activities with volunteers.

In August 1969 the Voluntary Workers Bureau started the English as a second language teaching scheme. I can remember a young man teacher who had come from somewhere in Yorkshire where they had a scheme for teaching English to Asian women. He came in saying that this is what he wanted to do. Although we were building up our own job cards of 'vacancies,' there was no apparent demand for teaching English to Asian women. There hadn't as yet been a big influx of Asians into Leicester; they came in the early Seventies. So, what I did was talk to people in the Education Department and to the Community Relations Officer, but they didn't know of any Asian women seeking English teachers. Then I thought who knows these women? Maybe the health visitors. I went to talk at a health visitors meeting, I well remember that. That was the summer of 1969. They were very interested, and very soon we had about 100 Asian women who wanted to learn English, and only one volunteer teacher. So then I wrote to the letters page of the *Leicester Mercury* asking for volunteers. We got a lot of replies quite quickly; it was a mind-blowing potential scheme, and fortunately we found an excellent woman, named Elizabeth Loosmore, to help with the organising of it. Elizabeth did this as a volunteer for a number of years, working from home and putting in hours of work. As a result we recruited a lot of volunteers and it became a very good scheme. Eventually, after she had done it for about five or six years, the Council of Social Service employed a part-time organiser, funded by the Leicestershire Education Department and then, quite appropriately, it was taken over by the Education Department itself.

That's the kind of thing that I love doing. We didn't go out and say, let's start things; we developed what came to us, of which this was one interesting example. Another example again in 1969, we were getting a lot of requests from the Children's Department for volunteers to go and work in children's homes. The Children's Officer was a member of the Council of Social Service executive committee and he was also on the committee of the Voluntary Workers Bureau. So I knew him well, he was a good mate, George Creighton. And we used to send volunteers to these children's homes, but it was chaos really. Nobody knew where the volunteers were going, nobody was following them up. There was no system for paying their expenses. Then Margaret Harrison came to the Voluntary Workers Bureau as a volunteer with experience of running playgroups, and she wanted to do something with children, so I said to her, 'Look, what they need in the Children's Department is an organiser of the volunteers!' I rang George Creighton and said, 'I've found you somebody you need.' Margaret became the volunteer organiser for children in care, and we sent her any volunteers wanting to work in children's homes. This ensured that the volunteers were realistically matched and were well supported. In 1973, Margaret Harrison got a Churchill Fellowship to go to the United States to look at the US Headstart idea where they paid para-professionals to work in homes where parents were having difficulties with their pre-school children. This helped her to develop Leicester Home-Start which offers support, friendship and practical help to young people experiencing difficulties. Home-Start went from Leicestershire to the whole of the UK and is now international.

Not every project got off the ground! I'm not sure whether it was the late Sixties or into the early Seventies when another woman came to talk to me. She was a primary schools adviser who wanted to get a number of volunteers to go into primary schools. But it was the wrong time, the teachers were rather defensive. So that could have been a great scheme, but we didn't really even dare to advertise for 'uncle' or 'aunt' for deprived children because the schools adviser realised that the teaching unions would be very much against it.

A good development, a little bit later in the early Seventies, was when a psychiatric social worker wanted to get some volunteers to work with some of his patients in the community. Again, we were very closely involved in that. We recruited his volunteers for him, and we used to have a monthly meeting which met initially in our dowdy offices. So that was another good experience, in a newish area.

For the first four-and-a-bit years the Voluntary Workers Bureau was run by volunteers. We were all married women with children. I worked as a volunteer at the Bureau one half day a week, and my colleague was there the other half day. The two of us, doing half a day each at the Bureau, would also work at home writing the reports and keeping some fairly careful statistics. I was always interested in keeping good records. In 1972 we got our Urban Aid grant for the Bureau to pay part-time staff so we were paid for the first time. The Voluntary Workers Bureau is quite well staffed now, and is open every day. But when you are working part-time, as you know, for voluntary organisations, you work much more than that. Going to meetings outside your working hours, that was all done extra of course. I remember saying to the Children's Officer, I think you get much better value from part-time paid people because when I'm gardening I'm thinking about the work, and I think you get people coming in fresher with more energy.

We were also trying to promote good standards among organisations which used volunteers. We were reluctant to refer volunteers to organisations who couldn't pay their expenses. We felt that volunteers have a right to have their travel paid, and so we were, I think, trying to push out the boundaries for good practice with volunteers. We were in a good position to refer volunteers to organisations which we felt used good practice, and not refer them to others.

I think what is interesting is that one strand of my life often leads to another, and they intermingle, and as you'll see later on they continued to intermingle. I was involved in developing the local branch of the National Association for the Welfare of Children in

Hospital in the Sixties and as a result of this involvement, in 1969 I was put on to the Sheffield Regional Hospital Board and was allocated to one of the local hospital management committees, the one covering the psychiatric and subnormality hospitals as they were then called. I was visiting these hospitals wearing my regional health authority hat so I could see some of the obvious needs. Glenfrith was one of the subnormality hospitals where I had got quite friendly with the chief nursing officer. They were just appointing voluntary work coordinators there, and we sent many people to them. Again, we had good links with the assistant chief probation officer. The Probation Department had always been forward-looking about involving volunteers and had good training schemes. We also referred volunteers to city schools, voluntary playgroups, youth clubs, city mental health department, hospital leagues of friends, and so on.

We had a card index covering about 120 jobs, and for each organisation we had a good link person, someone we knew. We would always go and see that person before we put their organisation on our card index. The available jobs were divided in our card index into daytime, evening and weekend.

The largest group of volunteers was always the group in their twenties, which was surprising. They weren't in a sense, and couldn't be, the most long-lasting volunteers. If you like, the most reliable and long-lasting were the early retired or people in their fifties who knew what their life pattern was, and could see that that they wanted to do this, and could stay at it. Obviously students, for example, are going to be much more mobile and might just come for a Christmas placement. But always our largest group of volunteers was in this twenties age group.

Right through the time that I was involved, we always gave each volunteer a half an hour first interview. For the first quarter of an hour you were trying to find out as much as you could about them: their needs and their desires and their skills, and perhaps the things that they might not be so good at, but that was more of an instinctive thing. Then the second quarter of an hour you were feeding back to them suggestions of things that fitted in with their time, their availability, their skills; what seemed to you might be suitable for them. You would say, well, what about this, and this is what it involves, and what about this, and this is what it involves. But you did use some of your female instinct about people – you had to, it was such a short interview.

Then we would give them a referral form with all the details of the job the voluntary organisations needed doing and they could go away and think about it. Or if they said they'd definitely go and talk to, say, Mrs Pickering at the Red Cross, then we would send a referral form to Mrs Pickering as well. We developed a sort of complementary system with a pink form that we sent to the agency which we asked them to send back to us. It was a rather nasty blancmangey pink, which we chose hoping they would want to get it off their desks quickly and get it back to us!

We did a follow-up with the volunteers after six months to find out how it was going. I think we developed some good systems, some of which I expect we picked up from the other volunteer bureaux. There wasn't at that stage a national volunteer centre.

The National Volunteer Centre started in the Seventies. In fact I was on the Volunteer Centre board in 1977. Mike Thomas was the first director and he brought his team to Leicester, really at my suggestion, to do a survey of what was going on in the voluntary sector and in volunteering. This resulted in a report on Voluntary Activity in Leicestershire. There was then somebody at the Volunteer Centre working on Voluntary Workers Bureaux whom we linked with and so we started to learn about other volunteer bureaux. That was a good development.

The Sixties and early Seventies were extremely exciting because there was such a lot of new development. I was really lucky I think to be involved just at that stage. In terms of my paid working life and voluntary work, the Voluntary Workers Bureau was definitely one of the most exciting and fulfilling times, because there were always new things to be sussed.

From my personal point of view, as I've implied, it gave me a great deal, because while I was very involved with the family here was a contact with the real world, and an opportunity to do something really challenging, in a fairly limited time-scale. I worked in the Voluntary Workers Bureau until 1979, part-time paid and then I went for full-time jobs. So we developed it over eleven years. And so, I reckon I was very lucky to have the chance to do a job like that.

———

I was born in Birmingham in 1933, so I'm now sixty-eight, and my parents were I suppose church workers. My father's father was a stoker in a mill in Heckmondwike in Yorkshire. He used to tell us vivid stories of finding a finger in the coal when he was stoking the boiler. He was a manual worker. My father was one of five and he and his sister were the first generation to go to university. Daddy got an MA, my aunt got a First in French. So that was a big jump, from Yorkshire, leaving school at fourteen to get trained and through university paid for by the Church. My parents met at one of the Selly Oak colleges, Westhill, where they were both training to be youth workers, my father for the free church called the Churches of Christ, my mother for the Quakers. They married, and I was the first of four children. My father became the warden and then principal of a theological college in Selly Oak called Overdale which trained ministers for the Churches of Christ. I was brought up and lived in Birmingham until I went to university. My mother had left the Quakers, and joined the Churches of Christ because in those days you couldn't really be the wife of the warden of a theological college if you weren't a member of the same church. But once we moved to Leicester in 1954 she resigned from the Churches of Christ and joined the Quakers again. She was always a Quaker at heart, and he was very loyal to the Churches of Christ because they had given him his education, his everything. Mother was quite a strong personality, so he used to come to Quaker meeting, and when he was eighty he joined Friends as well. So he was a dual member of both denominations.

I had three younger sisters, we're four girls, and we had a wonderful, wonderfully rich life. I mean, not rich, we were very poor, and because my father only got about £300 a year plus our keep we were on a very tight budget. We couldn't go on history outings or anything like that – we didn't even tell them there were such things – because we knew there wasn't any money for that. But, in terms of family life really very full, full of church things, music and choirs and sport. My father was a very keen sportsman but he couldn't of course play in the County tennis team because they had their matches on Sundays. We knew that there were sacrifices being made because this is the way they had chosen to live.

I went to Bournville Village School, and from there I went to King Edward's in Birmingham which was a highly selective High School for Girls. Astonishingly, from my primary school I was the only one to get in. It was a very academic school for girls, which I thoroughly enjoyed, especially the hockey! And from there I went to the London School of Economics, the first girl from King Edward's ever to go to the LSE. They'd never heard of it, it was too left-wing. I wanted to be a social worker of some kind, and so I read sociology in the very early days of sociology, and nobody much knew what it was. I don't think LSE was very clear either. But I had a great time there, and was the Chair of the Student Christian Movement, women's hockey captain and various other things.

When I left LSE I had to have a year off. I was too young at twenty-one to train as a social worker or a probation officer which was what I wanted to be, and I was told I had to get some experience of life. My parents had moved to Leicester where Daddy became a teacher of religious education. So I worked in the Chilprufe factory in Leicester making vests for a year. I was winding beautiful wool on a winding machine mostly. During that year I met my husband, David, who was the son of one of my father's best friends. The first day we moved to Leicester they asked us to tea. We got engaged and then married when I was twenty-three, so I never did the social work or probation training because in those days one didn't. David was a yarn merchant in the family yarn business, and was well off enough and everybody could see that I would have a safe life.

We were married in 1956 and then the first child was born in 1957, and then we had one every other year until 1963. I can't remember how I managed the child care but it wasn't a major problem. People say I've got a lot of energy, which is obviously a help. I never felt tired.

My fourth and youngest child had congenital talipes – he's all right now – so he had to have various operations at a local hospital. The visiting hours were only an hour a day, and this was between 1963 when he was born and when he had finished his treatment in 1966. And that's how I got involved in the National Association for the Welfare of Children in Hospital. When his treatment finished I started the Leicester branch of NAWCH, and we started campaigning for longer visiting hours – writing letters and holding meetings, and so on. Then in 1968 NAWCH was asked, had we got any members who would be suitable to go on the different regional hospital boards. Richard Crossman, the Minister of Health, was trying to get a few slightly more radical members on these very grey-haired, elderly committees. So I said yes, not knowing what a Regional Hospital Board was. I was a member of health authorities at various levels for the next twenty-nine years!

We've lived in Leicester all our married life. My parents only died in the last two or three years. They used to live over the road. And I suppose the motivation, just thinking about what we've been saying up till now, was a strong family Christian service element in our upbringing, and indeed I hope we've passed that on to our children. I was a member of the Churches of Christ, and then became a Quaker in 1981, as is my daughter. Our sons all went to the local Anglican church choir which they adored, and so they became Anglicans of various types. I think that my motivation has really been very much a combination of loving doing the things that I've done, but also a feeling it was the right thing to do. A sort of link between, if you like, faith and action. So it's been very fulfilling from both points of view.

I think it was the chairman of the Health Authority who nominated me for the OBE. I was very hesitant about accepting. I don't approve of selecting out people. But I felt the honour was one for Leicestershire Health Authority which deserved it. So I accepted the OBE for services to the National Health Service in Leicestershire. Then they obviously looked at my c.v. again, and when I got to the Palace it said, For services to the National Health Service, and voluntary services in Leicestershire.

As my children were getting older, in 1978 I got a full-time job for a year with the Council of Voluntary Service – formerly the Council of Social Service – and then the director moved to Sheffield so I applied to be the Director, a job which I held for eight years. It was the first time I felt able, given my home situation, to have a full-time job. I hadn't wanted to before and it all fitted in beautifully. I wasn't ambitious at all but it was just that the then Director left and I had to decide, would I rather do this job or have somebody else I don't know managing me. I rather reluctantly decided to apply for the job.

Our eldest son committed suicide in the middle of his medical finals. He was a strong-minded Christian who felt deeply about the injustices of the world. He had done an elective in the Gambia, and realised that what poorer countries needed was food and water, not medicine. His death continues to challenge us, but the family has been wonderfully supportive and united through the sadness.

My husband is six years older than me and he retired in 1986. Then I realised, he was at home and I was slogging my guts out morning, noon and night as the Director of CVS. He would never complain, he's very supportive, but I just started to see my life from his point of view and realised that it was rather silly. So I slightly wound down from paid work, rather like the way I got into paid work, in a gentle way, which balanced the family needs. I didn't have a sudden retirement, I gradually phased out. I applied for a part-time job with the Leicestershire Association of Voluntary Agencies. I chose to do that because it was a part-time job and I was the coordinator for five years. I had the Health Authority work running all the time. It's only from 1991 that I was paid as a Health Authority non-executive director. Up till then all the health work had been voluntary. I'm still the Chair of the Friends of Leicester University Botanic Gardens, I am also a volunteer Neighbour Mediator, and am also involved in a lot of national Quaker committees. I go up to Friends House in London a couple of times a month.

David is very keen on his allotment. He's got a good voice, and he reads as a volunteer for the Society for the Blind on their taped newspaper. And we both are involved in lots of other interests and local organisations of various kinds. So we keep busy. I've just taken up bird-watching. David has been a bird-watcher all his life but I've never been interested in it, and I've suddenly learnt how to look through glasses properly. So we go to Rutland Water which is a beautiful place, quite close, so that's another new interest. Our children are all happily married and living full and useful lives. We have a growing number of beautiful grandchildren – so what fortunate people we are.

I reckon I've been extremely fortunate in my working life. To have had openings which have met my needs as well as, hopefully, other people's too.

Putting colour into the environment

Martin Goodrich
Free Form Arts Trust

The starting point for us – myself, Barbara Wheeler-Early and Jim Ives – was that we were visual artists, painters, from east London. The three of us were leaving art school at the time when art was meant to hang in galleries, but whether your work was of any value to society beyond being decorative was very much in question. What value are you as a painter? What good is this talent you've got? What are you going to do with it? These were the underlying questions one was constantly asking. And of course at the same time the Sixties was happening, we were kids in the Sixties so we were part of the whole liberation thing and of doing things radically and differently, saying sod it let's just do it. We were moving away from parents whose upbringing had been to conform. We felt we were extremely privileged to get to college from a council estate. We were the first generation of Wilson's new world.

WE WROTE A manifesto which was called *Us Towards the Live Situation*. It said, there are people who have benefited from art education but they have to create the circumstances where others can start to respond to their ideas as artists. We were very much influenced by various socialist writings at the time. One of my predominant influences was a philosopher called Octavia Ugasit who wrote a very short book – I think that's why I liked it – about the demystification of art. He argued that for ordinary people art was becoming more and more mystified, and he believed that ordinary people needed art but for them to begin to comprehend it, or to be involved in it, art needed to be demystified.

The three of us produced this manifesto as part of my thesis in 1968. We were sharing a flat, banging these ideas about. Our starting point was can we as artists work together, can we do joint projects? All of our training had been how to learn as an individual, acquire individual skills and come up with individual ideas. At that time we were sharing a property but we didn't get round to calling ourselves a cooperative, I don't think the thought had even occurred to us, but the idea was that what is mine is yours and vice versa. I think that idea was going around generally anyway, I mean it was in the air, you could pick it off the trees.

That was the beginnings of Barbara's and Jim's and my professional career together. We were looking for projects to do based on our idea of how can you do things out there in the community? We were talking along these lines to some people who included an art educational adviser to a local authority in London and he said, 'Well, I like what you're saying; what I'd like to do is to see whether we can find a method where young people could learn about colour without being taught it.' In other words that colour would be in their environment, so they could observe it and therefore understand it. We developed a proposal to transform the environment of a school playground by including colour. We spent three months in the summer of 1969 working away in our bedroom studio trying to introduce colour into the school playground in a very ambitious way. I mean we were talking about the Yellow Brick Road, we were talking about completely transforming buildings. We produced models and drawings and ideas, and presented an exhibition at the school. The exhibition was applauded by all the art people as being wonderful, terrific, and we got the Arts Council interested. But we did begin to notice that the members of staff said nothing so you didn't know what they were thinking. Similarly when we showed it to the pupils we found that there was a mixed reaction. There was a small minority who liked it, and were even enthusiastic. I was getting a bit worried and I asked the unenthusiastic young people, 'What's wrong?' Some got up the courage to say, 'Yes well, this is all very well, but you're going to make our school stand out; we're not sure that we want our school to stand out. We think that we come to school to be at school.' So these young kids were giving us a conservative reaction to change, they didn't like the notion of change if it was going to affect them. We got a debate going and we quickly picked up that we had actually made a fundamental mistake in our own plans. Here we were devising ideas for the benefit of others, but we hadn't actually involved them in it at all. We'd presented our ideas as a *fait accompli*. So we came back to the studio and re-wrote our proposal, saying we realised that in fact we had been imposing ourselves and that we would prefer to spend three months working in the school to test our ideas, to challenge them, to pick up on where the staff and kids were. And our proposal was rejected. They tried to buy us off by just taking a little bit, you know, you could do this entrance way. We stuck to our guns and said no, we think that we've got this wrong, we have to own up to the fact we got it wrong, and really if we're going to propose this kind of project we have to work in partnership with this community, and we have to identify that they are the client, the real client.

That was the beginnings of the intellectual theorising about what I would call community arts. First, you identify issues and needs and don't assume that you know what they are. Second, in doing this you create methods whereby people can have a voice themselves so as to empower those with the creative tools to come up with their own ideas. This raised the question, how can an artist do that? You've got to create an opportunity for community participation, physical participation in both thinking through the creation of a design and the implementation of that design. That was the lesson of the late Sixties. If you were serious about working outside the gallery in public spaces, then you had to be socially responsible to those for whom you were producing the art.

There was this notion, yes you should work in the community but there was also this feeling that you had to take yourself seriously as an artist and present your art to the art world. We started to look around us and we found in fact that we weren't on our own, there were many other artists thinking along similar lines. These included Space Studios, Action Space, Space Structural Workshop. At this point we called ourselves Visual Systems. We began meeting with these artists and decided to mount a joint multimedia exhibition. The exhibition was to be in Waverley Market in Edinburgh in 1970. We worked as a group on this throughout 1969 deciding what we would be doing in this massive hall, what the art would be, and how we could get sponsorship, et cetera. These were the beginnings of our career as community artists.

We supported ourselves in those days in any way we could. I was on the dole for six months, and Jimmy was finishing his last year at the Royal Academy so he still had a student grant. Barbara was at college up in Manchester but spent all her time down in London with us. So we were surviving on a mixture of the grant aid system and a bit of subsidy. And then I got a part-time job in a factory doing metal work partly as a route to making some maquettes for the exhibition. Also by using their tools I could start to think how we might actually mount this exhibition. We began to realise that we needed materials, new materials, and so we started to pursue various sorts of sponsorship by writing directly to the manufacturers. And we found ourselves being remarkably successful at that. It seemed that industry were quite willing to give you the things they made, providing it wasn't the finished product but just a component of it. So you could get wire rope from one company, bulldog grips or bottleneck screws from another company, and then you could go to yet another company and get metal tubing. We ended up being the material gatherers for the whole group of artists.

We were looking for a studio and were offered a prefab construction on a wonderful derelict site. I think it was the last remaining bomb site in Plaistow in East London, where an old school had been demolished. We were allowed to occupy this prefab which was in the middle of a tip and surrounded by traditional turn-of-the-century two-up-two-down cottages, built by private landlords and rented to the working classes. It was also right next to Ronan Point and other new high-rise flats so the area was in the process of change. It was terrific but since the place was surrounded by housing the site was a natural kids' play area. As soon as spring arrived all of a sudden you had hundreds of kids running up and down. We thought, we can't cope with this, we can't work, they're just driving us nuts. School was out and in the evening it was just mad. And so we thought, we've got to do something, well let's become their friends. We started playing football and then they became curious and started asking, 'What are you doing in there?' We said, 'Look, we'll do a deal with you. We'll play games of football with you at certain times, and then we'll have an open studio for two hours in the evening provided you let us get on with our work.' So we actually started to do impromptu workshops which went reasonably well, and lots of kids came in and did things with various materials, played around, painted and were just curious. After a while they started to drift away but at least ten of them were still around, our mates.

As we were trying to organise this big multimedia exhibition in November, we thought, why don't we do a live experiment here on our patch of what we are proposing to do in Edinburgh? We called it *Free Form Fun Event*. Overnight we built a big structure out of scaffolding. We had masses of materials dyed and cut into triangular shapes, and we put up coloured sails. It was all about putting colour in the environment. The community woke up to an event like a fun fair, and they all came. We painted the grass and the Scratch Orchestra played saxophones and flutes and violins and oboes in various places around the estate. We had this huge inflatable structure, the kind of thing you see now but which has become commercialised. We also had a big mural painting exercise, the 'how not to paint a mural exercise' we later called it. It was a complete mess, kids going home covered in emulsion paint. But they had a terrific time. We were absolutely exhausted. We were actually a bit embarrassed by it, and the mural painting was disastrous. The kids wrecked lots of things, taking everything on as their own playground, so chaos reigned. In fact they took it over. So, we thought, well let's ask the neighbours what they thought, and we sent round a questionnaire with questions such as: What do you think it was? Should it happen again? Who do you think should pay for it? It was a kind of market research. Incredibly, we got 60 per cent response. Mind you, we did go round and say, 'Can we have our form back please.' Basically what they said was, yes, it should happen again, the Council should pay for it, and what it was, was a play scheme. At that time we had never even heard of anything called a play scheme. So given that response we wrote to the Council saying, here's the evidence of the success of the event, the neighbours think it should happen again, so maybe we should repeat it. After about a year of badgering we got some money to do similar events in other parts of the borough.

At the same time we were preparing the art event for Edinburgh but it was cancelled, so we transferred it to a huge building on the Euston Road opposite Madame Tussauds. We took over all the outside areas and had this multimedia event. This was much more self-consciously 'artistic' than the Free Form Fun Event; all the materials were sponsored and aimed at an art audience, and everything was much more controlled. The difference was, the first event was extremely interactive, lively, and involved hundreds of people, and the second was sterile because hardly anyone came. And those who did were other artists who responded to it as artists respond to other artists' work. There was this sense of anticlimax. We were able to compare the two events and say, well, which one of these was more successful? On the one hand we found the live action

Free Form event the most satisfying. On the other hand the community hadn't really allowed us to be artists, we were social entrepreneurs providing entertainment for their kids. We felt, well we haven't quite cracked it, what we want now is to introduce something that was actually 'art' into the community.

After a year and a half we had to leave the studio because it was being demolished. By this time we were getting small grants and a few commissions, £100 a time, three times a year or so. There was very little money but there was a huge amount of energy. And it was no longer just us. Whenever we did something in public many young people interested in art joined us. We were beginning to develop a network of young people who were interested in participating in our events, and experimenting. The three of us – Jim, Barbara and myself – were the organisers, we were the creative catalysts, and then we invited other people to contribute. We then started doing some multimedia exhibitions called Blow-Up for the Arts Council.

The Arts Council organised about six exhibitions over the course of a year, and we went on tour each time doing something different. First of all we built a big main structure which took a hell of a long time to put up and take down again. And then we decided on something that was really a performance using costumes, dyeing rags and stretching the rags all over the environment to create different forms. The events were becoming increasingly about performance, less about exhibitions and static art work. We did things like street parades which would go through the back streets, riding horses through Woolworth's and Marks & Spencer, and creating mayhem and provoking interest and reaction. We did an event called Artism Lifism at the Harrogate Festival which brought in lots of people but many were confused by what we were trying to do. I mean, the front entrance piece to our exhibition was totally invented on the spot. It was two powerful garden water sprinklers and then two swings which would criss-cross so that they created a pattern of water going shhh shhh, and then the swings doing the opposite with lighting projecting into it. Everyone got wet so they were provided with coloured umbrellas. Anyway, it was just wonderful fun, amazing stuff, and people were coming up and saying, really wacky, amazing. We constructed a large maze, Barbara started doing a piece called architectonic paint rag which was a huge box of muslin which was coloured and hung up, so it was like doing instant Jackson Pollocks in an enormous space. Lovely stuff really. We were part of the official Harrogate Festival but we were so alternative that the concert players began getting fed up with this, because we would go to the various arts clubs and evening events and cause mayhem. An artist called Robin Classic sprayed the grass with paint and a little poodle came past and he sprayed the tail of the poodle and it was headline paper stuff, 'Artist vandal...' And then the minister came and we sprayed him so the *Daily Mirror* was hunting us for the next outrageous stunt.

In retrospect Artism Lifism was something of a watershed between those artists interested in fixed exhibition forms, and those interested in the process and transitional, time-based work which created spaces for participation. We realised that our real interest was to create something in a community context, and to create original pieces of work. After that we never went back to an exhibition format. We then did a whole series of festivals in the community, minimally funded by the local rather than the national Arts Council. One was in Canning Town which was enormously successful done with hardly any money but using hundreds of volunteers. This featured the artist, Ian Dury, and the Kilburn Highroads giving them their first outdoor stage. We also realised that there was another person doing a festival, an artist called Maggie Pinhorn in the East End of London whom we got to know. Out of that connection and through other networking we formed the Association of Community Artists, which became a focus for all the artists who wanted to collaborate in this way. By this time we were living on the top floor of an old furniture factory in Upton Park which we got from the GLC. I created an arty penthouse suite on the top which had a view out over the Thames where you could hear the hooting ships. There was a genuine pride about being a Londoner at that time in the 1960s, and about being part of a community, about being East Enders.

Money was tight. Barbara started teaching, and then she decided to go to Goldsmiths' to do the art teachers degree but she still was part of Visual Systems. Jim started doing cleaning work to earn a living, and I did a bit of work in a factory. But then Joan Littlewood of the Stratford Theatre Royal in East London rang us up, said that she had heard about what we were doing in Canning Town, and thought that it was really good and it was what she had been trying to do for years. She had actually set up something called the Fun

Palace Trust but I think it had never got off the ground. She invited us explaining, 'Look, I'm going to do this show which is about people going on a package holiday.' At that time the package holiday industry was just getting going. It was called *Costa Packet*. It was dreadful. But what she wanted to do in the show was to say to the audience, 'You don't have to go to Torremolinos, you can get a holiday in Stratford if you look around you.' The job was to deliver the holiday in Stratford which at that time was in total chaos. I had an interview with the theatre impresario, Jerry Raffles, and was given a job to enliven the outside space. For the first time I was actually being paid, I was getting £20 a week, and they agreed to take me on for two months. I said, 'Well the first thing I've got to do is to raise some money.' For the first week Joan criticised me saying, 'What are you doing, sitting in that corner writing? You're an artist, get out, be an artist.' I said, 'No, I want to write this proposal, I'm trying to get some money out of the Arts Council.' Which I duly did. I got her her first Arts Council grant. We were awarded £2,000, which at the time was big money. And so we did this whole programme of animating the streets around the theatre as much as we could, animating the space and doing things mainly focused on the kids. We painted our first serious mural, and ran children's workshops making music, doing things about maths. It was all good, innocent lovely stuff. At the same time Joan was doing her show, and of course the relationship between outside the theatre and inside was nil. She said, 'Well when push comes to shove, I'm afraid this whole horrible box takes priority.' The theatre in the box as she called it was a compromise. The idea of coming out of the box, forget it, it was a dream in her head. But she was quite inspirational and through her we met lots of other people. You realised that there were all these architects and others who were interested in the whole notion of rejecting conventional mechanisms for doing art. You realised you were part of a groundswell movement coming out of the Sixties, which was about let's change things, let's do it differently, let's challenge the conventions.

Through Joan Littlewood I met the architect, Cedric Price, and he told this wonderful anecdote, making the point that an architect is also there to provide good social advice. His example was when he was asked to build a house for a couple. He began by telling them, 'In order to be briefed, I'll come and stay with you.' After staying with them for the weekend however, his advice was they didn't need a house, they needed a divorce. The point is that if you are an artist working to serve a community you have to understand the life of that community. You have to ask, what are the issues here? Well the issue could be there's nowhere for the kids to play; or the kids are bad, they're always in trouble with the police, so you've got to tackle those issues. Your art has got to address these issues.

In 1973 we moved to new premises in Dalston Lane and opened with a documentary exhibition called the Growth of Public Art which featured our work from the previous four years. We decided to call ourselves Free Form rather than Visual Systems since this reflected better the work we were doing. The term Free Form is taken from free form jazz. In other words, there are no restrictions to this area of work, you can actually follow your own thought process and arrive at a conclusion provided you are doing it in partnership with the community.

One of our projects was working with community groups in Liverpool. They had established the fact that their neighbourhood was littered with empty spaces which were full of rubbish, and they wanted to show the Council that the community could take on two particular pieces of land and transform them into an asset for the community. The local authority was planning to tarmac them over – I think the cost for the two of the spaces was £800 – and the local community said, don't tarmac them over, give us the £800 and we'll come up with a solution. The local authority wasn't going to do it, but eventually because of political pressure they agreed and engaged us, Free Form, as we had done a festival for them the previous year. One piece of land was to become a garden and one a play area. And so we worked with the neighbourhood over four weeks in the summer to transform the two areas, creating rockeries, mosaics, seating areas, planting areas, play areas with all the community involved. A little later the Urban Programme came in, and Hackney Council said, 'Well what can you do here?' So we did about twenty projects in Hackney within a year, transforming derelict sites with local community involvement. Some of them still exist – not always looking their best since the Council in their wisdom hasn't seen fit to maintain them, nevertheless they're still very good examples of art in the community.

The Urban Programme had been running for a number of years when we were invited by the Regional Arts Association of North Tyneside Council to start something in an area where there was very little arts activity at all. We were asked to do a feasibility study, identifying communities that we could work with on environmental projects. One was a fishing community in North Shields where we undertook the task of persuading the fishermen to create a symbol that would express confidence in the fishing industry for all to see. I met with the Fishermen's Association, all of whom were men, and there was I waxing on about art, and you could see their eyes were rolling in the back of their heads. I knew that I had to give a demonstration of what I was talking about. I had to be literal rather than abstract, so I looked at this chap's tie and on it he had the emblem for the association – a fish swimming – so I just said to the meeting, 'I can take this tie, put it on your photocopier and blow it up, and I can make it this big; but I can take the same thing and blow it up and make it 70 metres big on that bank side. That's what an environment improvement is. Now if I do that, would you support it?' 'Well do that son, and you're in.' So we adapted the emblem on the tie to make a large outdoor mosaic. That took a year to deliver, but in the meantime we organised a whole festival called the Fish Quay which was enormously successful and continued for eleven years. We engaged local artists, all from the north-east. We then formed a team who carried on working together under a franchise from us and they became a completely independent organisation, Northern Free Form. This project had a massive impact, the town's completely changed. It's true it would probably have changed anyway but Free Form had a hand in its change. It's not just me saying this, last year Free Form won the Guardian Jerwood Award.

Free Form is art. People sometimes say, community arts is a compromise too far but this is wrong. The quest for community art is about liberating what you as an artist can do, but at the same time creating a means by which it can be socially responsible, can actually make a net contribution to society.

———

I was born in London in 1943. My mother was an Irish immigrant, training to be a nurse at the London Hospital. She came from a middle-class family in rural Ireland, and she met my father at the local Catholic Youth Club. My father was a very handsome man, a tall fellow whose father had been a powerful local presence having been the MP for Hackney just after the war. All his family had strong links with the Labour Party. My father was a solicitor's clerk going nowhere, and then he became an insurance detective, and he went round the countryside on his motorbike, and he was going nowhere with that job too. They got married in 1940 during the war. He was in the RAF but didn't go abroad, he was stationed up and down the east coast. My sister and I were sent to Ireland for a year or so to live with relatives while the war was on.

I was the second child. My sister Helen is a year older than me. I've got seven sisters, no brothers. A big family you see.

When my father came back from the war he went to college, got on to the teachers programme which enabled you to become a teacher in two years. My mother encouraged him to do that. She was nursing and looking after, by that time I think three or four children. Once he'd trained he got his first job in a junior school, the school where he ended up being headmaster. And then he got offered a job in a Catholic secondary modern school in Walthamstow which was also tied to housing and it allowed him to move out of Hackney which he was desperate to do, so we went to live in Debden on a council estate. We had a three-bedroomed corrugated house on the housing estate. You know, homes for heroes. Debden is an extremely beautiful place on the Epping Forest borders, but I thought it was dreadful, I thought it was the pits. On the new estate you had all the ruffians having gang warfare, and then you had Loughton where all the posh people lived. The class divide was quite clear.

Eventually we moved out of the three-bedroomed home – there would be five of us by that time – to a four-bedroomed house on the same estate. My mum did nursing two or three nights a week, to supplement the income when she wasn't pregnant. Poor woman. A wonderful mum.

The estate of about 2,000 units didn't even have a pub. Most of the men who still worked in London spent a limited amount of time on the estate which became a female-dominated society until eventually after five years they built two pubs. The social provision was non-existent. In terms of social activity and cultural events it was limited to the Catholic Church and the Boys Brigade which celebrated with impressive street parades.

My first school was in Woodford. My sister and I used to be packed off on a little ordinary bus, it wasn't a school bus so you had to pay, I've forgotten what the fare was. A couple of times on the trot my older sister had lost the money and had to borrow from neighbours. Money was really tight and my mum was furious so she said, 'I'm going to give it to Martin this time.' So she duly put the bus money in my top pocket with my handkerchief. Come to going home time, 'Right, got the money Martin?' 'Oh yes.' But I hadn't. I was only five. And because we didn't have any money and my mum had lectured us about borrowing from neighbours, we walked home. And that's a long way, seven miles. Of course we got home about half-past seven, my mother was up the wall. She was so furious, she had been thinking the worst. And on the way home I got caught short, so I was in a bit of a mess.

My father worked all the time, he worked at school, he taught evening classes, and if he didn't do that he was working at Side Car Sids making motorbike sidecars. Just earning money – work work work. Even his holidays were work work work. So you had to entertain yourself really. Our entertainment was radio and the approved children's comics, the Eagle and Girl. We didn't have television, we were one of the last people to have television in our area, much to my annoyance. I used to make model aeroplanes and we used to play games, running mad around Epping Forest and enacting fantasies. Occasionally we would go to the cinema, very occasionally. I wasn't a great reader, no.

My father should have been a sculptor, he was just passionate about tools and making things. And I remember going to see my father at Side Car Sids, taking him his sandwiches or something in the evening, and you'd go in and he would be wearing a leather smock. It was a freezing cold place, and he would have a tin full of tacks, and he would empty the tacks in his mouth, organise them in his mouth so they came out head first, and put them on a magnetic hammer, and hammer them in. Years later you think, the poisons that must have been in that tin, and there he was with a mouth full of tacks. But as a kid I was dead impressed. Of course these days there are staple guns and pressure hoses.

My father started to specialise in technical drawing and art as part of his teacher training at college. They suggested he should do that but he had had no interest in it before then. My mother suddenly started painting when she was 80, she was so talented it was unbelievable. You say to yourself, 'Oh so that's where it came from.'

Secondary school was an all boys, fee-paying school. Dreadful, totally and utterly awful. There was a bit of victimisation but the worst was that it was just educationally zero. I was an 11 plus failure, and the stigma of that was quite heavy. I've since been told that I'm dyslexic, which I probably am, actually I think half of my family are. I left school after only getting two O levels, and I got this fantastic job as a drawing office junior at Lotus Cars. Lotus Cars are now a big racing car company but in those days they hadn't yet won a Formula One race. They were the amateur enthusiast's car makers, and they made cars to a quite revolutionary design by Colin Chapman, which were relatively cheap for people to buy. My job was to title up some of the drawings and make out cards, and then gradually they taught me how to do the dye-line processing. One day Colin Chapman came bursting in – over the two-day Christmas break he had designed a new car. He said, 'This is it, this is my new Formula One racing car. I want it up and running, built, in six weeks.' Because of his charisma the whole factory, which was about 200 people by this time, just set to. It was my first experience of someone who could draw and had power to motivate other people and create excitement and direction. So that was I think a formative influence of the notion of power related to creativity. I remember Chapman coming and saying, 'Who's Goodrich?' 'Him.' 'Well done son.' Anyway we built the car within six weeks, and Colin Chapman drove it down the Delamere Road in Cheshunt, and he got arrested by the police. At the South American Grand Prix in 1960 Sterling Moss had lost his car, so he took the new Lotus car out and broke the lap record in it. Two months later Lotus won the Monaco Grand Prix.

I left there to work on a farm because I could earn more money, and then I said to my father, I want to go to Walthamstow Tech to do some English and get some more GCEs. I went for a year but I did nothing, I played cards I think. My sister had gone to the art school. I looked at it and thought, my God! they're having a fantastic time, I wouldn't mind a bit of that. How can I get in there? I knew my drawing standard was nowhere near as good as the art students. But I found out that they were accepting people without art qualifications provided they showed some sort of interest or talent.

So I went to art school. And that to me was like opening a magic box. It's quite strange because I felt totally inadequate, I didn't know how to draw, I was nowhere near as good as any of these people, and all I could do was to work hard and learn. And fortunately, everything I did I just loved, I couldn't get enough of it; I was in there all the time, I just worked and worked. And within a year I was the top boy. I remember putting up my first painting, because you used to go and do your little paintings on paper, and then they used to put it all up as if it were the Royal Academy, all round the room, and then they had a crit, an open crit, all the thirty students and the four or five staff. 'Right, OK, first exercise is, I want five of you, you, you, you and you to choose the best paintings in the room.' 'OK. Now we're going to do the same exercise but the staff are going to choose the best paintings.' When the staff picked out five paintings, one of them was mine. And of course all the students in the room were staggered because most of the paintings the students liked were all superficially competent, and there was my muddy old painting. 'And do you know why this one's any good? Because this young man has understood that light outside is brighter than light inside. And that's why this is a good painting.' We learnt by peer group demonstration and by debate and discussion. Walthamstow was a really terrific art school, it was a very energetic place at the time with people like Peter Greenaway, the film maker, he was a year above us; people like Ian Dury, musicians and others. We were taught by people like Keith Albarn from the Arts Lab, and I was also taught to draw by Eric Heban, probably one of the greatest artist forgers going, a draughtsman who could teach anyone to draw. It was empowerment beyond belief. And within two years I felt that I was king, you know, my arrogance was second to none. Well it's that power of learning you see. So I progressed from feeling that I was useless to a sense that I could actually do something, and could do it well, I can compete, and I've got good ideas. And so I got my NDD (National Diploma in Design), and then went to the Royal College of Art. I did seven years at art school in all, a real privilege, three years at the Royal College, four years at Walthamstow.

Jim left Free Form in about 1975, and he works for community and arts organisations. Barbara and I have remained with Free Form. We're both directors of Free Form and life partners.

It takes a lot of work to break through: Being second is easy

ED Berman
Inter-Action

In the early 1960s the Turkish newspapers were whipping up great anti-American sentiment. And I suppose it was rather unusual to have an American who spoke Turkish fluently, living on the Asian side of Istanbul with no visible means of support. As a Rhodes Scholar I was well funded – for the first and last time in my life. I was reading a Sunday newspaper on my patio when two young Turkish Naval Officers home on leave crept up behind me, and tried to club me to death. The woman I was living with at the time came out, she was Dutch and had converted to Islam. These two 'gentlemen' of course wouldn't hit a lady, and she frightened them off. She then dragged me bleeding and semi-conscious to the Florence Nightingale Hospital in Skutari. They sewed me up and took X-rays. They had injured my back permanently and for five years I lost the stereoscopic vision in my eyes, so I couldn't do any academic work. I also had a blood clot on the brain, and I was told I had a year to live. My brother and I decided not to tell my parents.

When you think you only have a year to live you really have to think over what you want to do. What I wanted to do was to write socially meaningful and entertaining plays, to do community work; and I wanted to combine the two in some way. Also I had decided not to go back to America. After an anti-American incident like this, it seemed a perfect time to become British.

I HAD A friend who had a friend who knew the chap who was running the International Theatre Club at the Mercury Theatre in London. Anyway, the chap in charge was rather snooty about my plays so I rang Frank Hauser, director of the Oxford Playhouse, who invited me to come and see him but before doing so I told the snooty chap and he said, 'I'll put them on.' And they had a curious success in a funny old way. They were two one-hour plays called *Stamp* and *Freeze*. One of them I promoted with the reproduction of an American dollar bill saying, 'Is this worth the price of murder and slaughter in Vietnam?'

I became resident playwright – whatever that pretentious title meant – at this rather strange little theatre club at the Mercury Theatre. Impish I think is the word for a lot of the things that I did in those early days. I went to see a production up in Manchester by a fellow by the name of Naftali Yavin who was putting on a play of his, a rather Freudian piece about his mother. I was very impressed with the production rather than with the content. I suggested to the International Theatre Club that we should invite this guy down to work with us. Naftali and I hit it off like brothers. So we started working together. He directed my plays, except for the *Supersantas* which the La Mama Company did when they visited London. It was basically about a Santa Claus character who has a little girl on his knee and then the two of them get into the sack together and roll off the stage. This did not go down well in Kensington and Chelsea.

In the meantime I was doing community work with a technique I had developed when doing voluntary community work as a student at Harvard in 1957 and dubbed it the Inter-Action Creative Game. This was a means of working with an individual or a group based on my research and belief in the commonality of the structure of children's games throughout the world, games which may have different names in different places. For example, even within a mile the same game might have a different name: 'tag' becomes 'tiggy', or 'he' becomes 'it'. I was able to develop a very simple tool kit for getting groups to create things together; or for individuals to be able to unblock themselves and create. We use it to train actors and people working in the community including psychologists and psychiatrists. The reason why this method probably wasn't discovered before was that children's games formerly were undervalued.

I continued using the Inter-Action Creative Game Method in therapeutic communities, mental hospitals, day care centres, and in youth clubs and remand homes. When I started to train actors to do this we made it a condition that you actually couldn't act in any of our permanent companies unless you had learnt this method. By 1968 Inter-Action had three theatre companies. One was called

Professor Dogg's Troupe – also known as the Father and Mother Christmas Union. The Other Company, or TOC, was one of the leading experimental companies which Naftali and I directed, and the Ambiance Lunch-Hour Theatre Club was the first real off-West End Theatre.

There was a rather well-off chap who was devoted to our kind of theatre. He thought I shouldn't sleep on the floor of a flat in Queensway any more, and so he agreed to pay me £2.10s. to rent what was a very small room. If you leaned in all four directions, without moving your feet, you could touch all four walls. I haven't progressed very much. I have this little cabin office here on HMS President that you can't swing a cat in. I remember the Polish landlady didn't like the hours I kept. I didn't have money for food or anything so I used to go to the Ambiance restaurant and club, which was an Afro-Caribbean place run by a man by the name of Junior Telfer. He used to let me sit there and he would feed me and give me cups of tea. I couldn't drink alcohol because of my head injury. Anyway we started the lunch-hour theatre movement at the Ambiance. Junior had the right idea but lunch-hour theatre was about twenty years too early. It caught on with a few publicans but when I asked the Royal Court to let us create a late-night theatre they decided that they could do it without us. So there was no way for us to climb up any kind of ladder; in any case I didn't see a ladder because I thought commercial or large-scale theatre was not what I was interested in. These days all the fringe theatres are doing quite well for themselves with grants. We got the first grant the Arts Council gave for such a thing, but it was a pittance. We also got the first grant for street theatre, and for participatory theatre in education. It was a big breakthrough at the time. The Arts Council of Great Britain, with Lord Goodman as its Chairperson, controlled everything in the arts at the time: if they didn't put their imprimatur on it you were nothing. It was Junior Telfer and a very nice lady, Erica Marks, and a few others who helped me set up Inter-Action.

It takes a lot of work to be first in various new fields. I have a cousin whose favourite theory is: don't try to be first, always be second because first is too difficult, but being second is very easy. I have not followed his idea as it seemed so weak. So we did manage to make all of these things acceptable: street and community theatre, community arts, participatory theatre in education, participatory theatre in general, and lunch-hour theatre. There were aesthetics underpinning them that were sensible in my opinion, which had roots in very ancient theatre and arts. Street theatre had various components – including a lap of honour – and one could trace it back through time to, for example, the original Olympics or the Mystery Plays. I wouldn't say it was like a religious experience but it was certainly a communal experience in which there was participation and joy. The Sixties was a very affluent period which allowed for that kind of wildness, because you thought things were going to change, and there was a lot of money and opportunity around. In this country there was the freedom to oppose the Vietnam War, and we weren't involved in any big international problems. So people had both the time and money.

I had a couple of policies for the lunch-hour theatre: one was that the director or one of the actors or the writer had to be well-known, because they would then attract an audience that would enable the work of inexperienced actors or the new playwright or the young director to be seen. That was a successful policy. The other one was to have thematic seasons. Now it has become *de rigueur* but in those days it wasn't. I would create seasons: the Black Power season of plays, the first Gay season of plays, the first Women's season of plays. I also did a Human Rights season and so on. I convened a caucus of people who were interested in a specific issue, say women who were at the time being kept out of technical jobs or directorial jobs, et cetera. And I used the Arts Council grant for, say, a third of the year to have this caucus of interested people shadow our company's staff. From that shadowing the caucus would gain experience for the purpose of setting up their own company after the season ended. This led to many splits; indeed each of those first three groups that I mentioned managed at the end of the season to set up theatre companies of their own on both radical and non-radical sides of the fence, and they fought with each other because of their politics. To this day some of them still exist. I came out of it being hated by everybody of course, because I was just the guy who didn't belong to any of these groups. At the time it was easy to pick on me because I was a white male heterosexual with an Afro and an American accent to boot, and I didn't really fit in anywhere. However I've retained friends from those days till today. I hadn't yet written a book about what it is to be British if you are an immigrant, something I have been working on.

By this time I had lived ten years beyond my medically allotted

time, and I was able to read again. I had been going to Moorfields
Eye Hospital and I did eye exercises. But I had that permanent back
injury – now riddled with arthritis – which I still cope with daily
through exercise and treatment.

In 1972 I created the Fun Art Bus by re-designing one side of the
bus to look like it had three decks and the other side looked like a
normal red double decker bus. Except when it pulled up to a bus
stop, people would get on and the clippy – people don't know what
clippies are now – but the clippy would dole out a free ticket which
would be a poem by Roger McGough or somebody else who I had
commissioned to write 'tickets'. We had a picnic drawn on the roof
for people in high-rise blocks to see as we went by. That was done by
Liz Leyn who was a member of Inter-Action. She was the artist who
did the concrete cows in Milton Keynes later on. We did the sorts of
things that people now treat as normal like having cut-out figures in
the windows, poetry and pun cartoons by Ros Asquith as adverts.
We also did mime out of the windows. People got very confused as
they got on this bus which was wallpapered inside and looked like
you were entering somebody's home. People like Bob Gill and Theo
Crosby of Pentagram were helping me, all sorts of radical young
artists helped. If you want to reach the general public you run a bus
that happens to do theatre upstairs and downstairs, has mime
playing out onto the street from a window, has kinetic sculpture in
the luggage compartment, and is a three-decker bus on one side and
two-decker on the other side, and when you look down from a tall
building you see a picnic going by. You know, it depends on who
you want to reach and who you want to make smile and think. On
European tours we were paid a fortune to bring the Fun Art Bus and
we were much higher paid than any other company at the time. One
day we came back from running a bus route which went everywhere
and nowhere, and I was told that Naftali was dead. So I really lost my
appetite for theatre for quite some time.

My real complaint about theatre and why I don't go to it very
often is that it's still court jesters playing for a bourgeois court. The
sort of thing we were doing with the Father and Mother Christmas
Union was a kind of guerrilla type of theatre. The first one was in
1968 when we picketed Selfridges for using 'red-leg' labour which is
the kind of black-leg labour that a Father Christmas Union would be
against. We got arrested and it took, I don't know, a year to get
through the courts. It was very funny. I had had the foresight –

because of many previous incidents with the police – to have a solicitor with me whenever we went out and to have somebody with a camera clicking shots every ten seconds. Therefore we could prove whatever had to be proved in court. We caused all sorts of things to happen. I set up with the GPO a line for Santa Claus on one number. I was threatened by the government with sabotage as at the time if 500,000 calls hit one line this would eventually burn out the national grid.

Once we had twenty or thirty people going out in the street with Father Christmas creating National Hello Day, where you would say hello to people and note their reactions. The next day you would have a National Goodbye Day and you would have mirrors coming out of your shoulders, and you would walk backwards saying goodbye to everyone you passed. This kind of insanity was appealing in the late 1960s; it was very early performance art – I guess that's what it would be called nowadays – but it was done by groups with whatever name we were using at the time, the Father and Mother Christmas Union or the Dogg's Troupe.

Around that time I had been introduced to a woman who had a shop-front space which went right back into a warehouse. Her current tenant was very busy making people levitate and doing other pieces of art work with bubbles. After about six months of no levitation, nor even levity, she got fed up with him and she said to me, 'You can have this space until the lease runs out,' which was I think a year and a half. And I said, 'Thank you very much.' It was opposite the Roundhouse in Camden. One day we rolled up to our shop-front, and Arnold Wesker had put up a sign outside the Roundhouse saying, 'We need £280,000 to complete Centre 42'. So we put up a sign outside our little shop opposite saying, 'We do not need £280,000 yet.' Arnold and I never got along terribly well.

That winter, that first winter of our discomfort we slept on the warehouse floor and on the desks, as if it was a new frontier. I tell it as a joke but it wasn't. We lost all of our women, they quit except for one. The men wouldn't dare admit that they were uncomfortable. I freely admit that I hate the cold and I was so miserable sleeping on my desk.

Over the years I must have personally participated in over two thousand performances of street theatre. We would go with or without the bus, mainly on foot, into the back streets and housing estates from the south-east of England to the Welsh Valleys to

Easterhouse in Glasgow before Easterhouse was knocked down. So I knew England, Wales and Scotland really well. I didn't see the point of doing one or two performances so we would do nine shows a day. In the Welsh Valleys there weren't that many kids at each place, yet more and more kept coming until we figured out we'd seen these kids before. The kids would come back because that's all they ever had from the outside world. They had nothing. And so I learnt a lot about the society in which we live: the underclass, the working class, and through lunch-hour theatre – although it was always fringe – the middle class.

One day in the late Sixties, Tom Stoppard came into the Ambiance and said, 'You know I really think what you're doing is wonderful, especially work with children and lunch-hour theatre. Tell me, why is Dogg's Troupe called Dogg's Troupe?' I said, 'Well, my pseudonym when I write for children is Professor R.L. Dogg, and so when things I write for children go into a library they'll go under Dogg, R.L., doggerel.' He looked at me and he said, 'Anyone who can wait that long for a bad pun to explode that far away from where they are, and never really see anyone appreciating it deserves a bit better. Would you like me to write a play for you?' And that was the first of six short plays that he wrote for us. So there was a decade in which Tom and I collaborated on a number of things. He wrote *After Magritte* which we put on, and then he wrote *Dogg's Our Pet* which is an anagram of Dogg's Troupe, and then he wrote the fifteen-minute *The Dogg's Troupe Hamlet* which takes seventeen minutes!

If you take street theatre of our participatory form out into housing estates or on to the streets then your audience is the people in the housing estates or on the streets. They don't have a choice really. On the other hand once you decide that you are going to have people come to you, then you're only going to get people who are literate enough and who are motivated enough to look in the theatre columns. That was very clear to me from day one, and to me the worst thing that could happen was to have anything that Dogg's Troupe was doing listed in the theatre columns. It actually mattered to me that if you were in a 'proper' theatre you were only playing to a certain type of audience. In order to make sure you reach the people that you want to reach, you have to figure out how to do it. You know retail business is about three things: location, location, location. And if you want to reach an audience who won't come to a theatre you've got to go to them. If you want to do plays about for example, prisoners, you go to prisons. I think the worst kind of theatre is where you are trying to put across a message in a didactic way. You have to be very careful about thinking that you can impose a lengthy message in theatre, however good you think you are at what you're doing.

I remember in South London there was a very tough youth club we were asked to go into with the Inter-Action game method, and I went in personally every week. One of these very tough guys came up to me and he said, 'Hoy, this Inter-Action thing, it isn't theatre is it that we're doing?' I said, 'No, it's Inter-Action.' 'Somebody told me it was theatre, and I'm not going to come again if it's theatre.' I was using the Inter-Action Creative Game method but if it had been called theatre they wouldn't have come.

I wasn't class-bound in any way, I guess that is what has reinforced my keeping my American accent because I had no reason to want to lose it. The kids that I worked with loved it because I wasn't reminding them of some class structure where they were always bottom of the pile.

Most of the time we were paid. I mean, it didn't take much to get us to do things for nothing because we could just balance things up by taking the bus abroad and get paid a lot of money.

In 1973 we got Rank Xerox, as it was then, to give us the money to set up the first Community Media Van – a big Mercedes van. You could print community newspapers on it, you could do back projections of film slides, you could show videos out of the side, and you could do theatre from a theatre platform on the roof.

We also had a radio telephone, one of the first in the country. We put the microphone into an amplifier which pushed the sound out of big horn speakers. And in those days you had to get a line because there were a limited number of lines. In 1973 who had radio telephones? The Prime Minister and a few millionaires. So, we were paid to go into places by local authorities. We had the largest telephone kiosk in the world and we would then ring the Leader of the local council or the Director of Housing whatever, and we would have two or three hundred people asking them very pertinent questions. Well, we never got invited back a second time by a local authority. So I'd been using the radio telephone van as long ago as 1973. It seems impossible, when you think back, that the mobile phone in its infancy was used as a community action tool.

In 1968 we had started a kind of informal participatory group of young people in the Kentish Town premises originally leased by Erica Marks. She had passed away and her lease on the premises had expired so we were squatting – this was the largest squat in the country. I went to see the Deputy Director of Housing and I slammed the table and said, 'We have all these people who are doing all of this good work, and you've got all these empty buildings, and all we want is have to have a roof over our heads.' And all of a sudden I thought to myself, ED, you're a horse's arse. This guy is in his fifties, you're in your twenties. What was he doing when he was in his twenties? It was the Depression and he was doing more or less the same thing you're doing now, only he was probably a communist or a fellow traveller, which I wasn't, but he was doing the equivalent for his time. And then this guy looked at me and he said, 'You know, when I was your age I was a member of the Communist Party and then the war came. We all went off and when we came back there was the Election in 1945, and we thought that Jerusalem had arrived. A lot of us went into local authorities and into the Civil Service thinking we were going to change the world. And we've had our try at it, we've done some good things. I know it's all bureaucratic and so on, but we've tried, and things are better, we think. But you know, nothing's perfect. How many houses do you want?' And I thought, there's a whole different way of approaching people. You don't go out there pounding the table and being arrogant and thinking you've discovered how to save the world because there have been millions of people there before you. And there are millions of people out there now. So the question is, how do you work with bureaucrats, you've got to get them to help you.

Because I'm an immigrant I had to learn what most people take for granted, and what most people take for granted they don't see. I was very interested in what I saw when we were doing street theatre up and down the housing estates of the country. You had these broken glass-strewn tarmac or concrete yards in most housing estates, and just over the wall there was grass and then there was a railway line. And I had seen hundreds of these and I reckoned there were thousands of acres of land just where it was needed if you could somehow get your hands on it. Not having been brought up in this country I wasn't brought up in its class system. Most first generation immigrants have either a lot of fear and keep their heads down, or if they are young they have a lot of nerve and don't know the rules of the game so they're constantly breaking them whether they want to or not. I fell into the latter category. So I'd pick up the phone and ring Richard Marsh, who was the head of British Rail and had all this land that could be used for playgrounds and say, 'Could I speak to Dick please?' And the secretary would say, 'Who are you?' and I'd say who I was. She'd say, 'Do you know him?' 'No, but I'm very close friends with a friend of his who suggested that I rang. By the way, what's your name?' and she would say her first name, and then I'd go through my regular routine of 'Don't you have a surname?' And because it was a time of great raw nerve feminism, that would strike a chord. And so in the early Seventies I got to see Dick Marsh. I went in to see him, and said, 'You have 10,000 acres of land in the inner cities which is grassland which could be used for playgrounds or city farms.' He said, 'How did you know?' I said, 'Well I've been doing all this street theatre.' He said, 'But how do you know it was 10,000 acres?' I said, 'I extrapolated it from what I saw.' Apparently it was dangerously close to a figure they had, but I didn't know, I was just guessing. So he said, 'What do you want to do with it?' I said, 'Well I've set up with others this City Farm in Kentish Town where previously there had been stables for the old railway shunting ponies and disused allotments.'

The City Farm in Kentish Town which started up in 1972 had community gardens rather than allotments, and ready-made manure from the horses, and an indoor riding school which included riding for the disabled, and concrete sculpture with the help again of Liz Leyn. There was a building which we turned into a workshop for local people who wanted to fix things. Local adults involved in the farm often dealt with problems with 'tough' kids as they were all part of the same community. It was pointless to set up something just for one age group, I have never believed in that unless you are aiming at a single particular problem. If you put all the kids in one place they run rings around the youth workers, whereas if their parents are nearby the parents will take care of them, right?

I managed to make an appointment with a fairly senior civil servant on the grounds that I was a very large landowner. I said I had 10,000 acres of land which I wanted to give for the purpose of open areas within the city. 'Can we come and see this example you have Mr Berman?' And so they came to Kentish Town – I remember it was a very wet day – and we supplied them with wellies because they came in very shiny brogues, and they walked through and scratched their heads. There were horses, goats and chickens. We had ducks and geese, guard geese. We didn't have guard dogs, because geese are much more vicious and it's hard to make friends with them, in fact one bit me. The civil servants didn't quite believe what they saw, 'How do you have all this acreage?' I said, 'Do you mean the Kentish Town acreage?' 'No,' they said, 'you said you had 10,000 acres.' I said, 'Oh my friend Dick Marsh said I could have it if I could fence it off, so I need some money from you chaps so the children will be safe from the rail lines. If we can fence it off, British Rail will give us the land.' So, they said, 'That isn't exactly what you said.' I said, 'Well, it amounts to the same thing, there's 10,000 acres, and it's mine to dispose of if I can fence it off. I don't want to sell it, I want to see that people are allowed to set up City Farms.' And they said, 'OK, we'll give you a grant; we're not going to give you a grant to fence it all off, but we'll give you a small grant to start with to see if you can foster city farms.'

Eventually we were in a position to recommend grants for other groups. We gave a grant to a group in Bristol who were setting up a City Farm in the early seventies. Bristol later became the site for the National Association of City Farms. Inter-Action no longer has any farms, they've all been turned over to the local community. Now there are some sixty-five City Farms and over one thousand community gardens around the country, each locally managed.

Things continued to develop on the educational side. We now have one of the projects that I initiated in the Eighties, the National Inter-Action Computer Award Scheme which is accredited by the RSA Examinations Board. It has expanded to video, sound recording and photography. It even operates in eleven prisons in the country, and in a number of other institutions including ordinary schools and unemployment centres. So things have built on each other.

From the beginning we were using video. I remember Rediffusion Television gave me some outdated television studio equipment. We used to take it out in 1968 and 1969 to adventure playgrounds or just rough areas – bomb sites or whatever – and we would ask somebody on the ground floor of a tower block, 'Can we go through your window with our plug and buy some electricity from you?' We would pay them two shillings and sixpence, plug in a hundred-yard cable and take the studio equipment outside. In 1968 this was unheard of. This was before any kind of portable video. To me the question was always, what's the right medium? In fact in the mid-Eighties we were working on networks before the World Wide Web was set up. We had 200 youth centres in the UK on line together. Up to the late 1990s we were reaching 120,000 kids a year face-to-face in what we called 'Learning Domes' – inflatable learning spaces like a baby planetarium – that would pack up into the back of a car. With their own projector systems with teachers covering anything from astronomy to nutrition. So I'm much more interested in the appropriate medium for a given purpose.

None of these are now called Inter-Action. I don't want to have the responsibility for them; I'll gladly help others set it up, train the people, monitor it for a while. Now that we have helped spawn a number of movements here, I think we could help in other countries.

The voluntary sector needed to be professionalised. It is a huge sector turning over vast sums of money which have to be handled properly, carefully, honestly, and productively. And it wasn't going to happen in the old-fashioned way. It seemed to me in thinking about it interactively, you could bring in what was at the time the big management consultancy firm, McKinsey & Co. I approached them and said we want to set up an agency which will train people in the voluntary sector and set up models of good practice. They were very willing to do it and in the late Sixties/ Seventies they helped us to set up 1200 different agencies using a non-culturally biased approach and a peer training programme. Then other people started to do it and there was no longer a need for us to carry on. The breakthrough had happened.

Basically we're in a problem-solving business, trying to help other groups help their target populations or set up entirely new initiatives, which we rapidly try to get replicated. I've learnt over the years to dissociate myself to a large degree from the individual projects. Inter-Action exists without me, I hope.

I'm not terribly interested in the past nor do I think it's terribly important, but I was born in Lewiston in the state of Maine in 1941, my mother was Canadian, my father was American, and we were relatively speaking quite poor. Before the Depression my grandfather had owned quite a lot of property in downtown Lewiston but the town moved up and the property became a slum.

We lived for much of the time in an apartment above my grandmother's on the edge of a French Canadian slum. At the time the French in Maine were a large part of the underclass. There was great poverty, there was just no access to anything. Lewiston is a small town in a large state. The state is as large geographically as England but has less than a million people in it. I think it has more moose than it has people, and certainly more deer.

My father went from one kind of job to another. He was a dreamer and a very kind, nice, generous man who didn't have the wherewithal to be generous. My mother wanted to live up to the Joneses and it was impossible. So it was generally unpleasant. She was very shrewd and very sharp, but she and I never got along very well. I remember one thing she would always say, that I would always sneer at, which was, you can catch more flies with honey than with vinegar, to which I would reply, being a very bolshie young man, 'Who wants to catch flies?' But over the years I have certainly learnt that you might as well be nice to everyone, including your worst enemy, because frankly there's too much stress in doing anything else.

I was an accident and my parents were like grandparents to me. My brother was also like an only child as he was fifteen years older. I was precocious and my mother was I think as frightened as she was proud of me. She always thought I could fend for myself from a very early age.

I learnt to read at a very young age from a neighbour who was about three years older than I. I was very active in sports, and most of the activities I was involved in were at the school clubs, debating society, the annual school play, school elections, the newspaper, yearbook and so on. These are things that American schools do very well although usually tastelessly. There are dozens of these sorts of things that don't exist in the UK except perhaps in private education. I don't think that this aspect of learning is understood, even in the USA.

All of these clubs and so on are what I call micro-democracies. They all elect their peers to the various posts involved. That has two effects. It is a learning ground for democracy – and tastelessness; also it tends to elect the best-looking people, which describes a lot about American politics. So I'm writing a book on this called *Micro-democracy*.

I went two years early to Harvard without finishing high school. This was an unfortunate honour which I think led to my being out of sync all my life with the situations around me. Socially I was not really geared to students who were two to three years older than I. I may have been intellectually geared to it, I don't know. But I got thrown out and then I went back again and got a Rhodes Scholarship and came to Oxford, from which I got thrown out twice. At Harvard they 'sever your connection'. At Oxford they 'rusticate' you or 'send you down'. It's an interesting difference in the language.

At Harvard the Dean at the time – who later became famous as an assistant to JFK – was a tough character. He called me in one day and said, 'You are not returning your library books until about eleven in the morning.' And I said, 'I sleep until eleven.' And he said, 'Well, they're supposed to be back at nine. You are depriving your fellow students of these books.' I said, 'No, I'm not; they're supposed to be at lecture.' And he said, 'So are you.' I said, 'Well I stay up most of the night reading, so I don't see why I should go to lectures unless there's a particularly good lecturer. In any case I'd sleep through it because my body clock is just different, and so I write and read till four or five in the morning, and I'm not going to get up at nine to return the books.' And he said, 'But that's the rule.' And I said, 'You know there's no harm being done, because nobody's being deprived of the books. I'm not stealing them, every book is returned.' He said, 'We're not accusing you of stealing them, you're not obeying a rule.' I said, 'The rule's an ass, it just makes no sense.' 'Well, you don't seem to be taking this very seriously.' I said, 'Well, I'm not because I don't think it's a very serious issue. And you brought me here two years early, and there's some responsibility here if I can't cope with your hours. And he said, 'Right, you are to go and see the psychiatrist.' I went to see the psychiatrist and I explained the story to him, that I felt alienated and too young and so on. He said, 'It sounds like you're right, everyone here is two or three years older in your class, and I can see, coming from a small town in Maine, that you might have such difficulties anyway.' So I went back to the Dean and said, 'The shrink agrees with me.' He said, 'Did you tell him the whole story? Did you tell him that you were signing books out of the library under the names of Mickey Mouse, Donald Duck, Superman and Nietzsche and he didn't find that peculiar?' I said, 'Well, the guys behind the desk used to call me Mickey, so it didn't really matter, and I wanted to read all those books and you're only allowed one book at a time; as I say I wasn't depriving anybody of the books so it didn't strike me as a sensible rule.' They later computerised the system, I don't think Mickey would be able to take any books out of the Lamont Library any longer. They severed my connection.

I was rather wild: I knew Timothy Leary when he was a lecturer at Harvard, and we used to crush peyote balls from Mexico and mix them into milkshakes. It makes you sick, all that milkshake.

In Oxford on the Rhodes Scholarship I felt much more comfortable being British since my mother had brought me up on tea instead of coffee and I still have I think Coronation glasses, gold-rimmed glasses. My mother was very British from a Commonwealth point of view although it wasn't called the Commonwealth at that time, it was the Empire still when she was a girl. Then I got thrown out of Oxford, once for punching the proctor. I think I was drunk, I must have been drunk because I can't remember hitting anybody else in my life.

So I got sent down for a year. And then I came back and got sent down again. I was in digs above a dentist's surgery, and he had one of these coat racks with the metal prongs that come out of the top. I had a broken leg at the time as a result of playing cricket or some silly thing and I started jousting with cars in the street with this hat rack. The University authorities didn't think this was an action becoming a student of such prestige. So I got sent down again. I did however get invited back to Oxford to do my doctoral dissertation after I recovered from – if I ever did recover from – the attack on my life in Turkey.

You must remember that anybody under forty, forty-five will never have heard about Inter-Action. When I happen to bump into someone who used to know me – over, say forty or forty-five – they say, 'We thought you were dead.' And I say, 'Well I am.' It depends on which part you're talking about, you know.

To get our agenda on to other people's agenda

Peg Belson
Mother Care for Children in Hospital

My fourteen-month old son was playing outside the bedroom door while his eight-year old sister was bouncing with a friend on the bed inside the bedroom. The door shut on the first finger of his right hand. A neighbour drove us to the hospital with his hand crumpled up. He was clinging on to me and the young doctor who saw him said they wanted to cut the top off his finger. I said, 'What for, surely you can stitch it back on again?' He said, 'Well we can't even see if the bone is broken. And I can't take an X-ray because he won't open the hand to let me see it.' I said, 'Well he certainly will open his hand for me!' So we went to the X-ray department and they took a picture of Bruce's hand with my hand plonked across it to keep his hand in place. The radiographer was most impressed. Obviously they never had anybody accompany a child for an X-ray before, and they were intrigued with how well behaved he was – despite a four-hour wait in Accident and Emergency. After the X-ray they decided that they could stitch the finger back on. The interesting thing was that when we came back the following week to have the stitches taken out, they were so proud of the wonderful job that they'd done on this tiny little boy's finger. I didn't say a word!

WHEN THE CONCEPT of parents being with their children in hospital was presented to me in the 1960s, I didn't know it was necessary because since 1951 I'd been going into treatment rooms but none of my children had been actually admitted into hospital. The whole issue of children and parents in hospital began in the 1950s at the Tavistock Institute of Human Relations with the Robertsons and their research, and their films – starting with *A Two-Year Old Goes to Hospital*. When James Robertson approached the paediatricians originally they didn't see any need for parents to be in the hospital because, as far as they were concerned, children in hospital were suffering because of their illness or their injury not because of separation. Eventually a few of the paediatricians saw things rather differently and accepted what he was talking about. But he still felt that he wasn't getting anywhere with the professionals such as nurses, even the paediatric nurses, so he went public and he wrote a couple of articles for *The Observer* and did a programme on the BBC promoting his ideas.

Part of the work I had done for my psychology degree involved child development. I had been looking at the new work that was coming out which challenged routine patterns of looking after children, particularly the principle that babies didn't need to cry. I suppose I really put theory into practice when my first baby was born in 1951. She was born in St Thomas' Hospital and the practice then was for babies to see their mothers for one reason only, to be fed. In fact if they weren't being mother-fed they hardly saw their mothers at all, spent their whole time in the hospital nursery. I asked whether I could have the baby by my bed and this was astounding. I just think I was very lucky: she was an extremely amenable child. When we brought her home at nine at night she was still asleep at eight the next morning. She was nearly ten pounds, in other words she was the size of a two to three-month old baby. And that was it. I mean we did everything together. I took her to the theatre when she was about four weeks old and took her to the hairdresser at three weeks old and the shop, everything in the shop stopped. Remember this was 1950, 1951 when you hardly appeared in the street if you were pregnant or with a very young baby. My husband and I spent most of the time out of the house doing things with her.

The reasons doctors and nurses gave for not allowing parents to be in hospital with their children were the danger of transfer of infection, or not enough space, or parents will interfere with the care being given their children, or the children didn't need their parents, or the nurses are more than capable of looking after children. One reason after another. When a child psychiatrist's own child was admitted to Great Ormond Street Hospital in the early sixties he discovered for the first time how limited the access to children in hospital was. And he wrote to the *Times* saying how wrong this was, supporting Robertson's view. But most people didn't actually know what was the pattern of care for children in hospital.

Jane Thomas, a neighbour of mine who lives three floors above me and who was a television journalist, saw James Robertson's programmes and read the articles. She rang him up and asked what could she do to make sure that if her children went into hospital the pattern of care that he was advocating would be the one that her children would receive. The first thing he said was, 'You should make yourself very knowledgeable about the subject and confident that you know what you are talking about. Talk to people in your own district who have had a child in hospital to see what the pattern of care is and then go and visit the hospital. Then draw together a group of your friends to talk about it.' So that's what she did. She asked me if I would join her. It was April 1961 and I was expecting my fourth child in June.

The very early meetings took place on a bench in Battersea Park with the children underfoot. There were six people in the original group and then more joined. There were one or two people from Chelsea, but mainly it was Battersea people around here along Prince of Wales Drive and the side streets. They were all professionally qualified but were no longer working or were working part-time. The members of our group were all mothers. My oldest child was then nine coming up to ten, the others in the main had younger children. I think the idea was quite attractive, the idea that you would continue to care for your child whether they were sick at home or were sick in hospital. One of our members had been a nurse and was the wife of a psychiatrist. Another one was a dentist. Another was a teacher and there was I think a social worker.

A teacher, the wife of a schoolmaster down at the end of the road, was also involved so our very first public meeting was held in his school, Lechlade School. It's no longer there. So at that meeting the organisation to promote the welfare of children in hospital was born: Mother Care for Children in Hospital. James Robertson came and a paediatrician from the hospital we'd visited, and we had various people who'd had experiences with their children in hospital.

A lot of branches were started by people who had an objection to the pattern of care that their own children had received in hospital. I think the interesting thing about those of us who set the organisation up was that none of us had actually ever had a child in hospital as an inpatient. I mean obviously all of us had children going to hospital, going to outpatients. None of us had ever had to think about what it meant to walk away and leave the child in hospital. Thinking it over maybe that was an advantage for us because what we were doing was only to a limited degree personal. I think we had been in existence about two and a half years before the first person from our group had a child admitted to hospital, a child who was born with spina bifida. The child was admitted to hospital for surgery and the mother was not invited nor allowed to stay with her. With the support of our group she withdrew the child from hospital which was a major thing to do. The child was admitted to the Queen Elizabeth Hospital for Children in Hackney but the staff made it very plain that allowing the mother to stay with the child was something special.

We were around at the beginning of the consumer movement if you like, but I don't recall that we were aware of any of that at all. It was a couple of years later that the famous journalist, Mary Stott, wrote about us in the *Guardian* as part of the consumer movement. We also had a television programme quite early on.

We made a very early connection with the Department of Health. We went to visit one of the ministers who thought us 'a lot of do-gooding women' but he obviously saw us because it was the right thing to do. In later years a subsequent Minister of Health said that he saw the association as the people on the ground who could give him information about what was going on. Keith Joseph was very supportive and in fact was the minister, much later on, who gave us our first government grant.

Subsequent to James Robertson's first film the Department of Health set up the Platt Committee to look at the non-medical aspects of children in hospital. In 1959, The Department of Health instructed hospitals to accede to the Platt Report's recommendations: to ensure that all children who went into hospital had unrestricted visiting, and to provide the opportunity for parents to be with them and that hospitals were to implement these recommendations. However they made no effort whatsoever to monitor implementation. Early in 1962 Mother Care for Children in Hospital did the first survey asking hospitals about the implementation of the Platt Report and we got some fascinating responses. There were hospitals that said visiting was unrestricted, but parents should come 'only in the afternoons', or 'only stay for an hour or so'. One hospital allowed fathers to visit for an hour in the early evening, but this late visiting did not apply to mothers who could not come earlier in the day.

Further surveys followed. Quoting from one of my own papers:

> In 1964 when forty-five hours was an acceptable minimum for weekly visiting, the survey found only twenty-six percent of the hospitals in one region permitted such unrestricted visiting. In 1966 only forty-five percent of the hospitals permitted unrestricted visiting and mothers

were offered accommodation in only half-a-dozen of the fifty-six hospitals admitting children. By 1969 this proportion had increased to fifty-seven percent. Still, fewer than half the hospitals offered any accommodation for mothers and only in a small number of these was it offered routinely. No morning visiting was permitted in more than one-quarter of the hospitals. Our 1971 surveys showed the severely limited visiting policies of the past to be on the wane. Most hospitals offered at least five hours visiting a day, and more that three-quarters permitted visiting throughout normal waking hours. Accommodation for mothers, however, was still very limited.

We did various surveys including Ear Nose and Throat Departments and Burns Units. When we did the ENT survey we got a lot of publicity because at that stage there was an enormous variation in the length of stay in hospital. Nancy, who was our press and publicity officer, mentioned these variations in her press release as an interesting piece of information. We were not questioning clinical judgement in any way because we weren't in a position to do that. But it was an interesting fact that there was a variation I think, between three and six days in the length of time that children stayed in hospital. And that aroused the ire of quite a number of clinicians.

Until 1967 MCCH still worked from our own sitting-rooms or kitchens. The person who acted as the secretary was Mary who lived in the flat opposite ours, so we worked together. She was instrumental in putting people together, so that groups could be set up in various parts of the country. I was in charge of meetings. By the time we held the first annual general meeting in, I suppose, 1964, there were over twenty groups all over the country. The first Annual General Meeting was held in the Harrington Hotel in South Kensington. The speakers included James Robertson himself, Dermot McCarthy who was the first paediatrician to routinely admit parents into his hospital, David Morris who also did so, and Barbara Weller who was a ward Sister in Great Ormond Street and one of the first nurses to admit parents into hospital. At that meeting the national organisation was set up and a committee elected. It was quite exciting to have all those people from the various branches there and to have the professional people working closely with us.

The Islington branch were somewhat concerned about the name – Mother Care for Children in Hospital – because of the restriction that it imposed. In any case right from the very beginning we'd obviously had men in membership because we had paediatricians and so on working with us. The Islington branch wanted the organisation re-named so there was a consultation and various names were suggested and the name that Islington supported became the new name of the organisation, the National Association for the Welfare of Children in Hospital. This was of course the wording of the Platt Report of 1959, The Welfare of Children in Hospital. The association's long name became shortened to NAWCH.

One of things that I was doing was taking requests from people who wanted speakers in various parts of the country and then arranging for somebody from the nearest group to go out and do those sessions. I did a certain amount of speaking myself – in those early days it was quite frightening – also writing about the organisation and putting bits of paper together for publicity. My husband had been given an award by the Market Research Society, and we decided to spend the money on having a trained nanny which gave me much more freedom to do things for the organisation.

In 1967 we opened up of the office in Victoria in Vauxhall Bridge Road. I had written a letter to the Sembal Trust applying for a grant which was successful. Apparently the thing that appealed to the particular man who arranged for us to be given the grant was this phrase about meeting on the bench in Battersea Park. We had a part-time secretary and we shared one large room with another organisation; they were in one corner and we were in the other corner and I spent quite a lot of time there.

I did whatever needed to be done: packaging, answering people on the telephone, helping the chairman, setting up the talks. It doesn't seem very much looking at it now but we did get a lot of requests from all kinds of organisations wanting somebody to talk about children in hospital. By 1973 we had fifty-three branches.

The first big piece of work we did was the Hospital Admission Leaflet which we published in 1967. The leaflets were purchased by hospitals to send out to parents with the admission literature for the child coming into hospital. Millions of them wended their way to peoples' homes from the hospitals. So all that work of packaging and mailing had to be done in the office.

The Hospital Admission leaflet was reissued, slightly changed, many times. In that first leaflet we didn't actually include anything about living in hospital with your child because at that stage the number of hospitals which would do this was minimal. But then gradually that suggestion got fed into the leaflet with the result that hospitals that didn't have accommodation were sending out the leaflet and then of course getting enquiries as to what accommodation they could offer. The next change in the leaflet was sibling visiting and that was just slipped in! The information about parents' accommodation was never written in terms of rights. There were no patients' rights about it. It was all to do with 'this is the pattern and if you ask...'

I suppose that I'm one of the few people who stayed with the organisation all the way through, and now I act as advisor to the organisation. I was a member of their Executive for a long time. I was chairman for three years and vice-chairman for four years. I organised the annual conference for many years and did a lot of press work until the Association employed a paid press officer. I helped to set up organisations in Poland, Australia, New Zealand. My practice was to invite people to come over here and suggest to them a number of things. One was that they should meet with the Robertsons who were very generous with their time. The second was that I'd arrange visits to various hospitals so that they could see for themselves. You had actually to see what happened and how children's parents were welcomed and helped to play a role in the hospital. I had people come from Holland, Germany, Austria, Kuwait, Malta, Poland, Australia, New Zealand, South Africa, Japan, the Czech Republic.

Over the years there were many high moments for example, having the then Minister of Health coming to open the annual conference. We had Keith Joseph, we had David Owen, we had Baroness Serota. Enoch Powell was one of the first ministers we had. One very exciting meeting was with Princess Alexandra who came and opened the conference on accident and emergency care and she was very interested in what was happening.

Other great highlights were when questions were asked in the House of Commons. Questions were put by MPs to elucidate points on procedure and recommendations about what the pattern of care was to be for children in hospital. One of the most important answers to a parliamentary question was where the Minister of Health said there should be no restriction on the visiting of a child at all in hospital whether they were there for surgery or for infectious diseases – 'that all children in hospital should be able to have a parent visit them at any time when they would not ordinarily be asleep.' But of course hospitals also interpreted that to be the break after lunch when many children would ordinarily be asleep.

I suppose one of the most exciting things for me was when I was chairman I was asked to discuss with the then doctor in the Children's Division of the Department of Health what should go into the document that the Department of Health were publishing in 1971 to set standards for the child in hospital. I discussed with her what the organisation thought would be the appropriate pattern of care for children in hospital. It's quite interesting to go back and see one's words in print as it were in what became the effective document for the care of sick children in hospital, HM71/22 *Hospital Facilities for Children.*

One of the highlights for me personally was in 1973 when the National Health Service was changing and moving into regions, areas and districts, and the first Community Health Councils were being set up. I spent many days on the telephone talking to members throughout the country, persuading them that no Community Health Council could possibly work unless there was a member of NAWCH on it. We got fifty-two of our fifty-three branches to nominate somebody for their CHC, and all except one were appointed. And that was really exciting. From that, interestingly enough, has stemmed a major career for a large number of people who took up those CHC posts. Some of them became chairmen of their CHC. Some, at a later stage, became chairmen or vice chairmen of health authorities, and now a number of them are chairmen of hospital trusts. I became chairman of my local Chelsea Community Health Council and then a member of the Victoria Health Authority. Some people stayed with NAWCH but others moved on to other organisations or, as their children grew up, a great many went into paid work.

There's still an awful lot to do. For example we don't know how many children are still being nursed on adult wards. I am currently the UK representative on the European Association for Children in Hospital which NAWCH helped to set up. Our project for 1998/99 was to find out how many children were being nursed in adult wards in Europe. We prepared a questionnaire to go directly to all the hospitals but I haven't managed to get the money to do it for England. With the Chairman of the Welsh Association for Children in Hospital I have completed a study of the children in adult wards in Wales.

An issue I've worked on intermittently since 1972 is financial assistance to meet travel costs for people on low incomes to enable them to visit their children in hospital. Even when parents such as those on unemployment benefit are entitled to travel costs they don't always get it. They have to know that they are entitled to help and if you don't apply you don't get. There's nothing automatic about it so if they don't know about it and the social worker doesn't advise them, they won't get anything. If you think, just going from here – Battersea to St Thomas' – is £1.20 and that would be one of our local hospitals. And if you're taking another child with you or if you've got other children at home and you want to visit twice a day it all adds up very quickly. And now with so many hospitals closing, the travelling distance gets greater and greater. And if a child has a speciality condition for instance like burns, the parents may have to travel a very long way – twenty miles or more – to a burns unit to visit the child.

The work that I'm doing at the moment in the Czech Republic is fascinating because when we went there four years ago the pattern was just as it was here in 1961. Visiting was an hour and a half a day and no accommodation whatsoever for parents and in many hospitals you only saw the child if the child was well enough to leave the ward. The average length of stay was ten days but we saw a child with congenital dislocation of the hip who had been in hospital for months. But what's fascinating is how quickly it's changing over there. Within five years we've seen changes which took perhaps ten, twelve, fifteen years here. Six Czech paediatricians and three nurses came here and we took them on a hospital tour and they went back, and four out of the six immediately facilitated the setting up of a play programme in their hospitals. And within a year one of the paediatricians had more than fifty per cent of the children under five with a parent staying in the hospital with them.

I very much see myself as a facilitator. One of the things I've always been keen on is to get our agenda on to other people's agenda, for example very early on I got Dr. Kellmer Pringle, first director of the National Children's Bureau interested in our organisation.

I was born in Devonport in Devon on 30th August 1921 and my name then was Margaret Harris. My father, John Mark Harris, was a Scot and my mother, Lillian, was English. My mother was born and brought up in Plymouth. She had married her first husband early in 1914 before the First World War broke out. He fought right through the war and died in Nottingham from flu two days before the war ended. My father was his best friend, and they had served together as army schoolmasters for eight or nine years in India. My father met my mother when he came back from India and married her in 1920.

In 1923 we went to Australia to visit my father's parents and family who emigrated from Perth in Scotland. My grandparents were greengrocers in Scotland, but when they got out to Australia they had a farm and a sawmill. My father decided that we should stay in Australia where he trained as an accountant with an insurance firm. My mother hated Australia because it wasn't her kind of place at all. She was very much a city girl used to electric light, cars, buses, with theatres, shops and friends nearby. We were brought up not to think of ourselves Australians at all. Her total allegiance was to England.

When she came back here to visit in 1976, the England she knew in the 1920s had gone and she couldn't cope with how it was. She was a very old lady – eighty-eight – and no one even gave her a seat on the bus or train. It was quite a different place from the country she'd been living with in her head all those fifty years. She was very happy to go back to Australia where she lived for another thirteen years until she died in 1989, aged 101. My three brothers and my sister are all in Australia. My father died in 1964 when he was well into his seventies.

We lived in a lot of houses in various parts of Brisbane. They were what we now call Queenslanders. Now they are classics. A Queenslander is a wooden house on high wooden stumps with an area underneath, stumps with metal caps on to keep the white ants out. You spent a lot of time under the house because it's cool there. There was a verandah at least on the front of the house, sometimes on the back of the house and sometimes all the way round. We moved to the country when I was five. We had books – we had books, books, books. That's what I remember most about both my parents, but particularly my father. He taught me to read, he was very keen on mathematics: it was all part of life. The school day was long because we never lived very close to the school, and we had to walk each way. One house we lived in must have been two miles from school. When we moved to Kingston I had a five mile train journey to school which meant leaving at half-seven in the morning. What I remember most is running to the station with my hair hanging down my back and plaiting it in the train. Later on I went seventeen miles to high school in Brisbane on a scholarship – and caught the same train and plaited my hair.

Many of my father's family lived around the same area and we'd go visit them. He had four brothers and five sisters. My grandparents lived within reasonable reach, and they grew strawberries and tomatoes. We picked strawberries for my grandmother and she gave us a shilling a row. The rows were very long, uphill on both sides but that's how you grow strawberries. It was a very happy childhood, nothing unhappy about it.

I went from high school to teachers' college and trained as a teacher in Queensland. My father was a teacher and I think it was assumed that I would become a teacher. My parents weren't very well off so I don't think there was a possibility of my doing much else. And I expect I wanted to become a teacher. I quite like teaching now. My mother always wanted to be a teacher but I can't remember what stopped her. She went into catering instead.

I taught school in lots of places and then went out to West Queensland, to Womalilla, 400 miles away from home. This was a one-teacher school, just me and up to thirty children from five to fourteen years old. I had adventures there learning to ride a motor bike because you were twenty miles or more from the nearest town for dances. The children brought interesting things to school, like a snake in a bucket. It was an interesting place to be in, just a little wooden shack really, just large enough to take the children. I think it had three or four long desks with forms on either side. There was a verandah front and back and a tin roof. The children were scattered all over the place. Some of them were on sheep stations. Many walked quite long distances to school and others came on horseback.

I lodged on a sheep station. The house was built a bit like a log cabin but the logs were set vertical with Women's Weekly coloured pictures all over the walls. The ceiling was hessian, hung on ropes. It was the kind of place where the temperature is always above seventy but in the night time in the winter it drops to below freezing and there was no heating! You could wake up and your face cloth had frozen to the wash basin. We walked across the railway bridge – quite a long road to school. The thing that I can remember about it was of course the flies. You wore hats, bobble hats to keep the flies off. I took my landlady's two little girls to school – a child on each hand – so it was quite hard to dispose of the flies. I'd never lived in anywhere like that. No radio. Newspaper once a week and the phones were party lines so if you rang up you were absolutely certain other people were listening in.

I was teaching at Somerset Down School when war broke out. I can remember listening to the broadcast very clearly, listening to Mr Chamberlain. The other teacher and I lived in a small house at the side of a hill and we had all our meals in the canteen with senior members of staff and they had a radio. The day the war broke out a half a dozen of the senior men, the engineers and surveyors, went off to the nearest town and joined up – just like that. Six of them went and only three returned. By the time the Japanese came into the war I was teaching in another one-teacher school. The school committee came and dug trenches in the grounds of the school for the children to get into if the bombers came. We were miles away in the country in a very wooded area. How anyone would have found us is beyond me.

In the following year, July 1942, I applied to join the Australian Air Force. I stayed until just after the end of the European war. I was a radar operator right up in north Queensland. We were as far north as women went except for nurses. It was like being at school with little units, about thirty or forty people stuck up the side of a mountain or out somewhere near an aerodrome – always out of town. By the end I was back in Brisbane on another radar station beside the river at Pinkenba where my mother and I had landed all those years before.

After the war, at twenty-four, I went back to teaching, this time to a school in the city. At the same time I finished my matriculation in order to get to university. I had applied for an army postwar scholarship to do an Arts degree in Sydney. I studied English, History and Psychology and gained my degree. I met Bill, my husband at university. He was a year ahead of me taking an honours degree in Psychology. I was broke so I taught school for a year while I was at university – teaching in the morning, classes in the afternoons.

After I left the university I worked as a personnel officer in a big cotton mill for a year before we came to England. My husband had applied for a job with the BBC in their Audience Research Department. His thesis had been on the effects of advertising on radio programmes. He had been in England during the war when he was in the Air Force and he always wanted to come back. He had quite a long time waiting for the BBC job, but he got it. We married on a Saturday and went to England the following Saturday. The BBC refused to pay my travel costs because Bill wasn't married when he applied for the job. They said the appropriate thing to do was to come to England and take up the booked accommodation they'd arranged for him in one of the university residences and I could follow. So I cashed an insurance policy that my parents had taken out for me when I was small. We bought an extra ticket for me and came to England together. I was very excited.

We arrived at the very end of November and it snowed the first week we were here. It was so cold. We left Australia when their winter was over so there was no way of getting warm clothes in Australia, and when

I got here practically everything had been sold. The other thing I didn't realise in Australia was how very little there was here in the shops in 1950. The shops were practically empty. I'd been given a lot of china as wedding presents and I went back to the shop in Sydney to change it for something more portable. The shopkeeper said, 'I wouldn't if I were you because when you get to England you'll find you won't be able to buy any china there.'

I started teaching school – first near the Portobello Market, and then in Stoke Newington, which was quite a long journey from Battersea where we were living. By that time I was pregnant with my first baby. We got this flat – where we still are – in Battersea in 1952 by advertising in *The Times*. The rent was five pounds a week for four bedrooms and two big front rooms, a kitchen and a bathroom and a pantry and an extra loo outside the back door. The flat was in a terrible state, it hadn't been occupied for over two years. Most of the women along here were very young and had young children. I was thirty-one. Some of them were on to their second child, they'd all been schoolgirls during the war, and I felt like a fish out of water.

I saw an advertisement in the *Times* for somebody to do what was called Care Committee work. That was somebody being an unpaid social worker to help families to cope with their financial difficulties. I was a Care Committee worker for about six years. My job was to visit the schools and contact the families of any children who were giving them cause for concern. I remember one case where a couple of little boys always seemed to be falling asleep in the mornings and were always terribly hungry. And I had to go and visit the home and see what was behind that. What I found was a single mother with these two small boys. She worked in a bank in the City and these two little boys were looked after by the grandmother who lived with them. They were quite small, about five and seven, but the grandmother simply wouldn't get out of bed in the mornings so the boys came to school without breakfast. Their mother apparently didn't know, she had no way of knowing because she went off to work very early. I also had to go and interview the families, to see whether they were eligible to apply for free school meals or free school clothes or free school trips. Just before my third child was born I gave up Care Committee work.

Not very many women with children were working then. It was difficult to work outside the home if you had young children – there were no day nurseries. Nurseries which had operated extensively during the war all closed down once the war was over. In Prince of

Wales Drive we had two ladies who were 'Park Nannies.' Everyday they took a group of children into the park, and for half a crown you had your children taken off your hands from ten to twelve o'clock. Mrs Grimshaw, one of our nannies also took a child for the whole day; my day was Thursday and she took Jane who was only a few months old. That was the day I spent doing the Care Committee work and I had to be back by four.

I didn't have any living-in help until my third child Ross was a year old but I'd always had a cleaner for two, three days a week and I also had this wonderful 'Park Nanny.'

I made the decision to do voluntary work rather than go back to paid because I wanted to be with the children, four children. There also was an awful lot of to-ing and fro-ing because the children had to be fetched from school. My husband used to take them but I fetched them. Yes, there were various opportunities I could have had but there were so many things that needed to be done at home, and Bill had a very demanding job. In the early days of course it would have been difficult because his work for the BBC in the Audience Research Department meant he was working nights as well as days, in order to be able to meet people when they were available. When Jane was little, I used to bath her in the evening so that Bill could see her.

In April, 1961, NAWCH got going just before my fourth and youngest child was born. Things got a little easier because I had an absolutely wonderful woman who came to join me, Mrs Woods who stayed for ten years. She had done domestic work all her life and she sort of took over the house. She was the one who took the curtains down when it was necessary. That gave me far more freedom, that was part of the reason I was able to devote so much time to NAWCH.

Many, many years ago I was in the States reading in the newspaper of an older woman, slightly older than I was then, who was getting her Social Security cards for the first time. And the clerk said to her, 'Madam have you never worked before?' She said, 'No, young man, I've worked all my life but I've never been paid before.' I thought, that's me. I thought that really fitted me absolutely to a T.

Not just a cupboard full of toys

Roma Lear
Toy Libraries

A chance happening one gloomy afternoon altered the course of my life.
For once I was up to date with the daily chores and before setting out to
meet the children from school, I was listening to Woman's Hour. That
day Jill Norris was talking about the toy library for children with special
needs that she had started up in Enfield in 1967. As the mother of two
boys with special needs – and incidentally a Froebel teacher like me –
she often found it difficult to buy suitable toys for them. She was a
member of Enfield MENCAP and often lent to other parents the toys
which did not interest her boys. In return she would be offered toys that
other children had enjoyed and outgrown. This swapping and donating
of toys not right for one child but perhaps perfect for another soon
developed into 'the box under the spare bed' in Jill's house. Before long
this had expanded into a proper toy library. At the end of her radio
interview Jill invited anyone interested to contact her. In a few days my
letter was on her mat!

OVER SUPPER THAT night I discussed the idea with the family. I
felt that running a toy library would be a really interesting and
helpful thing to do alongside my part-time job as a home tutor to
children with special needs. My husband agreed, and of course the
children were all for it as they would have the chance to test out the
toys. With my family behind me all I needed was some advice from
Jill.

At that time there were only three toy libraries in the UK, the one
at Enfield, another nearby run by a social worker – a friend of Jill's –
who was involved with a hostel for girls with learning difficulties,
and one at Nottingham University set up by Drs John and Elizabeth
Newson – I think for the benefit of their patients and students.

It seemed I needed to consider four things before I plunged into this exciting project: potential users, money, premises and toys to stock. I visited the two special schools in my area and discussed the idea of a local toy library with the head teachers. They thought it was a good idea and promised to contact the parents of the children in their schools to see if any would like to be potential borrowers. Twelve parents replied out of a possible one hundred and thirty-five – not many, but encouraging. Next came the question of money. The local Rotarians run an annual May Fair and I decided to hire a stall. It would be stocked with second-hand toys donated by the children of all my school and playgroup contacts. Once the plea went out the toys rolled in! By the end of the day my stall was cleared and I had made £78 – wealth indeed for those days. Premises? No problem. As a Quaker I was generously offered space in the children's room at the Friends' Meeting House in Kingston-upon-Thames, and I bought a book cupboard from the local authority school surplus store for ten shillings, fifty pence in new money.

Next came the buying of the first toys for the toy library. I window-shopped at all the local toyshops and wrote away to educational suppliers for their catalogues.

Guided again by Jill I bought many of those she had already found to be successful. These were often unusual toys that would appeal to children with special needs but the toys also needed to be strong, easily cleaned, brightly coloured and not have too many pieces to get lost. I spent most of my newly-raised funds and it was time to make the big decision and fix the opening date for an inaugural meeting at my home. I contacted all the parents who had written to me as well as a reporter on the local paper who was interested in the toy library idea when we met at the May Fair.

On the great day in 1968 our wallpaper table was set up in our front room and covered with a sheet. All the toys – now marked and catalogued – were displayed on it. I think I am responsible for inventing the net curtain bags which many toy libraries still use for storing toys. It is such a simple idea. You just make a drawstring bag from net curtaining and sew on a label made from a piece of old sheeting. The details of the toy can be written on the label and the contents inside are easy to see. The bag can be washed in a jiffy when it gets grubby.

On that first evening none of the people I expected turned up but an article in the local paper was noticed by five parents of children with cerebral palsy who all attended a centre nearby. We were off!

We decided to meet again for the exchange of toys on the first Thursday morning in the month at the Friends' Meeting House which was easy to reach in the centre of Kingston. The membership gradually crept up and so did the stock of toys. We had the support of many well-wishers. We soon outgrew the book cupboard and I added two filing cabinets from a junk shop. One day the Rotarians generously offered to line the Children's Room with purpose-built cupboards. The Quakers were happy for this to happen, so our storage problems were soon elegantly solved.

In those early days all toy libraries that I knew of were for children with special needs and we often found it difficult to stock the shelves because for some children the choice of toys that they could play with was very limited. I remember one little boy with brittle bones, which were so fragile he couldn't even handle the weight of a Dinky toy. Luckily I had tucked away some realistic-looking farm animals made of celluloid. They are forbidden these days because of their flammability but in the 60s such toys were commonplace. These animals became the nucleus of a farm. I used thin card, matchboxes and tea cartons to make a stable, a pigsty, a haystack, troughs, a farmhouse and all sorts of extras as they occurred to me. This simple farmyard gave my new little friend hours of happy and imaginative play. It also started me off making many more toys for children with special difficulties when I found there was nothing really suitable to buy for them. And that eventually led to Butterworth Heinemann asking me to write a book on making toys for children with special needs.

Having decided I was writing a book for toy library Mums and Dads rather than for the professionals the question was how to organise so much information. It occurred to me that being disabled means that you're missing out on one of your senses. You may have a visual impairment, a hearing loss, or hands that do not work efficiently. I organised the book under five senses. Magic! Suddenly all the play materials sorted themselves into good for looking at, listening to or feeling. After the chapters on Sight, Hearing and Touch I added Taste and Smell. *Play Helps* is now in its fourth edition and has expanded into the *Play Can Help* Series of three smaller books. *Look at it This Way* is for children with visual impairment, *Finger and Thumbs* for children with hand function problems, and *Fun Without Fatigue*, for children with limited movement and energy.

Now, thirty-four years on, the toy library continues to open every Thursday at the same premises. The children are aged anything from six months upwards. Some only come to the library two or three times, others for ever and ever. They use it as they need it. As well as lending toys the toy library now includes a flourishing play session with plenty of time for free play and music, storytelling and making things, depending on which children are there.

The person who gets there first puts on the urn because we always have coffee on tap. The Meeting House has a large recreation hall, a very nice kitchen, and upstairs is the Children's Room where all the toys are stored. We take some of the toys downstairs to the hall and set up tables with puzzles and things to do. We have a safe area with 'nests' for the babies while the more energetic toddlers enjoy the ride-on toys and the push-alongs. Upstairs we set out all the business paraphernalia for loaning out the toys. We check the returned toys, and against the date we list the new toys borrowed and the hire cost. There is a modest charge for each toy – roughly 5% of its cost. If it's an electronic toy it could be 50p, or a Wendy House might be £1. Most toys are 5p or 10p. We haven't much storage space for large toys so they are out on extended loan around the district. We keep a list and if anyone asks for something like the slide or the Wendy House we can arrange a transfer.

We often need to adapt toys. Children with jerky movements, perhaps because they have cerebral palsy, may need suckers put on their toys. I have found that suckers are also used in car maintenance and for shop fittings. I often visit the garden centre or ironmongers in search of unusual treasures. Then there are magnetic toys which can often be the answer for a child with poor hand function. You can buy these, but it is easy to add variety by making more. Add magnetic tape to the back of any small flat surface and it will stick to the fridge or the right kind of baking tray. I make shapes for patterns-making, story telling and 'push together' puzzles, all backed with magnetic tape.

The toy library is the ideal place for borrowing jigsaws for instance. The child does one a few times, and that's it. She is happy to return it for a fresh one. We have a neat line in jigsaws of all standards, some inset puzzles with large knobs, some with hooks and many sturdy wooden puzzles with the number of pieces between four and fifty. The toy library is also good for children who need to practise a skill such as colour-matching or counting, in a number of interesting ways. They can borrow a different toy or game each visit.

From the beginning Jill Norris made it clear that a toy library was not to be just a cupboard or two, full of toys. The stock should always be selected with the children in mind. The object was to help them to play and incidentally improve their skills. Before setting up the Toy Libraries Association in the early 1970s she asked the advice of many professionals and invited on to the Steering Committee paediatric occupational therapists and physiotherapists, a head teacher from a school for children with special needs, an educational psychologist, a toy designer and a toy manufacturer, as well as those of us who were beginning to set up toy libraries.

Our founder members have all grown up and are interested in more adult puzzles, sports equipment and special items like switch-operated radios and tape recorders. No two toy or leisure libraries are ever alike. They have all evolved to serve the needs of their local community. A large number now are for children without disabilities. Some are housed in purpose-built premises, others, like us, share part of a building with others. In country areas the toy library may be housed in a mobile van or bus. In cities there may be a 'core and cluster' organisation with a large toy store supplying many small toy libraries around the city. Some are still run by volunteers, others by paid staff or a mixture of the two. Professional involvement is still crucial and training in becoming a toy librarian is now available. The TLA has become The National Association of Toy and Leisure Libraries, NATLL, the national organisation that supports all 1,000 toy libraries that belong to it. The toy library movement is now flourishing worldwide. Jill, with the help of Lesley Moreland who became the first Director of TLA, set up the first International Conference in London in 1978. It was a most inspiring occasion. Now we meet in a different country every three years and I have been privileged to go to all the eight conferences that have been held so far. Thanks to toy libraries I have friends everywhere. I am so glad I tuned into *'Woman's Hour'* on that fatal day!

My father was a solicitor and my mother would have loved to have been a nurse but in her day it was not suggested, although one of my aunts was a nurse. My mother married young and spent her life bringing us all up. That was her life and she made a very good job of it.

I was born in 1923 and am the fourth of what would have been five children. I had two elder brothers and a sister and after nine years there was me. The child between me and my sister unfortunately died, so I was a very precious baby. We lived on the Isle of Wight, very near the sea. In 1910 my dad bought a cottage there and when his fortunes improved, built our family home on part of the land. We still have the tiny cottage there but my childhood was spent in the large, five-bedroomed, red brick house next door. I had a governess three days a week until I was twelve. Can you imagine that happening these days? I spent the rest of my day down on the beach, swimming, sailing with my brothers, playing in the mud on the cliffs and building sandcastles.

My mother had a terrific sense of humour and having brought up the three older children during the war she was very practical, and never wasted a thing. Luckily she taught me her skills. I was using her ancient Singer sewing machine at a very early age and I think I was knitting by the time I had measles at four. She used to have that lovely rainbow wool put by, so that if it was a terribly wet day and we were stuck indoors she always had something new and interesting for me to do.

We used to make things for an East End mission, as people with spare time used to do in those days. My mother heard of a wonderful lady called a Farthing Bundle Lady, in Bermondsey I think, who used to make up little tiny farthing bundles of toys for the children to buy. A farthing was a quarter of a penny so worth very little. The bundle was wrapped in newspaper and its contents were provided by people like us. It was a lucky dip. A bundle might contain a Christmas card with a few blank pages inside and a stump of pencil tied to it, or a small toy. My mum used to make dolls, and my friends and I would stuff the arms and legs. On Saturday mornings an arch was put on the pavement outside the Farthing Bundle Lady's house and the children queued up behind it. If they were small enough to pass under the arch they could buy their bundle. It was hard luck on the taller children. I used to belong to the Brownies, went to the local dancing class and learnt the piano and violin. What a fantastic childhood!

My dad died when I was quite young. A few years later my mum and I moved to Hinchley Wood in Surrey to be nearer to my brothers and sister who were all working in the London area. We lived just round the corner from this house where I am living now. I went to

Surbiton High School. That was in 1936, not long before the war. It was quite a culture shock to be suddenly confronted with 300 girls in identical gymslips. The teachers sorted me out very nicely, because my part-time governess had left several gaps in my education. It was a very caring school, and each new girl had a volunteer 'mother'. She had to shadow you for a fortnight and if she didn't she was in serious trouble. She had to show you round and stick to you like glue. She played with you in playtime, made sure you got your milk and took you everywhere until you were used to the building and the routine. Of course by then 'mother and child' were best friends.

I was average at school, but used to play the piano for hymns in Assembly. I was so nervous I made every mistake in the book – forgetting the repeats, leaving out verses or playing too many. Music was really my favourite subject but I also loved PT, art and geography. I ended up with the School Certificate with exemption from Matriculation. By then the war had begun and I remember writing some of the papers in the air raid shelters in the cloakrooms under the school. There were three careers suggested to me – teaching, nursing, or secretarial. I guess if I had known about occupational therapy I might have chosen that, but in those days it mostly consisted of caning chairs and glove-making. I have turned out accidentally to be a paediatric occupational therapist without the training. Many of my friends are OTs and they ask me to make things for them and we exchange ideas. I either think about the child and wonder what does he need, or I look at the pile of scrap materials and imagine what I could do with that lot! The result can often be a very satisfactory 'ephemeral' toy which is both fun and therapeutic.

As a career I chose teaching and during the war I trained as a Froebel teacher. We were taught to see each child as an individual, to challenge the bright ones and encourage and help the slower ones. The idea was to lead each child to learn at his own pace largely by discovery and observation.

My interest in children with special needs dates from the last term of my teacher training when we were all sent to visit a special school. I went to a small school for physically handicapped children at The Oval in London. It was such a happy place. Until then I had probably only seen a couple of children wearing callipers and one in a wheel chair. In those days I suppose they were all in long-stay hospitals or in special institutions. Anyway, from that visit on I wanted to work with such children.

At the end of my teacher training I looked for a post in a special school, but of course the war was still on and they were few and far between. I had no luck. My first teaching job was in a kindergarten and then I found a job as a ward teacher at Lord Mayor Treloar Cripples Hospital – 'cripple' is a word you never hear these days.

My first term as a ward teacher was quite a shock after my cosy little kindergarten. Now I had a long ward of twenty-eight children aged between four and twelve. They were there to be treated for bovine TB, osteomyelitis and polio – all diseases thankfully seen rarely these days. Some of the children were lying on plaster shells, others were on high spinal carriages with weights attached to their limbs in an attempt to help them to grow straight. Open air was part of the treatment, so before school all the beds were pushed out on to the veranda where they would stay until bedtime. The windy days were the worst. The children were restless and it was impossible to talk to them all at once. Of course all the books and papers blew away and I was forever chasing some flyaway. I soon had to come up with ways of defeating the elements and preventing the children from 'accidentally-on-purpose' dropping all their school gear. This experience came in handy later when I needed to keep toys within reach of children who could not pick them up for themselves. It is wonderful what you can do with string, safety pins, and magnets!

After about three years I moved to a job nearer home where I divided my time between a TB sanatorium and the long-stay children at a nearby general hospital. My final move was to a medical ward at Guy's Hospital.

I got married very late, extremely happily. We met over our fiddles. We both played the violin at various evening classes and summer schools, and apparently John had got his eye on me a bit before I had my eye on him. And so it happened, and we've still got this lovely shared interest in music. After he served in the war John became a valuation surveyor for London County Council, and that was his career. I was thirty-nine when I had Andrew and forty-one when I had Eve. So I took a risk but was lucky. I was able to be at home with the children for all those gorgeous early years. I ran a little playgroup for them and three small neighbours, then we moved on to a large playgroup where I became the storytelling, piano-playing, and general factotum volunteer.

I suppose to be honest I was a bit on the lonely side because I missed the buzz of Guy's. When you have worked in a busy hospital for many years and then all of a sudden you are in a small house with two young children it can seem a long time before husband comes home with proper conversation! When toy libraries were starting it was all pioneering – there was no established way of setting about it. I thought setting one up would be a lovely thing to do, and it related back really to my working days.

I still visit the toy library every week and play the piano for the music session though the day-to-day organisation is now in the hands of the younger volunteers. I keep up my interest in making toys for children with special needs by running an Active Group. They were started by a wonderful man called Roger Jefcoate who has recently been honoured. His speciality is electronics and engineering, and he is a consultant for people with severe disabilities. Our group is less technical, but serves a useful purpose. We are divided into 'makers' and 'takers'. We 'makers' are rather handy with our sewing machines and can do simple woodwork. We make one-off toys for the 'takers'. These may be teachers from local special schools, therapists, carers or parents who really haven't got time to do anything extra. Among our members we have a therapist in a school for children with autism, and therapists from the local assessment unit, teachers of the visually impaired, the young deaf, children with physical disabilities and learning difficulties. We are getting quite well known and new members are coming from further afield. The 'takers' come up with some excellent ideas for individual children and we do our best to carry them out. We do not copy anything you can buy. One favourite request is for an apron with patch pockets all over it. Each pocket closes with a different fastening – zip, button, popper, Velcro etc. The therapist wears the apron and hides little surprises in the pockets. When the child comes to her she can see how he does or does not manage all the fastenings and she can then work on his weaknesses.

One of my favourite toys is the Colour Matching Game. It is so simple and versatile. It consists of several squares of cardboard, all different colours, and a large collection of objects to match to them. In my game I have a piece of glass worn smooth by the sea which I picked up on the beach when I went to the cottage, a fir cone, a button, a coloured clothes peg, a feather, and much more besides – simple items bringing a little bit of the world to a child who cannot find them for himself. If I were using the game with such a child I might add a lemon (for the smell) or a carrot or potato. It is amazing how many children think potatoes grow chipped or mashed! Another favourite design is a beanbag shaped like a starfish. It looks attractive and is much easier for some children to catch than the usual square or oblong.

In odd moments I make loads and loads of finger puppets. These are for 'Two Little Dickie-Birds' – Peter and Paul. I am sure you know the rhyme. I took 200 to Japan for our International Conference and have just left 300 in Johannesburg. I have several elderly housebound ladies who help me make these enormous flocks.

I have got a workroom upstairs now. My son moved out and has his own house which is lovely for him and although I'm sorry to see him go it has its advantages. I can leave things out while the glue dries.

I have a pipe-dream. Although we now have leisure libraries they are mostly for adults with learning difficulties. That is splendid, but I have friends who have Parkinson's, glaucoma, diabetes, arthritis and other restricting conditions and time can often hang heavy on their hands. I know the time can come when people just want to be left in peace, but before that time arrives it would be nice to think that congenial activities are available for them. For instance, hand-cut wooden jigsaws with attractive pictures and not too many pieces, and adapted board games. Of course I am too ancient to start a new project now, but wouldn't it be wonderful if someone reading this would feel the urge to start leisure libraries for the Third Age?

A learning experience for all of us

Jill Faux
Pre-school Playgroups Association

I was listening to the radio one day, I think it was Woman's Hour, and there was some pompous man saying that if you hadn't been talking to your child since he was born then he was bound to be backward in speech. William at thirteen months was a very silent child and I actually found it quite difficult to chatter away as a mum. And I just thought, I just felt God, I've failed completely and I burst into floods of tears and felt desperate about the whole thing and couldn't cope.

I PICKED MYSELF up and went with William to a little public playground just at the back of the house. I didn't know anybody as we had only just moved from the north of Scotland to Wombourne in Staffordshire. OK, I'd not made much effort to get to know anyone and I thought now I must. There was another woman with a small child there too. William toddled over to see this small child and the woman said, 'Come away dear and leave that child alone.' I went up to her and said, 'I don't know anybody here, I'm quite new in the area. It would be good for William and me to get to know other people and do you think they can play together?' She picked her child up, looked at me and walked off. I was very very upset and didn't really know where to turn.

I didn't want to go out to work because I did want to look after William if I could do it adequately. So I decided I'd better go to some classes about child development. If this talking bit was that important then I ought to find out more. So I signed up – actually at the school where my husband, Geoffrey, was teaching – for an evening class on child development. It turned out to be run by the local playgroup leader, Christina Forder.

The playgroup movement started in 1961 when a young London mother, Bella Tutaev, wrote to the *Guardian* newspaper about how, in the absence of a state nursery place for her daughter, she had set up a group of her own. The response to the *Guardian* letter was overwhelming.

I went to the evening class which, I think, was six weeks. It wasn't very long and it was fairly low level. Looking back on it I think I had two motives. One was certainly to learn a bit more about children and secondly, I thought there was a good chance I'd meet other people who had young children. That turned out to be so. I quite rapidly began to knit into the local young family community. But the biggest boon was meeting Christina. I think she recognised a fairly distraught and lonely soul. She's still a firm friend, still lives in that area. She said, 'If you're passing, why don't you pop in and see the playgroup.' It was on our way to the shops so we would pop in. Christina was very clever at getting you quickly involved one way or another. She said William was too young to leave alone in the playgroup because he was only eighteen months old and it wasn't a parent and toddler group, it was a playgroup for over-threes. But she'd say, would I like to just nip out and get some sugar for them. She was excellent at appearing to be disorganised enough to need help but actually being very organised into drawing people in. I went there I think about twice a week and spent anything up to an hour in the group doing errands or odd jobs for them. William was perfectly happy with me doing that, and this carried on till he was three when he started to go to the playgroup.

I was involved in a peripheral way as the parent of a young child in the playgroup. But it was a key element in establishing myself in the community. However my husband got the job as head of mathematics at Abraham Darby school in Telford near Ironbridge. So we moved to Broseley in April 1969 when our second child, Andrew, was six weeks old. I was really sad to be going to yet another new place, another new set of circumstances to work out. But Christina said, 'Does this new place, Broseley, have a playgroup?' I said, 'I don't think so'. And she said, 'Oh well you're going to have to start one aren't you!' And the Wombourne playgroup made me a member of the Pre-school Playgroups Association as my leaving gift. The Association's aims at first were: mutual support to those running groups; and lobbying of government to emphasise the importance of pre-school provision. I got their magazine, *Contact,* every month and received all the literature, and I had this imposed mission to start a playgroup in Broseley, quite a run-down little village, and I always say about that particular neck of the woods – I think it's a bit better now – anyone who had any get up and go had got up and gone! We bought an end-of-terrace Victorian house and we did have a car which we really couldn't afford. I was actually one of the few women in the village who a) could drive and b) had occasional access to a car during the day.

I started talking around in the shops and met up with various people. The child clinic was held in the village hall, and I'd go to that and I'd say, 'What about a playgroup? Why haven't we got something like that here?' People started saying yes, it would be a good idea. Gradually, we got to the stage where we decided it was worth having an open meeting and we put up notices all around the village which said come along and talk about having a playgroup. The last thing I wanted to do was to be involved in a professional sense, that is to be a playgroup leader. I had a young child, and a baby only a couple of months old and I had never done any training of any sort, I'd just been to this one six-week course on child development. We got a group of people together who were all quite determined but none of them thought they could actually be the playgroup leader. So we advertised for a playgroup leader and we negotiated a rent for the village hall and we started fund-raising. We ended up by appointing a trained nurse, the wife of the local grocer, a lovely person but quite strait-laced. There were a lot of things that were not acceptable to her, but never mind; she was very good with the children though she wasn't particularly active about their development.

We asked the Health Department for advice, it wasn't Social Services then, it was pre-Seebohm. All they were interested in was the number of loos we had – the standard number was something incredible like one per five children – and the number of square feet we'd got per child. They didn't give us any advice on play at all. Almost exactly at that moment the Pre-school Playgroups Association had done a survey on how many times children went to the loo in the morning to try and prove we didn't need all these loos. It was quite funny, lots and lots of playgroup leaders had been randomly chosen to tick every time a child went to the loo. They discovered that children went to the loo when they finished playing, far too busy playing to think about it, and there was a rush at the end of the session or just before milk. Basically, nobody went to the loo the rest of the time and we could well do with fewer loos than we had. Anyway, we had to have some potties because we didn't have enough loos.

We got the playgroup going and I acted as Chair of the committee which seemed to me to be the best bet. You'd got some control as the Chair and, let's face it, I like some control! Also, because I had the car I could say to people, let's go on a course somewhere. So I took the playgroup leader and various other people to Wellington and to Bridgnorth and all over the place to any course we could access, because the one thing I was quite certain about was that we'd got the nucleus of something that was quite good. But we needed to go on learning to make it better, so although I didn't help very regularly in the group because of Andrew, William went to it regularly. I would push the pram up with Andrew and spend an hour there every so often. I chaired all the committee meetings, and we had a lot of them. Actually I'm quite a believer in committee meetings; I work best when I'm working with a group of people who spark each other off, and I can develop things quite quickly in that context. On my own, I find it much more difficult.

We started our playgroup in Broseley in 1970. We had one of those typical parish halls with high windows you couldn't see out of, and antiquated heating. We had quite a lot of storage space. We begged and borrowed, and a lot of the toys and equipment we got was totally unsuitable because it was designed for use by one child in the home. If you've got twenty-five children using it in a group it doesn't last very long. Initially we went for the large climbing frame type of play activity. We also had a lot of creative materials: all relatively cheap, paints and brushes; and we made dough, we didn't have clay at that time. We had sand, which was a bone of contention because people played badminton in the hall and they couldn't get the sand off the floor. And we had water-play.

The playgroup leader liked to get in early, she always wore a neat overall and she liked to get all the equipment out and sorted so she was there to greet the parents. Which was fine but it left very little room for anyone else to do much helping. So whenever I could I'd be down there saying to other parents have you ten minutes, can you stay for a little while just to do this that or the other. Only the playgroup leader was there all the time, so we had to have parent helpers. We had a rota, two parents each session. In the two and a half years I was there those were the people – about half a dozen – who I was taking on courses and who went to branch meetings.

I think we provided an opportunity for parents to get to know each other, and it was a break from the children. Certainly the children were happy there doing the things they were doing. I'm sure they were learning, they're learning all the time anyway. But it wasn't structured in any sense, it was very much free play, not quite a free-for-all, but free play. And there were times when it did get out of hand and we needed to learn how to impose rules. We did this through the materials. So it wasn't a question of ticking children off for doing something wrong. It was just a question of saying it doesn't go there. It stays there: water stays there, sand stays there, the Lego goes over there; and you'd take the child to put it there. It was very much a learning experience for all of us.

I learnt a lot about children and was much happier at home with my own kids. I could now organise play activities for them which kept them occupied and I could get an intellectual satisfaction from watching them develop through the play I was offering to them. Which made the whole business of having children worthwhile! Before that I won't say it was a bore but I wasn't aware of what was happening so I found it much more difficult to get that kind of satisfaction out of it. But having said I was going to stay at home with the children, at least until they went to school, it was imperative for me to get some sort of satisfaction. I couldn't just do it without understanding because I would probably bawl them out or hit them. I always had the utmost sympathy for anyone who ended up bashing their kids because literally but for the grace of God… And that's why I've always felt it's so important to help people to understand their children better. And that's why as far as I was concerned the playgroup movement's most important aspect was the adult education rather than the child education. You'd see things happening, children in the supermarket being swiped for touching things. And you think, oh God what can I do about this, you know there's the mum picking up things, looking at them and putting them back on the shelf and when the child copies her he's told not to do it. And yet imitating is the natural way children learn. You see terrible scenes, a complete lack of understanding of the child's current stage of development, what he needs to do in order to grow at that point.

I always used to say when people criticised playgroups for not being as good as nursery schools, that they are not trying to be nursery schools. What they're trying to do is provide an alternative form of pre-school activity which is equally valid. It has a different focus which is about parental involvement, it's about parental growth, it's about helping parents to understand their children better. I've watched so many parents begin to understand through being with a group of children including their own and through talking to other parents. That's why I don't like children going off to nursery without their parents. However, I know the world's changed and everyone goes to work now and it's not going to happen so there you are. But that was my *raison d'etre* for working in the movement. However I always was more interested in the organisational bit than I was in the actual play itself. That's not to say I didn't appreciate that side.

While I was in Broseley I became a member of the local branch committee of the Pre-school Playgroups Association, so I started getting involved in that wider context. I think I was vice-chair of the branch committee at one stage. And then each branch had to send somebody to the county PPA, and I was sent to the county committee. At the county level PPA was involved in writing responses to consultative documents. For example, about the time the Seebohm changeover was coming to Social Services we did a lot of lobbying as to what should happen to the Nursery and Childminders Regulation Act 1974 and how these responsibilities should switch over to Social Services.

I became PPA's newsletter editor for Shropshire. It was just at that time that you could get colour duplicators. So I'd go into Geoffrey's school where they had one of these magnificent machines and we'd design a front cover for the newsletter – usually a child's painting in several different colours – and we'd cut stencils for each colour and put them through. It took us ages, I can't think how we had the patience. Through the newsletter we ran surveys to find out what people wanted and why they wanted it. We started to apply for grants to the county council to help us establish a network of fieldwork support for groups, and we also applied for small grants to help playgroups buy equipment, or to go on training courses.

We weren't in Broseley very long, that was the next problem, always moving you see. After two and a half years we had moved to Keswick, William was five and Andrew was three. So William went to the local school. Poor lad he'd been really shunted about. In 1971 we moved again to Curthwaite in Cumbria and he went to primary school in Thursby. So by the time he was six and a half he had been to three different schools and two playgroups. And that's always had an effect on him. He found it very difficult to make friends when we finally settled. I said to him one day, 'Michael Cutforth seems a nice little boy, do you like Michael Cutforth?' And he said, 'Yes.' So I said, 'Shall we have Michael Cutforth for tea?' And he said, 'But we might go away.' And I said 'No, we won't go away, we'll stay here, you can make friends we're not going away, nothing's going to happen.' The next term it was Michael Cutforth who moved away, so poor little thing was stymied by this and it actually took him a long time to make friends.

Andrew went to Thursby playgroup which was run, funnily enough, by someone like the playgroup leader in Broseley, a woman whose husband ran the local post office. Again, she was a homely figure. She had a lot of good points, she also did things which drove me absolutely crazy like line the children up to blow their noses. I used to end up totally frustrated because I was regarded as just a mum. She was very certain in her ways and she didn't take kindly to advice or criticism. If you get the right leader the group can work in organic, community work terms which involves everybody and provides opportunities for growth which is quite phenomenal. But if you get the wrong person, the person who won't let people in, and gets into this boxed-in framework then there's no room for others. And I can't pretend that all groups are, or were, the ideal organic ones. Probably twenty per cent of them were, another twenty per cent were definitely boxed-in and then you've got the sixty per cent who were middle of the road. But the good ones were so exciting, they were wonderful to be with. You don't get, can't get that excitement in a much more formal and structured system.

It was really the fact that I couldn't get myself and others further involved in the Thursby group which drove me to apply for the job I saw advertised for a Development Officer for Pre-school Playgroups. So I switched from being a volunteer to a staff member.

The Development Officer job was funded by the first grant that the Pre-school Playgroups Association got from the Department of Health in 1973. At the interview the only thing I remember is right at the end they said, 'Are there any questions you want to ask?' And I said, 'Yes can you tell me exactly what this job is?' The Chair said, 'We're rather hoping that you might be able to tell us that in about six months time!' I got the job and I may say the pay was very good, the full-time at that point was £2,000 and it was on a scale that rose to £2,700. My husband had just been appointed on a very similar pay scale as Maths Adviser for the county so it was quite remarkably high. However it didn't go up for the next ten years. The expenses were abysmal, but never mind it was an extraordinarily good starting point. This first job, the training/development officer job which I worked in tandem with a colleague, was from 1973 to 1985 and after that I did ten years as a national adviser.

The playgroups were really a training ground for people to get involved in other community activities. If I look round now at people who I knew at the time, many parents whose children had outgrown the playgroup would go off and do almost anything having gained an enormous amount in self-confidence. One friend who'd gone right through the association now works for the Leonard Cheshire Homes training volunteers as home carers, so she's still in the voluntary movement. Other people I've known have moved into Age Concern, Citizens Advice Bureau and a great friend is now regional treasurer for Riding for the Disabled. Other people would use the skills they'd acquired by getting involved in Parent Teacher Associations or the Brownies and Guides, growing up with their children in a sense.

I was born in the war – November 1940 – in a little village called Molesworth in Cheshire where my father was stationed. He was a barrister in the army in the Judge Advocate General's department. I was the second of four children. I have an elder brother and a younger brother and a younger sister. So it went boy, girl, boy, girl. Very well organised my parents. We were sort of camp followers for the next six years, moving to various rented accommodation, mostly in the Manchester/Cheshire area. Then my parents bought a small house in Cheadle in Cheshire. I'm not quite sure when they bought that but I know my younger brother was born there because it created a family disappointment. My grandfather was keen that he should be born in Lancashire so he would qualify to play cricket for Lancashire.

We were a fairly typical middle class family. My grandfather on my mother's side was a cotton king who lost most of his money in the slump in the 1930s. He travelled across the Atlantic over and over and I've still got things like wonderful menu cards off the Queen Elizabeth signed by various people like the Vanderbilts. He was always at the captain's table. It was a very posh sort of existence. And they actually lived in America for a short time, when Mother was between two and five. My father's father was also in cotton. They were merchantmen, fine spinners in Manchester.

Mother was brought up really not to work but at the same time the crashes of the 1920s and 1930s led to her getting a job with the BBC in Manchester. She did some newsreading and some minor secretarial work and then got a job as the secretary to the Principal of Didsbury College in Manchester which was a Methodist teacher training college.

We moved from Cheadle to Cheadle Hulme which was not that far away, in 1946, after my younger sister was born in 1945. We moved to an enormous Victorian pile which had been used by the Home Guard during the war. The windows had all been painted black because they couldn't be bothered with black-out. My parents had to hack their way up to the front door; we actually had a wonderful time there as children because it was a completely wild garden. It was absolutely full of beer bottles and we were given a penny for each bottle we collected. I think we collected 550 beer bottles and we scraped the paint off the windows with pennies. We lived there very happily. I was about twenty when we moved out. In those days it was quite hard because although they came from middle class families, both families had lost most of their money in the slump. And of course after the war Father had to rebuild a career with four children to support. So he was always broke, there was never any money. We did wonderful things like pre-heat the draughts by putting paraffin stoves outside the doors in the porch. We salted beans and we isinglassed eggs.

My mother's parents came to live with us. And that I think was a tremendous strain for Mum and Dad but from the point of view of us kids it was wonderful to have Granny and Grandpa on hand. We would rush back from school and go to see them in their room and they'd always have time for us. But when I was about seven or eight my granny died, and grandfather died when I was about twelve.

In that particular era and in that particular culture and community, it was just natural for my parents to send their sons away to school. My grandfather paid for some of their education. They both went to Clifton which was where my father had been, and his father, and my grandfather on my mother's side, and my mother's brothers. It was a bit divisive because my sister and I both went to local schools. I think my sister and I were the first two ever to go to a state school. I passed the eleven plus so I was sent to Withington Girls School in Manchester.

Again it's all part of that culture. Boys were considered slightly more important than girls, so careers for us two girls were never really considered to be important, although we were bright and intelligent children who did well. I got ten 'O' levels at good grades. The options after that were fairly limited. My mum said to me, either you can go to Switzerland for a year or you can go to university but at that time there wasn't really the choice because my brothers' education was draining the trust my grandfather had set up.

So I went to Switzerland for six months to a so-called finishing school. It was actually quite a hard-working place and I polished up my French fairly well and got a diploma from Lausanne University which enabled me to teach French in England. I enjoyed that and it was the first time I'd really been away from home. It was assumed that I would go to secretarial college, get married and have kids and live happily ever after. So I wasn't prepared for any sort of professional life.

When I came back from Switzerland I did two or three terms teaching French in a local school, the old school that I used to go to before I went to secondary school. And then I went to London and did my secretarial training, and got a job at the Royal Institute of British Architects where I worked as a junior secretary to the deputy director for six months, and then I was his PA for a couple of years.

At that time, the family was beginning to fall apart. My father had depressive illnesses of one sort or another as well as arthritis of the hips. He was under stress and started drinking very heavily – he became an alcoholic. We always knew that there was something wrong although my mother did her best to cover things up for us. I have to say we were all very very fond of both our parents, and my father in particular gave us a tremendous sense of security despite his shortcomings. He always used to say to us – I never forget this because I think it's terribly important for children to know – he used to say, 'If ever you're in any trouble whatever part of the world you're in, it doesn't matter how stupid you've been to get in it, give us a ring and I'll be there in the morning.' And he meant it, he would have been, he'd have borrowed down to his last penny to have got there. Anyway he walked out of chambers one day when he was about fifty-six, about my age, and said he wasn't going back. Mother had to cope with the mess and there was a mess: he hadn't opened any letters for yonks, he hadn't paid any bills for ages. It was just at this time my brother was starting at the Bar in Manchester and he, my brother, in fact did very well out of it. He earned more money than any young barrister had ever done in their first year because he got all of Dad's cases, all the solicitors were so sorry for my mother. Mother got a part-time job as a receptionist at a doctor's surgery. Basically she helped organise the finances after Dad collapsed and really managed the house sale, moving to a flat in Wilmslow and then up to Kendal.

Meanwhile I became secretary to the Manchester Society of Architects and PA to the director of the Building Centre in Manchester, and lived at home so that I could help and contribute to family expenses. Geoffrey and I got married from there. We had met years before, when I was about fifteen or sixteen so we'd known each other for six or seven years but he was at the University of Liverpool and then he was teaching in Scotland so we just occasionally met. But we both knew that we were right for each other although we had other boyfriends and girlfriends. We finally got married in 1963 when I was twenty-three and he was twenty-six. He was teaching at Gordonstoun at that time, so we went to live at Gordonstoun and left Mum and Dad to cope. But my younger brother by that time was up and running and was able to help. Geoffrey taught at Gordonstoun for a year. I got pregnant almost immediately and lost the baby and then became pregnant again. So I seemed to spend the first fifteen months of our married life pregnant.

Geoffrey had two teacher friends at Gordonstoun who were going to start a new school. So we moved from Gordonstoun at the end of the first year to Dunrobin about seventy miles south of John o' Groats. It is the home of the Countess of Sutherland, a beautiful castle actually. We were living there and the three of them started the new school which was a great exciting adventure but doomed to failure right from the beginning because who on earth is going to send their children that far unless they're as thick as two short planks and couldn't get in anywhere else?

That only lasted for about eighteen months when Geoffrey came home one night having given in his notice – he's done this twice to me in his life without having another job – at which point I was pretty cross. Geoffrey hadn't a job and he hadn't a decent reference and we had a baby. He said, 'We're going to teach in state schools. I'm fed up with this. We've got all these parents who expect the earth and don't take any notice of their children.' Even at Gordonstoun it was the same.

Geoffrey had gone straight from university to Gordonstoun so he'd never got a teacher training qualification which meant if he went to a state school he had to go back to square one, become a registered teacher, do a probationary year. So from having a free house and a reasonable salary, we landed up just on the outskirts of Wolverhampton at Wombourne, and he had to do a year's probation at a comprehensive school before he could get anywhere.

So we had no house, no money, nothing. We had a joint overdraft when we were first married and we couldn't afford for us both to go and look at houses right from the north of Scotland down to the Midlands. Geoffrey went to look one weekend and he found a little canal worker's cottage in Wombourne which cost £3,200. We had £320 in the Gordonstoun pension and we had to cash it in because it was the only way of getting money for the ten percent downpayment. In April, we moved down and installed ourselves and off Geoffrey went to school to teach. It sounds silly now, I think his pay was £75 a month and we were paying £26 a month on our mortgage so we really hadn't got any spare cash. I did various things to try and make ends meet. I used to leave William with Geoffrey over the summer holiday period and go and do temporary secretarial work, sometimes in London and sometimes in Birmingham.

So that's really me up to Pre-school Playgroups Association taking over my life. I stopped working with them in May 1995. I had always believed that I would stop work altogether when I was about fifty-five and Geoffrey could carry on for a bit longer and we might have a little window of time when we didn't have the kids to finance. And then all of sudden Geoffrey gets made redundant, and I have to pull out all the stops to earn the money, and then I also get made redundant. Bang goes any window of opportunity, travel or anything. I was really angry when Geoffrey was made redundant, and upset and hurt when I was made redundant too. Our hopes and aspirations were dashed.

I now do some work in developing consultative processes in the county on a freelance basis. I just don't feel that I want to spend my time doing a lot of voluntary work now. I also do some freelance work for the Cumbria Social Services Inspectorate. So I inspect pre-school playgroups. The other thing I've done since I came away from PPA was to undertake a review of the children's library services for the County Council and I also conducted the 1995 Section 19 Review of Children's Services for them.

Geoffrey does mostly in-service training for teachers. He's always worked as a volunteer for the Association of Teachers of Mathematics. And he does some training for other agencies too.

I think if I hadn't done the playgroups I would have had to find some other outlet. I don't know what it would have been. I probably would have gone to university actually. There was one point when I did apply. I wanted to go to Lancaster to do a degree in organisational behaviour because that's actually the area that fascinates me, about how organisations work. I got in despite the fact that I hadn't got any A-levels. But just at that time my mother-in-law became very ill with cancer and I had to spend about eight months nursing her. When she died my eldest was about to go to university and we really couldn't afford for both of us to go at the same time! I always regretted I didn't go to university.

Geoffrey and I always had a pretty equal relationship, but it wouldn't have happened if Geoffrey hadn't been a) good with kids and b) interested in me having something which I wanted to do. Which not every man in Cumbria wants! And c) that we had the school holidays, had the time.

It's difficult to remember what a crazy idea it was at the time

Sonia Jackson
Advisory Centre for Education

It was at the Institute of Community Studies, in the East End of London, that Michael Young started ACE in 1960. An advisory service for people telephoning or sending in their questions on education, ACE also published WHERE?, first a quarterly and then a monthly magazine modelled on the Consumers' Association's Which? magazine. In the beginning ACE largely depended on the efforts of a wonderful man, Len White. He was an Education Officer in Hampshire and almost single-handedly answered all the enquiries. In 1961 Michael was appointed a Fellow at Churchill College, Cambridge, and as he was always inclined to take his organisations with him, he asked Brian Jackson to take over ACE and run it in Cambridge. Brian had just published his book Education and the Working Class. Having accepted the job to run ACE Brian happened to be on the train coming back to Cambridge from London and he met my then husband who invited him back to supper. A few days later Brian came to call, and asked whether I would be interested in being a half-time administrative secretary for a new organisation, the Advisory Centre for Education. He made ACE sound so attractive that I couldn't resist saying yes!

I COULD TYPE pretty well because my mother had insisted on my doing a secretarial course before I went to university but I knew nothing about running an office, because I didn't expect ever to do secretarial work. I'd never seen a filing system, I couldn't understand why there were all these buff files in green folders. I thought they looked rather untidy so I started taking out all the contents until Brian pointed out to me very kindly that they were an essential part of the system! But the filing was in a total mess anyway.

My job was running the organisation and Brian mainly did publicity and starting new projects. He also wrote about three quarters of every edition of *WHERE?* When we started we were completely amateur and had to learn as we went along. I mean it was all terribly primitive. I remember Brian had a blue ledger in which he wrote down numbers of enquiries and applications for membership. This was long before the days of computers but we did have secretaries. And I suppose we must have had quite an expansion of staff because we couldn't have coped otherwise.

People were constantly wandering in and out of rooms talking to each other. Every morning I would arrive and would find about six suggestions of new things to do from Brian. He just had a constant stream of ideas. At first I tried to do everything and then I realised it was impossible.

When I first went to ACE I just had the one child but I had terrible child care problems. And then I got pregnant with Rebecca, my second child, and I went on working for ACE until the day before she was born. I started working again about six weeks later because I just loved doing it. By that time ACE must have moved to the old Fitzwilliam House which was 32 Trumpington Street, because what brought Rebecca on a bit early was that I ran all the way from one end of Trinity Street to Trumpington Street and I can't remember why now! But it wasn't a good thing to do when you were eight and three-quarter months pregnant.

My main task was to manage the advisory service which answered the questions people sent in. At that time, well always, people joined ACE in order to be able to ask questions. It was mostly about which school to choose. They wanted to know which was the best school in say, Bolton or Solihull, or what their rights were if they wanted to appeal. Len White always knew the answers, I don't know how he managed to do a proper job as well. As a child psychologist I was very happy to deal with psychological questions. Some of them were about children who had what we'd now call dyslexia – 'my son is terribly bright but doesn't seem to be able to learn to read.' People would often write in with questions relating to subjects in articles in *WHERE?*.

Part of ACE's mission was to be within the consumer movement. It was to give more power to the consumers. And I must say in those days we rather saw the parents as the consumers, not the children. And although it's wrong, we did. One of the first articles published in *WHERE?* once Brian and I took it over was No Parent Beyond This Point and we illustrated it with a great chicken fence! There was a line on the playground that parents actually weren't allowed to cross. That was very common, even if it wasn't a particularly bad school, the idea was you kept parents well away. When I was teaching I remember my very first day with a reception class. There were the parents standing outside the wire fence looking in, and there were these forty-eight children at least half of whom were screaming their heads off. I thought there's something wrong here.

I think that *WHERE?* did make a tremendous difference in changing attitudes. Somehow before that schools and teachers were unchallengeable. Nobody criticised them. So part of the campaign was to inform parents and to enable them to play a much bigger part in their children's education. But the other part of ACE's mission was to improve the educational chances particularly of working class children and to use the middle class parents who belonged to ACE to provide us with the resources to speak for both. At the beginning we didn't have much idea about the disadvantages of black children, later on we did. I think that the improvement of educational opportunity was very much where Brian was coming from, thinking about the children he'd grown up with.

Sasha Young, Michael Young's wife and the first editor of *WHERE?*, decided to give it up when she had her second child. Brian then asked me if I would take it over. By that time I knew quite a bit about writing and editing because I worked closely with Sasha and she taught me an awful lot – a wonderful journalist.

One day when *WHERE?* was just about to go to press Michael Young gave me this very boring looking paper about four pages long and he said in a rather tentative way, you might put it in *WHERE?*. Actually that edition of *WHERE?* was already full but I forced myself to read the article. It was all about distance learning and the Chicago College of the Air which he had recently visited. It was just incredibly exciting. So I actually stopped the press and put in a four-page spread and I called it *Towards an Open University!* This was before Harold Wilson's speech in 1963 about the University of the Air which he based mainly on Michael's thinking.

Every time *WHERE?* was published we'd have a lead article and a press release, and usually we held a press conference. We'd go to a hotel and we'd focus on one subject which we thought was new, and we usually got all the education correspondents and quite a lot of other journalists as well. Sometimes we'd have a story in every single daily newspaper, and also on television and radio, so that would bring in a lot of new members. I do remember in particular one press conference in London at the Waldorf Hotel in the Aldwych. It was just at the time when Mary Quant was the thing and we'd only just stopped wearing terribly middle-aged clothes. You know the 60s. I was really very pleased with my outfit which was a very short grey pinafore dress and long black boots. Frightfully daring. I felt the absolute pinnacle of fashion. I don't know whether the success of the press conference was due to that!

It's very difficult to know which were my ideas for subjects in *WHERE?* and which were Brian's, we worked so closely together. From time to time we'd issue a pull-out supplement on a specialist subject. The public school supplement as it happened wasn't our idea at all. A man called John Wakeford who was at Cardiff University came to see us and said that he'd got an idea. Like all of us, he wanted to get rid of private education, that was the top of the agenda really and he said, 'Well some of these public schools are rubbish and parents don't know about this and it would be right for *WHERE?* to show that there is a lot of variation in public schools. Just because you pay fees doesn't mean it's a good education.' What he had done was compare the fees against the A level results from all the public schools. The idea of league tables in those days was considered outrageous, especially the sacred public schools. Originally we were going to run it as an article in *WHERE?* but then we thought what a waste, why not do a whole issue on the public schools. This we did in February 1964 and it cost 3s 6d a copy post free.

We had a lot of letters from parents whose families traditionally used private education, and to whom it was unthinkable to send their children to state schools but actually they were quite dissatisfied with the culture of beating and fagging. Brian was terribly good at thinking of connections. He'd known Harold Evans quite well earlier on when he was editor of the *Northern Echo* in Darlington, Durham. We went to see him – I think we had lunch at the Gay Hussar – and asked if he'd be interested in publishing our league table, and he jumped at it. Anyway, it was published in the *Sunday Times* and we were absolutely inundated over the next two or three weeks. We had literally hundreds of letters coming in every day and membership just jumped from two or three thousand to 20,000 in the following weeks. It was all tremendous fun. That was the start of our association with *The Sunday Times*. We regularly got features in, did joint projects with them.

Although UCCA, the Universities Central Council on Admissions, had been set up for getting into universities there was nothing for the polytechnics, you had to write separately to every single polytechnic. We had the idea of running a clearing house for polytechnics and technical colleges. We set that up with the *Sunday Times*. Of course now every newspaper publishes these huge lists of all the vacancies for higher education every summer and we actually started that.

We began to publish guides in response to the questions people were concerned about. These included, for example, How to Choose a School, Grants for Higher Education, Holiday Courses in Europe, University Entrance: the Basic Facts, etc. So sometimes we could just send people a publication with a standard note instead of an individual reply. Quite often the questions prompted articles which we published in *WHERE?* People wrote in to tell us what was wrong in education as well as to ask questions. One woman who had recently moved to Scotland was horrified when her little boy was hit on the hand with a tawse (a three-pronged leather strap) for rubbing out. I was horrified too, and found there was a firm in Lancashire which supplied the implements of torture used in schools. This one place made all the canes, all the tawses, everything. They had a catalogue, and in this catalogue was a nursery tawse – would you believe it. Anyway, that made a very good story for *WHERE?*

Then we ran a seminar. We held it in a pub, the Panton Arms in Cambridge, and AS Neill, the Headmaster of Summerhill and Mike Duane, the Head of Risinghill Comprehensive School in Islington and various other eminent educationists came along. It was very successful. It was such fun – all squeezed together in this funny old pub.

STOPP, the Society of Teachers Opposed to Physical Punishment, was an independent organisation, but you know it was part of the climate. You think you think of things by yourself but you don't; it's in the air.

The reason I gave up editing *WHERE?* was because I'd just been in the process of editing Supplement No 2, called Changing Tracks about changing careers in midlife. And I commissioned an article from a professor of psychology. He produced quite a long article so I cut it in half, typed it and got it set – because as usual we were working to deadlines – and sent it off to him. He phoned me up absolutely furious that I'd cut his precious article and insisted on reinstating several thousand words. At that moment I was sitting on the storage heater in the hall at home holding a baby in one arm, the phone under my chin, and trying to write with the other. The baby was screaming in one ear and the professor was screaming in the other. And I thought, this is too much. And I gave it up, something I really enjoyed doing.

Brian's idea was always to take advice to people where they naturally are, instead of sitting behind closed doors in town halls waiting for them to come in with their questions. It's difficult to remember what a crazy idea that was at the time. I think he floated it either in a newspaper article or in *WHERE?* and the manager of the Ipswich Co-op wrote and said he thought this was a great idea and would we like to open an education shop in his store, just for a short time. And Brian asked me to run it.

I remember we had great discussions because the Co-op wanted to tuck us away in some corner. Brian said no, it must be between the cornflakes and the shoe counter. And so they did give us a very good site on a natural shopping route. We took lots of reference books and set up with banners and posters. We ran it on a rota system during shopping hours and basically we just waited for people to come and it was absolutely fascinating. The questions were utterly different from the ones we received at the office and they were about incredibly simple things. So often all we had to say was well it would probably be a good idea if you went to see the head. It was just a revelation that people were so terrified to go and see the head.

Nobody ever thought of giving advice to parents before that, certainly not outside the school setting. So of course after this Brian took the principle further and ran advice centres in Butlins Holiday Camps because there people were on holiday and had time. ACE workers did it in a lighthearted way, joined in the games so they were part of the life in the camp. People asked important questions, for example teachers were still forcing left-handed children to write with their right hand. Parents were very nervous about challenging the teachers. They just had a feeling that the teachers were doing the wrong thing but they didn't have the confidence to question them.

The press were very helpful. Peter Preston of the *Guardian* gave very good support and so did other people who are terribly famous now. When we ran the education shop Brian said, 'Why don't you ring Harry Evans and ask him to take an article on the education shop?' I'd never written an article for a major newspaper before but

I wrote this article which was absolutely hopeless and Harold Evans rang me up and said, 'I've been doing some work on your article on the train, and I think it's come out really well.' He'd completely rewritten it! And he published it on the centre page of *The Sunday Times*. It was so sweet to take so much trouble over a bad article by an insecure young woman. Those five or six years: wonderful.

I've left out a very important bit which was the founding of the National Extension College, launched in *WHERE?* 14, Summer 1964. What happened was that *Which?*, the Consumers' Association magazine, did a study of correspondence courses and found that most of them were absolutely awful. And one day Brian said, do you think we should start a correspondence college? This was the way things happened you see, the most casual conversations. I said I thought it was a good idea. And so we recruited a very nice man called David Grugeon who afterwards became the Pro-Vice Chancellor of the Open University. There was a long established correspondence college in Cambridge which had been started by HG Wells. It was called the University Correspondence College and it was run by two extremely ancient women in wonderful antique offices, and its courses were simply dreadful. So what we did was take it over and start commissioning new courses and advertising them, and that was the basis of the National Extension College. Brian did a tie-up with ITV to do television programmes in association with the correspondence courses. We had a meeting at the top of Senate House with Michael Young, who by then had been made Director of the Social Science Research Council, and Peter Laslett. At that meeting we decided to start the Open University. Just like that! And in the 60s that was fine because you could always get money to do new things if you had an idea. Of course later on Harold Wilson made his speech about an open university and gave the job of establishing it to Jennie Lee, Minister of State with responsibility for the Arts.

Not all ideas came off but ACE was the catalyst for ideas that were around. An awful lot of things that were considered pretty way out then are now completely accepted. The idea for example of involving parents in education, the idea that the parents are their children's first and most important teachers; it's hard to remember now that that was a radical idea in those days. I think there are an awful lot of teachers who still haven't grasped it.

I was born Sonia Edelman in Mill Hill on 7th September, 1934 the same day as Queen Elizabeth I. It's nice isn't it to share a birthday with an extremely famous person.

My father, Maurice Edelman, came from a very poor but intellectual family in Cardiff and my mother from a very wealthy business family. My father's family were rabbinical scholars from Poland on his father's side and large landowners from Russia on his mother's. His parents emigrated because of his father's involvement in the 1905 Revolution. My father was brought up in Cardiff and always considered himself Welsh. And if people said to me when I was a child, What nationality are you? I'd say, 'Half Welsh and half English.'

My mother's family was from Romania. Her father's name was Yager and he was a tremendously interesting man. Because of anti-Semitism he came over from Romania as a boy of fourteen on his own, and he worked for his uncle who was a cabinet maker in the East End. When my grandfather got a bit older he made panels for coaches and hackney carriages. He and a friend set up a workshop doing cabinet work for motor buses which later became Park Royal Coachworks and which made all the red double-decker buses. At one time – it's really funny, fortunes come and go so quickly – he owned a whole string of factories along the river at Ponders End and he also owned White City, the greyhound race track. But unfortunately my uncles gambled all the family money away.

My maternal grandfather gave my parents a house when they married in 1932. I remember great excitement because a few years later my parents decided to have a swimming pool. They started digging and then war came and it had to be turned into an air-raid shelter. But for us children the air-raid shelter was rather fun as well. We were evacuated, first of all I think in what must have been 1939 to a farm in Shennington in Oxfordshire. It was lit by oil lamps and had a bath which didn't actually have taps, but it had a drain so it had to be filled by hand. Everybody in the village used to come and take turns in the bath.

At that time my father was a war correspondent, and half the time he seemed to be in the British Army and the rest of the time he was attached to the American Army. He was in Algiers for most of the war, and actually there's a photograph of him with Marlene Dietrich come to entertain the troops in Algiers. Then he went to Normandy, for D-day. So we saw very little of him during the war but my mother used to go off and meet him on his brief leaves in London.

Coming from a wealthy family my mother was not expected to work but she did do a bit of voluntary work. When we were very young my parents had a cook, a maid, a nanny, a French governess, and a gardener. And then, later on, I mean when we all came back together again, which I think was in 1944, my parents bought a large house in the country in Chesham Bois, near Amersham. We had a very nice orchard, and a tennis court but I think things were quite difficult. My mother did absolutely everything: she kept chickens, she even killed chickens when necessary, and grew vegetables, all kinds of things that she must never, never have done before. Before the war my father worked for my grandfather as a timber buyer but he absolutely hated it, and then he got a job as a journalist on *Picture Post*. He was a very attractive and interesting person, he wrote twelve novels, he was a very good painter, very good musician; he spoke French, Italian, German, Welsh and Russian. He was elected to Parliament in 1945 and was Labour MP for Coventry until he died in 1975.

I had a rather isolated upbringing because my sister went to Frensham Heights. I didn't want to go to boarding school so I stayed at home and went to local schools. After we moved to Chesham Bois I went to a school called Belle Vue which was exactly the opposite to my first school where although there were physical privations – I can still remember being agonisingly cold – it was a friendly, affectionate kind of school. Belle Vue was a really vicious, horrible school. They were obsessed with the idea of the girls getting out of control, and seemed to be dedicated to making you feel as bad as possible. I was very unhappy. I was there for four years and then I took the scholarship for Berkhamsted and I got a place there. I think I did quite well academically but it was the sort of school where all the girls became secretaries or physiotherapists, and I wanted to be an architect. I was told girls can't be architects, and I don't know why I believed them. By the time I'd got to the upper sixth to do A levels, I think there were only three girls left in my year. I did English, History, French and Latin but my main interest actually was doing the other things in school which was taking part in plays and music. I learnt the cello and I was a good pianist in those days, in fact I actually was offered a place at the Royal Academy of Music.

My mother was very keen on our acquiring skills, so she encouraged us to do physically adventurous things like skiing or skating. But I was never allowed out except to social occasions which were organised by my parents. I think the most exciting thing I ever did was to go to a village dance. But there were very good things about Chesham Bois. There was a family who lived down the road called Kahan, and they were the centre for all the Jewish refugees in that area. Every Sunday afternoon they used to have a Viennese type salon to which we were invited and to which amazing artists, musicians and opera singers came. I just wish that I had realised how privileged I was.

I always knew I was going to go to Cambridge because my father's adventures at Trinity were part of the family mythology. When I was seven years old I remember being taken to Cambridge and having lunch on the grass in front of the Wren Library – you were allowed to do that sort of thing then. I was determined I was going to go. Anyway, I didn't actually get a place at Cambridge, there were only six places for women to read history, and I didn't get one, and I was absolutely devastated, and disgraced myself by rushing out of school without saying goodbye. My father took me skiing to console me. But while we were skiing I got a telegram from my mother saying, 'Stop worrying Sonia, you have a place at Newnham.' So that was a most wonderful moment. Before going up I did a secretarial course at a place in Bedford Square run by a Mrs Finlayson who ran it for 'her gels'. It was like going back into the 19th century and I actually enjoyed it.

Newnham was just so incredible. At first, I had a horrible little room above the ironing room. It had an ugly gas fire which gave off noxious fumes, but I didn't mind that because I just loved being there so much. I remember walking to lectures on the first day – we had to wear gowns in those days – and walking across to Mill Lane where the lectures were on one of those incredible freezing blue October mornings. I just thought, I am in heaven.

I made the most ridiculous mistake; I imagined that there would be a piano in my room. And there wasn't for two whole years. It wasn't until the third year that I discovered you actually had to go to the local music shop and arrange to hire a piano. So I didn't have a piano for two years and that was fatal because musicians have to practise all the time. And I've never really got back to it although I play the cello and viols, and music is an important part of my life.

There were eight men to every woman at the time so even a quite average girl was besieged. The college rule was that you had to be in by midnight, and I can still remember how good it was to hear the door slam behind you, leaving the men outside. It was funny, I didn't actually meet anybody that I liked particularly at all though there were lots of men trying to take me out. I did go out with a young man who was an Olympic fencer. His project was for me to be a champion fencer too. So I joined the fencing club. About forty other people went along to the first meeting of the fencing club including Brian as it happened, and I think I was the only one out of the whole lot who carried on. I was considered eccentric by my intellectual friends, and in the end was awarded a Half Blue for fencing against Oxford in the Varsity match at Hurlingham. Interestingly, my mother was a fencer as well when she was young, but I didn't know that.

The college was divided into halls; I was in Peele and we ate in hall in those days. I remember once coming in to breakfast and somebody hissing into my ear, 'That's the poet'. I can still remember Sylvia Plath quite vividly, what she looked like, stunning. She was a very striking person. I did make very good friends with two people. One of them was Anne Taylor, now Triesman, who is now Professor of Psychology at Princeton, and the other one was Elizabeth Cochrane. Anne had some connections with a family in Italy, and so the first summer vacation I went to Italy for three months as a companion to a young girl, Costanza Benini. And that was an extraordinary experience because her father had been governor of Albania under Mussolini and they were connected with all the great Florentine families. All the names that you see in Dante or in history books, they all used to come round, come for meals, so it was a very interesting insight into Italian aristocratic life which I would never have had otherwise. They led such a boring life. They had nothing to do except go and visit each other, and go to parties. I had a great time, because I was taken up by her brother in a very mild way, you know we were so innocent in those days, there was absolutely no question of sex. The life of this family was just so amazing. You threw your clothes outside the door at night when you went to bed, and in the morning they would be returned washed and ironed. After lunch, which was served by someone behind each chair, you went to bed from 2.00 until 5.00 in the afternoon Well I couldn't possibly sleep from 2.00 until 5.00 so I worked through Hugo's *Teach Yourself Italian*. A combination of that and of course only speaking Italian, within three months I had absolutely fluent Italian. So it was a very valuable experience.

In my third year I met my first husband, Philip, and he asked me to take part in a review organised by the Cambridge University Socialist Club. Previously I had kept out of politics altogether, having been brought up with it all those years. But in my third year I was doing

Theories of the Modern State and I was bowled over by Marxism. This involved many difficult arguments with my parents who had been to Russia in the Thirties. But although my father was a socialist he was bitterly opposed to Stalin and to Soviet Communism.

When Philip asked me to marry him I didn't think he could possibly be serious because we had barely done more than hold hands. But I said yes and then of course I got carried along, and it was nice to have an engagement and Philip was tremendously interesting. But I knew it was a mistake somehow, somewhere. It was very much the thing that people did, you know, you came down from Cambridge not to have a career but to get married. We used to sit in the University Library admiring each other's engagement rings. I did go along to the careers service and all they could suggest to me was that I should go and teach in a finishing school in Switzerland, which wasn't a very entrancing prospect.

Philip had already decided to spend the next year working on the Locke manuscripts in the Bodleian. He looked in the Oxford University Calendar and saw that you could do a Certificate in Social Studies at Barnett House. And so that's what we did. We got married in September 1956 on my twenty-second birthday at a registry office although my parents would have liked me to have had a grand wedding in London, and we lived in a bungalow in Kidlington, a few miles north of Oxford. Barnett House was wonderful. There were mature students, mostly from Ruskin, who were fascinating people, some of them from developing countries who were going back to be Foreign Ministers and Prime Ministers. And I enjoyed my social work placements in the Oxfordshire Children's Department and the Bristol University Settlement.

Then we came back to Cambridge. Peterhouse gave Philip a Fellowship, which was really intended for single men. The stipend was only £6 a week, and our rent was £7 a week, so we sold all our wedding presents, and I got a job, two jobs actually. The first job was part-time research assistant to Edmund Leach, the anthropologist. That sounds exciting but actually it was frightfully boring because all he wanted me to do was to type endless drafts of his book about land tenure in Ceylon. In the afternoon I used to cycle about three miles to my second job which was in a blanket factory.

Then I got pregnant, and that was difficult because I didn't really want a child then. Philip felt even more strongly; he even tried to make me have an abortion but neither of us had any idea how to go about it. Eventually when I was about eight months pregnant I knew something was wrong and went to the doctor who said, 'You've got to give up the blanket factory work.' The funny thing was I loved working in the blanket factory, it was much more interesting than working in the Museum of Anthropology. The owner of the factory was Hungarian, and he made two products. One was radiators and the other was those electric blankets which were always catching fire. My job was dealing with the complaints. There was a great atmosphere in the factory, and it was such fun answering letters and thinking of excuses, and offering the customers new blankets. It was the last thing they wanted!

About three weeks before the baby was due I went on the first Aldermaston march. I was a passionate anti-nuclear person so I was determined to go along even though I was eight months pregnant. A few days later I started to have suspicious twinges. I was all by myself with no car and no telephone and had the most hazy idea about what was involved in giving birth. Philip had gone away without leaving a contact number or address. Luckily my sister came down to see me, and we went to the phone box and called a taxi to go to the hospital. I was in labour for thirty-six hours, most of it on my own. Then miraculously my mother appeared and she was there when the baby was born, which was a moment of indescribable joy.

Eventually Philip arrived and we went back to our flat with the baby in whom he showed no interest. He told me to put the baby in its cot in the spare bedroom. My mother had organised a maternity nurse who turned up just after we got home. She was a tremendously efficient woman of the old style, she must have been about fifty-five. I remember asking her, 'Why is the baby crying?' And she said, 'The poor little thing's freezing cold.' Anyway, how poor Dominic survived I just don't know, but he did, and he's a Professor of Psychology at Kent now and seems to be relatively unscarred by his early experiences.

Philip was a registered conscientious objector so he got taken on by the Co-op to deliver milk. It was quite hard because it involved getting up at 4 o'clock in the morning, and at the same time he was finishing his PhD. I had to go back to work when Dominic was only seven weeks old. I can still remember the agony of handing him over to the nursery nurse that morning. For about a year I did temping. I was grateful to my mother for insisting on the secretarial course which gave me a way of earning money and I enjoyed the variety. Then I went back to University to do the Part II in Natural Sciences, a two-year course. In the afternoons I had a job at the Cambridge Child

Psychiatric Clinic. This was hard going but all went well until Philip fell off a ladder putting up decorations for a party at the youth club we ran in one of the Cambridgeshire villages. He broke his arm very badly and could no longer carry milk crates, so he lost his job at the Co-op. It was obviously unrealistic to think of studying for another year, so I switched from a two-year to a one-year course and as soon as I had finished my Tripos exams went to work full-time at the Clinic as a trainee psychologist instead of as a social worker. That still left us only £4 a week after we'd paid the rent but I was very well organised and had boxes on the mantelpiece to save money for coal and electricity and child care. Philip hated not to have money to spend on the house, like cushions and lampshades and things we couldn't possibly afford, so we had terrible rows about money.

Philip and I had a lot of interests in common. We were both active in the Labour Party, politically we were in accord. But our marriage never really worked. Every time he knocked me about he would be terribly remorseful afterwards. I led a complete double life. Outwardly I was quite confident and successful. At home I was always in terror of provoking a violent outburst. I never thought of leaving or telling anyone. It was only when the violence started to spill over on to the children that I started to feel I must get out for their sake but I couldn't think how to do it. Years later when I read Erin Pizzey's book *Scream Quietly or the Neighbours Will Hear* I recognised that I had been a typical battered wife but at the time I didn't know about marital violence.

Brian and I fell in love with each other without realising what was happening. That was wonderful, but I was still incredibly naïve at the age of thirty. I thought that adultery happened in books, not in real life. And I was completely unprepared, I just didn't have any defences. It gave me the courage to decide to leave Philip because having a relationship which was so different made me realise that life didn't have to be like it was.

The break came when Philip found a letter from Brian. Philip told all our parents and they somehow formed a united front to force us to stay together. Philip's father organised a temporary job for him, a lecturing post as Professor of Sociology at the University of Chicago, and I was subjected to enormous pressure to go with him. But the reason I went really was because I felt very unhappy about the idea of breaking up somebody else's marriage, so I thought I should go and give Brian a year to decide if he really did want to leave his wife, and his children who he was absolutely devoted to. So Philip and I went to Chicago. I don't know what might have happened if Brian hadn't been absolutely determined to hang on to me, but he was, and wrote to me every day. He also organised a job for me as American editor of *WHERE?* and I in fact produced a special issue on Education in America. By May of that year I had made a firm decision to return to England and end my marriage.

Brian and I found a house to rent in a village outside Cambridge for ourselves and the children. I got a morning job as a part-time teacher in a village school and in the afternoon I worked as director of yet another new organisation that Michael Young had set up, the Home and School Council. When it became known that Brian and I were living together people who knew us both were terribly shocked and the *News of the World* ran a front-page story. This was terribly painful to everybody. Dominic was the only one of the four children old enough to understand. I remember Dominic tried to buy all the *News of the Worlds* from the corner shop and put them in the fire. I was so upset. Going back to school the next morning was one of the hardest things I'd ever done.

I don't know if this was why my teaching contract was not renewed at the end of the year or if it was my unorthodox teaching methods. Anyway I had to find another job. After an unsuccessful attempt at working in a pub – I just couldn't add up prices of the mixed drinks in my head – I found one of the best jobs I've ever had. It was being a part-time Welfare Officer for the County Council. The Chief Welfare Officer was a wonderful man called Dennis Hitch who was far ahead of his time in thinking about how to help people with disabilities and how to manage residential care for older people.

Then in 1971 the recommendations of the Seebohm Committee were implemented and overnight we all became generic social workers instead of specialists. I was better equipped to work with children than some of my colleagues but I knew virtually nothing about mental health. All the same I was issued with a card saying I was now a Duly Authorised Officer which meant, along with a GP or psychiatrist, I could admit people to hospital under a Section and was also part of the out-of-hours duty rota.

I continued to work for the Social Services Department until 1972 when I was offered secondment to upgrade my social work qualification. When I went for the interview at LSE I was seven months or eight months pregnant but they didn't even notice. So they gave me a place and that was a very hard year, because by that time the baby was born and I had to commute from Cambridge to London. I got my Certificate of Qualification in Social Work, and that has been very valuable to me.

Brian then applied for a Simon Fellowship at Manchester University to do research and we moved to Huddersfield which was Brian's home town. We lived in a mill house in Elland which is a wholly working-class town between Huddersfield and Halifax, it's got quite trendy now. At that time, it was quite lonely. I did research on child-minding which was the first time anybody had been interested in the subject at all. In the mid-Seventies, things started to get harder and harder financially. It was a time of great inflation, and we had six children between us, and there just wasn't enough money. And so I decided at least one of us had got to have a proper job with a regular salary, and we both started applying. The job that Brian had applied for was Chair of Education at Bristol which he absolutely should have got but didn't. At the same time I applied to the Extra-Mural Department at Bristol University and I was offered the job as Staff Tutor in Social Work.

We lived in Bristol from 1976 to 1983. Brian was given a grant at the Institute of Child Health at Bristol University and worked on a longitudinal study of child health and education. It was there that he did his work on fatherhood, far ahead of its time. Brian also continued to run the National Children's Centre in Huddersfield. In 1983 they organised a Fun Run with the Rugby Club up there and Brian took Seth, our seven-year-old, with him. It was a very hot day and I didn't want Brian to run. Just at the end of the run he had a heart attack caused by heat stroke. He collapsed and was dead by the time they reached the Infirmary.

I remarried in 1990. Before he retired my husband, Derek Greenwood, was a Senior Lecturer in Physics at Bristol University.

I've never told my life story to anyone before ever. People always tell me their life stories because I'm a social worker – you get the social worker expression on your face.

It was more than a full-time job

Marian Hirst
Task Force

I was checking the old people who needed to be visited and I arrived at this house and knocked on the door and the neighbour said, 'Oh the old lady's died.' As I was chatting to the neighbour she said, 'It's a pity you didn't come earlier, because none of the family ever visited her. I was the only person ever went in there. Then these relatives all turned up to the funeral. They couldn't wait to get at her goods and chattels, but they couldn't come and visit her when she was alive and lonely.' Loneliness was the problem. You would knock on doors, and the vast majority of old folks would say, 'Oh come on in,' and they'd be so pleased to see you, 'Come in, will you have a cup of tea?' The difficulty always was getting away. You could see they really really wanted you to stay and were delighted to tell you about the old days. That's one of the things I always used to say to the older boys and girls, 'if you're doing history, you're getting first-hand history here; get them talking about the war and whatever, and you'll get better marks because of that.'

AT HIS YOUTH CLUB in the East End Anthony Steen had involved young people in helping the elderly. He had an idea that he would like to have a big organisation, not just limited to what was happening in his own club. So he had started going round London visiting as many youth clubs as possible to persuade the leaders to take up this idea. He would contact the local social services and old age pensioner organisations to get the ball rolling with some names of old people wanting a visitor and/or practical help such as decorating or gardening. I was a full-time teacher but I was also voluntarily in my spare time running two youth clubs in Camden. This was I suppose a couple of years at least before 1964 when Task Force was formally founded. I got involved by getting the kids from my youth clubs doing this, and I started to involve the children in my school.

So I was one of the early few that became part of an inner circle of people Anthony could rely on and, except for me, they were mainly people from his social circle. I liked Anthony immediately, it's very easy to have a rapport with Anthony, an amazing mind, one of those rare and irritating people who can finish your sentence before you've started it. And I liked his energy, and his commitment to the elderly which was absolutely real. Before Task Force was official he had already built up a very big organisation with nobody being paid anything.

For several years I suppose in a way I became Anthony's right hand. I ran the first office in the north of London, in Camden Town, and Jane Ridd ran the first southern office down in Lewisham.

Anthony's major task as front man was obviously PR and raising the finance. The money we actually got from the local authorities and from the Government wasn't enough if you needed a van and to pay the staff so another of his tasks was writing to charities, trust funds. He was very good at that, and of course he had quite a lot of personal contacts. When I eventually became Director it was £100,000 a year that had to be raised, and I had to take that task on, because Anthony after five or six years with Task Force founded the Young Volunteer Force Foundation, which was a national organisation, a community development project. Anthony was an absolute power-house of enthusiasm, totally disorganised, and a great delight really.

I think one of the reasons that Anthony was so keen on me was that the original group of people helping him came from his privileged background and they often had the sort of accents and approaches that the local social services could be wary of. I had actually worked in the borough where I became organiser of Task Force, and I think that built up credibility. Anthony always found a key person in each London borough because although Task Force had central government money, it also needed to persuade that local borough to give us a grant and office premises. The key officer in Camden was the Medical Officer of Health, Dr Harding. That was rare as normally it was the Director of Social Services who was the key person, although it could be different people. It was the Mayor of Hackney that I persuaded, that was the one borough that I brought into the fold eventually. Anyway, we had Dr Harding in Camden, and he gave us a prime site, a very good central office, and sufficient money. The boroughs also had to pay for the transport.

Every Task Force office had a van to transport volunteers and decorating equipment.

We also had to recruit staff. We took on Gillian Edgar who had been helping as a volunteer, and a couple of other people. We generally had a staff of four to each office. And what we had to set up was a very efficient organisation, because within a short time – eighteen months – we had 1,000 volunteers in Camden. We had to coordinate both the contact with the organisations dealing with the elderly and contact with the organisations or schools to recruit the volunteers. I went for the younger, more radical staff, staff who wanted to change the world and they're the most difficult to manage, and one or two of them wanted to take Task Force away from the mainstream of what we were doing. Another recruitment disaster was if you got somebody who wasn't efficient. One of the things about Task Force, it was really pacey, you had to be up and out.

Apart from centrally organising things, we, the staff, had to recruit volunteers. When we started I think Anthony said everyone should be under twenty-five; that soon went up to thirty when he became thirty, and I think eventually we were up to thirty-five. We targeted youth clubs, schools, young people's hostels, young nurses' hostels, and wherever we felt that we would be able to get through to people in that area. It meant going into schools, persuading the heads, arranging meetings, going and talking in assembly or to smaller groups, and then getting somebody there to organise the volunteers.

We had to persuade the local agencies that we were sufficiently responsible to hand over names of the elderly to the volunteers, and then very often – this is the staggering thing, I suspect it's exactly the same today – you get a list and you go through it, go out and visit the elderly to see first of all whether they needed any help and then whether they wanted practical help such as gardening or decorating or shopping or whether it was just that they were lonely and wanted a visit. And time and again they were either dead or they had moved. You really had to check the list, that was the first criterion. What you didn't want is for a volunteer to visit, go to an address and the old person's dead. That's going to put them off for life.

School-leaving age was raised round about the time Task Force was operational so that instead of leaving school at fifteen you had to stay on till sixteen. The secondary schools didn't know what they were going to do with boys and girls who had got another year and who weren't going to take exams. So something like Task Force was a great boon you see. Not all Heads were enthusiastic. One particular Head, later a senior politician, was in charge of a boys school in North London. When I talked to him about involving some of his boys in community service, visiting old people, he was very patronising, and said, well, he might just allow me to talk to the boys in the lower forms in the fourth year. And I said, 'Well, I would be very grateful for that opportunity but what about your sixth form?' 'Oh they are high-flyers, they are the ones who are going to go somewhere.' And I said, 'Well, that's great, but this helps them to become a rounded person, not just concentrating on studies. It gives them the opportunity to see a different way of life and to extend sensitivity as well as intelligence.' And he more or less went, 'Bah! what are you talking about?' He was terribly rude. No, he wasn't going to have his sixth form boys deflected from the greater glory of good examination results. But most schools did perceive that it was a two-way process.

Part of the initial recruitment talk was about why the old people wanted to be visited, that what they really wanted was another granddaughter or grandson really, that they probably hadn't got them or they'd moved away. I'm trying to remember whether we took them along the first time to visit. I don't think we did. I think we left it very much to them. It was in the early heady days of the Sixties when to volunteer was enough to be accepted, without all the later emphasis on validation and proof of whether you were a suitable person and fit to visit, and whether you should go through training in how to visit. I think we tended to take the view that if people wanted to help an elderly person then they would put themselves out and be responsive to them. I can see there are all kinds of potential pitfalls, but I have to say in all the years that I was involved in Task Force there were very few mishaps where for example old people had their purse stolen or something like that. Obviously we got to know about that from the school, or from the old person by checking back, or they told the social services which came back to us. And when those very rare examples happened, we took that very seriously and it was pursued with the school, with the young person, and with the old person. I think that we have to be very proud of the fact that that was a rarity.

The people we tended to visit were people who were just very grateful that you had got in touch and the sort of old folks who wouldn't ask for social security because they would think that was wrong, you know, you shouldn't be taking money from other people. Yet very often they would want to offer you money, and that's one of the things we would say very clearly to the young people, that you don't take money. On the other hand if they wanted to make you a cup of tea, or if they wanted to give you a bit of cake or something, that's all right because it's important too that they feel that they can offer something back to you. Sometimes one old person would refer other people in the street. They might say, 'Have you been to my neighbour?' or, 'I think so-and-so down the street might like a visit.'

Before we handed over decorating, we used to have what we called decorating weekends which one of us staff would always go on. My father was a builder so I was a decorator, knew all the techniques. We had quite a few university volunteers, and in my area we had some very good chaps who were skilled at decorating, so we asked them to train volunteers in decorating on the weekends. It was a practical hands-on training for decorating. The old folk had to pay for the decorating materials. Obviously a lot of elderly people couldn't afford to be decorated so we eventually – it took a long time – had a system, for those who were on pensions and social security, to charge Social Security for whatever paint or materials we used. After we handed out a decorating job to a school, we would double-check back and see that it had been done.

When you got in a list of elderly people that needed visiting and you had nobody to visit them, that was the worst nightmare of all. Suddenly social services would come through with a list, and you didn't have anybody in that area. You didn't have a youth club, you didn't have a school, and you had got twenty or thirty old folks who, you'd been nagging away at the social services saying, give us these names. Sometimes you actually took on an old person yourself. I always had a couple of old people that I was visiting, but that wasn't the answer. So you really had to dig into either your pool of individual volunteers or go and find another local group or another hostel or actually go back to the schools and try and find if you could extend the group into that area. And the same with the decorating, you'd have a pile of decorating jobs, and you couldn't just hand the jobs out to anybody. It had to be done well, and you couldn't descend on old folks with a raggle-taggle group of people, you had got to be sure you could do the job before invading an old person's home because for a while it would be uncomfortable. They didn't have all that many rooms, so we had to get the work done to a certain timetable because you couldn't let it drag on. Very often you were doing the one room they lived in or their bedroom. So you had to get enough people together to do it in as short a time as possible.

I've always been good at chaos management I think. When I left Task Force I ended up running a unit for disturbed adolescents, and when you've got children who are potentially violent, it's not a regular routine. Task Force was good training for that.

The organisational system was very important, the back-up, the records system. Gillian and I set up a card system. I've got an extraordinarily good memory, and I actually could always remember which of the thousand volunteers were with which old lady, so I never needed to have the system, but we had to have a back-up. When new centres were set up after that, the system was replicated in another area.

We would generally start the day by having a meeting of all the staff. I would need to go through the post, check what was coming in. We would compare notes, who might be going to speak at this school, who had got something coming up, some people were going out checking, I might be going off to another borough to give some talks there or I might be preparing for the trustees' meeting. And then we would all go our appointed ways. There was always a secretary at each centre, sometimes it would be a volunteer if we hadn't got enough money, preferably it would be at least part-time paid. I would have about five centres in the northern area that I was responsible for as well as Camden, and Jane in south London would have the same. We had ten centres eventually, fifty staff, and about 10,000 volunteers.

I moved around a lot, got to know London very very well, better than a taxi driver really. I would have to pick up the pieces of any crises. Very rarely did I finish a day before ten o'clock; very often with my secretary or with another member of staff we'd go and have a meal and still be checking through things and planning ahead. We'd have regular meetings for all the staff to get together where we'd have speakers from other organisations as part of in-service training for the staff. I set that up with Anthony's wife who was an educational psychologist and is a very skilled and gifted woman. She and I together used to plan training programmes and that was a regular event about every three months. So we were offering top-flight training to our staff. And I went off on several of the Tavistock Clinic group work training programmes and so did Sally, my deputy. Where there was a possibility of extending skills for our staff, we did so.

Working for Task Force was a wonderful opportunity. Various staff who worked in Task Force have gone on to very very good jobs afterwards. What was extraordinarily stimulating and challenging and rewarding was that one minute you were talking to the Medical Officer for Health, the key man in the borough and to similar key people in the other boroughs and the next minute you would be out assessing poverty-stricken, extraordinary elderly people, and then you would be having to exercise your skills of acting and projection by talking in front of a whole school, enthusing them with the need of what had to be done in terms of these elderly people, and then you might be sitting composing letters to persuade people to give you money, and the sheer humdrum routine of recording and checking your diaries and sorting out what was happening. And then, the trustee meetings, working alongside people like Selwyn Lloyd who I used to regularly go and update because he was chair of the trustees for quite a while. It really was a high all the time. There were several articles in the local press, and then Jonathan Aitken was at that time writing for the *Evening Standard*, and he wrote an article on the two queens of the voluntary service scene, Liz Hoodless at Community Service Volunteers and me. And shortly afterwards, about six months afterwards, I got an invitation to a cocktail party at Buckingham Palace, and so did Liz Hoodless obviously as a result of this article. And so things like that happened. Quite extraordinary. There were lots of perks, and one of the perks was actually having work breakfasts with Anthony at the Ritz, or the Savoy or whatever. Your working environment at times was heady; at other times it was decorating an old lady's home where all you can do with a wall is stuff it with newspaper and paper it over because the whole fabric of the building is so ghastly, and you're offered a cup of tea and the cup is utterly filthy, and you've got to drink it because otherwise you would offend. It was from one extreme to another. My days were very very long. I was not married at the time, and very committed, as Anthony was, to the organisation. So, you know, it was more than a full-time job.

I was with Task Force from 1964 until 1971. It was an extraordinarily heady time to be involved. There was so much optimism around generally in the world. I don't think for one minute we thought we as an organisation were changing the world, but I did trumpet very strongly the community service ethic. The philosophy was that it should be young volunteers for the elderly because it would enrich both.

———————

I was born Marian Would on 12th November 1938 in Cleethorpes, on the coast in Lincolnshire. I was first generation university. My father was a builder and his father was a self-made builder. My other grandfather was a self-made fish merchant. So they had both done extraordinary well. My dad went to grammar school, but then he went into the family business so he didn't go to university.

My mother came from a fishing family. There were six in the family, well seven, but one died young, as did one of my father's brothers. None of the girls were expected to work; boys, my mother's brothers, were expected to go into the fishing business, which was awful for both of them, because one was a brilliant engineer, and the other one was very artistic, very musical. All the girls were very beautiful. My mum used to say that her eldest sister was so beautiful that people literally used to stop and turn to look at her in the street. I didn't inherit that; my sister has, she's very lovely. Granddad actually was an illegitimate son of a local sea captain and the local prostitute. He was adopted at nine by a local antiques merchant, and, because he was so bright, he was taught to read and write. Obviously the antiques merchant must have left him his money, because he eventually had a fishing fleet. Mum remembers their yacht, and they had a garden and a huge orchard, and all the girls went to a Roman Catholic French convent in Boston in Lincolnshire. It's now silted up but the port of Boston was a big port at that time. When it did silt up, they had to move the fleet to Grimsby, and it didn't do well, so Granddad gradually lost his money although he still had a big house. When they moved to Grimsby, Mum used to go to the local library, and the head librarian took a liking to her and he trained her to become a librarian.

I grew up in Cleethorpes and I remember the war there. My father inherited the building business which was thriving, but he was a godly man and never really made a lot of money. I remember we had a very large showroom with a works yards behind. We lived in this huge flat right across the top of the showroom. There was the air-raid shelter, and I remember my mother used to carry me down into it. The sound of that air-raid siren, I'll never forget. It used to start low, wooooooooh and it goes right up, and even as a little child, three or four years old, there's that feeling in the pit of your tummy. You caught it obviously from your parents, but also it was the sound that was really really frightening. The only thing we didn't like in Cleethorpes was when the trippers as we used to call them came in the summer. They poured in from Lancashire and Yorkshire because all their mills would close for a week. We used to dread them coming. It's ironic that I then ended up in Yorkshire, home of all those trippers.

I got a scholarship early at ten. I was a bright lass which was really very fortunate because I went a year early to grammar school, and then when I was thirteen I got a TB knee. We'd gone to a farm for a holiday and I drank some non-TB tested milk. There's two kinds of TB, there's tuberculosis of the lung which is caught through breathing the air, and there's bovine TB which you get in your bones through drinking milk. I always say I am four years younger than I am, because at that time I was hospitalised for two years with this TB because they had no treatment other than lie on a bed, bed rest they called it. So I was seventy miles from home in this orthopaedic unit. The second year they had brought in streptomycin, but it was too late, my knee had been eaten away. When I got up after two years I had callipers and I was fifteen, it was a very crucial year for me as a young woman, devastating. But you develop empathy if you've been institutionalised. I came back to grammar school, and because I had been a year ahead I only lost a year, so that wasn't too bad. While I was in the second year my mother and dad moved to Woodhall Spa in the middle of Lincolnshire. It's a beautiful spa village. Dad's business had crashed because he was not very good with financial matters. His brother, who had a different nature from my dad, had got out and had taken a lot of the capital and set up in Woodhall. Dad went to work for him. I had to stay on in Cleethorpes with some neighbours for a year, to finish my O levels. It wasn't a nice year, they were so different from me. So I was pleased to get back home to Woodhall to do my sixth form.

I was the only child for ten years. My father wanted a son to take on the business, so, ten years later my sister was born, much to Dad's disappointment. Then three years later my brother was born. And sadly for Dad my brother wasn't interested. He's an artist, he writes music, he writes books for children, very successfully. When my brother arrived, I had already gone into hospital, so it was a very fractured time for me, once those children were born. I didn't get on with my brother and sister when I came back, they were much younger than me. I always remember the very first guitar that my brother had when he was about five. By accident, although you do things by accident which perhaps you mean to do, I stood on it on Christmas Day. They used to kick my bad leg, they were so horrid. I mean I love them both dearly now. We were called by the local people in Woodhall 'Mrs Would's three clever children.'

Mum's library training stood her in good stead when we were in Woodhall and again we were short of money. Mum used to go and run the local library in Woodhall. Dad was happy about this because it was books, it wasn't work as it were.

At my grammar school the art teacher was a great influence, and I had a very good English teacher but the history teacher was exceptional. He was very witty, and helped to train my mind, and knock the Tory out of me. I believed at that time that Britain should be run by an élite because the aristocrats are the only people who could run the world. He scoffed at that, and he was very good, very very good. And there was also a good French teacher, who kindled my love for languages really. I read voraciously.

And so when I went up to the London School of Economics I did, unusually, history. In my year there were only seven people doing history, because it's politics, sociology, economics really at LSE. But I was extremely fortunate continuing with art and language. I specialised in the Renaissance, and Ernst Gombrich, the history of art man, was still lecturing at Imperial College, so I went to lectures by him, and I went to the Courtauld for lectures in the art history of the Renaissance. And I had to learn mediaeval Italian to read Machiavelli in the original. You had to have Latin at that time to get into LSE, so I did Latin to scholarship level, just picked it up in the sixth form. I had the best of both worlds. I had an incredibly international politically aware college base, and all the esoteric refinements of art history and mediaeval Italian and Latin for my reading. It was a marvellous period, I loved it, really loved it.

While I was at university I was involved through a boyfriend from Woodhall Spa days in his youth club. He went to Marlborough, and Marlborough has a youth club in the East End, so I started getting involved in youth work very early on in my time in London, way before I met Anthony. That's where I cut my teeth on youth work. I was sort of assistant to this brilliant man who was so good. There are two styles, or there were then, of a successful youth club leader. One is get up and lead from the front; and the other type, equally effective, perhaps even more effective, is the very quiet man or woman who you don't really even notice, but the kids really respect, and really trust, and he was one of those, and I learned an enormous amount from him. I also had a friend at LSE who was living in an East End Jewish settlement. She took me down there, we did a lot of youth camps. I never did any formal youth work training but I had a good grounding.

I decided to become a teacher, it was a toss-up between journalism and teaching. But I decided to be a teacher, do good in the world, and went to do my postgraduate diploma at the Institute of Education, University of London. And towards the end of that year my knee flared again, the TB had never been cured properly, and I had another two years in hospital. I actually took my exams, my Dip.Ed., in hospital. But it was marvellous, I had the corner bed of this huge ward in St. Pancras, and there was never a day that I didn't have visitors. I was in a wheelchair and these friends would come and carry me, put me in their car. I went to the Mermaid Theatre, I went to the Tate Gallery up in the lift which carried the paintings! People were wonderful, I had a lovely social time. But I had lost two years again, so that was my second two years.

I wanted to teach in a tough area of London, that's why I went to Camden Town. It was St. Michael's Secondary Modern, next to the Greek church in Camden Town. I don't know whether it's still operational. At that period in the Sixties a lot of Indians had come into the country, a lot of Greeks had come in, so it was Camden Town locals plus young Indians plus Greeks, Greek Cypriots. We had a corrupt headmaster. He was embezzling the school funds with his secretary. And the deputy head he had appointed was ancient and vast, she had hairs coming out of moles. She was a Roald Dahl type figure. I don't think she smelt but she looked as though she did, she was terribly untidy and had absolutely no control. Wherever she went, kids were throwing over tables. It was just like something out of *The Blackboard Jungle*. The headmaster never had a timetable, you would be in the school for a week at the beginning of term and you would get your timetable at the end of the first week, so it was chaos. I was given everything. I was given PE, even though I had got my bad leg; and I was given science. The first few weeks I was there we broke every Bunsen burner in the science lab because I had not a clue. But I was determined that these youngsters weren't going to get the better of me. And by the time I left, I could go into a room and say, 'Right, we're going to have a debate today,' and I would go and sit at the back of the room and there would be four kids at the front and they would be debating on whether we should have school uniform or not. In the midst of chaos it gave me a marvellous, heady feeling of achieving something for these youngsters. I used to take the whole class, thirty or forty boys and girls, down to the Commonwealth Institute on the bus on my own, because there was never anybody to do anything with you. We would go for the day, and we would look round the Commonwealth Institute, and we'd come back again. And of course when Anthony came along my class was delighted to get involved with me in the evening or the weekend doing decorating and visiting old folks. I suppose I've always been anti-authority really, and I certainly was anti the headmaster. He used to stand up in assembly and tell them they had all got to bring white gloves because we were going to church on Wednesday morning. It was a rabble, he was ranting at these kids from the poorest background to wear white gloves. Three of us staff talked to the vicar, fortunately we had a nice vicar who listened. And by hook or by crook, we managed to get the head removed, and we would never have done it if it hadn't have been a C of E school. Absolutely amazing, that's one of my major achievements I think. So that was quite a formative experience really.

While I was teaching in Camden I ran two Church of England youth clubs. One was in Kentish Town, and one was behind the Everyman Cinema in Hampstead. I used to take the boys and girls off on the boat to France for the day or go on camps. I spent a lot of my time in the probation courts with them because they would go through this great phase of stealing but then I used to have the satisfaction that once the boys had got a girl, they became so respectable and would settle down. A lot of them visited me for a long time. One frightening experience was the night when we got a gang in from Somers Town. They were actually flashing a knife down at the end of the hall. I was quite fearless, and I think that's the only way of running an adolescent unit with these very very volatile, sometimes violent boys and girls. If you ever are frightened you have to give up. In those days I didn't have a fear of anything, and I went and took the knife off the boy. I was not prepared to have anybody in the club with a knife. And they went off jeering, but I was very lucky. But the most frightening time was when some other lads came from another club and they brought with them a deaf mute who was incredibly strong, and said, 'Could we talk to you in the office?' He was in there, and they locked the door. He had been set up to rape me. I was strong but with my leg, my balance isn't all that good. I was beginning to despair. And then somebody had obviously thought, where is Marian, and somebody got in the door somehow or other, and I was saved as it were. In all the years that I've worked with tough kids, that's the nearest I came to being hurt. Shortly after that Anthony came along, and I got involved in Task Force.

I was at St Michael's School from 1961 to '64, when I left to go to Canada. Don't ask me why. I think I felt that I wanted to work in another country for a while, to live in a different culture, to observe how people lived. Sense of adventure. And I would have stayed in Canada but for Anthony. Task Force was a different form of adventure I think, pioneering something with Anthony. He wrote and asked me to come back and set up Task Force with him.

After I left Task Force in 1971 I wasn't sure what I wanted to do. I'd got to a pinnacle, and although I was very involved both in voluntary organisations and as a teacher – I mean if I'd stayed in teaching I'd have been a head by then – I hadn't got any formal qualifications in social work or youth work. What was I going to do? And then I saw an advert for the Community Development Project up in Batley. It was the sound of the job: Harold Wilson's Government was going to do something about poverty and there were going to be ten of these projects throughout the nation, each one being given the freedom to evolve in its own way. There were no guidelines, it was set up incredibly naively. People bid to have it, and Alec Clegg who was the renowned Director of Education in West Yorkshire bid to have one based in Batley, because Batley at that time, it's the next-door town to this, had many problems and many large families – Irish Catholics and Indian Muslims. There were problems with education, unemployment, and housing, a huge number of houses had no inside toilets. So I applied and I got it. It was a joint action research project, so we had a research team based at York University, and an action team. And I took as my specialism the Indian community. I could do a whole treatise for you on how badly they were received by the town, how now twenty years later – partly as a result of early rejections and misunderstandings – they have been forced into a much more traditional community. I still have some very close friends within the community. So I worked with them and tried to make bridges between them and the local councillors. The Labour councillors were so reactionary. A head of a local primary school thought we would be as anti-black as he was, and he told me a story which was quite lascivious really, about how these Muslims sent their little girls, little five-year-olds, in loose trousers and how he wasn't having anything of that. And when he made them take them off to put skirts on, they had no knickers underneath. Absolutely appalling racism. There was nothing CDP could do really, because of there was opposition to anything. For example, when we got tenants' groups going we were accused of rabble-rousing. I was there from 1971 to1974, when I got married.

I met my husband because when you are setting up a community development project, you need to get into the community networks, find out where people meet, what they think. The local community network here was one of the most vibrant, I think it's less so now but then the mills were still working and there were the local working men's clubs. There were two Irish ones, and Derek was vice-president of one of these. Fate has its hand because I should have met the president and he wasn't there, so I met Derek. He offered to show me around the other working men's clubs in the area. We were totally totally different. Here was I with an academic and fairly high-powered background, and Derek had left school at fifteen, he was a turner in the local mill. I'd only been proposed to three times before, but I had had lots of relationships, and a lot of men by this time were daunted by me. Derek wasn't. He was so sweet and so lovely. And I must say the other factor was that I was ready to have a family. I wanted to settle. So we got married. He was my rock and my rudder. So I was very lucky, because I had this huge sort of personal love, but I was still able to do what I wanted really. Derek wasn't interested in art so I was able to, if I wanted to, go away with a friend for a weekend to Florence. Derek went into the prison service when we got married, and was the most marvellous, effective prison officer. He could talk to the men where they came from, and he had immense compassion.

If Derek were still alive we would have lived together for twenty-seven years this year, it would have been our 25th wedding anniversary last month. My mother and Auntie Doffy lived with us for about twenty-one years for two reasons. One was financial, and the other was to help with the babies. Derek didn't have any funds, and I had never saved, I had always been a high earner but I'd always spent it. Like my mother, I love clothes, and a good life, nice restaurants, you know, wine and so on. And, so we really needed to have a home. Dad had died, and Mum and Auntie were living in a lovely bungalow near Woodhall Spa. I had taken out a mortgage on it because Dad hadn't got enough money even to pay the mortgage towards the end. And so we sold the bungalow, and put that down as a deposit for a bigger house in Batley. It was very good of my mum, because Batley compared to Woodhall, she felt oh, grim grim grim. But she became a supply librarian here and went round all the towns in her little car, she worked until she was seventy, and they thought she was sixty-five. They said, 'Now you're sixty-five Ms Would you really, I'm sorry, we don't want to lose you but you have to retire.' She never looked her age.

It didn't happen, we didn't have any children, which was a great sadness to both of us. I went on fertility pills, and when that wasn't working the specialist said, 'Oh well we'll have to put you on double dosage, that might work.' And Derek said, 'I don't want it Marian. Because that would be too much for your health, it's you that I want really.' I would have liked to have gone on but I could also see the point that although we desperately wanted to have a baby, he felt strongly it would not be good for me and potentially dangerous. And so we didn't go on to the double dosage.

When I got married I did supply teaching for three years. And the last supply that I did was at the forerunner of a purpose-built residential assessment centre. I was asked to apply for the post of head which I did, and I developed the school unit as the residential centre declined until there weren't any children residents, it was just my school unit really. Many of these units in schools for difficult children don't survive, but my unit had a very good reputation. The commitment was to the young people, to value them because so often that's the principal problem. They haven't been valued, they've been so abused or shunted from prison to remand home to yet another school. I did that for sixteen years.

I had retained friends within the Muslim community so as soon as I retired, they collared me and for two and a half years until Derek got ill I was involved voluntarily in being a sort of deputy head for the local Muslim girls' high school here. I believe that if it's a traditional community, the way forward for the women is to be educated. So the aim was to help to build educational standards with the head, who I have tremendous time for, who is a good mate. In the three years nearly, their exam results improved so they became third in the authority from practically nothing.

For the past two years I've been involved with an organisation set up by a friend, John Lipetz, called LEAD, Lobby To End Age Discrimination. We've been launched in the House of Commons, Anthony is one of our supporters, we've got fifty MPs supporting us. It's a campaign organisation so once we've achieved the aim it will be disbanded. The aim is to get age discrimination on the same basis as sex and race, and to get legislation, to get a commission to set that up and monitor this. I'm still involved in quite a lot of things, and I've got to build up more of a local network of friends if I'm going to stay here, now I haven't got Derek.

I do have stepchildren who have been tremendously supportive, and I have these gorgeous grandchildren. The eldest boy is really quite bright and, I think, going to be gifted in art, he draws extraordinarily well. I said, 'Well Jake, when you're older, you and Grandma will go on a sketching holiday together.' And he looked straight at me and he said, 'You'll be dead by then Grandma.' So just to out-fox him I'm determined that I will survive long enough so that we can go sketching together.

There are no losers

Bob Curtis
Young Enterprise

How did I get involved? The works manager at ICI came up to me one day and said 'I'd like to see you in the office for a minute please.' I was a manager and I thought, what the hell have I done now? He said, 'How would you like to do a voluntary, unpaid job for the company with Young Enterprise.' I said, 'I'm sorry, I've never heard of it.' He said, 'Neither did I till I got this letter.' So I went to a meeting where somebody explained it, and I got hooked. Reason: there are no losers.

IN 1969/1970 YOUNG Enterprise was still in the process of establishing themselves. There were only about three Young Enterprise schemes in the whole of the UK, and they were looking for people from industry to become Advisers to help start Young Enterprise in Doncaster. I went to the meeting and the full-time Young Enterprise representative said that a local school was interested in the scheme. Well the young people came along, and we formed the first Doncaster Young Enterprise company, and I thought, this is good.

The main programme which was started in 1963 has in principle never changed. The pupils are all volunteers, from the fifth form to the upper sixth. Young Enterprise is a unique nationwide education business partnership. It provides young people with an exciting, imaginative and practical hands-on business experience, and enables them to develop their personal awareness, self-confidence, and vocational skills. They gain an understanding of basic economics and how business works. Young Enterprise is not a game, it is about running a business, with volunteers forming a proper operating company.

You need a minimum of six volunteers. If it's over twenty they are encouraged to split into two teams. It's difficult but I've known a company of fifty-four to be very successful. You then need two or three outside Advisers, either from industry or commerce with marketing, accounting, production experience. It's very difficult to get three Advisers these days, we're lucky to get two because they have a regular two-hour-a-week commitment. They make no financial gain from this whatsoever, but over the years Young Enterprise has realised how much the Advisers themselves benefit from just being with the young people and guiding them. In many cases the Advisers have never seen the complete working of the company they themselves work for: at work they sit in their little departments, but in the schools they see the whole thing through. Once we get these Advisers the school has to nominate a link teacher to act as a liaison person between the school and the Advisers. The teachers facilitate but they should not participate.

When the Adviser meets the young people for the first time he brings a box, what we call the company kit; it contains all the documents you need to run a company. You can actually take it into the outside world and run your own business with it: from accounts to production records, share certificates, everything is included. So the young people, Achievers as we call them, get together and within forty-eight hours after their first meeting they should have completed a registration document with names of the members, what they are going to call their company, name of school, etc. This document is forwarded to the Young Enterprise national office for registration and the company is set up for one academic year. They then have to decide on a complete management team including managing director and production, sales and marketing managers. The most difficult decision they have to make is what they are going to produce. We encourage them to create their own product, because that's when the problems arise. They have to do some market research on what might sell. But a lot of them decide, 'Oh I can buy so-and-so cheap, bring it back, re-package it and re-sell it.' Yes of course they can learn from that, but not as much as if they actually produce something themselves.

They have got to decide how much money they need to start their company, so we allow them to raise – I think it's gone up now – £250 through the sale of shares; I think the share has gone up to 50 pence each, but you can't sell more than ten to any one person. We insist that each Achiever buys at least one share in their company. The moment they've done that they become a director of that company, though it's more like a cooperative they are running. At company meetings everybody is encouraged to participate. That's the only way each company member gets maximum benefit from the scheme.

They have to pay rent wherever they operate, which is usually at their school. They also pay Young Enterprise a £75 registration fee. That covers the administrative costs of our national office in Oxford as well as total insurance cover which contains a number of exclusion clauses, for example, regarding the production and sale of explosive material. Some of the companies, especially those with more sophisticated products, go to their bank for a loan and they have to submit a complete business plan. If they ask for and receive, say, £100 from the bank and that loan is not repaid it becomes the bank's loss. Like any other business. I have never come across any wholesaler or retailer saying a Young Enterprise company owes them money. We try to imagine a real-life situation, and in real life nobody gets anything free, for example, firms charged for the use of their machinery.

I was an Adviser for about two or three years, and then Youth Enterprise decided to form an Area Board in Doncaster because other schools had also become interested. I then became a member of that board. In 1981 I became a full-time employee as Regional Director for eleven years.

Walter Saloman, who started Young Enterprise, was a merchant banker who emigrated from Germany to the UK. Whilst visiting the States in 1959 he was introduced to what the Americans call the Junior Achievement Movement, founded in 1919 as the 4H Movement: Head, Heart, Hands and Health. It was aimed at training young farmers in the efficient running of their farms. It was based on the famous 'learning by doing' principle, that had not been up till then applied to the industrial world. On his return from the United States in 1959 Walter Saloman sought the support of leading business people and educationists for the idea which became Young Enterprise. It was not until 1962 that they really got down to the nitty-gritty of employing the first paid person, and organising a pilot Youth Enterprise scheme in the Medway towns. Walter was knighted in 1980 for his services to Young Enterprise.

In the beginning Young Enterprise started from a one room office in London, with one lady who did everything. There was no filing system till they moved in 1989 to proper office accommodation in Oxford. These days the UK is administered in the field by about 250-plus Area Boards. In the early days we were supposed to rely on donations but now we are widely sponsored by many employers and a variety of educational institutions.

What these Young Enterprise companies have produced – the list is endless. Everything you can imagine. Winning products include: teddy bears, garden ornaments, cushions, cookery books, wooden magazine racks, music cassettes, calendars, badge holders, designer dresses, track suits, clocks in all shapes and sizes, wrought-iron gates, key rings, table lamps, coasters, engraved mugs, clipboards, magnetic noughts and crosses game. Somebody designed a bicycle alarm based on an electronic circuit; they were actually on Midland Television. A fifth-year company in Lancashire produced a card game for junior school pupils who have difficulty learning music; and it took off, they couldn't produce enough. And when after a year this Youth Enterprise company had finished the participants decided to continue privately, so they put a business plan to the Midland Bank and got the backing. One of our companies was sponsored by Express Lifts who gave the students scrap sheet metal, which was cut into various sizes to make clocks. The students bought the clock mechanism, and then took their clocks round churches, businesses, etc in Northampton and said, 'We are prepared to screen-print any logo you wish, or sales slogan, on to this clock.' They sold over 1500. And a clock bearing the Midland Bank logo was presented to the Chairman of Midland Bank who was also the Chairman of Young Enterprise at the time.

A magic roundabout designed as an educational toy was produced by Lancashire Achievers of no more than fifteen years of age; it was tested by Trading Standards, who recommended the strengthening of the centre pole after it had been dropped from an upstairs window! On completion of the modification, the product with the aid of the Chamber of Commerce was also marketed in Scandinavia.

But I think one of the most innovative products was from Scotland where a group of sixth-form girls wanted to produce a calendar, and they thought, we'll take photographs. And they decided, what's wrong with a calendar of topless boys? So they asked for volunteer sixth-formers, of course they got plenty, and the calendars sold like hot cakes! What's interesting now, is how many Young Enterprise companies get themselves on the Internet

The majority of companies regretfully are now school-based, operating after school hours. I found a change of environment so much better. When I was doing it in Doncaster the students used to walk through the ICI gate where I worked at the time, and they loved it. Nowadays, in the middle of winter, parents do not like their children to travel by bus from one end of town to the other. It's understandable.

I feel the Advisers have a very difficult role. We advise them not to interfere with the direct running of the company even if it means the project falls by the wayside. If a group of youngsters which has gelled from the beginning brings a problem to the Adviser, the Adviser will help them in such a way that in the end the resolution comes from the Achievers. But if they are the type of group that turns around and says, 'What the hell are you doing here? We don't need you,' the Adviser may let them get on with it even if it results in the company folding. As a result of this the Achievers might find they've benefited more than if they had made £1,000 profit. The shareholders, well, it's their bad luck. On the back of every share certificate, it states, 'This is a charitable organisation. You are helping young people to develop. If the full amount cannot be repaid, consider this a donation to charity.' Nobody objects! At the end of the company year, which is usually about April, May of the following year, they go into voluntary liquidation, they dispose of everything they have, submit a full company report as per the criteria laid down by Young Enterprise National Office. They should have paid themselves wages throughout the life of the company, but a lot of them decide, let us wait and see what we've got in the kitty at the end. If they have made a profit, they should pay a dividend to the shareholders. After payment of any outstanding wages the balance can be disposed of as agreed by a full board meeting.

To put in a little bit of competitiveness, although we hate the word, we do offer awards for the best products. We now offer eleven awards in Doncaster. Other areas have a lot more. We don't believe in money prizes. For example South Yorkshire Police in Doncaster, especially the Thorne Division, last year decided to support the best Achiever. The Young Enterprise companies nominated their own candidates and the Superintendent took the top three to London for a day. They had lunch at the Institute of Directors, then went across to the House of Commons. Everything paid for by the police.

There are dozens of examples of Young Enterprise Achievers having the opportunity to go abroad. Cambridge had extremely good links through the Rotary Club with their opposite numbers in the States, and for a number of years two or three Achievers went across to the States. Likewise, some of the chemical companies in Cambridge have head offices in Switzerland or Germany, which Achievers visited. BMW also gave a national prize for a number of years. They sent them to Munich, and the Achievers lived with local employees' families. They visited the company factory, and when they came home they had to report back, and on one occasion the report back was at the German Embassy. What an experience!

Young people learned to make decisions, they learned to stand up for themselves. Don't forget a managing director could be running a company made up of their best friends, and they've got to be able to tell them off. In real life you can't pick and choose who you work with. I've seen the best of friends fall out.

I remember once the teacher saying, 'God! they have elected so-and-so as the managing director; she's about the worst person they could have chosen.' However, she was still the managing director at the end, they hadn't removed her from office. But they staged a strike for two weeks because they got fed up with her attitude. They formed a union, and they had a meeting with her, the personnel director, and their union representatives. And in the end they settled their dispute.

What's very interesting is, the majority of participants each year are girls. When I was working for Young Enterprise full-time I noted how many male managing directors were removed from office by Christmas, and a girl elected in his place.

A lot of Achievers have found their future and have gone into industry or taken up business studies. Others say, 'It's the last thing I want to do. I don't want the hassle we had.' The majority will tell you the gain was that they themselves had benefited from the experience. Great, if that's what occurs. Teachers who watch them far more closely than we can as Advisers, comment on how much the students mature and gain in confidence, and parents confirm this, too.

Some of the companies were absolutely wonderful. With others you go back home after a two-hour meeting in the evening, and say, what the hell did I waste my time for? Half of them didn't turn up, or you are trying to knock their heads together. But something must have rubbed off. One of the companies, Entercraft, gave me an inscribed Parker pen and Biro, and I treasured that.

I helped to develop the special needs material, for a separate project called Team Enterprise, which works with special needs schools and is very close to my heart. With the children with special needs the Advisers have to be hands-on. They don't take a back seat like they do in their Young Enterprise company programme.

We don't like to differentiate to the outside world that Team Enterprise is for pupils with special needs. To us they are the same as the six-formers or fifth year, but as I say the teacher and the Adviser are far more directly involved. In many cases the Achievers cannot count or read. I've got one company in Doncaster running a breakfast bar in the local church hall every Thursday morning. They're doing really well. The vicar's only charging them £5 rent for three hours. The Achievers' involvement is very restricted, it mainly consists of serving the customer. But of course the teacher and assistant is around. Before that, the same school ran a grocery trade where on a Wednesday the pupils wearing their Team Enterprise badge went round to a prearranged number of people with an order form. Next day they collected the order. The teacher and staff consolidated the orders to be delivered in bulk from a local greengrocer and on Friday they split up the goods and the Achievers delivered them. In Lancashire last year it was a Team Enterprise company which won the area's best company award.

Young Enterprise doesn't stand out as much as it did in the Sixties. It was new, it was fantastic. But that's all faded away because of National Vocational Qualifications and so many simulated schemes at school now. Everybody is talking about enterprise now, and being entrepreneurs, and in newspaper articles you read about young enterprise, the young entrepreneurs.

The interesting part was that at the end of each year I was wiser than when I started, because the Achievers were all so different, and you learnt so much from them.

———————

I was born in 1925 – an only child – in Krefeld near Cologne in Germany. My parents were being persecuted for their outspoken beliefs and opposition to the Fascist regime. They were both killed in a concentration camp. I never forget my parents, obviously, but you can't dwell on it. To me, although you don't forget, the past was the past; I've always been one for looking forward, even today. My wife Erna still has her sister in her eighties and a niece living in Germany. We do occasionally visit but my wife says she couldn't live there any more. She is always glad to get back home. She says, 'My home is here.'

At the age of eight I came over here and I was adopted by a Quaker family in Sheffield. They had met my parents, but how that came about I either can't remember or I just don't know, and I haven't ever asked. They came up last year for our 50th wedding anniversary. He used to teach out in Kenya and finished up as headmaster. There was only a fifteen-year difference between him and me.

I joined the regular Army from school when I was eighteen, that was in 1943. I was taken prisoner in Arnhem with the Parachute Regiment. The family were notified that I was reported missing, presumed prisoner of war, which I was, from September till the following May, 1945. In those days, and at that age, one was still very innocent. I grew up.

After release from prison I came back to the UK, and I was taken quite ill, perhaps connected with the food, or the cigarettes – oh it was dried tea wrapped in papers from a Bible. In 1946 I went back to north Germany attached to the Control Commission, and that's where I met my wife, Erna, who was a refugee from Silesia, now Poland. By that time I had signed on for a twenty-two year engagement in the Regular Army and I never regretted it.

My wife eventually joined me in Berlin. She never worked from the moment we got married. She said, 'I didn't get married to work!' From there we came back to the UK. When I went to Cyprus for the Jordan emergency, I left her alone in Scarborough with my two lads in the Army hostel, for families when the husbands were overseas.

I was just forty when I left the Army and I applied to ICI, a nylon plant. I had no idea of industry but they gave me a six-month course, and I was very lucky to be taken on as a shift manager. In 1981 when I left ICI, Young Enterprise offered me something I'd always dreamt of doing: working full-time for them. I got a letter saying, 'If you ever consider working as a director for Young Enterprise, please let us know.' So I rang the Chairman back and we met in London. And he said, 'When can you start?'

I worked full-time for Young Enterprise, until I was sixty-eight. I'm not blowing my own trumpet now, but while I was doing the director's job I was also looking after the Young Enterprise annual conference at Warwick University, all the administration in my little office, single-handed; everything prepared upstairs in my house here. And I enjoyed it, but eventually I got tired of all the travelling.

It was fun while you were a bit younger. When I finished as a director, I took on the task of writing the history of Young Enterprise. And the founder's son, William Salomon, has agreed to underwrite my expenses.

When I retired from full-time employment I went to the Doncaster Council for Voluntary Service and said, 'Here I am, what have you got?' WRVS were looking for somebody to keep accounts, so I started doing three of their hospital accounts. Then they said, 'Why not try the WRVS shops in the hospital?' So I said to my wife, 'Come with me'. She did. So we do one week at one hospital, and the following week in the evening at the women's hospital, and I still do the accounts. And again we enjoy it.

Now at seventy-five years of age, I am still an active member of the Doncaster Board of Young Enterprise and continue to act as an Adviser to a Team Enterprise company. I will keep involved with Team Enterprise as long as they want me, because I think it's wonderful to be with those young people.

Last year I got crazy. I saw an advert for a correspondence course for bookkeeping with the Mid-Kent College. On completion I took the Institute of Certified Bookkeepers exam, and passed. I would have gone on to the next stage, the computerised stage, but Erna said, 'Enough is enough!'

We rejected nobody

Elisabeth Hoodless
Community Service Volunteers (CSV)

When I trained as a medical social worker at the London School of Economics, my tutor found the word 'volunteer' intolerable. Indeed, there came a moment when she was reviewing some of my work in which I had spotted some opportunities for a volunteer to help the family, and she indicated to me that if I wished to qualify as a medical social worker I would be wise to discontinue all talk about volunteers. After all, we were trying to establish social work as a profession, weren't we? I decided I needed my meal ticket so I desisted from mentioning volunteers again. But when I saw a post advertised for assistant director for Community Service Volunteers, I applied and was offered the job. The salary was significantly less than I could have got as a medical social worker, but the prospects were better. It was 1963 and I was twenty-two.

COMMUNITY SERVICE VOLUNTEERS had been founded by Dr Alec and Mrs Mora Dickson the previous year, 1962, and the Gulbenkian Foundation had given them enough money to recruit a member of staff. Therefore I was going to be the only member of staff until I did something about it. Alec Dickson had founded CSV to enable young people to serve in the UK much like young people were able to serve abroad for Voluntary Service Overseas (VSO) which he had founded in 1958. When a young person applied to VSO and was considered not suitable for work overseas, he found it very uncomfortable having to say, 'Thank you very much for offering to invest a year in community service but no thank you very much.' However, CSV had one particular rule which was that we rejected nobody. As long as they were between sixteen and thirty-five they didn't need any specific qualifications. Only a willingness to move away from home and commit themselves to anything between four months and a year. And those same rules still apply.

Our first office consisted of one room – about the size of a rather small single bedroom – which contained Dr Dickson's desk, my desk, and later the secretary or what Dr Dickson called a stenographer, and a huge filing cabinet, all tucked in this room which I'm sure flouted all the rules on space and air and so on. Nevertheless, it was within the premises of TOC H at 3 Trinity Square, overlooking the Tower of London where the famous Methodist minister, Donald Soper, used to preach on Wednesday lunchtimes. So it was a wonderful place to work in. And of course because my desk was at right angles to Dr Dickson's I learnt a great deal from everything he was doing.

Dr Dickson actually gave away the prizes at most of our major public schools, and so people used to tease us and say, 'So long as you keep speaking to only the very best public schools, and our finer grammar schools, you'll be OK.' This carried on for quite some time. There then came a moment when we thought that we should respond to all this teasing about only taking the easy kids. And so we thought, who are the young people least likely to be thought of as volunteers? We thought: young offenders. So we went to see the Home Secretary, James Callaghan – Dr Dickson didn't waste any time with underlings – and said, 'Look we think using young offenders as volunteers would be a good thing,' and Callaghan said, 'Oh that's interesting.' And since that day we've had several hundred young offenders in their last month of sentence coming out to work as volunteers. And it has transformed their lives because lots of them had never been allowed to help anybody before, let alone ever been thanked. Many of them stay on as volunteers, and lots of them get paid jobs. If there's one thing a young offender needs, it's a job. So that was an exciting moment.

Then we decided to diversify. People kept saying to us, 'Not everybody can go away from home to do voluntary work for four months to a year, but all our young people in Wolverhampton would like to do something on a wet Wednesday afternoon, what could you suggest?' So we started CSV Education, and tomorrow we will have succeeded because the Secretary of State is going to announce that every young person in school will spend one period a week on citizenship education. This is not just learning about how society works but how you can influence society, how you can make a difference. So that was a good move.

Dr Dickson was more interested in the boys than the girls. He would always say, 'Oh well, if you really want a girl, I'll put you onto the distaff side.' I didn't know what a distaff was but I did know that it meant girls. And so when exciting opportunities came in, if he had a suitable young man to carry out the task, that is what would happen. And if he didn't, girls might get a look in.

Dr Dickson's wife explained to me early on that she had married a very great man, and I had the privilege of working for a very great man, and it was our job to work round him. Indeed it was. He had been a journalist, he had written for *The Yorkshire Post*; he had done a lot of work getting kids out of Germany before the war; he had worked for the British Council; and in 1956 he had gone to rescue Hungarian refugees as they were trying to swim across rivers into Austria. He had never been anywhere more than two years, and he generally left after a big row. However he was a man of huge vision who divided the world into people who were for us and those who were against us, there was nothing in between, they were either our great supporters or our enemies. He believed there was a flashing red light which went on whenever we phoned the Home Office so they could all think up their excuses before they lifted the receiver.

I remember at a very early stage he told me to send out the young people's pocket-money, and I asked where the files were. 'Files?' he said. 'This isn't MI6!' I said, 'How am I to know their addresses?' 'Well,' he said, 'whose address do you want?' I said, 'I've got the girls, what about the boys?' 'Well,' he said, 'where do you want to start?' So I said, 'Shall we start at the beginning?' And they were all in his head, the phone numbers, the addresses, everything. And then I said, 'Right, now what is the level of pocket-money?' 'Well,' he said, 'what do you think?' 'I've only been here three days.' So, he said, 'Let's go through the list. Michael Brown, yes, well his father works on the railways, I think you'd best send him about £5, he certainly needs it. John Smith, oh! his father's a barrister, he doesn't need any pocket-money at all.' Now this is not how we conduct ourselves in medical social work, no. But we got there.

He agreed to keep files to humour me, but then he kept all the boys' files in his case, and he used to travel huge distances and take them with him because he might want to telephone them from a railway station and see how they were getting on. He was devoted to the boys, terrific, but it was not the way I'd been brought up to run an office. I didn't have any writing paper or account books or leaflets. The application forms were done on a duplicator. But somehow we muddled through. I also did the books, and I once found myself with sixpence more than I could account for. The honorary treasurer who was an accountant went berserk. He opened up all the books, where could this have happened? I wished I'd put it in my pocket, I really did. The accountant insisted on receipts from Dr Dickson for what he'd spent in the period prior to my arrival. I put this to Dr Dickson who said, 'What's the matter with this man? Haven't I run it properly?' 'Oh,' I said, 'it's not a question of running it properly, I mean, did we spend it on train fares, or buying typewriters? Can you give me any indication? I could go along to the shop and find out what we've spent.' 'Am I not to be trusted?' he said. 'Not at all, it's just, you know, accountants like this sort of thing.' And so finally he reached for a piece of paper and he wrote on it, 'To running CSV effectively and economically, Alec Dickson, £2,000.'

He was an absolute believer in young people, in their vision, their strength, their energy, their commitment, at a time – well it remains the same today – when young people were getting a very bad press. He used to say, 'Fifty young people get on their Vespas on the sea front at Brighton, it's front page news. A hundred of them go and do something good in Wales or anywhere else, nobody takes a blind bit of notice.' CSV's aim was to give young people a chance to serve their own nation for up to a year, and at that time there was no problem in recruiting young people; the challenge was to persuade adults to allow them to serve.

Nothing stood in Dr Dickson's way. He was so ahead of his time it's unbelievable.

In 1963 there was an earthquake in Skopje and he wanted to be able to send help quickly. He was in touch with a firm that sold or produced prefabricated panels that could be put together but you needed some basic skills to do it. And he knew a personnel manager for a manufacturing company, and said, 'I need a dozen apprentices for a fortnight.' And within about three days they were in Skopje. But I did try to persuade him that we should draw a line if we weren't going to be in pointless competition with VSO. They were abroad and we were at home, and we've held to that line more or less.

Now we place nearly 3,000 volunteers in the UK a year working with the elderly, people with disabilities, young offenders, children with special needs; volunteers work in night shelters, hospitals, day centres and so on. I think in the first year – 1963 – we placed thirty. Well that was pioneering stuff. The people who welcomed the volunteers were pioneers too because everybody else thought they were mad to take on volunteers, let alone young volunteers.

I remember Miss Cooper, who was the Children's Officer for East Sussex, saying to me, 'And Miss Plummer, what makes you think that my children's homes could possibly be improved by some of your untrained, inexperienced volunteers?'. And I said, 'Well Miss Cooper, I don't know how many of your trained and experienced house mothers take the children to football matches, or climb trees, or do building work.' She became a great friend for years and years, and had dozens of volunteers in the Children's Department. They tended to be the pioneers, the confident people, not the kind of grey-suited men that we have to work with today.

Tim Cook, who has just retired from the City Parochial Foundation, used to run a hostel for people with alcohol addictions and he had volunteers working with him; Robin Guthrie, who's head of economic and social affairs at the Council of Europe, he ran Cambridge House Settlement and he had volunteers; Elisabeth Filkin, who became the first Parliamentary Commissioner, she was working in south Birmingham in a settlement house, and she loved having volunteers there. Volunteers worked all the hours God gave them, they were keen, they were energetic, they wanted to be there. It was a time of very high employment and, as things turned out, many of them developed careers in the fields where they'd been placed as volunteers.

Dr Dickson made enemies very readily. Some of the people at VSO were very unhappy that he had set up another organisation, as they saw it in competition. He hadn't really. You know, VSO could send so few; we send three times as many young people to projects now. It wasn't really competition. And then, oh! the most hilarious thing – well it is to me but I suppose it's not for the people involved – CSV had actually been brought to life by Dr Dickson drafting a letter which he got a number of people to sign. One of them was a Dean and various other prestigious people. And over a period of time they all claimed to be the founder of CSV. I wasn't there at the time, but on the knowledge available to me there's absolutely no doubt who the founder was. They all helped or they signed the original letter but the idea that any of them founded it is ridiculous. But they were implacable enemies because they all claimed that they had done it.

I soon decided we would have to move the office, and we found wonderful accommodation at Toynbee Hall where the warden,

Walter Birmingham, had a block of tenement flats at the back that were empty. He said that we could move in right away and rent-free. So we did. I had the offices painted and, radically enough, I didn't have lino on the floor but sisal, coloured sisal. The bursar at Toynbee Hall rang up to complain. How lavish. And when I pointed out it was easier to clean coconut matting than lino and rugs, the sort of thing she had, she went apoplectic. When I bought new desks, she pointed out I could have got them second-hand. So I explained to her they would all be at different heights, and I needed to cram them in close. It was just another culture clash really. She thought charity meant uncomfortable and I didn't. We knocked a hole into the next empty flat, and when that flat was filled up we put a hole in the ceiling and went upstairs. I think we got up to three floors in the end. Those were very exciting times.

My husband and I had been thinking of having a second baby, and so I consulted the warden about our tenure and he said, 'Oh yes my dear, you can stay there as long as you like.' I said, 'Well it won't be forever I know, but could we stay three years?' 'Oh yes,' he said. I said, 'Well in that case can I have it in writing?' They sent me a letter to say CSV could have security for at least three years. Good. Mr Profumo had recently joined Toynbee Hall as a volunteer. I remember – I was six months pregnant – he knocked on my door, 'Elisabeth my dear, I know you're going to be so pleased to know that I've secured the funding to redevelop this site.' And then he said, 'Ah, the letter. Yes I know about the letter. But you wouldn't want to stand in the way of our new Old People's Day Centre would you?' It was the height of a property boom, and I was thinking, well yes I would. I had a vision of us sitting down in front of the bulldozers, you know, cruelly and illegally evicted. Not at all. He was such a charmer. We all used to have lunch together round a big table, and he would pick us off one by one. You know, politician to the tips of his fingers.

Suddenly one day the Greater London Council rang up and said, would we like a tenement block in Pentonville Road? And I said yes. And they said, 'You haven't seen it yet.' I said, 'If you knew how desperate we are!' And that's where we still are.

Then in 1975 we got involved with radio and television, and now we recruit volunteers through 80 radio and television partnerships. Around that time youth unemployment began to rise, and we tried to persuade young people in Liverpool, Sunderland and Glasgow to be volunteers. No they wouldn't. So we thought, well, if they won't come to us we'll go to them. We took a decision to move into training, and we set up a programme in Sunderland. We now have eighteen programmes nationwide which prepare young people for careers in what we call the caring professions, very broadly interpreted, as well as carpentry, painting and decorating, broadcasting and the media. We now train over 5,000 people a year. So those were good moments. They were risky moments as well.

I remember a civil servant saying to us, 'Look, I've never made a grant as big as this before, and if you fail you'll never get another penny of government money, and I'll be looking for a new job.' And we said, 'Mike, we won't let you down.' And interestingly he was an ex-VSO. We've always been helped by ex-VSOs, but we've reached a pinnacle today I think. Do you know that the second permanent secretary of HM Treasury was a CSV?

We constructed our fastest growing programme ten years ago, which is our Retired Senior Volunteer Programme. Extraordinary. It has 6,000 volunteers who organise their own groups and are a complete cross-section. We have retired postmen, the retired deputy chief executive of the Prudential, London regional director of IBM. Evidence coming out proves what we've always known, that volunteering reduces blood pressure, reduces cholesterol level, and prolongs life!

We've got a wonderful programme at the moment for mentors with young offenders. Lots of these kids are just bored. What shall we do tonight? Break into a shop, do a burglary, or go skating? Well I haven't got any money to go skating, so we'll do a burglary. Now they have these mentors attached to them twenty-four hours round the clock, except when they're at home with their parents, and the mentor's job is to introduce them to alternative activities to crime. It saves the nation millions in terms of crime avoided and prison places empty.

Some organisations think that scale is the imperative – and God knows we employ 300 staff which is bad enough – but the more responsibilities you've got to your existing staff, the more difficult it becomes to innovate. So first of all we're into constant product review, we're always looking for new ways of delivering the services better. Secondly, we enjoy innovation, we enjoy diversity in all its forms. We run open systems. There is a hierarchy, there has to be some kind of accountability, but people work together in groups appropriate for the task. Lots of our senior managers have been here twenty years, and we have learnt to work together. I really do believe that human beings have a capacity to work with each other, you don't have to be competitive. I agree with the Chief Constable of Sussex who refused to take performance-related pay because he said, 'Look, we all work together here. If the performance of the force goes up, fine, give us some more equipment but don't pick on individuals and give them more money. They've only been able to succeed because other people have pulled their weight.'

I have noticed in the last ten or fifteen years how much more time we have to spend on raising money. More and more civil servants are sitting there crawling over grant applications. They talk about joined-up Government but they can't even agree on a standard application form. So every department asks for different information.

I became Executive Director of CSV in 1986. Dr Dickson died in 1994 when he was eighty. He looked no different to me than he did the year I first met him. He'd been working a lot in Africa and the Far East, he was in the King's African Rifles, and his skin had dried as people's skin does when they work in hot countries. He always looked old to me, he also behaved quite old, he was a slightly old-fashioned sort of man.

My mother had a tragic life really. Her father died when she was two in the First World War, and her two brothers died in the Navy in the Second World War, neither of them yet eighteen years old. Her stepfather died when she was seventeen and just about to go to Oxford so she had to learn to type to become a secretary and keep the family. It was always a matter of great regret to her that she hadn't gone to university. In those days, if you missed it at eighteen you'd had it. I was born in 1941 in Boscombe in Bournemouth where my grandmother lived. My father was in the Army, leaving my mother on her own so she lived with her mother. We moved to Bristol when my father came home from the war. My sister was born three years later. My father was in advertising.

When I was eight the zoning didn't allow me to go to the school of my parents' choice, and so they sent me to an independent school, Redland High School for Girls in Bristol. It was a very liberal school although it didn't feel very liberal at the time, and indeed I remember being naughty. I can't remember what I did but I was so naughty that

I was not allowed to volunteer at the Union of Girls Schools Settlement for a week. Now there's a punishment.

Another time it was April Fool's Day and we knew where to get the key for the staff room, and we locked them all in there at playtime and they couldn't get out. But subsequently I was made a prefect and head girl, and that was a very good training. I've never had such excellent management training as when I was head girl. And then, to everyone's surprise I also passed my A levels. Very pushy young women Redland produces; I think it did give us a sense that there was nothing we couldn't do. I didn't know about things like glass ceilings or prejudices against women or anything like that till I'd started work, it never occurred to me that there was anything I couldn't do because I was a woman, quite the contrary. What I do recall was that the teachers were devoted to us. I felt deeply for my children when their teachers were going on strike because at my school the teachers would come to school at 7.00 in the morning to help you with your Latin or stay till 8.00 at night to help with your French. We were their only purposes in life. I didn't know that was anything special till I discovered that in other schools teachers could have calculators adding up their hours, saying they'd done their 1265 hours for this year thank you very much.

I think my school was always committed to service, and although nearly all the girls were there because their parents paid the fees, we were always given strong messages about our duty to repay privileges we enjoyed, not later but now. The school was ahead of its time in terms of involving the girls in service. We used to have an annual party for children from the school for spastic children up the road. But there was this strong sense that there was nothing special about it. And that we had obligations to society.

I think I always had a strong sense that you could make a difference and there was something you can do. There's recently been some research into altruism looking at families in the Netherlands which sheltered Jewish people during the occupation, and families that didn't; and why did some people risk their whole family's life for someone they'd never met before, and some people didn't. And they found that it was that they'd been brought up in altruistic families, and they'd continued to behave in that way. When I was four Willi and Carl used to come to tea with us on Sundays. They were nice to me and I was nice to them, and I knew they lived in a camp which wasn't very comfortable which was why

443

they liked to come to tea. And I now realise they were German prisoners of war.

My parents moved in a kind of socialist network amongst which were a lot of conscientious objectors. My nanny – when my mother started work – was married to a conscientious objector who had been sent down the mines. Although my father had been a conscientious objector he joined the Army because he finally got tired of Hitler.

My friends and I used to joke that there were only three careers women were allowed to do: social work, teaching, nursing, or if you were very clever, medicine. If you didn't want to do any of those, tough. And I remember one of my particular friends told the headmistress she wanted to be a cowgirl. 'Really Susan, and if you weren't able to be a cowgirl?' 'But I am going to be a cowgirl, Miss Peters.' 'Yes, well, yes there is a very good teaching course, you could teach at a country school.' Anyway she didn't put up with that, she went to an agricultural college and married a cowman.

Being able to stay on at my school in Bristol when my parents moved to Kent was lovely. You know, in the Middle Ages knights used to exchange their sons because they were always intolerable to live with, but other boys always seemed so much nicer. And for me I was able to live with other families and in the holidays their daughters used to come home with me. I think that saved a lot of mother and daughter harassment in both families really.

Then I chose universities as far away from home as possible. I had considered going to the London School of Economics when I was eighteen and they told me I would have to live at home in Kent, and I thought, oh my! This is not what I had in mind. So I went to Newcastle. Although it wasn't deeply intellectually challenging it was an extremely useful training which I could recommend because it included economics, law, anthropology, statistics. I did the New Testament and the Old Testament, I just chose to do it. There was a good mix, a good range of choice, nice teachers, lovely place to be. Met nice young men. From thence to LSE to do applied social studies to be a medical social worker.

In Newcastle I met my husband, Donald, who was an economist. It was absolutely love at first sight. Here I was a third-year student, Queen of the May, I think almost anyone I wanted to take me out would have taken me out. And in the college chapel freshers' tea I saw this tall blond, and I thought, wow! And I made myself known to him. He joined the congregation of the college chapel, and he used to come every Wednesday morning and sit next to me but did not ask me out. And it came to the day before my finals began, and he asked me if I wanted to go to the pictures. I said, 'My finals start tomorrow.' Donald said, 'Suit yourself then.' Anyway I managed to squeeze him into my busy diary.

When we finished our exams I went to Israel for three months to work as a volunteer, teaching Hebrew. I was recruited by Greville Janner's Bridge in Britain. We learnt Hebrew in the morning in English, and we taught it in the afternoon in French to Jews expelled from North Africa. No qualified teacher would have even attempted it. But we worked hard and they worked hard, and of course they had this tremendous incentive. Teenagers up from North Africa, dumped in the Negev, and about eight weeks to learn Hebrew.

I forgot a wonderful thing. Just between qualifying as a medical social worker and starting work I went to America as vice-chairman of the United Nations Students Association, and I heard Martin Luther King deliver his 'I Have a Dream' speech. 'I have a dream the day will come when my children will be valued for the quality of their character, not for the colour of their skin.' Fantastic. My granddaughters are mixed race, so I think about that every time I look at them. I think, you're going to be valued for the quality of your character.

Anyway, then I started work at CSV. And we were married in 1965. Dr Dickson had helped President Kennedy set up The Peace Corps, so in 1966 I went over to help set up VISTA (Volunteers in Service to America) which survives to this day. Our eldest son was born in 1969, and the next one in 1972. I used to go into work at half-past nine, and then at one o'clock I would have a break for lunch until two o'clock, and then I would go home at 5.25 to just miss the rush-hour. And I thought that was a hard day's work. Whereas today I start at 9.00 and I finish about quarter past six, and three evenings a week I generally have to do something else, and at weekends I'm catching up on the week before. I think that's true for the whole world. My youngest son works a twelve-hour day sometimes.

We've always been involved. Donald and I used to run a newsletter for the Labour Party for years and years. My parents also used to run newsletters. I was an Islington Borough Councillor which taught me more than any university ever taught me. That was very useful because we were taking over services from the Greater London Council, and I was learning about social services and childcare and other local services from the public administration perspective rather than the social worker's angle. Donald, who is director of Circle 33 Housing Trust, became an Islington Councillor at the time I stopped being a councillor. Indeed he was Leader of the Council for a while, Chairman of Social Services and Chairman of Housing.

For breaks we were always lucky enough to have – well since the boys were tiny – a house in the country. You see when Donald was a councillor it was really quite hard, people coming to the front door or ringing up. We used to go down to the country on a Friday, and on Sundays we'd give the boys their supper and a bath and bring them back and put them straight to bed. So that was a good break. I forgot to mention that I'm deeply into ballet; I'm a qualified teacher of ballet. In ballet there are two routes you can go up. If you've got slim legs and the right height you become a performer, otherwise you learn to teach ballet. And I'm happy to say that my eldest granddaughter goes to ballet every Tuesday. I pick her up from school, and we have tea and we go to ballet, and she is an absolute perfect shape.

I am of course a shopaholic. That's one of the things I missed about being a working mother really, you never have any time for pointless shopping. But I go to America every year to take part in a conference, and shopping there is wonderful. They do much nicer clothes for larger ladies than they do in this country, and the staff are so much more polite. I always give myself a day or so.

HelpAge: The act of helping

John Pearson
Help The Aged

I remember in the Sixties, after we started Help the Aged, how excited
we were to have raised £100,000 in a year. I mean now they think in
terms of 50 million. But that £100,000, my God that was a landmark for
us. We were really over the moon. We were starting what most people
thought was an unpopular charity. People were quite amazed that we
should actually want to raise money specifically for old people, why not
for children?

HELP THE AGED started by raising money for emergency aid for the
elderly overseas but then went on to fund UK projects such as day
centres, geriatric hospitals, minibuses, and especially housing
associations for the elderly. One of the methods of raising money
was by inviting people to name a flat, so £150 put your name plate
on somebody's flat door. Mixed results from that one actually, as you
can imagine. Now, a lot of people would name the flat in memory of
somebody, and I remember the embarrassment in the Scottish
Association when one man named it in memory of his young sister
who had died, and he actually created in the flat a sort of shrine to
her with a picture and flowers and so on. The poor old lady who was
living in the flat was really perturbed about this. But he thought his
£150 more or less gave him ownership of the flat, he could do what
he liked. The scheme had to be modified as time went on to putting
names on a board in the reception area because some of the tenants
didn't like the idea of having 'In Memory of' on their door. But the
Help the Aged Housing Association – now Anchor – really developed
to a tremendous extent. I don't know how many flats Anchor have
now in England and Wales and Northern Ireland, but certainly
they're in excess of 10,000. And the Scottish one, Bield, they have
over 4,000. We've got a big project on at the moment for housing
homeless old people in Glasgow. So it's growing. I mean it's still not
meeting the entire need obviously, but it's done very well.

On the housing side it was the bringing in of the Finance Acts in the late 1960s, which made it possible for housing associations to be formed. And you know, the marvellous thing is that they get a 60-year interest-free mortgage. So, that made it possible to provide housing with very very little charitable finance. We used to reckon that a whole housing scheme of thirty, thirty-five flats would only require a charitable input of about £5,000, and that was virtually to provide extras.

In 1959 Cecil Jackson-Cole invited me to join the committee of Voluntary and Christian Causes, which later became Voluntary and Christian Service. This was his 'umbrella' charity, which was responsible for the formation of Help Aged Refugees, Action in Distress which became Actionaid, and in the 60s for Help the Aged. VCS was set up by Jackson-Cole to encourage OXFAM by raising cash and used clothing through the Christian churches. When OXFAM decided that it no longer needed this help, we moved on to form Help the Aged to raise funds mainly for helping elderly people in the UK by providing day centres and housing and also for emergency aid overseas. Cecil Jackson-Cole had worked for many years with Oxfam of which he was a co-founder with Canon Milford. He always told me that, 'It's my first love.'

He was also Chairman of Andrews Estate Agencies and Andrews Furnishing when I was working as a salesman in their shop in Highbury Corner, London. After the Secretary General of Help the Aged had resigned he called me and said, 'I'd like you to sit in his chair for three weeks while I go on my holiday.' So I said, 'Well I don't really know the first thing about what the secretary-general of a charity does.' 'Oh that's all right old chap,' he said, 'I'll explain it to you in the morning. Pick you up at nine o'clock.' So at nine o'clock he arrived in a taxi, and between Highbury Corner and Piccadilly was the only briefing that I got on how to be the secretary-general of a charity.

And that was it. I went and I sat in this chair, and the atmosphere wasn't very good in the office because Jackson-Cole had created quite a bit of mayhem. I was very naïve actually, I didn't realise I was looked on as his personal Gestapo so I had a rather chilly time. I was allowed to spend half a day there and half a day at the furniture business so I never had any lunch hours, I spent the lunch hour shunting from one place to the other. I thought, well I'd better get some understanding and do something useful here. Gradually I was managing to win trust and create a calmer atmosphere. Anyway Jackson-Cole came back from holiday, and he said, 'They haven't found a replacement yet so will you still hold the fort?' This went on for eighteen months.

One day Jackson-Cole came back to the charity and he was in one of his rather bad moods. He said, 'I've just come from the business and there are some things not right there.' I said, 'Well you're absolutely right, and there are a lot of things not right here, and that situation will continue while you expect one man to do two full-time jobs. You'll have to make up your mind, one way or the other.' That put a stop to his temper. He said, 'Well which would you prefer?' I said, 'I rather like this charity work.' 'Well, would you be director of development and founder's deputy?' I said to him, 'That will do.' So that was what I became. Eventually Hugh Faulkner became a full-time director of the charity.

Until Jackson-Cole died I had the most exciting life really with him. We got on extremely well, we had no disagreements, which was a miracle actually, because nobody had ever achieved that. I argued with him you see; nobody else did.

People listening would have thought we were having a real old barny, but we weren't. We were both being very positive. We spent an awful lot of our time discussing and planning fundraising ideas, and so I gave as good as I got. But it was all perfectly friendly. You see he was a night bird, he wouldn't get up until eleven o'clock, and he would stay up till two and three in the morning. I stayed with him in the evenings, oh, till nine, ten, even eleven o'clock, and he liked that. Before then he had driven everybody mad by phoning them in the middle of their dinner, the wives hated him, needless to say. He was probably BT's biggest customer. He would take a piece of paper and fold it in three, and at the top of each section he'd got the name of the person, and he would have an agenda for his phone calls, and throw it in the bin when he'd finished. He travelled light. But when I started working with him, he had company in the evening, he had somebody to discuss things with, and in fact one of the directors in the company came to thank me for the way that I had calmed him down.

He was quite a genius on stocks and shares, he had made his living from playing the market. He refused to take a salary from his businesses because all the profits went into his charitable trust. I mean when he died he was worth £130,000, that was all. He was quite good at tax avoidance, you know, he wanted to make quite sure that his money didn't go to the taxman but went to the charities. And those trusts are still in existence.

He lived very prudently. He could be most generous in entertaining other people, but for himself he was really frugal. He bought his clothes from charity shops. I remember, I came back from lunch one day and I said, 'You know Meakers in Piccadilly, they've got a sale on and they've got some quite decent shirts for £8.99.' He said, 'I don't pay £8.99 for a shirt. I get my shirts from the Oxfam shops.' Well, he used to wear shirts with the collar about eighteen sizes too big, you know. He didn't care about things like that. He was eccentric and he could be very warm, could be very affectionate, but at the same time he also could be an absolute fiend when he was aroused. At committee meetings, I've seen him slam his fist on the table – a great big solid oak table – and the cups and saucers would rattle.

I started the minibus campaign which has now provided well over 1,000 buses. That would have been in the mid-Seventies – like many things of course it's a matter of grasping the initiative when it appears. A day centre in Edinburgh had asked us if we would provide an ambulance as they called it, and this was the first request we'd had of that kind. Anyway, I got the committee to agree. I went up to Edinburgh and I saw this lady who ran a very good day centre in a listed building, a beautiful, very ancient building. And this lady knew what she was about. She asked us to help to get a bus converted, so we provided her with the money and she did the rest. She got the conversion done and then she rang me and said, 'The bus is being delivered, and I'd like you to come up and present it.' I mean I wasn't much into the up-front stuff but anyway I went up to Edinburgh. When I saw this bus of course it was the answer to my prayers because – without my asking her to do it – there was Help the Aged emblazoned on every side. I was astonished at the amount of publicity this woman had been able to generate. We had Scottish Television there, we had all the press, radio.

I came back and I said to the committee, this is the sort of exposure that we need.

We had given money to day centres and we had at that time provided a geriatric hospital in Ipswich, and were involved with another one in Brent, quite big for a project at the time. And what happens? What publicity mileage does Help the Aged get out of it? We got a plaque on the wall. Who sees it? I said, 'This thing is going to be driving all round Edinburgh, day in, day out, flashing 'Help the

Aged', 'Help the Aged'. At last people are actually going to say that's something that Help the Aged did.'

The minibus campaign went from strength to strength. Was it £10,000 per bus? And very quickly the demand exceeded the amount of money. We used to go and interview these people, and I used to say to them, 'Well OK, if you could raise half, we'll give you the other half.' And I found that local projects had very little difficulty in getting £5,000, because it was about the sort of target the local Lions Club or Rotary or Round Table wanted. So that was great. We put Rotary's name on the bus, put our name on it, and everybody got a slice of the cake. And so that doubled the number that we were able to provide.

Our forte is raising funds and giving them out. And Jackson-Cole was quite adamant that we never actually wanted to get involved in the caring side like Age Concern. When Age Concern's funding from the Government diminished, Help the Aged stepped in and we in fact gave them an administrative grant every year for many years. With housing associations you see, you were able to form a separate organisation, let them get on with it. He reckoned that our fundraising would grind to a halt if we started actually running projects ourselves here or abroad.

We were very successful at press advertising, we were probably the first charity in the UK to use the press. Everything that we did was copied. I mean Jackson-Cole used to say to me every time I threw a new idea to him, 'Yes, fine; you'll have it yourself for six months before others copy it.' And it's very largely true. Everybody else jumped on the press advertising wagon, but the bottom fell out of it eventually, there was too much of it. We were very good on postal appeals, I mean we really produced good money from people once they were on our list, and we had very successful appeals. The schools fundraising, the sponsored events, we were virtually the inventors of that. Again in time that was copied.

In 1973 we employed our first professional fundraiser, the Wells organisation, because we wanted to set up the Help the Aged Scottish Housing Association, and that needed some major funding to kick it off. So I spent a lot of time up in Edinburgh and Glasgow with the Wells campaign director as they called him. They were the greatest American fundraisers. I spent a lot of time shadowing this guy, learning the ropes, and I was fascinated by it. And we raised the money that was wanted, and we formed a development trust which was part of their technique. I am still a trustee. And it thrives. They changed their name from Help the Aged Housing Association, Scotland, to Bield, which is an old Scottish name for a sheltered place. But who knows that?

In other words you have a fundraising committee of big shots who are capable of raising money, but also are capable of getting other people to do it too. It's the old pyramid selling actually. And it works, it works if it's done correctly. And it works very well. But then, you need to form an ongoing trust to administer those funds. to make money available for things for which there is no statutory funding.

I think charity fundraising has progressed quite a lot. The competition has multiplied enormously, that's the first thing. But to combat that, if that's the right word, more sophistication has come into charity fundraising. Charities are into just about everything you can think of. A big item of course is charity shops. And they have mushroomed haven't they. Now, strangely enough Jackson-Cole held us back on having Help the Aged shops. He had a set of shops called Helping Hand gift shops which he formed into a separate company. This gave him the freedom to put the proceeds to Action Aid, Help the Aged or anywhere else he wanted to use it; he kept it in his personal control. You see there was this problem with Jackson-Cole that he would not do anything to upset Oxfam which have something like 900 shops. But it actually held back Help the Aged, and it's only in the, oh, mid-1980s that Help the Aged has really got started on gift shops, I think there are about 400 now. That's one thing that's developed enormously. And it is probably the biggest money-spinner of all because you really get your stock for free.

There used to be a lot of opposition from shopkeepers because charities, as you know, get fifty per cent rate relief. In fact councils even had the ability to give them one hundred per cent if they so wished, and there were one or two who did. Local traders saw that as unfair advantage. One of the excuses that they would also put up for not wanting them was that they were scruffy and they brought down the tone of the neighbourhood. So there was a lot of opposition. I think it's died out now.

Press advertising has virtually died the death, except for specific things like Help the Aged's Adopt-a-Granny scheme. They do put press adverts in for that and that does pay because you're not relying upon just the initial donation, but the fact that it's likely to continue sponsorship for three, four, five years. The donors agree to pay whether by covenant or otherwise, a given amount per month, per quarter or per year. And even in fact, if that old person dies, Help the Aged immediately offers another one, and they continue.

When Help the Aged was forming a trading company we needed a name for it, and I said, we'll call it HelpAge Limited. And so HelpAge has become the name for HelpAge International, HelpAge India, HelpAge Sri Lanka, HelpAge Kenya, HelpAge Korea, they're all using it. It's a coined noun. It can mean help the aged, but it can also mean the act of helping, helpage.

After Jackson-Cole died in 1979, I don't think the committee quite knew what to do with the founder's deputy when there was no longer a founder. I had always wanted to develop the trading side, the mail order trading, so I just hived myself off to Edmonton, took on a warehouse there and built up a very successful trading operation for Help the Aged.

I was born in Glasgow, 29th of July,1928. And lived there until 1946 when I was eighteen and was called up. I went into the Air Force for three years, after all the fighting was finished of course.

We were pretty poor. Dad was a simple, poorly-educated man. Both his parents were dead by the time he was fourteen, and he was brought up by his older brother. He was unemployed from the day I was born until the day war broke out, so that was more or less eleven years. He got his first job really on the 3rd of September 1939 in the shipyard, and he stayed there until he was seventy-four or so. Financially I suppose we had a tough time, but it didn't seem like it. I remember when we were in a poor Indian village, an Oxfam colleague said to me, 'Does it shock you, this sort of thing?' I said, 'No, not all that much, because poverty is the same whether it's an Indian village or a Glasgow slum tenement, it's still the same.' Where the problem comes is when the consumer society takes over, particularly in the cities, and then to be poor is hell because everybody else has got what you haven't got. In a poor village nobody's got it, so you're not envious. And that's the way we were – out of 150 families, one man had a job. It was the Depression. The son of the man with a job had the hardest time from all the other kids, because he was different. His father made him wear shoes. The rest of us wore boots with real hob-nails, yes, real killers, that were supplied by the parish but he insisted on his son wearing shoes. The boots were a very useful weapon in a tight spot. I have the chips on my shin bones even now.

Looking back on it, it was a pretty deplorable way to live but as I say it was the way everybody else around us was living. And the community spirit was very strong, you know. It was very friendly, everybody helping everybody. We had for the six of us two rooms about two-thirds the size of this room, that was our total. Now, if you wanted to decorate the place it had to be done in a day. And everybody else would come up to strip the wallpaper with table knives, and a painter would come in and do the painting. The street tended to be a community in itself; in fact with us kids any sort of enmity was towards people in another street, not towards the ones in our own street. So the whole street would gang up. It was a pretty rough area actually. All demolished now. It's a car wash where I was born. They could have thought of something a bit more imposing than a car wash, but there we are!

I had one brother and two sisters. I don't really remember much of my early schooling. But I got the equivalent of the 11-plus, and went on to grammar school. I was evacuated three times: once to the town of Ayr, the second to a remote part of Perthshire, the third time was back to Ayrshire to a mining village. My father stayed in Glasgow, Mother went off with us.

I loved school, I really did. It was a very good school. I thrived, and I excelled, and in those days strangely enough I had a photographic memory, which was a hell of a help in passing exams because I could literally just copy the page from my head. I wish I had that facility now. I can't remember what I'm supposed to do tomorrow.

I took my Highers when I was sixteen, which was in fact younger than I should have done but, I took them then. That was the sort of A level of Scotland you see. And I had a bit of fun actually, I took a job as a doorman at the cinema believe it or not. Then I got a job in a shipping office as an assistant cashier, God knows with what qualifications, but it was twenty-five shillings a week. Then I saw a notice in a furniture shop window, wanting a stock clerk for £2.10s, £2.50 as it would be now. And so I thought, oh I'll apply for that. I don't know what a stock clerk does, but I dare say I can do it. And I got the job strangely enough. So I doubled my wages overnight. That was where I got the taste for selling, because on a Saturday all the office staff had to come out on the sales floor and I really got into this. I did quite well actually, and I was very popular with the customers. The customers used to come in to pay their accounts and bring me bags of sweets because they recognised that I was still a young'un. I was in that until I was called up.

When I came home on leave near the end of my RAF service my old furniture shop colleagues said, 'One of the directors is here from London, why don't you have a chat with him about getting a salesman's job.' So I did. And he said, 'When your demob comes we'll find you a place.' I told him I wanted to go down south because I had had my eyes opened that life was not always like Glasgow slum tenements and that there were actually people down here in London who lived in decent houses.

And so I arrived down here, and I stayed for one night with a distant cousin of mine who was in London. I went into the job, and said to the manager, 'I need some digs.' 'Oh,' he said, 'that cashier's auntie lives just round the corner from the shop, and she lets rooms.' So he took me and introduced me to the cashier, and there she is today, out there in our kitchen! The first and only girl that I met. I had to wait two years for Joyce to be twenty-one because her father wouldn't let her get married before. That was it. The right person comes at the right time and the right place. And here we are, forty-six years on. So I missed all the wild London scene.

I stayed in that shop but I wasn't particularly happy, because we had a pretty dreadful manager. He was a real pig. But anyway, when I saw a job advertised with a company called Easterns, I went after it. Of course when I told the manager I was leaving he said, 'Oh you won't last five minutes with them. They're murderers, they chuck salesmen out left right and centre.' So I went to work at Easterns in West Ealing where the average life of a salesman in that company was six weeks! You only had to fall short on your sales target one week and you were out. They were ruthless. I was with them for four and a half years.

Then I saw an advert in one of the trade papers for a job in Oxford, and it said, 'Help with housing'. Well we were in a top-floor attic flat, in her auntie's house. Joyce had been evacuated to Oxford and she loved Oxford. And I said, 'What do you think?' She said, 'We'll have a shot.' So I wrote off for this job, and I heard nothing, got no reply. I think more than three months elapsed and we got a letter from the company secretary of Andrews Furnishers saying that the reason they hadn't replied was because the chairman, Jackson-

Cole, was abroad on one of his winter holidays. But now he would like to see me.

I had to go to their Hammersmith shop. There was this long narrow office with a door at one end, and sitting down the other end was Norman Maynard who was in fact Jackson-Cole's brother-in-law. Jackson-Cole was there and every question I asked he would say, 'Excuse us for a minute,' and so I had to go back out again till they'd conferred. This went on several times and at no time was I actually given a straightforward answer, they had to have a conference each time! I was thinking, do I really want to work for this lot? You know, I've looked at their shop and it's scruffy. Poor quality furniture. I'm in a flash shop with up-to-date stuff. And so while I was hesitating, he doubled the amount of pay. I thought, it's got to be worth a gamble. He told me it would not be in Oxford at all, no, no, the Angel, Islington, and he'd like me to meet the rest of the board. I mean, you would have thought I was applying for a job as the chairman wouldn't you? I was given the date for a meeting at Highbury Corner. In the meantime I went along and had a look in the shop at the Angel, and I was appalled. It was absolutely filthy. The windows inside hadn't been cleaned in a year I shouldn't think. The floor, instead of carpet, was tatty old lino. The furniture was all covered in what we call bloom which is a sort of film that you get with cellulose finish, you know.

But anyway, I went for it. And I transformed the place actually. I pushed for some freedom, and I went out and bought carpets and put them down. One of the problems was that the door opened right onto the pavement with bus stops right outside the door, so all the filth blew in every time a bus went by. It was very hard to keep the place clean. We had an ancient cleaner called Liz who used a dustpan and brush. She didn't have a vacuum cleaner. So I bought a vacuum cleaner. But, bless her, 'I'm not using them new-fangled things you know.' She wouldn't use it. So I finished up vacuuming all the carpets myself. But that's the kind of weird set-up that it was. It was very paternalistic. When Jackson-Cole came on his tours any one of the staff at any level could go up to him and talk to him, and ask him for all sorts of personal things. He knew them all by name, he knew their families, everything. It was very Victorian, Dickensian. This was 1954.

I progressed through various parts of the company after that. And, as I say in 1959 Jackson-Cole knew nothing about me apart from the fact that we had had one glorious barny. He came on one of his tours on a Saturday. Now, on a Saturday in a furniture shop in those days you had to earn your week's takings, that was your busy day, and it was concentrated in about a two-hour period in the afternoon. That was when the customers all came in. If you were a clever salesman you had to be a bit selective. You are looking to give priority to people with the biggest potential order. You didn't want the people that wanted a companion set for the fireplace or anything like that during those two hours. We were all really haring away, and I was very fast on selling, I mean, particularly the paperwork, I had it down to a fine art. A lot of it was prepared in advance and I talked to the people while I was doing it, all the time. Well Jackson-Cole came in. He had a customer who wanted to spend £4, whereas I was dealing with people who wanted a bedroom suite, a dining suite and a three-piece suite. I said, 'No, I'm serving.' Anyway, as it calmed down, he said, 'You lost that customer, they went off,' and he started railing off at me. Of course I gave it back to him as fast. He ran out of the shop. He ran all the way up the road, and I ran after him. And in the middle of Chapel Market the two of us were having a right old ding-dong. He said, 'I want you to report to the board of directors on Tuesday.' I more or less told him to stuff his board of directors, that I wasn't reporting to anybody thank you very much, and I went back to the shop. As I say, I was a cocky young salesman. In 1959, what was I? Thirty-one then. I thought, this old fool, telling me how to do my job, and he obviously hasn't got a clue. He wants to make a big fuss of somebody who wants to spend £4 when the shop's full, people buying serious furniture. I was very much a salesman, a very successful furniture salesman I must say, went to sales manager, then director, but was happiest as a salesman quite honestly, because there is a great deal of difference between doing your own selling and having to depend on other people to do it.

If you could sell furniture sure, you could sell charity. The successful salesman is the one who believes in his product. And when I told people that it is the best made furniture that you can buy, I meant it. And I knew my product. I could tell them exactly what was inside the cushions on the suite. You know, I really enjoyed it. And when I was guiding people, it was for their benefit. It wasn't just to sell them the most expensive items. And carpets, I will say I was brilliant on carpets, I really knew my carpets.

I am a firm believer in charity work, that the right person appears in the right place at the right time. I think that applies to Jackson-Cole. I fitted in with him, and I did things which I'm proud of, particularly overseas. In the 1970's over a ten-year period I was spending six months a year overseas for Help the Aged. I was doing four trips to India, six weeks at a time, fundraising. I was working the schools, from the back of motorbikes, from buses, from auto-rickshaws, just about everything. And it was great fun, it was great excitement you know. I then became President for HelpAge India for seven years. But even with Help the Aged in the UK the things that I started are still thriving like the minibus campaign and the American-type fundraising – they now have a big department doing that. Various other activities like mail order catalogue trading, I did that until I retired in fact.

I was brought up in a Catholic family, and that was the beginning of my charity ideas. But the amusing part was that when Jackson-Cole brought me onto his committee and eventually into Help the Aged he had no knowledge at all of my Christian background, I mean that had never come into any discussion with us. And when I first went on that committee, I remember the first time when I made some remarks which indicated that I was a Catholic, and the look of shock round that table, my God! we've got a papist amongst us, how did we get him? Because they were all from the Free Churches. I mean that sort of thing died down, and indeed if you're in charity work overseas it's very hard to avoid the Catholic intake, or output, very difficult, because to be quite honest the most reliable methods of distributing are generally through Catholic sources.

Joyce is not a joiner and I've never tried in any way to involve her either when I was in business, or in charity work. Jackson-Cole was a great one for pulling the wives into everything, and I resisted that because I knew what happened, the wives began to hate him. I mean he wanted me to take Joyce to India and said, 'I'll pay, I'll pay.' I said, 'No, she doesn't want to go.' Because in any case when I was on this sort of job I was single-minded, and she did not like being deserted, no. On the few occasions where we were together, I would unfortunately forget that she was there, and go off talking to people and so on, and she didn't like that. And it certainly would have applied overseas where I was totally immersed in what I was doing. Apart from which she can't stand the heat and there were three boys and an adopted daughter to care for.

Absorbing interests

Alastair Heron
The Pre-Retirement Association

It was a tragic commonplace that the Monday after a man retired he would be hanging round the gates of the factory to say hello to his mates when they came out, and what's more, would keep on doing it every day or twice a week before eventually tailing off. Because that was his life. The meaningfulness and the significance of life for these men was their normal employment, and when that stopped there was a very big hole, and a great many of them didn't know how to fill it. Therefore what could we do about it?

IN 1955 I was appointed the Director of a new Medical Research Council unit attached to the University of Liverpool to carry out studies on human ageing, with particular reference to the occupational aspects of ageing. We carried out a very large-scale survey in the early years in twenty-three representative companies, that is representative in terms of the industrial census categories. Arising out of the survey was a recognition of how obviously ill-prepared men – and women though not in those days to the same extent – were prepared for what happened when they reached sixty-five and sixty. It was very rare to find people kept on beyond the statutory pensionable age. One had this very very strong picture that you rolled up to work till you were sixty-five and that was it, and the people who were retiring most effectively were those who had gardens or allotments.

With this picture in my mind, I got involved with an initiative of the National Old People's Welfare Council, which was the predecessor of what we now call Age Concern. The NOPWC formed a small committee and invited me to be a member of it. In about 1959 the committee proposed a series of short booklets on relevant topics around retirement, and they asked me to do the first one. I don't think the full series was ever completed, but I produced *Solving New Problems* in which I outlined the situation as I saw it, particularly in terms of this lack of preparedness for a life after work. If you had been working – as you were in those days – fifty hours a week on a manual job, and your wife was not working, you stopped work and then you found there was nothing to get up for in the morning and nothing to do all day; you were under your wife's feet, to use a frequently used expression. And so I came out with a list of what I perceived to be the main requirements for a reasonably satisfactory retirement from full-time employment:

- good physical and emotional health
- adequate income, substantially above subsistence level
- suitable accommodation
- congenial associates and neighbours
- one or more absorbing interests
- an adequate personal philosophy of life.

These eventually became known as Heron's Six Points, and they are to this day, forty years later, still known, notably in this country, but also to a limited extent in Australia, North America and the Scandinavian countries. And these six points were to be the topics of a six-part course on preparation for retirement.

A problem then became very evident, and that was, where on earth could we put this course to the test? To keep the story reasonably short, I was given an introduction to Sir Alfred Owen, the managing director of a group of manufacturing firms, mainly working for the motor industry, in the north Midlands. He was very encouraging, a very enlightened man, and he had already launched a workshop for retired employees. The workshop was on a small scale, a dozen retired men using mostly hand tools but also one or two very small machine tools, with an experienced, retired foreman or supervisor in charge of them. The men just came along and worked when they wanted. It was meant to be a way of meeting this painfully demonstrated need that many men had for working, that work gave their lives significance and meaning.

I was also introduced to Sir Alfred's daughter, Grace Owen, who was in the personnel department. And he said, 'Well, if you and my daughter discuss what might be done and come up with a scheme, we'll look at it.' That obviously involved not just discussion with managers but with the trades unions, which I was fairly accustomed to because of my part-time activities in adult education. Eventually,

I found myself one day in a room where, apart from Grace Owen and one or two other staff people and the trade union men, all the other men in the audience were exactly fifty years old, which was an incredible experience. The firm and the union obviously cooperated, and these men were allowed to come in the last hour of the working day, so they weren't losing any pay. Well I looked around that room, I suppose there were about forty-five to fifty men there, and it was the most striking illustration I had experienced of seeing the difference in people in relation to age. In other words, they were all exactly the same age but the differences were visible. Some of them looked relatively younger, and some looked relatively older, and some looked very old, much older. Some of that had to do with the nature of the work that they had been doing for donkey's years, and some of it had to do with the nature of their non-working activities. But certainly the differences were very striking.

We got the course going. I involved the local Workers' Education Association which was in those days extremely active, pretty well nationwide. The local secretary, an experienced adult educationalist, was very keen so I got him to come along and lead the discussions. And it went down quite well. I think we got substantially more than half of the original roomful signed up to actually do the full course. Their motivation varied greatly. And again you see, it was all part of the differences between them, some of these men may have had life experiences that blunted their imagination, or their risk-taking spirit, whereas others might have always been let's-have-a-go kind of people. I did emotional health, recruited the works medical officer to do the purely medical aspect, and on finance we had somebody from the pensions department give a talk and then answer questions. I forget who I got to do the others, but anyway we went through the six points. I was actually quite dependent for feedback on the trades union representatives, the shop stewards, and they were generally approving and encouraging, glad that it had happened. They were of course naturally alert to the whole business of the financial side; in those days the state retirement pension was even worse than it is now, and these manual workers had no company pension; they might be given an *ex gratia* payment but there was no occupational pension scheme.

Grace Owen and I felt quite strongly that we really ought to bring the wives in on this, so some time later, she asked her father and his brother, the other principal director, if the company would stump up for a residential meeting in some local college, where the husbands could bring their wives if they wanted to. Obviously it was not compulsory, but to provide an opportunity for the wives to find out what their husbands had been doing. Of course we knew that some of the husbands wouldn't say a word to their wives; others would tell them all about it. We had a residential in 1961, and I managed to bring in Nora Phillips who was very active in the trade union movement herself – she eventually became Baroness Phillips under one of the Labour governments. So we built her into the programme, and the women had her to themselves without the men about. And that went down quite well.

I ran the course for three consecutive years. As a new wave of men became fifty they were offered the course and those who accepted it were put through it. I also set up what you might call a revision course which happened after I left. Those who were still around at fifty-five years old were offered a refresher.

I think the fundamental flaw in my concept was that it was over-ambitious to have started the course fifteen years before retirement. I mean that was ideal but it was too large a gap. Being clever after the event, or learning from practice, I would have thought that ten years at the most and five years at the least would have been better. I remember being asked, 'Why are you doing the course so early,' and I used to say, 'Well look, if there's something that a man and his wife would like to do when he is retired, and if it's something you have to save up for, they've got to have saved up for it for quite a long time, and it's no good getting the bright idea a year before your pay's going to stop.' It was primarily on those grounds that you had to start earlier rather than later. The whole business of maintaining your health was something you didn't leave till the last minute and then hope that you were suddenly going to be fit; if you were going to do anything even slightly systematic, then the sooner you started and maintained it the better.

I did try to spread the message. Companies set up meetings at my request and I would talk to them. I could be sure that there were some gardeners or allotment holders out there in the audience so an example of what I would say to them was, 'Look, none of us know what our joints are going to be like when we're a bit older and maybe it won't be quite so easy to keep on doing all the tough stuff, and wouldn't it be nice to have a small greenhouse, and wouldn't it be nice if it was warm? It doesn't have to be very special, just a heater in it, but at least a place where you can do some potting up.' This went down very well, they saw the point. Now, many of them, unless they were foremen, weren't going to be able to afford even the raw materials to erect the greenhouse, so therefore it was going to be an objective that they would have to save for, and that took time.

One can't emphasise too often the matter of individual differences. There were men who had hobbies, there were pigeon fanciers of course, lots of them had lofts, and not necessarily racing pigeons but homing pigeons. Some men had little workshops, did carpentry, and one or two did carving. But then there were others who did nothing, absolutely nothing. One of the six points was to have one or more absorbing interests. And when I was actually talking about that subject I would point out that it was desirable that one of them should be an indoor interest, because of weather. Don't have all your eggs in the one basket like gardening; have something which you are keen on doing and which you could do indoors, all through the winter or when the weather's lousy.

Whoever it was who did that particular topic – one or more absorbing interest – would also indicate where they could sample local possibilities, an adult education college or something of that sort. In those days there were a lot of adult evening classes, and it was quite possible for example for the Workers' Educational Association chap to say, well, you could go along to X and just see what you think of it. In other words you had to provide them with ideas, and then persuade them to have a go.

Meanwhile the National Old People's Welfare Council set up a provisional committee which did a lot of drumming up of interest in preparation for retirement around the country. That functioned for a relatively short time, I think a year or so, and got enough people interested to say, 'Let's launch a national body.' The Pre-Retirement Association was formed in 1963, two months after I left Britain, so I wasn't involved in the official beginning of it. I had been a significant figure in its inception, in the thinking and the development of it, but it fell to others to actually launch it. The Association had a very thin time when it couldn't attract grant support, and was always in financial straits: an office with one person who answered the telephone and did correspondence, took the minutes when they had a committee meeting and so on. A shoestring affair. It had a long period of about a decade in which quite frankly a lot of the educational objectives got less and less attention, and the pension people began to dominate the scene, so many of the courses that were offered within companies were offered only in relation to financial planning.

I think it's very easy for people in administrative positions to think in planning terms, and if you're talking about something as concrete as how much money a retired person is going to have the week after their retirement, then yes, you do talk about financial planning. But PRA was mainly about *preparation* for retirement and it struggled to sustain the notion that it wasn't just about planning to improve the financial position or to make it as good as possible, but there was the whole business of opening up new horizons, the other five points really. It was about trying to interest people, before they retired, in paying attention to their health and having some positive interests so that they could happily and meaningfully utilise all this spare time.

When I came back from abroad in 1976 I reintroduced myself into the Pre-Retirement Association's activities. And then in about '78, which was fifteen years after I'd left PRA, I became its Chairman. Some of the pioneers were still there, they were a bit discouraged, and certainly the association was finding it hard to keep its chin above water financially. One of the things that I found out fairly quickly in conversation was that even when local companies were offering their employees full-length courses, the tutors who came and ran them often made quite a good job of the first five points and simply couldn't tackle the sixth – an adequate personal philosophy of life. It was obvious to me that I'd got to discuss this problem with those who were actually at the sharp edge. The one thing I was very concerned about was that I didn't want there to be any suggestion that PRA was saying that everybody had, for example, to have a deep religious faith in order to retire successfully. That's why I came up with 'an adequate personal philosophy of life.' When I was asked to put it to the test and do it myself, I didn't find it difficult at all. I mean, it is pretty important, particularly in later life when one's got time to think about it, to have some idea about what life's all about, the meaning of life, and is there any purpose in it and so forth. And that's what an adequate personal philosophy is basically about. And then what you make of it is very much a matter of who you meet, what sort of discussions you get involved in, if you're a reader what you read, and so on. Bringing this right up to date, quite recently I went over to Manchester, by invitation, to the annual meeting of the local Pre-Retirement Association, to talk about the six points forty years on. And so I did. And we had quite an interesting discussion about the sixth point. They knew what I was talking about all right.

The biggest problem the pre-retirement movement has always had – going back to my being too ambitious with the fifteen years in advance of retirement – is the number of companies that could not be persuaded to offer the course even as late as one year before retirement. They thought they were doing a wonderful job if they provided a course at six months or less before retirement, and sometimes even then in an attenuated form with the pensions business to the fore, probably a bit of health education thrown in. What's happened recently I think is really very important. The Pre-Retirement Association has responded to the realities of a changed culture and they are now offering mid-life courses which simply recognise that people are being forced into retirement in their fifties, and so they're trying to get people who are forty, forty-five. So the Pre-Retirement Association now has got a very heavy emphasis on mid-life.

The variety of courses is enormous. You're very much in the hands of the personnel departments, and then it's how well does the personnel officer or manager go about it, how seriously he or she takes it, the resources on which they call or don't call. Unlike the early days when almost all our people who actually ran the courses did it for nothing, today everybody expects to be paid a fee. Of course the other thing is, that if you have relatively few people in a company approaching pensionable age, it's uneconomic to put on courses for them, and the Pre-Retirement Association's answer to that was and is to send the employees to a course arranged by the local Pre-Retirement Association. These courses are held in adult education colleges, further education colleges, usually in the evenings. Again you're up against company policy. There are some companies which let employees attend in an afternoon. On the other hand, what you call middle rank people, in production or in the office, quite often employers couldn't spare them, or said they couldn't.

PRA runs courses to train their tutors in pre-retirement education. Some of them actually earn a living doing it, and they build up a clientele of companies. PRA has had and continues to have a significant input into the general field of what you might call prophylactic measures in ageing. It has a significant preventative potential. The extent to which that has been realised varies from place to place, and from individual to individual, and to the extent to which a man or a woman is able temperamentally or through circumstance to take advantage of it.

I think PRA is one of the most worthwhile things I have done in my long life.

I was born on 10th October 1915 in Edinburgh, Scotland. My mother had been before her marriage, a nursing sister in a London teaching hospital, and my father had an engineering qualification, but this being the beginning of the First World War, was already in uniform.

Edinburgh was my father's family's home. His father, my grandfather, was the Secretary of the Merchant Company of Edinburgh, and a distinguished solicitor. The Merchant Company was a bit like one of the livery companies in London. Several of the famous schools in Edinburgh are Merchant Company schools, including George Watson's College, which my father went to for thirteen years, and I went to for only two.

My mother was English. She was born in London, and her father was the head of the telegraph section of the General Post Office in the City of London.

I was an only child. My father was an only child – two consecutive only children. So I had almost no relatives on my Scottish side; my relatives were my mother's brothers and sisters, and that brought with them a couple of cousins.

I think the only way to describe the early years of my life was that they were peripatetic. My parents just moved about. It was almost certainly wholly because of my father being an engineer. He tended to go where there were contracts but I think also in his younger adulthood he was inclined to be itchy and to want to move on to the next place. It meant that I went to six different schools which is quite something.

My two last schools were in Montreal, Canada. I went to Canada when I was nearly ten. I was in the care of the captain of a cargo boat sailing to Montreal which had a few passengers from the port of Leith, Edinburgh's port. My father and mother had gone out the previous year and left me in lodgings and attending George Watson's in Edinburgh. At the age of eleven I went to the High School of Montreal, in the centre of the city, right next to the university, and I was there for four years, which was the full high school course in those days.

I was the youngest in my class, but more seriously I was the smallest. From the day I entered my first school at five till the day I left Montreal High School at fifteen and a half I was the smallest boy in my class, every year. It wasn't funny. But I figured out ways of dealing with that, usually by being a bit passive about the physical side of the bullying, and then using my tongue, which was fluent from an early age. After I left school at the time of the great Depression, my father and I were mostly unemployed. I then grew five inches in twelve months and so my trousers came up my legs, sleeves came up my arms, and my toes curled up in my shoes.

My first job was as office boy in the head office of an oil company in Montreal. The second one was what I wanted to do: I went to an analytical chemist's, in a very junior capacity, and I was getting on fine, but they went out of business. I reckoned later on in my life that I probably did about twenty different jobs for periods varying from two or three days to two or three months before I was twenty years old. Good preparation for life.

My father and I managed to earn enough to pay my mother's passage back to Britain. Then he and I worked our passage back, and by very good luck we were on the same ship, he as a substitute fifth engineer and I worked in the black squad heaving coal. Twelve days across the Atlantic. I had my nineteenth birthday in mid-ocean. After a few months of trying to find jobs in London, unsuccessfully, I got fed up and walked into the Army recruiting office in Whitehall, joined the Royal Corps of Signals, and went up to Catterick in Yorkshire. That was in 1934.

I was very happy in the Signals, although it was tough, it was very tough, the second toughest training depot in the British Army after the Guards depot at Aldershot. But I'd been in the cadets at school and after school I'd been in the Canadian equivalent of the Territorials, so I had a big advantage over other recruits because I knew what to do, what to expect. But we weren't very well fed, nobody was, the Army was under-funded, and as I said, it was the Depression. I ended up in the military hospital in Catterick with pericarditis, an inflammation of one of the linings of the heart, and in due course was discharged from the Army less than a year after joining, very much to my regret. I would have been very content to make a career in the Signals.

I came back to London for a few months staying with my parents and then I had a relapse and was in a hospital in Earl's Court for three months. A few months later I got a job as an articled clerk in an accountant's office in the City, which started me off on the way to becoming an accountant. I took a job down in Southampton where I met the people who turned out to be the parents of Margaret, my wife-to-be. I met her father and her mother and three of her sisters, and then I met her. I owe a great deal to the original Oxford Group through which I met Margaret and her family. However, eventually Margaret and I dissociated ourselves from the Oxford Group which became Moral Rearmament; there were various aspects of it we weren't happy with.

I did quite well in accountancy, and I took my intermediate exam, but then the call-up came. By that time I had decided, very surprisingly in some ways for an ex-regular soldier, to become a conscientious objector. But it was entirely on religious grounds: I simply could not credit Jesus killing anybody, and that weighed more with me than anything else. The tribunal accepted that position, and I spent a short time in the Ambulance Service in Southampton, including responding to the first daylight raids from German bombers. Then I went up to London and was more than three years in the Rescue Service in Islington digging people out when the house fell on them. Margaret and I married in 1940, and when we were living in Muswell Hill in London we started going to a Quaker meeting because we weren't really very at ease with prayers for the war effort in the churches we attended.

In order to train for overseas service with Friends Relief, I was allowed to leave the Rescue Service by the government bodies that supervised conscientious objectors. The Friends Relief Service sent me to Italy to work with non-Italian refugees while the war was still on, very early 1945. Then in January of 1946 I went to Germany to work with German refugees from the east, driven out of East Prussia and Silesia by the Russians. I knew that I would only be there for nine months because by then I had a place at the University of Manchester at the beginning of October '46. So I finally got to university full-time at the age of thirty-one.

I had settled my wife and children – son Keith was born in 1942, our daughter Joy thirteen months later in 1943 – in Manchester before I went off to Italy. I had decided not to continue with accountancy because somewhere along the line I got an interest in the possibility of doing something in psychology. When I was still in the Rescue Service, when the major blitzes on London were over and we had nothing much to do, I got permission to go to classes on Saturdays and Sundays at Birkbeck College, which was the only college of the University of London not to leave London in the war. It was a college wholly for adults, and I spent a couple of years there, perhaps a little longer. In fact I ended up as president of the student union just before I went off to Friends Relief Service training.

Because I had done a diploma course at Birkbeck the professor of psychology at the University of Manchester rather skilfully used a regulation that had been brought in to help refugees from the Nazis with rather strange qualifications, and that allowed me to do an MSc course in three years. I chose as my thesis education for parenthood, which I suppose arose out of the fact that I was very conscious of being an incredibly unsatisfactory father of two young children. Having done some child psychology, I gained enough insight to realise that being a good parent was a trickier task than is usually recognised. And that made me say to myself, if you can learn other things, why can't you learn, not exactly how to be a good parent, but at least how to deal with young children and how to relate to them, and when to be firm, when to be tolerant and so forth. So I thought, wouldn't it be good if that was available in school before the earliest likely time of being a parent, they would have some impression in their minds as to what was relevant to parenthood. So I constructed a fairly detailed questionnaire, and did two studies in Devon and in Oldham. The overall finding from the two studies was quite clear: education for parenthood was an acceptable school subject by the age of 15, unsurprisingly to the girls but very surprisingly to a substantial proportion of the boys, about forty per cent. And nobody had ever discovered anything like this before, it was a first. But of course nobody paid any attention to the published results although it gave me an MSc in psychology.

My external examiner apparently mentioned me to the late Sir Aubrey Lewis, the honorary director of the Medical Research Council unit based at the Maudsley Hospital in London, who was starting a little occupational outpost in Manchester. Margaret and I had been living on a three-year post-war grant, and we kept pretty close accounts – it was very Dickensian because we ended up about ten shillings on the right side at the end of three years. So I hitchhiked to London for the interview, and was offered a one-year appointment, and on the basis of that I took the bus back. That started fourteen years of service in the Medical Research Council for the last eight of which I was a director of the unit on ageing in Liverpool. Out of my work there I derived the concept of functional age. The models used for both parenting and ageing were what I suppose you would call prophylactic. In other words, just as I thought that it ought to be possible to arrive at parenthood with at least some idea of where you were heading for – a few tools at your disposal – so you ought to arrive at the end of full-time employment similarly prepared.

While our children were young, Margaret and I had always wondered if an opportunity would ever arise to work abroad, particularly in Africa. We had become aware of the debt we owed to the African people, and we wanted to put our little bit in towards paying it off. But psychology was not a very good subject, there weren't any openings, except in the Republic of South Africa and that was out of the question. We couldn't possibly have worked under apartheid, we would have been thrown out anyway. Oh, out of the question, really out of the question. Totally repugnant to us. At the end of 1962 I saw an advertisement, popped out of the page as sometimes things do, which said that they were looking for a director of some place called the Rhodes Livingstone Institute in what was still Northern Rhodesia. I got an interview and the upshot was, I was offered the job. When the University of Zambia was set up, as I had correctly foretold when interviewed, the Rhodes Livingstone Institute was incorporated into the new university. I then became the first Professor of Psychology in the University of Zambia, in fact one of its first two professors of anything. There was no way the name Rhodes could appear once the Institute became part of the University of Zambia. So I discussed it with all the relevant people, and came up with the neutral term, the Institute for Social Research, the ISR, a nice euphonic title.

It was a tremendous experience. But I also got an education. Africans taught me a lot about what being a human being is about. Quite a lot about basic equality. And it was very interesting to notice the parallel between their method of decision-taking, you know, going all round the subject until they had consensus, and the apparently similar Quaker method of taking decisions in their meetings. But the important difference is that the Quaker is seeking to cooperate with the purposes of God, not just to reach consensus. What they do have in common is the openness to everybody to contribute.

The major piece of work I did there was to devise, deliver and supervise the initial running of the secondary school selection system for the whole country. It was rather bizarre to be producing for a newly independent African country an 11-plus examination that we were trying to get rid of in Britain: but it was for good reason. It was the only practical way to do it because Zambia consisted of about five or six major ethnic regions and about twenty or thirty tribes, and the one thing the incoming government was scared stiff of was that they would be accused of tribal favouritism. I produced a system which was above it, and it was never ever criticised. The system had its imperfections but it worked, it was pragmatic. I just based it on the British model, but with some care about the actual tests that I used. It included a non-verbal test and a vocabulary test instead of what you might call a verbal intelligence test which I eliminated as much too inappropriate a tool. Primary school leavers in Zambia in those days, their command of English was not good, and that was why it was essential to give them a non-verbal test. They would still be disadvantaged of course vis-à-vis an European educated child of the same age, but amongst themselves, and it was entirely amongst themselves, it would certainly sort them out and it did. They were going to go into brand new secondary schools, and they were going to be faced with all the problems that you could think of. And so problem-solving was quite important. I modified that to produce the first ever civil service selection examination in Zambia. It worked too and it gave a lot of people who were humble clerks in government offices a chance to show that they had got something more to offer.

We left Zambia in 1968 because Margaret had a recurrence of her depressive illness. I became fairly convinced, and nothing ever happened subsequently to change my mind, that she was missing her family in both directions, missing her sisters, but also missing our son and daughter. She did a fantastic job with the African women at the institute and enjoyed that enormously in the early years. But as they became more able to stand on their own feet Margaret in her part-time way was doing what the rest of us in our full-time way were doing our best to do – work ourselves out of a job. So I recognised that the time had come to go. Then we discovered along with a lot of other people, that in those days anyway, I don't know if it's still true, that if you left the academic life of Britain, for more than three years, you would have trouble getting back again. I had been away six, and every job I applied for I didn't get.

Fortunately as part of my ordinary life as an academic in Zambia, I already had a half-year's visiting professorship organised in Canberra, at the Australian National University. So we went out to Australia to do my six months on the assumption that while I was away one or more of the jobs that I had applied for in Britain would turn up. None of them did. I came to the end of my six months in Canberra in effect jobless. But during that last week I got a phone call from Melbourne, where I had given a few invited lectures some months previously, telling me that I was about to be formally offered the headship of the Department of Psychology at the University of Melbourne. So what Britain didn't want, Australia did. I had a very interesting, very challenging, unexpectedly successful period as a senior Australian academic. I left there in September 1974, having resigned because Margaret was not only back in England, and had been for some time, but she was in hospital.

Through a contact that I had made earlier in Australia, I arranged to see the head of a centre which formed part of the Organisation for European Cooperation and Development, OECD, in Paris, and the outcome was that I finished up in Australia knowing I had got a one-year job in Paris. It was right up my street: I was to be a consultant in early childhood care and education. So I went and lived in Paris for a year, which meant I could visit Margaret quite easily and frequently. Meanwhile I told all my close friends in Britain to be alert to even the remotest possibility of my getting a job there a year later, because I was already fifty-nine. One of my former colleagues and friends was very well-known for his work on the treatment of mentally handicapped children, and he had been appointed as the Department of Health's representative on a committee in Sheffield University to appoint somebody to set up a unit to evaluate the services for the mentally handicapped in Sheffield. I applied for and got that job, and it saw me through to pensionable age five years later.

I retired in 1980 for the second time, aged sixty-five. The first time was of necessity in Melbourne. I decided to clear the decks in 1985 when I was seventy. Yes. For example, I gave the Pre-Retirement Association a full year's notice that I was going to step down as Chairman, and worked together with my successor in that twelve months and he took over in a smooth transition. That's right, that was my third retirement – I gave myself a computer on my 70th birthday.

From 1982 to 1988, I was mainly involved in Quaker activities. So, when I stopped at the end of 1988, I was beginning to see myself moving to a fourth retirement although I was still involved in the planning and equipping of the new meeting house for Quakers in central Sheffield, which occupied me on and off for five years.

When I reached my 80th birthday in 1995, I felt that this was the time to retire in the sense that most people think of retirement; in other words I would no longer hold office of any kind, Quaker or other, and I wouldn't serve on any standing committees, but I would be available on call for one-off things, or for very short service if they wanted to set up a committee to look into something. I am still mobile, can drive long distances without difficulty. And, now at eighty-four I've produced one Quaker book a year for five years running, as well as my 1998 autobiography, *Only One Life: A Quaker's Voyage*.

Education for parenthood has now 'arrived', fifty years later. The idea of preparation for retirement was probably twenty years ahead of its time before it was recognised as not a luxury but a highly desirable thing, if not indeed a necessity. The eight years of work in Liverpool on ageing resulted in a book called *Age and Function*, published by Churchill. On the last couple of pages I raised the question as to whether there was a possibility that the efficiency of what we call cognitive or intellectual processes in the brain are dependent upon the speed at which the brain can operate, whether you are talking about a child or a young adult or an old person, that the really important thing is the speed of processing within the brain. Well, just a few months ago there was a special issue of the *Australian Journal of Psychology* on various aspects of research into ageing which contained two papers addressing the question of the speed of mental function. I e-mailed the authors copies of the last two pages of my 1967 book. And I had enthusiastic reactions from both of them. The most flattering and heart-warming one describes the work nearly thirty-five years after publication as 'thoroughly modern,' and that made my day. It's all about living long enough when you were born about thirty years too soon!

Appendix

ORGANISATIONS STARTED IN the UK in the 1960s, as they are today and listed in chapter order. The information is taken from the *National Voluntary Agencies Directory 2003* with kind permission from the National Council for Voluntary Organisations, except where the entry is asterisked and provided by the organisation itself.

Chapter 1   Advisory Service for Squatters (ASS)
            2 St Pauls Road, London N1 2QN
Objects: To give legal and practical advice to squatters and homeless people.
Activities: Telephone advice 5 days per week. Publication of *Squatters Handbook*. Assistance with civil proceedings.

Chapter 2   Shelter
            88 Old Street, London EC1V 9HU
Objects: To campaign for decent homes that everyone can afford.
Activities: Providing advice and assistance to people in housing need. Running regional housing aid centres and charity shops, in addition to the London office. Running a national 24-hour free helpline. Campaigning and fundraising across the UK.

Chapter 3   Centrepoint
            Neil House, 7 Whitechapel Road, London E1 1DU
Objects: To improve the lives of a significant number of homeless and excluded young people.
Activities: Providing emergency shelters and a range of supported accommodation throughout London. Running projects offering counselling, healthcare, advice on jobs and benefits, and help finding a permanent place to live. Helping local groups across the country to set up their own housing and advice projects for young people locally. Publishing research and information about the causes and effects of youth homelessness in order to influence policies that affect young people.

Chapter 4   Crisis
               64 Commercial Street, London E1 6LT
Objects: To run a national charity for single homeless people.
Activities: Working year-round to help vulnerable people through the crisis of homelessness rebuild their lives, reintegrate into society and live independently, providing access to support for mental health and addiction problems. Also provides accommodation and training and employment opportunities and undertakes research. Probably best known for its Open Christmas shelters that run every year from 23 to 30 December.

Chapter 5   Alone in London Service (ALS)
               188 Kings Cross Road, London WC1X 9DE
Objects: To relieve the homelessness of young people aged under 26. To enable young people to live as independently as possible. To provide practical and emotional support for young people at risk of homelessness. To bring young people's homelessness to public attention.
Activities: Providing a range of residential and non-residential services for homeless young people aged 16-25; advice and counselling centre; advocacy project; shared housing with low support; resettlement support; access to local authority and housing association nominations; post-resettlement support; providing family mediating service. Our supporting services include finance, administration, fundraising, human resources and volunteer management.

Chapter 6   Simon Community
               PO Box 1187, London NW5 4HW
Objects: To provide relief, care and comfort to those people sleeping rough and with no fixed abode; to campaign for improvements in the quality of life for the homeless and rootless.
Activities: One night shelter and two residential houses; street-work to reach those people who most need help; medical care; campaigning at national and local level; tea and soup runs; twice weekly 'street café'.

Chapter 7   Alcohol Recovery Project (ARP)
            68 Newington Causeway, London SE1 6DF
Objects: To provide advice, information, counselling and
            residential services to people with alcohol problems.
Activities: Running open-access centres across London, including
            one for women only and one for black and minority
            ethnic people which offer individual counselling and
            group work. Running residential schemes where residents
            must be abstinent from alcohol, two of which are for
            women only. Providing floating support services to people
            in their homes. Providing training to agencies.

Chapter 8   Child Poverty Action Group (CPAG)
            94 White Lion Street, London N1 9PF
Objects: To promote action for the relief, directly or indirectly, of
            poverty among children and families with children.
Activities: Providing a national service of welfare benefits advice
            and training courses for advisers. Taking legal test cases
            to ensure that poor families receive the benefits due to
            them. Researching family poverty in the UK and
            informing the public, MPs and the media. Campaigning
            for improved policies and legislation to prevent poverty.

Chapter 9   *Claimants Unions exist as autonomous organisations
            engaged with the politics of work and unemployment.
            Several centres pursuing these aims are scattered
            throughout the UK.

Chapter 10 Community Transport (CT)
            PO Box 66, Manchester M19 2XT
Objects: To promote charitable purposes for the benefit of the
            community through the provision of transport advice or
            assistance.
Activities: Projects in the Midlands, North-East and North-West
            provide furniture for needy families and operate box
            vans and minibuses for use by voluntary and community
            groups.

Chapter 11 Law Centres Federation (LCF)
Duchess House, 18-19 Warren Street, London W1T 9LR

Objects: The Law Centres Federation encourages the development of publicly funded legal services for those most disadvantaged in society and promotes the Law Centre model as the best means of achieving this. To improve access to justice we promote good Law Centre practice and innovation.

Activities: The LCF provides support and developmental services covering the whole range of Law Centres needs, including training, information, facilitating the sharing of knowledge and resources, and improving standards. Through its policy and education work it aims to achieve improved access to legal services, highlighting the link between social exclusion and access to justice.

Chapter 12 Joint Council for the Welfare of Immigrants (JCWI)
115 Old Street, London EC1V 9RT

Objects: To work against racism and for social justice in British and EU immigration and nationality laws. To advise and represent people with problems caused by these laws.

Activities: Advising individuals, groups and other advice agencies; taking up cases with the Home Office and immigration authorities. Public lobbying, campaigning and media work on immigration and nationality issues. Producing information on the laws and their effects. Training other advisers in immigration and nationality law and practice.

Chapter 13 Release
388 Old Street, London EC1V 9LT

Objects: To give advice on drug and legal problems. To educate the public and relevant bodies on these issues.

Activities: Advice and referral on drug-related legal problems; emergency help in cases of arrest and training consultancy services.

Chapter 14 Prisoners' Families and Friends Service
20 Trinity Street, London SE1 1DB

Objects: To assist the families and friends of people in prison with any of the immediate problems which arise as a result of imprisonment; to provide information and advice to the families of prisoners on any matter resulting from imprisonment; to offer friendship and support to families and friends of prisoners during the period of imprisonment.

Activities: Visiting by women volunteers (in Inner London only); offering information, support and advice on a wide range of problems to callers nationwide. Presence in Inner London Crown Courts to offer information and assistance to relatives and friends of prisoners.

Chapter 15   *Consumer Advice Centres ceased as a network when their activities were taken on by local authorities and advice agencies

Chapter 16   *National Consumer Federation
180 High Street, West Molesey, Surrey KT8 2LX

Objects: To consult with, and represent grassroots members, to circulate, publish and disseminate their views, and where appropriate to respond to consultation on their behalf; to identify and promote the interests of consumers, with reference to the key guiding principles of Access to good and services, Choice, Information, Representation, Fairness, Safety and Redress and to provide a channel for consumer opinion and representation and assist members to put forward their views locally and nationally; to increase the awareness of consumers to those issues that affect them and to provide means communication with government, industry, the regulators and other interested parties; to encourage and support members and member organisations to work together better and to promote their activities locally and nationally and to provide consumer information and education.

Chapter 17   Campaign for Homosexual Equality (CHE)
PO Box 342, London WC1X 0DU

Objects: To seek social and legal equality for lesbians, gays and bisexuals.

Activities: Drafting amendments to the law and campaigning for their adoption. Research into discrimination and its consequences. Publishing education and lobbying material. Local groups work on local Authority issues. Promoting equal opportunities and opposing discrimination.

Chapter 18 Brook
421 Highgate Studios, 53-79 Highgate Road, London NW5 1TL

Objects: Protecting, promoting and preserving the sexual and reproductive health of young people by educating them in matters relating to sexual behaviour, contraception, sexually transmitted infections and unwanted pregnancy.

Activities: Running a network of 19 centres throughout the UK. Centres help provide free confidential sex advice and contraception for young people under 25. Students, teachers and other professionals can obtain advice and publications from Brook Publications.

Chapter 19 British Pregnancy Advisory Service (BPAS)
Austy Manor, Wootton Wawen, Sollihull, West Midlands B95 6BX

Objects: To help and advise women faced with unwanted pregnancy.

Activities: Providing a full abortion service including counselling for all patients. Pregnancy testing, emergency contraception, male vasectomy and female sterilisation and reversal. Clinics are approved and inspected by the Department of Health and patients are admitted on referral by a BPAS branch or under arrangements with GPs and other healthcare agencies.

Chapter 20 Carers UK
Ruth Pitter House, 20-25 Glasshouse Yard, London EC1A 4JT

Objects: To help anyone who is caring for a sick, disabled or frail friend or relative at home.

Activities: Providing information and advice service for carers. Publishing a regular magazine *Caring*. Bringing carers' needs and problems to the attention of government and media. Working with professionals who help carers. Putting carers in touch with one another.

Chapter 21 National Women's Register (NWR)
3a Vulcan House, Vulcan Road, North Norwich NR6 6AQ
Objects: To offer women the opportunity to meet in each other's homes to participate in stimulating and wide-ranging discussion. Women of all ages welcome.
Activities: Meeting the needs of women who want to develop their own range of talents. National and regional conferences offer a choice of wider exchanges.

Chapter 22 Women's Aid Federation of England (WAFE)
PO Box 391 Bristol BS99 7WS
Objects: To provide advice, information and temporary refuge for women and their children who are threatened by mental, emotional or physical violence, harassment or sexual abuse.
Activities: 204 autonomous, locally based member groups who provide information, advice and refuge. National office provides helpline service and information and publications to the general public, and resources to member groups. Lobbies on domestic violence and related legal issues.

Chapter 23 Gingerbread
First Floor, 7 Sovereign Close, Sovereign Court, London E1W 3HW
Objects: To develop services to meet the needs of lone parents and their children, and enable their voice to be heard in the national debate.
Activities: There are over 190 local Gingerbread Groups. The freephone Gingerbread Advice Line is open from 9am-5pm, weekdays, offering personalised help and support to lone parents. The organisation promotes the needs of lone parents to policy-makers and offers an information service for all organisations working with lone parents.

Chapter 24 Disablement Income Group (DIG)
PO Box 5743, Finchingfield, Essex CM7 4W
Objects: To work to improve the financial circumstances of disabled people through a programme of: advice;

advocacy; fieldwork; information; publications; research and training.

Activities: A registered charity with group members and individual members. DIG's main functions are research, advocacy, lobbying and advice.

Chapter 25 National Association of Volunteer Bureaux (NAVB)
New Oxford House, 16 Waterloo Street, Birmingham B2 5UG

Objects: To increase public awareness of Volunteer Bureaux; to assist in their establishment and development; to exchange information between Bureaux; to encourage and promote training for Volunteer Bureaux staff; to promote research into maters of concern to Bureaux; to produce publications and to arrange meetings, courses and conferences; to represent the views of Volunteer Bureaux and to liaise with statutory and voluntary bodies.

Activities: Providing an information service on matters related to volunteering; producing a directory of Volunteer Bureaux, and other publications; organising an annual conference and training events for Bureaux staff; providing regular mailings to members, and general advice and support to Volunteer Bureaux.

Chapter 26 Free Form Arts Trust
Hothouse, 274 Richmond Road, London Fields, London E8 3QW

Objects: To broaden the influence of arts practice through community environmental work. To enrich the quality of life by enabling wide community involvement and consultation throughout the work.

Activities: Undertakes all aspects of community, environmental and public art projects from inception to project management and implementation. Provides accredited work-based training and career guidance to practitioners for urban art forms to NVQ Design Level 3, as an approved BTEC EdExcel Training Centre. Runs 'Building Communities', supported by the DETR to promote the involvement of local people in housing and neighbourhood regeneration.

Chapter 27 Inter-Action Trust of Associated Charitable Trusts and
Companies
HMS President (1918), near Blackfriars Bridge, Victoria
Embankment, London EC4Y 0HJ

Objects: To apply entrepreneurial skills to obtain social and
community benefits. To set up model projects, especially
digital media and social enterprise training and
educational ones, which incorporate these aims, and to
offer training and consultancy to other groups locally
and internationally; helping them to adapt model projects
to their own communities' needs.

Activities: Encouraging a wide range of community education/social
enterprise projects; offering consultancies to the voluntary
and statutory sectors in all aspects of management and
organisation; setting up a centre for social education,
enterprise and technology on an historic ship moored on
the Thames in central London. Does mainly outreach
work and is currently helping to establish 30 independent
international centres.

Chapter 28 Action for Sick Children
8 Wakley Street, London EC1V 7QE

Objects: To join parents and professionals in promoting high-
quality healthcare for children in hospital and at home.

Activities: There is a library and information service. Liaison is
maintained with other concerned organisations and
individuals working in the child health field. Local
branches (27) offer practical help and support to parents
and professionals in their own hospitals.

Chapter 29 National Association of Toy and Leisure Libraries
(NATLL) (Play Matters)
68 Churchway, London NW1 1LT

Objects: To loan carefully chosen (and sometimes specially
adapted) toys to families with young children, including
those with special needs physical, mental, emotional,
social and learning difficulties. To aim to provide
friendship and support for parents and other carers, and
through leisure libraries a meeting place for adults with
special needs.

Activities: Maintaining links at national level with therapists, psychologists, teachers, research workers; statutory agencies; manufacturers and toy designers; existing societies for childcare and people with learning difficulties, and among toy libraries themselves. Giving guidance about the choice of toys and play through training courses, conferences, etc. Publishing *Play Matters* magazine for members and *The Good Toy Guide* annually, and other publications relating to play.

Chapter 30 Pre-school Learning Alliance
69 King's Cross Road, London WC1X 9LL
Objects: To enhance the development and education of children primarily under statutory school age by encouraging parents to understand and provide for the needs of their children through community groups such as pre-schools, parent and toddler groups, family centres, opportunity groups and full/extended daycare pre-schools.
Activities: Promoting the value of pre-schools in the education and care of under-fives and in providing opportunities for their parents to be actively involved in their young children's learning. Undertaking research and encouraging the study of needs of under-fives and their parents/carers. Providing training for people working with under-fives including their parents/carers. Support by 500 local fieldworkers in over 400 branch sub-committees.

Chapter 31 Advisory Centre for Education (ACE)
1C Aberdeen Studios, 22 Highbury Grove, London N5 2DQ
Objects: To provide a free advice service for parents of children in state-maintained schools. Advocates changes in state schools to help them to become more responsive to the needs of parents and children. Training offered in specialist areas of education and to support local organisations giving advice on education.
Activities: Disseminating information; running an advice service; offering direct help to parents when dealing with schools and education authorities. Publishing handbooks, information sheets and periodical publications.

Chapter 32   *Task Force renamed itself Pensioners Link in 1984. Pensioners Link disbanded as a network in the early 1990s. However, a few local groups operate under the name of Pensioners Link.

Chapter 33   Young Enterprise
Peterley House, Peterley Road, Oxford OX4 2TZ
Objects: To educate young people in the organisation, methods and practice of commerce and industry by direct practical experience; to give school and college students the opportunity to acquire a basic understanding of the world of work and wealth creation.
Activities: Giving young people between the ages of 15 and 19 the opportunity to set up and operate companies on their own responsibility and in an atmosphere of complete commercial realism. Assisted by volunteer business advisers, they act as shareholders, management and workforce in actual business undertakings.

Chapter 34   CSV
237 Pentonville Road, London N1 9NJ
Objects: CSV creates opportunities for people to play an active part in the life of their community through volunteering, training, education and the media.
Activities: CSV provides: young and older people with volunteering opportunities; training for unemployed and excluded people; materials for teaching citizenship; develops new approaches to volunteering through employee involvement, mentoring and one-off volunteering schemes; consultancy and advice for organisations setting up volunteering programmes; community action desks for TV and radio; support services and media training and develops community-based environmental projects; training and consulting.

Chapter 35   Help the Aged
207-221 Pentonville Road, London N1 9UZ
Objects: To provide practical support to help older people live independent lives, particularly those who are frail, isolated or poor.

Activities: Promoting and developing practical programmes by identifying needs, raising public awareness and fundraising. In Britain, emphasis on day centres, community alarms, minibuses, research, sheltered housing and Dignity on the Ward. Offering free advice through SeniorLine and via information leaflets. Campaigning for fair provision for older people. Overseas, priorities are urban destitution, health and ophthalmic projects and promoting projects to maintain the independence of older people in over 50 countries worldwide.

Chapter 36 Pre-Retirement Association (PRA)
                9 Chesham Road, Guildford, Surrey GU1 3LS

Objects: The PRA works to enable people to manage change from mid-life onwards and as the national focus for this activity.

Activities: Pre-retirement education. Training pre-retirement tutors. Research and development.

Index